Living in
Historic Cairo

Living in Historic Cairo
Past and Present in an Islamic city

Edited by
Farhad Daftary, Elizabeth Fernea
and Azim Nanji

Azimuth Editions in association with
The Institute of Ismaili Studies
and University of Washington Press

IN MEMORIAM
ELIZABETH WARNOCK
FERNEA
1927–2009

Published in the United Kingdom
by Azimuth Editions in association with
The Institute of Ismaili Studies and
University of Washington Press

The Institute of Ismaili Studies
210 Euston Road, London NW1 2DA
www.iis.ac.uk

Azimuth Editions
7 Egerton Gardens London SW3 2BP, UK
3310 R Street NW, Washington, DC 20007, USA

Distributed throughout the world
by University of Washington Press
4333 Brooklyn Avenue NE, Seattle
WA 98195–9570
www. washington.edu/uwpress

British Library Cataloguing-in-
Publication Data
A Catalogue record of this book is available
from the British Library

ISBN: 978-1-898592-28-0

Printed in Italy
Cover shows minarets of Cairo with
the dome of the Khayrbak complex in
the foreground, AKTC Historic Cities
Programme, 2006

The Institute of Ismaili Studies

The Institute of Ismaili Studies was established in 1977 with the object of promoting scholarship and learning on Islam, in the historical as well as contemporary contexts, and a better understanding of its relationship with other societies and faiths.

The Institute's programmes encourage a perspective which is not confined to the theological and religious heritage of Islam, but seeks to explore the relationship of religious ideas to broader dimensions of society and culture. The programmes thus encourage an interdisciplinary approach to the materials of Islamic history and thought. Particular attention is also given to issues of modernity that arise as Muslims seek to relate their heritage to the contemporary situation.

Within the Islamic tradition, the Institute's programmes promote research on those areas which have, to date, received relatively little attention from scholars. These include the intellectual and literary expressions of Shi'ism in general, and Ismailism in particular.

In the context of Islamic societies, the Institute's programmes are informed by the full range and diversity of cultures in which Islam is practised today, from the Middle East, South and Central Asia, and Africa to the industrialised societies of the West, thus taking into consideration the variety of contexts which shape the ideals, beliefs and practices of the faith.

These objectives are realised through concrete programmes and activities organised and implemented by various departments of the Institute. The Institute also collaborates periodically, on a programme-specific basis, with other institutions of learning in the United Kingdom and abroad.

The Institute's academic publications fall into a number of inter-related categories:

1 Occasional papers or essays addressing broad themes of the relationship between religion and society, with special reference to Islam.
2 Monographs exploring specific aspects of Islamic faith and culture, or the contributions of individual Muslim thinkers or writers.
3 Editions or translations of significant primary or secondary texts.
4 Translations of poetic or literary texts which illustrate the rich heritage of spiritual, devotional and symbolic expressions in Muslim history.
5 Works on Ismaili history and thought, and the relationship of the Ismailis to other traditions, communities and schools of thought in Islam.
6 Proceedings of conferences and seminars sponsored by the Institute.
7 Bibliographical works and catalogues which document manuscripts, printed texts and other source materials.
This book falls into category two listed above.

In facilitating these and other publications, the Institute's sole aim is to encourage original research and analysis of relevant issues. While every effort is made to ensure that the publications are of a high academic standard, there is naturally bound to be a diversity of views, ideas and interpretations. As such, the opinions expressed in these publications must be understood as belonging to their authors alone.

Contents

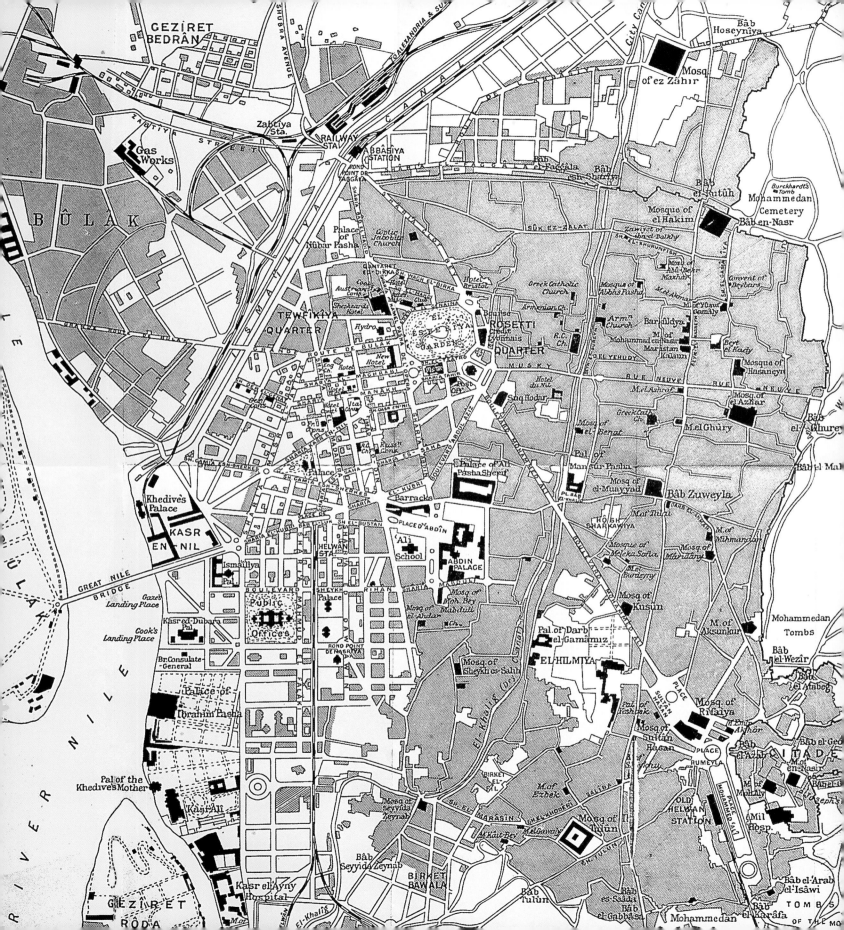

Foreword

The city of Cairo was founded in AH 358/AD 969 as the new royal capital of the Fatimids, an Ismaili Shiʻi dynasty that ruled over a flourishing empire for 262 years until its demise in 567/1171. Subsequently, Cairo maintained its status as a major metropolis under the Ayyubids and the Mamluks, who established their own states over extensive parts of the Muslim world. In the course of its history up to the end of Ottoman rule over Egypt, Cairo rivalled, and at times indeed surpassed, in its urban and cultural development, the achievements of other early Muslim cities of the region: Baghdad, Damascus and Cordoba. With the dramatic changes in political fortunes and demographic shifts, these cities entered the modern era in various stages of decline. Cairo was no exception. By the time a multitude of European archeologists, adventurers and orientalists of the 19th and 20th centuries rediscovered Historic Cairo and its antiquities in the aftermath of the Napoleonic invasion of Egypt, the city had become a ghost of its past, though not entirely devoid of a certain charm and romanticism which continued to appeal to generations of European travellers to the land of the Nile.

Subsequently, a host of developmental problems, notably population growth, a vicious cycle of poverty and regional conflict led to a neglect of the old city as attention tended to focus on the promotion of ancient Pharaonic monuments. As a major exception, a window of opportunity was provided in more recent times for a part of Cairo known locally as al-Darb al-Ahmar, through the activities of the Aga Khan Trust for Culture (AKTC) in collaboration with a variety of other agencies including the Egyptian Supreme Council of Antiquities. The aim of this collaborative undertaking was not only to restore the historic monuments of al-Darb al-Ahmar, a worthy cause in itself, but also to improve the socio-economic fabric of the area so as to enhance the living conditions of its artisans and other inhabitants. This book, originally conceived as a companion to an educational film (*Living with the Past: Historic Cairo*) produced in 2001, aims to capture the full story of this collaborative project within the broader context of the history of the city of Cairo.

The late Elizabeth W. Fernea (1927–2009) was the moving spirit behind both the film and the present companion book. That she did not live to witness the completion of this multi-dimensional project is indeed a source of immense sadness for all of us. This book would not have seen the light of day without her untiring efforts and initiatives, and it is now our honour and pride to dedicate *Living in Historic Cairo: Past and Present in an Islamic City*, the collective work of numerous scholars who have looked at Cairo through different professional lenses, to her memory. It remains for us to extend our deepest gratitude to the authorities of the University of Texas at Austin, originally chosen as the book's publishers for having relinquished that privilege to The Institute of Ismaili Studies, and to Isabel Miller who meticulously edited the various chapters of this book over the past few years. We would also like to acknowledge with many thanks the contributions of Elizabeth Fernea's secretary, Diane Watts, as well as Nadia Holmes and Patricia Salazar, amongst other colleagues for variously facilitating the production of the book. We should also like to acknowledge the creative talents of Lorna Raby and her team at Azimuth Editions, who have designed and published this book.

Farhad Daftary
The Institute of Ismaili Studies

Azim Nanji
Stanford University

Map of Cairo, 1900, showing Historic Cairo including al-Darb al-Ahmar, and the new city created by Khedive Ismaʻil in the late 19th century, from Stanley Lane-Poole, *Cairo* (after Standford's)

Introduction

Elizabeth Fernea

The history of Cairo is usually presented in terms of periods and dynasties: Fatimid, Ayyubid, Mamluk. This is called pre-modern history. The modern history of Egypt is generally held to begin in the last decades of the 19th century with the emergence of a new, modern city, reconfigured by the Muhammad 'Ali dynasty along the lines of European cities. The book that follows is an effort to examine Cairo across those historical lines considering, in the period from the 1st AH/ 7th AD century until the present, what sort of relationships between the physical layout of the city, its historic buildings, its economy, its social, cultural and religious life can be perceived? Perhaps this is a somewhat ambitious endeavour, but one which seems sorely needed now as planners and restorers work to refurbish the city.

In 2001, an educational film was produced, in English and Arabic, *Living with the Past: Historic Cairo*. Funded by the Ford Foundation, it sought to present the city in both the past and the present. This book was originally conceived as a companion to the film; both projects were to be used in classrooms, in both East and West, to document the processes that were then in progress for a) restoring historic monuments in the old pre-modern city and b) reviving and improving the social and economic life of the old city. It also sought to discover what the residents of the old city thought about these projects and how they affected their own individual futures; to clarify what, if any, was the felt relationship between the great monuments like Bab Zuwayla and the people who lived nearby and what lessons could be learned from this experience, by other people in other parts of the world facing similar restoration projects?

Early on, library research for the film demonstrated, as might be expected, a plethora of admirable scholarly works on the various historical periods and the cultural products of those periods. But no over-arching work dealt with the city across all those periods. And no work examined the relationships between the inhabitants and the space they occupied. Hence this volume.

In the beginning, the scope of the book was to be limited to the neighbourhood that was filmed – al-Darb al-Ahmar – the restoration of monuments being undertaken by both Egyptian and non-Egyptian institutions, and the ambitious project to revitalise not only the spaces, but the lives of the people in al-Darb al-Ahmar, undertaken by the Aga Khan Trust for Culture (AKTC). But the borders of al-Darb al-Ahmar proved more porous than expected. The economics of the area in medieval times was influenced by earlier history and these, in turn, influenced economic practices of later eras. Thus the scope broadened: relationships between past and present emerged; Mamluk architecture, not surprisingly, influenced post-Mamluk construction, and so on.

Thus, the final text touches on subjects beyond al-Darb al-Ahmar. The religious practices of Muslims, Christians and Jews in Cairo have reverberations in the present, as indicated by Roy Mottahedeh's masterful account of the Muslim liturgical year.

In the end, the volume was divided into two parts – the past and the present, with a brief middle transition section concerning 'Ali Mubarak Pasha's blueprint for the new Cairo envisioned by the Khedive Isma'il: *al-Khitat al-tawfiqiyya al-jadida*. Part one opens with an historical overview of the development of the city, written by Ayman Fu'ad Sayyid; Nasser Rabbat follows with an introduction to processes of reconstruction in the specific neighbourhood of al-Darb al-Ahmar.

A discussion of Nasir-i Khusraw's travelogue describing 11th-century Cairo sets the stage for essays with more specific subject matter

Panorama of Cairo showing
the Citadel, with the minarets
of the Muhammad 'Ali
Mosque in its centre, *circa* 1908

examining different facets of life – economic institutions (Kassem A. Kassem, Pascale Ghazaleh and Kristen Stilt), education (Heinz Halm), marriage and the family (Amira Sonbol), faith and practice (Roy Mottahedeh, Norman A. Stillman and Febe Armanios), art and architecture (Caroline Williams and Fahmida Suleman), and music (Jonathan Shannon). Part one closes with Randa Abou-bakr's observations on how the old city reverberates through the modern literary works of Naguib Mahfouz and Gamal al-Ghitani.

Robert K. Vincent, Jr., Nairy Hampikian and Agnieszka Dobrowolska, describe institutional efforts. Salah Zaky Said discusses the cooperative renovation of old houses and Hisham and 'Ali Mahmoud outline the successful local community undertaking to restore the Qijmas Mosque.

Accounts of the restoration of the social and economic fabric of al-Darb al-Ahmar, which the observers view as a possible role model for other depressed urban areas, fill the next section, written by Stefano Bianca of the Aga Khan Trust for Csulture, Mohamed El-Mikawi, General

The paper by Elizabeth Bishop shows the reader some of the considerations that went into 'Ali Mubarak Pasha's blueprint for a new, modern Cairo.

Part two looks at the present, but always in relation to the past. Two young members of the team of the Aga Khan Cultural Services (Egypt), Karim Ibrahim and Seif El-Rashidi, record their own traveller's observations 'on visiting al-Darb al-Ahmar for the first time in the 20th century'. Kamran Asdar 'Ali and Martina Rieker present the background for the understanding of the 'Ali Mubarak Pasha blueprint and the subsequent changes in modern plans for improving Cairo. Ragui Assaad points out the connections between the historic guilds and the expectations and practices of Egypt's contemporary labour market. Then follows a group of essays about specific monument preservation in Historic Cairo:

Manager of the Cairo Project Administration, and Mohamed Abdul Hafiz, whose work focuses specifically on the social and economic aspects.

Two quite different essays conclude the volume. Dina Shehayeb and Ahmed Sedky offer a new way of looking at these now depressed, but formerly glorious, neighbourhoods as repositories of cultural and social values and national heritage, and Maysoon Pachachi, who directed the documentary film *Living with the Past*, describes the challenges of representing al-Darb al-Ahmar on film.

Is this an ambitious undertaking? Clearly, yes. Yet, perhaps this volume will lead to further interdisciplinary research into society and life in the setting of structural formations in historically important areas of the world's great cities.

Part one:
al-Darb al-Ahmar in Egyptian history

Detail of Ottoman residences
with *mashrabiyya*s, 1880

1 The historical development of Cairo, 20–923/642–1517: an overview

Ayman Fu'ad Sayyid

Cairo is the capital of the Arab Republic of Egypt and one of the most important religious, cultural and political centres in the Islamic world. Ever since its foundation over a thousand years ago, Cairo has been considered the main centre of the Arabo-Islamic civilisation. Furthermore, it is regarded as a unique city in the Islamic world due to the diversity and abundance of its antiquities and buildings of historical interest, since we do not find such an accumulation of religious and secular antiquities in any other place. The various styles of these antiquities enable us to study the development of Islamic architecture.

The origins of Cairo, 20–567/642–1171

Cairo occupies a unique place at the apex of the Delta triangle, the point of its conjunction with the southern part of the Nile Valley (the north-south axis). This unique site is determined by the nature of the Egyptian land and the historical process. Capitals were founded in this general location at different sites (Memphis, On ['Ayn Shams, which the Greeks called Heliopolis] and Babylon – Babalyun). They were never established anywhere else, except for limited periods and at exceptional times in Egyptian history.

When the Arabs conquered Egypt in 20/642, al-Fustat was built as the first Muslim city in Egypt near the Roman fortress of Babylon. After nearly a century, a quarter was added to it in the north-east to house the official residence of the 'Abbasid amirs and their military encampment, beginning in 132/750. Because of this, the quarter was called al-'Askar (the troops). Again in the north-east a new district or small city was laid out by Ahmad b. Tulun, the first Muslim ruler to control Egypt independently of the 'Abbasid caliphate, in 254/868. This city was called al-Qata'i' because it was divided into separate quarters which were granted to detachments of the army. These three separate cities soon became virtually one city, with al-Fustat as its commercial, social and industrial centre.

The fourth step in the evolution of this city was yet another expansion to the north-east. This time a large area was left between the city and al-Qata'i' – which had been largely destroyed – so that there would be security and privacy for the Fatimid caliphs in whose name the fourth city, which was the actual al-Qahira, was built. However, it consisted only of the palace, barracks for the soldiery and the offices of the administration (*dar al-wuzara*). Al-Fustat remained the market for the sale of goods and a centre for culture and business.

Al-Qahira did not become the metropolis and ruling centre of Muslim Egypt until after al-Fustat had been deliberately set on fire in 564/1168. The walls of Salah al-Din were built to incorporate everything into a properly unified capital, since they were designed not simply to surround al-Qahira but also to include the Citadel and what was left of al-Fustat and al-Qata'i'.

This site, of which al-Qahira was an expansion nearly three centuries later, contained all the right conditions for the founding of cities and for guaranteeing their continuity. The choice of site was a success in every regard. The city was defended from attack in three directions: by the line of hills to the east, the Nile to the west, and the conjunction of the hills and the Nile to the south. The area opened up only to the north where the city was provided with space to expand. It was there that al-'Askar, al-Qata'i', al-Qahira and its present suburbs, were subsequently built. Moreover, the eastern hills provided stone which was valuable raw building material, and the river provided the raw materials of clay and water for making bricks.

The second Islamic capital of Egypt, al-'Askar, was erected by the troops of the 'Abbasid commander Salih b. 'Awn in 132/750 in the place which was known in early Islamic times as al-Hamra' al-Quswa. It was located north-east of al-Fustat in the area which is now bordered on the south by Qanatir Majrat al-'Uyun and on the north by Maydan al-Sayyida Zaynab. This city was planned in a manner similar to the layout of other centres of regional government (*madinat al-amir*) in order to be the permanent capital of the 'Abbasid governors in Egypt. Its congregational mosque (*al-masjid al-jami'*) – of which we have lost all trace – was built by al-Fadl b. Salih in 169/786.

Ahmad b. Tulun ruled Egypt independently from 254/868 and he built the new capital known as al-Qata'i' to the north-east of al-'Askar.

Copy of the World Map of
al-Idrisi (6th/12th century),
showing Egypt and the
Nile, with the Mountains of
the Moon top right and the
Mediterranean bottom right

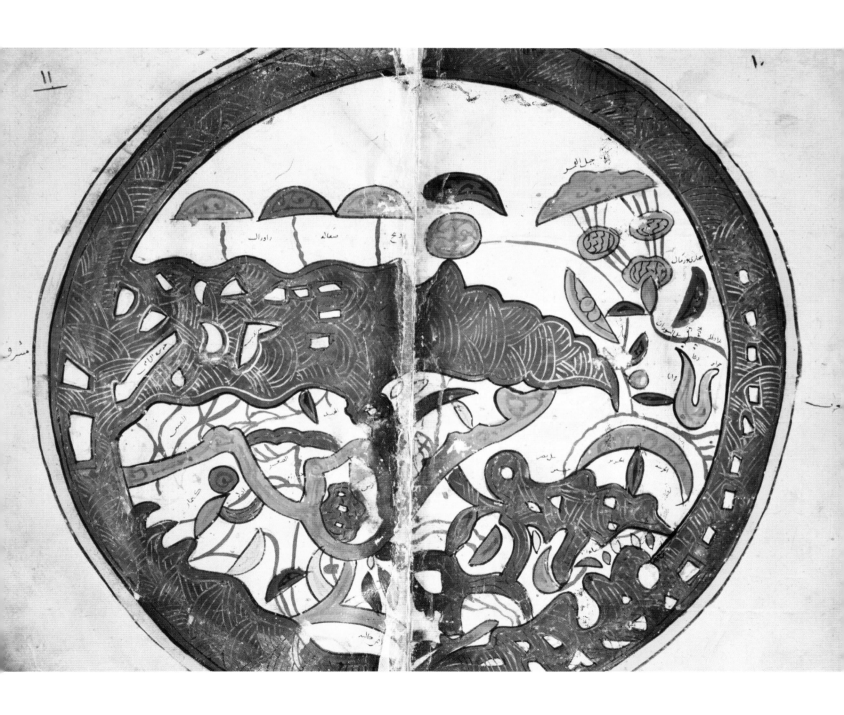

It lay in the area between Jabal Yashkur in the south and the foot of Jabal al-Muqattam in the east – where the Citadel is now situated – and between al-Rumayla – below the Citadel where the mosque of Sultan Hasan is now – and the mosque of Zayn al-'Abidin in Tilal Zinhum (an area of about a square mile). The new governor's city contained a *maydan*, a mosque and a hospital.

Furthermore, each division of the troops was assigned a quarter (*qati'a*) all of which made up the city of al-Qata'i' ('the quarters'). The name of the city seems to reflect the *iqta'* system which dominated this period. Furthermore, it was the first capital in Islamic Egypt that was planned following aesthetic criteria for the laying out and building of cities. Indeed, the city was greatly influenced by the plan of the 'Abbasid capital of Samarra' in Iraq. However, the monument which has actually perpetuated Ibn Tulun's name is his mosque, which was the only monument that was left after the city was sacked by the 'Abbasid soldiery and its subsequent decay due to neglect. It was in Ramadan 265/May 879 that the mosque was completed and could be used for prayer. This mosque is held to be the oldest mosque in Egypt that still retains its original architectural detail and structure. It was built to imitate the style of the Great Mosque at Samarra' in Iraq with its unique minaret. The mosque became the model which influenced the design and building of mosques in Egypt from then on until the construction of the mosque of al-Mu'ayyad Shaykh in 818/1415.

The Fatimids and the founding of Cairo, 358–567/969–1171
The arrival of the Fatimids in the middle of the 4th/10th century was regarded as a serious development and a unique transformation of the contemporary political and religious map of the Islamic world. For the first time, power in Islamic world was to be the object of a real contest between two caliphates seeking domination at the same time; each of them, that is to say the 'Abbasid caliphate in Baghdad and the Fatimid caliphate in Egypt, considered itself the rightful ruler of this world.

As soon as Jawhar al-Saqlabi – the commander (*qa'id*) of the army of the Fatimid caliph al-Mu'izz li-Din Allah – arrived in Egypt in

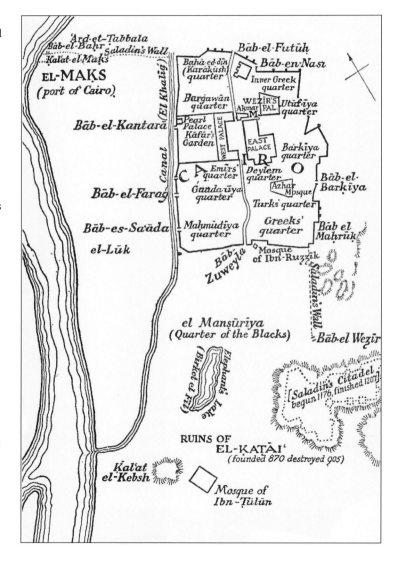

Madinat al-Qahira of the Fatimids, from Stanley Lane-Poole, *Cairo*, after Ravaisse

358/969, he began executing his master's orders to build a city which would stand in relation to al-Fustat as, in Ifriqiya, al-Mansuriyya did to Qayrawan. So on the night of 17 Sha'ban 358/6 July 969, Jawhar crossed with his troops from Giza to al-Fustat and camped on the sandy plain to the north of al-Qata'i'.

Jawhar built the first wall of the city with baked mud bricks and arranged in a square, each side measuring 1,080 metres. So al-Qahira, at its foundation, covered an area of 1,166,400 square metres; 240,141 square metres solely for the palace, 120,050 square metres for the Garden of Kafur and a similar amount of land for the *maydan*s. On the remaining land, which was some 686,000 square metres, the districts of the city were set out. However, part of the land was left undeveloped for further expansion. A large part of the eastern side of the walls was apparently still in existence at the time of the historian al-Maqrizi (d. 845/1442) and it ran behind the walls of Salah al-Din for about 50 cubits (*dhira'*) (92,890 metres) between Bab al-Barqiyya and Darb Battut, which was pulled down in 803/1400.

There were nine gates in the wall, two in the northern wall: Bab al- Nasr and Bab al-Futuh, two in the eastern wall: Bab al-Barqiyya and Bab al-Qarratin, three in the southern wall: two of which being Bab Zuwayla and Bab al-Faraj; and two in the western wall: Bab al-Qantara and Bab Sa'ada. A third gate called Bab al-Khuf was later added to these last gates. There now is no trace left of these gates although al-Maqrizi refers to the fact that he saw the remains of the arches of some of them.

At first, Jawhar thought that if he called the new city al-Mansuriyya – (meaning 'the Triumphant' or 'the Victorious') in imitation of the capital of the Fatimids established in Ifriqiya by al-Mansur the father of al-Mu'izz – he would curry favour with his master, al-Mu'izz. However on his arrival in Egypt four years later, al-Mu'izz changed its name to al-Qahira particularly because he gave an order to Jawhar – at his leave-taking in Ifriqiya – to build a city and call it al-Qahira ('the Vanquisher') because it would vanquish the world. (See also the report about its name, al-Qahira, in relation to the planet Mars, the Vanquisher, which was in the ascendant, when the city's foundations were laid.)

At first, the plan of al-Qahira took the shape of a square, and then 120 years later its shape was changed to a rectangle when the Fatimid vizier Badr al-Jamali widened the southern and northern walls and moved them to where the surviving gates now indicate their positions. A principal thoroughfare cut through al-Qahira from Bab Zuwayla in the south to Bab al-Futuh in the north parallel to al-Khalij. It was called al-Shari' al-A'zam or Qasabat al-Qahira and it divided the city into two equal halves. However, throughout the Islamic period there were no streets running off al-Shari' al-A'zam. There was also a road parallel to it – nowadays Shari' al-Jamaliyya indicates where it ran – which used to lead from Bab al-'Id, one of the doorways of the great Fatimid palace, to Bab al-Nasr. This street played an important role in the caliph's public acts since his processions used to pass down it in order to go, for example, to the *musalla* (place of prayer) located outside the northern wall.

Jawhar asked each of the ethnic groups that had accompanied him on the conquest of Egypt to choose a place to inhabit, and each of these was known as a *hara*. At that time *hara* did not refer to an alleyway between houses as it does now. Rather, it meant a part of the totality of the city's buildings which constituted an entire quarter penetrated by streets where communities, markets and mosques were located. Al-Qahira first had about ten *hara*s and they began to increase with the expansion of the city and the arrival of new communities. Each *hara* had a gate that was closed after the night prayer and opened before the dawn prayer with the knowledge of the night watchman (*mutawalli al-tawfi laylan*) or patrol men (*ashab al-'asas*).

At first, the name al-Qahira used to refer to everything that was surrounded by Jawhar's mud-brick wall, and later to what was surrounded by the stone wall built by Badr al-Jamali. As for what lay outside these walls and which was augmented with the city's regular expansion, it was called Zahir al-Qahira (al-Qahira extra-muros). At the beginning of its life, there was nothing outside the city's walls except the Musallat al-'Idayn, or Musallat al-Qahira, which was laid out by Jawhar outside the northern wall near Bab al-Nasr.

The tombs of the inhabitants of al-Qahira were outside the southern wall to the left of Bab Zuwayla on the land that extends from there as far as the foot of Jabal al-Muqattam. This space was occupied later by the mosques of al-Salih Tala'i'and al-Maridani, in the area now called al-Tabbana and Shari' al-Darb al-Ahmar as far as Bab al-Wazir.

If, in general, the *masjid al-jami'* (congregational mosque) should be the key for the topographical and historical study of any Islamic city rather than the residence of the ruler, then the situation viz-a-viz al-Qahira is different, since the Fatimid palace was the heart of the city, occupying some seventeen acres, that is to say nearly a fifth of the city's total area. It is true that the mosque of al-Qahira was the centre on which the Fatimids depended for spreading Fatimid intellectual culture and the Ismaili *da'wa*. However, the palace shared this function with the mosque since the chief missionary (*da'i al-du'at*) used to hold meetings for the Ismaili faithful in a part of the palace called al-Muhawwil, and the Fatimid caliph himself would occasionally be present at them.

As soon as the caliph al-Mu'izz arrived in al-Qahira, he ordered a place of burial to be laid out in the south-western corner of the palace for the interment of the coffins of his forebears, which he had brought with him from Ifriqiya, and for the burial of future Fatimid caliphs, their families and children. The construction was known thereafter as Turbat al-Za'fran (the Saffron Mausoleum).

The palace had nine doorways: in the west facade there was Bab al-Zahuma, Bab-al-Dhahab, and Bab-al-Bahr, and in the north facade there was Bab al-Rih. In the east facade there was Bab al-'Id, Bab al-Zumurrud, and Bab Qasr al-Shawk, and finally in the south facade there was Bab al-Daylam and Bab Turbat al-Za'fran.

This description does not include half the magnificent foyers and halls described by William of Tyre and al-Maqrizi. They consisted of a group of buildings, small palaces or pavilions, audience halls and porticoed courtyards, all of which made up the palace or the Luminous Palaces (al-Qusur al-Zahira). Unfortunately, we are ignorant of everything concerning the architecture since all traces of them have vanished and were replaced by the *madrasa*s (colleges) built during the Ayyubid and Mamluk periods as well as by Khan al-Khalili and the quarter of al-Jamaliyya. Our source of information for the palace is what al-Maqrizi says in his *al-Khitat*, that is either material transmitted from the Ayyubid sources or based on what he himself saw of its ruins. These ruins were demolished in 811/1408, during Jamal al-Din Yusuf al-Ustadar's despotic vizierate. Thanks to the pieces of information provided by al-Maqrizi, through studies undertaken separately by Ravaisse and the author of this paper, it has been possible to reconstruct the great Fatimid palace.

The most ancient of al-Qahira's mosques is al-Masjid al-Qahira which was later known as al-Jami' al-Azhar, whose foundations were laid by Jawhar on 14 Rabi' 359/25 January 970 and which was inaugurated in Ramadan 361/July 972. It was built on the exemplar of the mosque at al-Mahdiyya in Ifriqiya and its ground plan, when it was first built, consisted of three *iwan*s (porticos) disposed around a courtyard: the east *iwan* was made up of five colonnades (sing. *riwaq*), and in the other two sides there were three *riwaq*s. The part of these *riwaq*s that overhung the courtyard was supported by buttresses. The west side had no *riwaq*s and in its centre was the main entrance, over which was the minaret, and it is possible that the entrance projected from the facade as was the case with the mosque at al-Mahdiyya. Thus, little of the mosque now standing is the original Fatimid mosque, but rather it consists of a group of monuments which were added onto it in later times. Of the Fatimid mosque there is only the *majaz* (aisle) that leads to the Fatimid *mihrab* and its arches, which are all that remains of the original arches.

As for what is now known as the mosque of al-Hakim, the caliph al-'Aziz bi'llah started building it outside the old Bab al-Futuh in 380/990 and called it Jami' al-Khutba. Then the works on it stopped for a number of years until his son, al-Hakim bi-Amr Allah, finished them in 393/1003. However, it was not officially inaugurated until 403/1012–1013. In its design the mosque brings together both North African and Egyptian elements. It undoubtedly follows the plan of the

Ibn Tulun Mosque which was built after the style of the Great Mosque of Samarra'. The main portal, however, opens in the centre of the mosque's rear wall directly facing the *mihrab*, like the portal of the mosque at al-Mahdiyya. It projects from the line of the rear wall and it takes the form of two towers with a passage between them leading to an entrance. As a result, its design resembles a vernacular gateway or arch set in wall. Previously, it had been usual for the main entrances of mosques to be opened in the two lateral walls rather than facing Mecca and in the rear wall. This approach was repeated, however, in the mosque of al-Aqmar (519/1125) and in the mosque of al-Zahir Baybars (665/1267), but with different dimensions. Both minarets of the mosque have a design unique among minarets in Egypt. They were built of stone in the form of a cylindrical core surrounded by a square mass: one in the north-west corner of the mosque and the other in the north-east corner. The ornamentation of geometric and vegetal forms found on the base of these minarets and on the mosque's main entrance represents a conclusive stage in the formation of Islamic ornamentation. Stone did not appear in Fatimid architecture before the mosque of al-Hakim. So it was now possible to dispense with plaster wash for covering and dressing mural surfaces. Sculpted stone ornamentation gave value to the facades of Fatimid mosques, and it is distinctly apparent in the mosques of al-Aqmar and al-Salih Tala'i'.

After the mosque of al-Hakim, there was no further mosque building in al-Qahira for about a hundred years. The first to be built afterwards was the mosque of al-Aqmar in 515/1121 during the reign of al-Amir bi-Ahkam Allah and the vizierate of al-Ma'mun al-Bata'ihi and it was inaugurated in 519/1125. The walls and the facade were built of stone. This was the first time care was taken to construct and ornament the facade of a mosque in al-Qahira. This ornamentation was not merely confined to the portal but covered the entire facade of the mosque at the opposite end to the *qibla* wall. The facade of the mosque included a pair of analogous wings, to the right and left of the entrance and, for the first time in the architecture of al-Qahira, *muqarnas* was deployed as ornamentation. All trace of the mosque of

al-Afkar, built by the caliph al-Zafir in 543/1148 has vanished; it was replaced by a new mosque in 1149/1736 which was built by Amir Ahmad Katkhuda Mustahfizan.

The mosque of al-Salih Tala'i', built by the vizier al-Malik al-Salih Tala'i' outside Bab Zuwayla in 555/1160, is regarded as the last of the congregational mosques to be built by the Fatimids in al-Qahira. It was a raised mosque (*masjid mu'allaqa*) built over an underground floor which was used for shops and warehouses. The mosque experienced many upheavals and was much repaired until it was restored and rebuilt by the *Comité de conservation des monuments arabes* in the second decade of the last century.

It can be observed that the area of individual mosques built in the Fatimid period after the mosque of al-Hakim began to decrease due to an increase in the number of congregational mosques. It can also be observed that in the planning of Fatimid mosques there is a widening of the nave (*uskub*) of the *mihrab* and its pavement. This occurred in order to create a square base for the dome which was erected in front of the *mihrab* at the intersection of the nave and the pavement of the *mihrab*. The square base of the dome meant that its sides were equal and thus it became a new element in the design of mosques.

In the Fatimid era another kind of religious construction, the mosque with a shrine or *mashhad*, became known in Egypt. These are shrines that were built in order to commemorate the Family of the Prophet (*Ahl al-Bayt*). Most of them were sites where visions had been experienced and most of them are in the place known as al-Mashahid, between al-Qahira and al-Fustat. Their dating is by and large uncertain. However, based on the study of their architectural and ornamental elements, it is likely that they belong to the Fatimid period. Usually the *mashhad*, or the mosque used as a shrine, retains all the design elements of a mosque. The most important of these *mashhad*s are: Mashhad al-Sayyida Sukayna, Mashhad Atika, and al-Ja'fari, Mashhad al-Sayyida Ruqayya, Mashhad Ikhwa Yusuf, Mashhad al-Lu'lu'a, al-Mashahid al-Tis'a and al-Qibab al-Sab' in al-Qarafa. We can add to these the Mashad al-Juyushi which was erected by Badr al-Jamali on

Jabal al-Muqattam in 478/1085, perhaps as his own mausoleum. He was the first person of note in the Fatimid period who had a commemorative inscription made carrying the term *mashhad*.

What remains of the walls and gates of al-Qahira built by the general Badr al-Jamali between 480/1087 and 485/1092 are a part of the northern wall and three gates: Bab al-Nasr and Bab al-Futuh in the northern wall and Bab Zuwayla in the southern wall, as well as Bab al-Barqiyya which was opened in the eastern wall. The gates were built of stone and they were huge constructions, in the area that each of them occupied, in their height which exceeded twenty metres, and in the amount of stone used in their construction. Two great salients or towers precede each gate, projecting from the line of the wall, with the exception of Bab al-Barqiyya. On Bawwabat al-Nasr is displayed the oldest example of assembled interlocking stone elements, or joggled voussoirs, on a flat lintel to be found in the history of Cairene architecture, if not in the history of architecture as a whole.

The influence of Armenian architecture is evident in the gates. Al-Maqrizi says that the three brothers, the builders, came from Edessa and it was they who built the first three gates, whereas Abu Salih al-Armani says that the engineer for the walls and gates of al-Qahira was a man called Yuhanna al-Rahib.

Throughout the first period of the Fatimid caliphate, al-Qahira remained a secluded royal city; the people who lived in al-Fustat – the country's commercial and industrial capital – were not allowed to enter it except by special permission and for the purpose of serving the people of the Fatimid caliph's retinue (*khawass*), his ministers and the military.

Although al-Qahira was not basically established in order to be – literally in the proper sense – a residential city, residential areas began to spread outside its walls in an imperceptible and unorganised way. This expansion was the reason the city collapsed so rapidly when confronted with its first financial and political crises.

The first expansion of al-Qahira occurred beyond the northern and southern walls built by Jawhar. The expansion evidently happened at the beginning of the 5th/11th century when a large *hara* was chosen and marked out beyond the Bab al-Futuh and it was called al-Hara al-Husayniyya after the commander-in-chief, al-Husayn b. Jawhar. Moreover, the caliph al-Hakim also completed building the mosque of al-Anwar which his father had begun outside the northern wall in 404/1013. This phenomenon was repeated outside the southern wall where several *hara*s were established for the Sudani, Masamida, Yanisiyya, Hilaliyya and Manjabiyya troops. Furthermore, the caliph al-Hakim built a new gate beyond Bab Zuwayla (or Zawila) – at a date not specified in the sources – in order to define the furthest limits of the land that had been granted to them.

The severe economic crisis and the political anarchy that Egypt endured in the middle of the 5th/11th century put a stop to al-Qahira's first period of expansion. The effect of the crisis was clearly evident especially in al-Fustat. It had a brutal impact on the ancient 'Abbasid and Tulunid quarters of al-'Askar and al-Qata'i' to the north of al-Fustat where a large number of the houses were destroyed during the troubles.

This crisis, in addition to the administrative and political anarchy under which the country deteriorated and the bloody conflict between the Turkish and Sudanese soldiery, were the reasons that impelled the caliph al-Mustansir bi'llah – powerless himself – to seek the help of the governor of 'Akka (Acre), the *amir al-juyush*, Badr al-Jamali, to restore order and stability in the country. One of the most important reforms which the *amir al-juyush* carried out – after subduing these rebellions and hunting down corrupt individuals – was to permit whoever was capable of constructing something in al-Qahira to choose a piece of land for themselves inside the Fatimid walls (most of which, however, were now in ruins). He exploited the stone and other remains of buildings which had been destroyed during the upheavals. Thus, al-Maqrizi says, 'that was the first time that ordinary people acquired land inside al-Qahira'. As a result, al-Qahira temporarily lost its position as a royal city; however, Badr al-Jamali corrected that afterwards, preserving the city's shape and special character when he strengthened

Cairo viewed from the west
bank of the Nile, engraving
from *Description de l'Afrique*
by O. Dapper, 1686

its defences, rebuilt its gates and walls, and expanded it to the north and south between 480/1087 and 485/1092.

If the system of Badr al-Jamali and his successors restored the youth of the Fatimid state and delaye d its fall for another one hundred years, Fatimid al-Qahira reached the height of its efflorescence at the beginning of the 6th/12th century during the time of the caliph al-Amir bi-Ahkam Allah (495–524/1101–1130) and the vizierate of al-Ma'mun al-Bata'ihi (515–519/1121–1125). During al-Bata'ihi's vizierate, construction expanded into the southern area between Bab Zuwayla and al-Mashad al-Nafisi. Al-Bata'ihi also ordered his *wakil*, Abu al-Barakat b. 'Uthman, to restore and repair the *mashhad*s located on the edge of the district.

As for the region on the west bank of al-Khalij, it was built up only very slowly, notably after the Fatimids established an arsenal for the construction and repair of ships (*dar al-sina'a*) in al-Maqs area (now Maydan Ramsis and its surroundings). However, the shipyard could not have been in use for long since the histories do not mention it after the 5th/11th century. Furthermore, construction reached the west bank of al-Khalij after the caliph al-Hakim built a mosque, which became known as al-Maqs Mosque, in this district. In the middle of the 5th/11th century, the caliph al-Mustansir granted the land south of al-Maqs between the Khalij (the canal) and the Nile and to the north of the Birka (pond) of Batn al-Baqara (which afterwards became known as Birkat al-Azbakiyya) to a female musician and performer, known as the Drummer of the Caliph, and her descendants, after she had sung in his presence lauding Arslan al-Basasiri's victories over the 'Abbasids and Saljuqs in Iraq. Thus it became known as 'Ard al-Tabbala (Land of the drummer-girl), and is nowadays the district of Qantarat al-Dakka. A number of houses were built there and were, according to Ibn 'Abd al-Zahir, 'among the beauties and splendours of al-Qahira'. These places were abandoned as a result of the hardship in al-Mustansir's reign, so that the gang, called al-Farhiyya, chose a *hara* which became known as Harat al-Lusus (of thieves) because they, along with others, preyed on whoever passed through this district or on the people of the neighbouring districts. The *hara*s were not clearly laid out on the west bank of the Khalij and no real settled population was established there until the beginning of the 6th/12th century. Stability and security were restored in the reign of al-Amir bi-Ahkam Allah, when Ibn al-Tabban, the *ra'is al-marakib* (lit. 'the chief of the ships'), built a mosque, garden and a house in front of al-Kharq and to the west of the Khalij. And so, this selected piece of land (*al-khitta*), was known as Barr al-Tabban, after Ibn al-Tabban. Construction continued until the situation required the appointment of a governor solely for al-Jamikiyya, independent of the governor of al-Qahira, to oversee the west bank of the Khalij.

Throughout the Fatimid period, al-Fustat was the principal city of Egypt and the centre of its economic, industrial and scientific activity. In contrast, al-Qahira was the residence of the Fatimid government, the administrative and political centre of the state and the seat of the Ismaili *da'wa* or missionary organisation. The two cities together form the Egyptian capital in the Fatimid era.

Towards the end of Fatimid rule, in 564/1168, a fire which had been started deliberately on the orders of the vizier Shawar devastated al-Fustat during the Crusader invasion of Eyypt. The conflagration continued for over fifty-four days and destroyed most of the buildings around the mosque of 'Amr and in the north-western district known as al-Hamrawat (the areas to the east had been in ruins since the crisis of the mid 5th/11th century). The people of al-Fustat fled to al-Qahira: initially to seek protection there and then to protect it from attack by Amalric I, the king of the Frankish state of Jerusalem. Amalric was later compelled to lift the siege of al-Qahira when he learnt of the arrival of the armies of Nur al-Din under the leadership of Shirkuh and Salah al-Din (Saladin in Crusader sources), founder of the Ayyubid dynasty and nephew of the former, and their threat to his possessions in Palestine. Later, Shirkuh managed to defeat Shawar and eliminate his power base (as vizier of the caliph al-'Adid). He also managed to convince the people of al-Fustat to return to their homes and rebuild their city. It seems that the rebuilding process was actually carried out during 572/1176 and Abu Salih al-Armani regarded this year as the start of the reconstruction of many of the churches in al-Fustat. Furthermore, Ibn Jubayr, who visited Egypt nearly five years later, says that most of the city had been renovated and that construction was going on at the time of his visit.

Cairo in the Ayyubid era, 567–648/1171–1250
When Salah al-Din achieved control over Egypt in 567/1171, his primary concern was to leave Cairo and return north to Syria. Therefore, he thought of building a well-fortified citadel which would be defensible and which would overlook both al-Qahira and al-Fustat. This desire has already been observed in the ruling families who built the cities of al-'Askar, al-Qata'i' and al-Qahira. Salah al-Din chose the lower slopes of Jabal al-Muqattam on which to build the Citadel. The Citadel thereafter became the residence of the Mamluk sultans and then Ottoman pashas. In 572/1176–1177, Salah al-Din entrusted Baha' al-Din Qaraqush with building the Citadel and the stone walls that enclosed al-Qahira, the Citadel and al-Fustat. By 579/1183, Qaraqush had completed most of it, after demolishing numerous small pyramids scattered around Giza in order to use the stone for this purpose.

Although scholars have differed on the reason behind the building of the Citadel, it is most probable that when Salah al-Din built it he was following the common traditions of his homeland, Syria, where each city had its own citadel or fortress. Past experience had demonstrated that when a city fell into enemy hands, its citadel remained invincible and hence it was possible to regain the city.

During the short periods which Salah al-Din spent in Cairo, he did not reside in the Citadel permanently. Rather, he, together with his son al-Malik al-'Aziz 'Uthman and his brother al-Malik al-'Adil Abu Bakr, used to move frequently between the fortress and the *dar al-wuzara*, the administrative centre. Al-Malik al-Kamil Muhammad was the first to move permanently from the *dar al-wuzara* to the Citadel, in 604/1207. Thus, al-Qahira lost its prestige as a ruling centre, and commercial and artisan activities moved into it and spread out over the site of the Fatimid palaces around al-Shari' al-A'zam or Qasabat al-Qahira.

Nevertheless, al-Fustat remained – despite the horrors it had endured – an overpopulated city, since the general public and the poor went back to live there.

Paul Casanova, Keppel A. C. Creswell and Nasser Rabbat have all described the Citadel and Salah al-Din's wall in detail, following the literary sources and the archeological investigation of the site.

Nowadays, there is no mosque in Cairo that dates from the Ayyubid era. Furthermore, no Ayyubid archeological inscriptions have been found indicating the restoration or maintenance of the mosques of 'Amr and Ibn Tulun by the Ayyubids. These two mosques and the Hakim Mosque to the north of al-Qahira are those in which the Ayyubid rulers permitted the Friday sermon to be delivered, and this was done to undermine the importance of al-Azhar which had been the centre of the Fatimid *da'wa*. Thus Salah al-Din abrogated the delivery of the Friday sermon in it and this remained the case until the Mamluk sultan al-Zahir Baybars reintroduced it in 665/1267.

In general, the Ayyubids directed their concerns to the establishing of *madrasa*s; Salah al-Din built a large number of them in al-Fustat. What is more, his successors followed him in building *madrasa*s in al-Qahira in order to complete the Sunni reform he had undertaken and to combat the activities of the Fatimid *da'wa*. The Ayyubids established some twenty-three *madrasa*s in al-Qahira and al-Fustat. However, they did not survive the passage of time, though some of their remains can still be found, including those of al-Madrasa al-Kamiliyya and al-Madaris al-Salihiyya, not to mention the mausoleum (*qubba*) of al-Imam al-Shafi'i, the mausoleums of the 'Abbasid caliphs, the mausoleum of al-Salih Najm al-Din Ayyub, the mausoleum of Queen Shajarat al-Durr and the mansion of al-Tha'aliba.

Excluding the military constructions which the Ayyubids built in Egypt (the Citadel and the wall around Cairo), there is no extant public construction dating from the Ayyubid era. The Ayyubid elements of the aqueduct which used to supply the Citadel with water were incorporated in the works carried out by al-Nasir Muhammad b. Qalawun and al-Ashraf Qansuh al-Ghawri. However, there are still the remains of two bridges to Giza on which there are inscriptions in the name of Qaraqush dating from the reign of Salah al-Din. There are also other inscriptions which indicate the restoration works that were carried out by al-Nasir Muhammad b. Qalawun, al-Ashraf Qaytbay and Husayn Pasha.

Towards the end of the Ayyubid period, the seat of government moved temporarily from the Citadel to another fortified site at the western edge of the capital. This fortress was built by al-Malik al-Salih Najm al-Din Ayyub on the island of al-Rawda, using a large number of Crusader captives as labour. Al-Malik al-Salih had the palace surrounded by a wall fitted with sixty towers. He moved into it with his court and his family in 638/1240–1241. Al-Salih also established a regiment of Mamluks, whom he had brought up and trained in the citadel of al-Rawda. It was they who succeeded the Ayyubids under the name of the Bahri Mamluks. An audience hall (qa'a) from al-Malik al-Salih's palace survived until the end of the 18th century when Jean-Joseph Marcel, one of the scholars of Napoleon's expedition, presented a detailed description and an accurate plan of it in the section of *La Description de l'Egypte* devoted to the study of the island of al-Rawda and the Nilometre (*al-miqyas*).

The last years of the 6th/12th century witnessed an acute economic crisis, more severe than that which had hit Egypt in the middle of the 5th/11th century. 'Abd al-Latif al-Baghdadi described this crisis in detail in his *Kitab al-ifada*. As before, the people of al-Fustat were more affected than the inhabitants of al-Qahira.

The expansion of Cairo in the Mamluk era, 648–923/1250–1517
When the Mamluks attained supreme political authority in Egypt, the expansion and growth of Cairo took on a new shape. After the fall of Baghdad to the Mongols in 656/1258 and the transfer of the 'Abbasid caliphate to Cairo, the Islamic east came under this formal religious authority established from then on in the Egyptian capital. An increase of the population of Egypt resulted from these events:

First, because of the migration of a large number of refugees who fled to Egypt from the east in the face of the Mongol invasion. They settled especially on both sides of al-Khalij, around Birkat al-Fil and in the district of al-Husayniyya to the north of Fatimid al-Qahira where Sultan al-Zahir Baybars established his Great Mosque in 665/1266.

Second, after the flight of part of the army of the Mongol Hulagu to Egypt in 660/1262, al-Zahir Baybars lodged them in 'houses which he had built for them in the land of al-Luq', on the west bank of al-Khalij. Then, later on, Mongol immigrants called *wafidiyya*, or the newcomers, arrived and settled in Hikr Aqbugha, the area furthest north of al-Fustat where al-Sab' Siqayat was and near Qanatir al-Siba'. This bridge, which was built by al-Zahir Baybars (and is now in the district of al-Sayyida Zaynab) in order to link the banks of the Khalij, brought about the revival this quarter. There were also Mongol refugees known as Oirats who fled to Egypt after the Mongol invasion during the reign of al-'Adil Kitbugha (694/1294–1295) and settled in the district of al-Husayniyya to the north of al-Qahira.

Mamluk Cairo reached its greatest recorded level of growth during the third reign of al-Nasir Muhammad I b. Qalawun (709–741/1310–1341), which is considered to be an important turning point in the city's history. The growth was basically concentrated outside Bab Zuwayla and in the district below the Citadel (qal'at al-jabal) where the Mamluk amirs erected a large number of new constructions at the sultan's behest. This included – in addition to houses and palaces – building a number of congregational mosques. Thus, up to 718/1318, the opinion which stated that the Friday sermon should be delivered in only one mosque of a city had prevailed (and this was the opinion of the Shafi'i school of law which had been followed by the Ayyubids). Therefore, there now was in Cairo: al-Azhar in the south, the mosque of al-Hakim to the north and the congregational mosque (al-masjid al-jami') of 'Amr in al-Fustat. Furthermore, Sultan al-Mansur Lajin had restored the mosque of Ibn Tulun in 696/1296–1297 to serve the area south of Bab Zuwayla, and then the Citadel had its own mosque which was built by al-Nasir Muhammad b. Qalawun in 718/1318. However, between 730/1329 and 740/1339 four new congregational mosques were built between Bab Zuwayla and the Citadel. These mosques were Jami' 'Ulmas al-Hajib in Shari' al-Hilmiyya (730/

1329–1330), Jami' Qusun in Shari' al-Qal'a (formerly Muhammad 'Ali Street) (730/1329–1330), the Bashtak Mosque in Shari' Darb al-Jamamiz (736/1336), and Altunbugha al-Maridini Mosque in Shari' al-Tabbana (739/1338–1339) which was the largest and most magnificent of them. In addition, there were a number of mosques and *madrasa*s built elsewhere in the city, such as Madrasa Mughultay al-Jamali (730/1329), al-Khutayri Mosque (737/1337) and al-Sitt Hadaq Mosque (740/1339).

After the death of al-Nasir Muhammad in 741/1341, his amirs continued building in this district which became that of the Mamluk aristocracy. Thus, three new mosques were built: Jami' Aslam al-Silahdar al-Baha'i in Darb Shuglan (746/1345), Aqsunqur al-Nasiri Mosque in Shari' Bab al-Wazir (747/1346), which was restored by Ibrahim Agha Mustahfazan in 1061/1651 and became known as al-Jami' al-Azraq, and Jami' Shaykhu al-'Umari in Shari' Shaykhun in al-Salibiyya (750/1349).

The flourishing state of this southern district of Cairo outside Bab Zuwayla had a negative impact upon the development of the northern quarter outside Bab al-Futuh where al-Hara al-Husayniyya was located. This was particularly the case after the Black Death when the area was abandoned. Then its buildings were pulled down and it was completely destroyed after the privations of the year 806/1402. Nevertheless the Black Death could not stop the process of construction outside Bab Zuwayla and so the Jami' Shaykhu was built during this period, Dar Sarghitmish in the region of Bi'r al-Watawit (753/1352–1353), the palace of Amir Taz in Shari' al-Suyufiyya (755/1354) and the mausoleum and *khanqah* of Shaykhu (757/1356). However, the most important of these constructions was the mosque and *madrasa* of Sultan Hasan (757–764/1356–1363). It is one of the greatest *madrasa*-mosques and it cost over twenty million dirhams, which makes it the most expensive building ever erected in Cairo. In order to build it two of Cairo's most luxurious palaces were pulled down, Yalbugha al-Yahyawi Palace and Qasr Altunbugha al-Maridani.

The building of these mosques and *madrasa*s does not – as one might think – indicate an increase in population. On the contrary, the population of Egypt decreased at the time as a result of the Plague. However,

the large number of deaths led to an increase in inheritance tax (*al-mawarith*) and *al-mawarith al-hashriyya*, that is to say property left without inheritors which was appropriated by the state, and this therefore permitted the rulers and powerful amirs to implement an ambitious construction policy.

During the Mamluk period, Cairo was not a fortified city; the Fatimid wall had disappeared among the quarters of the Mamluk city. What is more al-Qasaba, or al-Shari' al-A'zam, was not only the commercial artery of the city, but also the route for processions and the place where the sultans would parade past the people. These celebrations bring to mind Cairo's Fatimid inheritance which could still be perceived, even at that time. As al-Shari' al-A'zam had been regarded as the main political and spiritual centre of Fatimid al-Qahira, so in the Mamluk era it became a sort of university city. All along al-Qasaba – especially around Bayn al-Qasrayn – were laid out a series of *madrasa*s, Dar al-Hadith al-Kamiliyya (622/1225), al-Madaris al-Salihiyya (641/1243–1244), al-Madrasa al-Zahiriyya Baybars (660–662/1262–1263), the mausoleum and *madrasa* of al-Mansur Qalawun (673–684/1274–1285), al-Madrasa al-Nasiriyya Muhammad b. Qalawun (695–703/1295–1304), al-Madrasa al-Zahiriyya Barquq (786–788/1384–1386) and al-Madrasa al-Ashrafiyya Barsbay (829/1425). Slightly to the south there is the last mosque of the Circassian Mamluks: Jami' al-Ashraf Qansuh al-Ghawri and near it there was a new complex: a mausoleum, a fountain and a *kuttab* or Qur'anic school (909–910/1504–1505), then the mosque and *madrasa* of al-Mu'ayyad Shaykh al-Mahmudi (818–823/1415–1420), near Bab Zuwayla to the south of the Fatimid city.

On both sides of al-Qasaba and the streets parallel to it there were also a large number of religious buildings: the *khanqah* of Baybars al-Jashinkir (706–709/1306–1310) and al-Madrasa al-Qarasunquriyya (700/1300–1301), which was next to the *khanqah* to the south of Shari' al-Jamaliyya. Jami' Sabiq al-Din Mithqal (763/1361–1362) was in Shari' Darb Hurmiz, the *madrasa* of Jamal al-Din al-Ustadar (811/1408–1409) was in Shari' al-Tumbakshiyya and the mosque of Abu Bakr b. Muzhir (884/1479) was in Hara Barjawan. The *qadi*'s court was held in Bayn al-Qasrayn in

N 855 Panorama du Vieux Caire et Pyramides

al-Salihiyya al-Najmiyya *madrasa*. There was also al-Maristan al-Mansuri, which was the medical centre of Egypt until the 19th century.

To these can also be added the foregoing: Madrasa Umm al-Sultan Sha'ban (770/1369) in Shari' Bab al-Wazir, Madrasat al-Ashraf Sha'ban (777/1376) on the rise in front of Bab al-Qal'a, and Jami' Aytmish al-Bajasi (785/1383) in Shari' Bab al-Wazir. Thus the greater part of the Islamic monuments of Cairo came to be concentrated inside the limits of Mamluk Cairo where the districts of al-Jamaliyya, al-Darb al-Ahmar and al-Khalifa as far as Shari' Saliba and the Ibn Tulun Mosque to the south now indicate its existence.

As for the houses and palaces built in the Mamluk era, of which al-Maqrizi in his *Khitat* mentions sixty-one, most of them were erected in the 8th/14th century. However, only four palaces have come down to us, three of them outside Bab Zuwayla to the south of al-Qahira, Qasr Alin Aq in Shari' Bab al-Wazir, Qasr Qusun Yashbak behind the mosque and *madrasa* of Sultan Hasan, and the palace of Amir Taz in Shari' al-Suyufiyya. The fourth palace, Qasr Bashtak, lay inside the limits of Fatimid al-Qahira in the district of Bayn al-Qasrayn.

Thus there is still an immense amount of Mamluk heritage in Cairo; and thanks to these surviving buildings, it is still possible to imagine the shape of Cairo in this age; and we can picture it full of mosques, *madrasas, khanqahs* (sufi centres), *sabils,* houses, palaces, commercial and artisanal complexes and *wakalas* (complexes for foreign merchants), so many of which have now vanished.

Panorama of Historic Cairo
with the Nile and the pyramids
of Giza in the distance, 1865

The mausoleums and cemeteries of medieval Cairo (al-Qarafa)
A final note should be made on the subject of the cemeteries and mausoleums of Cairo. Up until the middle of the 5th/11th century the cemetery for al-Fustat was situated east of the city. Its oldest sections lay between Masjid al-Fath and the foot of the Muqattam hills. The cemetery included the quarters known today as Batn al-Baqara, al-Basatin, 'Uqba 'Amir and al-Tunisi, and it is now called al-Qarafa al-Kubra, 'the great cemetery'. The area bounded by the mausoleum of Imam al-Shafi'i and the foot of Jabal al-Muqattam did not contain a burial ground until, in 608/1211–1212, the Ayyubid al-Malik al-Kamil Muhammad buried his son near the tomb of Imam al-Shafi'i and erected the great cupola, which can still be seen, for the imam's mausoleum. As a result, people moved their tombs from al-Qarafa al-Kubra to this area and built tombs there and so it was known as al-Qarafa al-Sughra (the small cemetery). During the reign of al-Nasir Muhammad I b. Qalawun, the Mamluk amirs built new mausoleums between the shrine of Imam al-Shafi'i and Bab al-Qarafa until construction became continuous from Birkat al-Habash in the south to Bab al-Qarafa in the north.

There is another cemetery whose origins go back to the 2nd/8th century. It was located at the northern edge of al-Fustat al-Misr and it used to cover the region south-west of Bab al-Qarafa as far as 'Ayn al-Sayyira. At the beginning of the 3rd/9th century, a third cemetery was established at the foot of Jabal al-Muqattam where the shrine of 'Umar b. al-Farid now is. The district used to be known as the Graveyard of Mahmud.

Finally, perhaps at the start of the 4th/10th century, a new phenomenon occurred in this quarter of architectural development. The quarter got its name from Banu Qarafa, one of the clans of the tribe of al-Ma'afir. All of Cairo's cemeteries, all known as al-Qarafa, are named after this tribe. Ibn Jubayr and Ibn Sa'id both say that they spent several nights in al-Qarafa. Ibn Sa'id adds that there are 'tombs which have attached to them buildings which are maintained and several graveyards which have religious endowments (sing. *waqf*) for reciters of the Qur'an and a great *madrasa* for the Shafi'is. Furthermore, there is always singing, especially on moonlit nights, and it is where most of Egypt's social gatherings take place and is their most famous park.'

After the Fatimid conquest, new cemeteries were established first in the south-east of al-Qahira and then expanding to Bab Zuwayla in the area now occupied by Jami' al-Salih Tala'i', Shari' al-Darb al-Ahmar, Shari' al-Tabbana, Shari' Bab al-Wazir and the streets that lead off from them. After the death of the *amir al-juyush*, Badr al-Jamali, in 487/1094, another cemetery was established outside Bab al-Nasr to the north of Cairo and the *amir al-juyush* was the first to be buried in it. The site is at present occupied by Qarafa Bab al-Nasr which lies between Hayy al-Husayniyya and Shari' al-Mansuriyya.

As for the Qarafa of the Mamluks which is located in the Sahra' al-Mamlik to the east of the road known as Tariq Salah Salim, it was only established in the Circassian Mamluk period at the end of the 8th/14th century when the Mamluk sultans and amirs began erecting mosques and *khanqah*s in the area and adding their tombs onto them. By the end of the 9th/15th century, this had become a unique assemblage of religious constructions and mausoleums all gathered together in one place. Among the Circassian Mamluk sultans, the one who devoted his attention to building in this area was al-Malik al-Sultan al-Ashraf Abu al-Nasr Qaytbay (872–901/1468–1496), and so it is known in the sources as 'the Graveyard of Qaytbay', Turab Qaytbay.

The urban character of al-Darb al-Ahmar

Nasser Rabbat

In an Islamic world rudely and almost belatedly awakened to the deteriorating splendours of its structural heritage, Cairo, unquestionably the Islamic city richest in significant architecture, has also one of the most endangered historic centres. This fragile, exceedingly crowded and relatively small, urban corridor (approximately 5 km × 2 km) has been threatened in recent decades by a severe population explosion accompanied by a mixture of official neglect, greedy and speculative development, and chaotic overbuilding. The degradation went on almost unnoticed until the earthquake of October 1992, which concentrated the attention of concerned organisations on some of the perennial problems of Historic Cairo and prompted the implementation of a number of conservation projects at various sites around the city. Some of these projects were carefully planned and executed, such as those for the *sabil-kuttab* of Nafisa al-Bayda (with its concomitant spirited rehabilitation of al-Darb al-Asfar) and the houses of al-Sinnari and al-Suhaimi. Others were akin to plastic surgery whereby the monuments acquired an ornate finish but their structural deterioration was left untreated, as in the case of al-Azhar Mosque and the mosque of al-Mu'ayyad. In contrast to this one can cite the restoration of four of the most important Fatimid monuments: the mosques of al-Hakim, al-Aqmar and Lu'lu'a, and the mausoleum of al-Juyushi. These projects, which began before the earthquake, were sponsored and carried out by members of the Ismaili Bohra community, whose concern was to reconstruct these monuments as places of worship for use in the modern age.

Cairo undoubtedly deserves sensible urban management, balancing the requirements of preservation and development. After all, the deterioration of the historic core in the 20th century is a direct outcome of the overall mismanagement of the contemporary metropolis. Moreover, the myriad restoration projects carried out thus far have not conformed to an overall plan of urban conservation, a subject which in its turn was not discussed until the late 1990s. In fact, it is only in the last few years that we can speak of a rhetorically articulated vision – but not yet of a clear policy – which moves from conserving individual monuments to advocating the preservation of the old city as a living and economically viable, social and physical entity. The first project to adhere to this vision is the Darb al-Ahmar Project, an ambitious undertaking that aims at nothing less than the rehabilitation and reinvigoration of this substantial historic neighbourhood in the heart of Cairo.

Al-Darb al-Ahmar is one of the five divisions (*aqsam*, sing. *qism*), of Historic Cairo. The other four *aqsam* are Sayyida Zaynab, al-Khalifa, al-Jamaliyya (Gamalia) and Bab al-Shar'iyya. Between them, these *aqsam* contain most of the Fatimid, Ayyubid, Mamluk and Ottoman monuments of Cairo. Within the walls of the Historic City, and with more than forty registered monuments from the various periods of Islamic history, al-Darb al-Ahmar is second in historic importance only to the Fatimid city. Administratively, al-Darb al-Ahmar belongs to the central district (*hay wasa*) of Cairo, which also includes the districts of al-Jamaliyya and Bab al-Shar'iyya. It encompasses fourteen subdivisions (sing. *shiyakha*), with a total area of 3.87 sq km and a population estimated at more than 350,000, making it one of the most densely packed districts in a very crowded city. The pressures of overcrowding and congestion render al-Darb al-Ahmar an extremely precarious domain for historic conservation. They also challenge the restorers and planners to produce solutions that meet the requirements of the inhabitants as much as they respond to the deteriorating condition of the monuments. Experience has shown that in the pursuit of the true preservation of historic centres, these two factors are closely interconnected.

The Darb al-Ahmar Project, sponsored by the Aga Khan Trust for Culture (AKTC) along with other Egyptian and foreign organisations, is being implemented by AKTC's specialised arm, the Historic Cities Support Programme (HCSP). It was initially envisaged as an offshoot of al-Azhar Park, another major project funded and executed by the same agency on the nearby Darassa Hills. Early on in the process, it was rightly observed that a modern landscape project such as al-Azhar Park, complete with lavish tourist services and the restored 6th/

12th-century wall as a backdrop, could not border on a dilapidated and depressed, though historically rich, district. Moreover, it was realised that only the strategically planned rejuvenation of the urban surroundings – besides the legal and zoning devices – could insure the survival of the park at this critical location in the constantly growing metropolis. Thus began the involvement of the AKTC with al-Darb al-Ahmar district. But the revitalisation project soon took on a relevance of its own as an integrated experiment in urban conservation, involving a serious investment in the welfare of the neighbourhood and the maintenance of its infrastructure and services, as well as its historic monuments. This was coupled with an educational campaign designed to teach the inhabitants the merits of conservation and to highlight the ties that bind them to their district and to the city at large. This campaign was meant to penetrate all social levels via both formal and informal channels.

The task of educating the inhabitants of the district must have been overwhelming, and not because reasons to be proud of belonging to al-Darb al-Ahmar were few or hard to find. Quite the opposite: the difficulty must have stemmed from the abundance of historical events to recall and monuments to anchor in the consciousness of the inhabitants before they could be properly rehabilitated as functioning structures and thus reincorporated into the life of the district. The area has indeed had a glorious past that has left indelible marks on the inordinate number of largely neglected landmarks lining its thoroughfares. These monuments, each protectively cocooned in the organic urban fabric of Cairo, span the entire gamut of styles that distinguished the Islamic city from the 6th/12th century onwards. Most of them, however, belong to the Mamluk period (648–922/1250–1517), which produced an extraordinary urban architecture, synthesising the achievements of previous ages and symbolising the city for centuries

Mamluks exercising in the square of Murad Bey's palace, Luigi Mayer, *circa* 1755–1803

View of al-Darb al-Ahmar
from the Darassa Hills,
showing the dome of the
Amir Khayrbak complex in the
foreground and the mosque
of Sultan Hasan in the
distance, *circa* 1865

to come. Grounding these structures in their historical context can help the reader empathise with the emotions that the denizens and restorers of al-Darb al-Ahmar must have experienced as they became reacquainted with the celebrated district in which they had had to negotiate their partnership.

Looking at a map of Historic Cairo, one is immediately struck by the irregular alignment of the main thoroughfare in al-Darb al-Ahmar, whose various sections are called also al-Darb al-Tabbana and Bab al-Wazir Street, al-Darb al-Ahmar being the name both of the district and its principal street. Beginning immediately outside Bab Zuwayla (Zawila), the imposing southern gate of Fatimid al-Qahira, the street runs almost due east behind the mosque of al-Salih Tala'i' (555/1160) along the Fatimid wall for about 200 metres. It then takes a turn to the south-east in front of the late Mamluk mosque of Qijmas al-Ishaqi (885–886/1480–1481) and runs straight for another 100 metres to the corner of the mosque of Ahmad al-Mihmandar (725/1324–1325). At that point, it takes a sharp turn further to the south and continues more or less uninterrupted for almost a kilometre until it comes to the side of the mosque of Aytamish al-Bajasi (725/1324–1325). There it turns very slightly to the south-west and goes on for almost 2,250 metres until it meets al-Sikkat al-Mahjar at the foot of the hill on which the Citadel stands. After that intersection, the street tilts considerably to the south-east and metamorphoses into the famous Sikkat al-Mudarraj, a wide stairway (*mudarraj*), carved in the rock which led originally up to the main Ayyubid gate of the Citadel, Bab al-Mudarraj. An inscription from the reign of Salah al-Din, dated 579/1183–1184, still exists above the gate's slightly pointed arch which formed the only entrance to the Citadel from the city throughout the Ayyubid and Mamluk periods.

At first glance, the wide arcuate shape of al-Darb al-Ahmar is incomprehensible as it clearly diverges from the dominant orientation of the north–south streets connecting al-Qahira with al-Fustat, the pre-Fatimid capital to the south. The two other main Mamluk streets, known today as al-Khiyamiyya and Suq al-Silah streets, follow the alignment of the main north–south streets of royal al-Qahira,

especially Bayn al-Qasrayn and al-Jamaliyya streets. They all clearly conform to the orientation of al-Khalij, the main canal that brought water from the Nile to the Fatimid capital, and thus the basic axis in that urban environment. Only al-Darb al-Ahmar deviates from this clearly deliberate planning scheme, and this must have been for an overriding reason. This reason has to be sought in the main function of al-Darb al-Ahmar as it developed with the growth of the city in the early Mamluk period to fill the sparsely populated land between Fatimid al-Qahira, the Citadel, al-Khalij and the northern reaches of al-Fustat.

Al-Darb al-Ahmar became the umbilical cord that linked the old Fatimid capital al-Qahira, which had become the hub of economic life, to the Citadel, the new seat of government and the centre of the empire from the beginning of the 7th/13th to the early 10th/16th century. The street provided the most direct passage for goods and people between these two poles of urban life in the conglomerate that Cairo had become after Salah al-Din decided to encircle al-Qahira, al-Fustat and the Citadel with one long, defensive wall that left huge swathes of land vacant within it. Goods were transported daily along al-Darb al-Ahmar's spine to supply the Citadel, home of the Mamluk army and court, with its necessary provisions. The citizens of Cairo traversed it to reach the part of the Citadel that was open to them, especially on the two days of *dar al-'adl* (the court of justice), Monday and Thursday, when the sultan held a public audience to look into acts of injustice (*al-nazar fi'l-mazalim*) brought to his attention. Conversely al-Darb al-Ahmar was the favourite route for the Mamluks when they came down from the Citadel to the city for official business or pleasure. It formed the last stretch of the processional route taken by the sultan in major ceremonies, such as coronation day and victory parades. The sultan would ride through al-Qahira from the north, through Bab al-Nasr and come out from Bab Zuwayla riding along al-Darb al-Ahmar to the horse market below the Citadel. He then would enter the Citadel from Bab al-Silsila and proceed up to the great *iwan* or portico, the scene of the culminating ceremony, the royal banquet.

Mosques, *madrasa*s, palaces and commercial structures lined the ceremonial route and vied with each other for maximum street exposure. In that busy public space, their designers had to resort to a number of architectural tricks to catch the attention of the passer-by. For instance, they constructed tightly composed facades with layered surfaces and cleverly placed recesses, which nonetheless followed the contours of the street, almost to a fault. Spatially, they emphasised the verticality of certain choice elements such as attenuated portals with trilobed conches and geometric decorative patterns, tall and tiered minarets with bulbous finials, and slender, carved stone domes with high drums and tapered profiles. They also used polychromatic surface articulation, the most ubiquitous technique being the one called *ablaq*, consisting of alternate courses of black and white stone designed to highlight important elements in the composition. Throughout the Mamluk period, architects and designers seem to have been constantly striving to refine what might be called an 'urbanistically' sensitive approach. The end result, which was specifically Cairene and Mamluk, was an accented street facade composed of distinct structures, ingeniously arranged to both accommodate and dominate their urban surroundings. This quality can still be admired today along the processional route from Bab al-Futuh to the Citadel, despite both the disappearance of numerous Mamluk structures and the dilapidated condition of most of the ones still standing.

The section of the processional route inside al-Qahira (the old Bayn al-Qasrayn of the Fatimids between Bab al-Futuh and Bab Zuwayla) seems to have been reserved exclusively for royal religious complexes. By the end of the Mamluk period, at least ten of these complexes lined the street from north to south. The oldest was the *madrasa* of al-Kamil Muhammad (known as al-Dar al-Hadith al-Kamiliyya) (622/1225), which seems to have inaugurated the process of building in the formerly restricted area of the Fatimid palaces. The last was the complex of Qansuh II al-Ghawri (906–922/1501–1516), which conscripted the street to heighten the spatial continuity between its two separate structures. Four other royal complexes congregated around the *madrasa*s of al-Salih Najm al-Din Ayyub (built over the period from 641 to 648/1243 to 1250) in the central section of Bayn al-Qasrayn. They comprised the complexes of al-Zahir Baybars I (660–662/1262–1263), al-Mansur Qalawun (683/1284), al-Nasir Muhammad I (693–708/1293–1309) and al-Zahir Barquq (784–791/1382–1389). Religious structures built by amirs were apparently not permitted to border on Bayn al-Qasrayn, only, although infrequently, their palaces and commercial establishments. This royal exclusivity would appear to indicate that it was only religious structures that imparted to their builders the prestige and good reputation they sought from bestowing their patronage. Palaces and caravanserais, though still recognised as major structures, did not carry the same meaning, at least not as far as our written sources are concerned. Moreover, because they did not command the same inviolability as religious buildings, amirs and sultans had no qualms about expropriating secular structures. They would either replace them with new constructions or remodel them to fit their tastes and then rename them after themselves. This process was only exceptionally, and in extreme political circumstances, carried out on religious structures (such as when Sultan al-Nasir Muhammad appropriated and completed the *madrasa* in Bayn al-Qasrayn which was started by al-'Adil Kitbugha who had usurped the throne between 694/1294 and 696/1296).

Amirs built their religious monuments on the side streets leading off Bayn al-Qasrayn, or along the second part of the processional route, al-Darb al-Ahmar, which in fact has no royal religious buildings. However, al-Darb al-Ahmar's prestige was second only to that of Bayn al-Qasrayn; the route between the city and the Citadel was attractive to Mamluk amirs as a site for building their religious structures, which in turn helped to embellish the street and raise its standing still further. Three major buildings, all mosques built by high-ranking amirs of Sultan al-Nasir Muhammad, mark the beginning of the monumentalising of al-Darb al-Ahmar. They are, from north to south, the mosque of Ahmad al-Mihmandar, the mosque of Altunbugha al-Maridani (739–740/1339–1340) and the mosque of

Aqsunqur (747–748/1346–1348). (The Fatimid mosque of al-Salih Tala'i' cannot be seen as belonging to al-Darb al-Ahmar since its main facade is on al-Khiyamiyya Street). Building activity slowed down after the prosperous reign of al-Nasir Muhammad but never stopped. In 770/1368–1369, the *madrasa* of Umm al-Sultan Sha'ban (the mother of Sultan Sha'ban) was constructed to the south of the three mosques of al-Nasir Muhammad's reign. This was followed by the mosque of Aytamish al-Bajasi, situated at the southern tip of al-Darb al-Ahmar, which was the first structure erected on the street by an amir in the Burji or Circassian period. Then came the elegant complex of Qijmas al-Ishaqi, which was placed at the northern bifurcation of the street, just by Bab Zuwayla. The last Burji complex on al-Darb al-Ahmar was that of Amir Khayrbak (907–926/1502–1521) which was built in two stages, the second after the fall of the Mamluk empire. The first construction was a mausoleum for Khayrbak (907/1502–1503) built when he was still a rising amir under Qansuh al-Ghawri. It was attached via a secret doorway to an earlier building, the palace of Alin Aq (691/1292) which Khayrbak had appropriated. The second stage comprised a mosque and a *sabil* (water fountain) (926/1520) erected when Khayrbak became viceroy of Egypt under the Ottoman sultan Selim I. He was given this highest of positions as a reward for his betrayal of his Mamluk master, al-Ghawri, at the battle of Marj Dabiq (25 Rajab 922/ 24 August 1516) which sealed the fate of the Mamluk empire. (The architecture of these monuments is discussed in Caroline Williams's article in this volume).

The trend for endowing flamboyant princely religious buildings along al-Darb al-Ahmar came to an abrupt end after the Ottomans took over Egypt. Cairo was reduced to a provincial capital whose governors were appointed from Istanbul for very short terms. Subordinate status is not conducive to either magnificent processions or grand architectural projects. Nor did al-Darb al-Ahmar preserve its role as a processional route, even on the modest scale required by a regional seat of government. The Ottoman pashas took to coming to Cairo by boat along the Nile, and to leading a procession of entry from Bulaq to the Citadel along the outskirts of the city, totally bypassing al-Darb al-Ahmar. The one procession that remained from the old days, the Mahmal procession (Litter procession) that marked the opening of the Pilgrimage (*hajj*) season, could not sustain the ceremonial aspect of the street on its own. Slowly, al-Darb al-Ahmar retreated to the status of a principal commercial avenue in the shadow of the Citadel, whose inhabitants constituted its main customers.

Throughout almost three hundred years of Ottoman rule, al-Darb al-Ahmar acquired only a handful of unassuming *sabil-kuttab*s, endowed by a number of powerful *agha*s (officers) of the Janissary corps, foot soldiers of the Ottoman army, stationed in Egypt. Some *agha*s appropriated Mamluk religious monuments and retrofitted them to suit their tastes and the circumstances. On the other hand, these same army *agha*s invested large sums in income-generating structures, such as shops, khans, *rab*'s (the uniquely Cairene style of tenement house), and residences. These new buildings lined both sides of the street and changed its character from a ceremonial avenue to a mixed-use street dominated by a commercial function. Things did not change much during the reigns of Muhammad 'Ali (1220–1264/1805–1848) and his successors in the 19th and early 20th century, who imposed a series of capricious modernising projects on the city. A number of new houses for government officials were built along al-Darb al-Ahmar, emphasising the residential aspect of the district. The architecture of these housing units, like most other cultural aspects of the period, vacillated between traditional and modern influences creating an air of quaint formal uncertainty that still affects Cairene residential architecture today.

Al-Darb al-Ahmar is thus essentially a Mamluk creation. Its overall orientation was dictated by the need to link the Mamluk Citadel, which became the focus of a truly imperial court, to the economic centre of the city, which occupied the former walled city of the Fatimids. Its plan was gradually adjusted to fit the refinements of Mamluk royal processions, which involved numerous halts along the ceremonial route. Mamluk amirs endowed all the religious and most of the secular monuments along the street. They competed with each other to command the best locations, those which would give the highest degree of visibility to their buildings. As a result, like Bayn al-Qasrayn, al-Darb al-Ahmar was transformed into a venue for exhibition where the Mamluks displayed their elaborate spatial, visual and ceremonial grandeur. Not only the forms and functions of the buildings, but also their artful manipulation of the street, were designed to enhance their overall architectural impact. All were mobilised in the service of an expressive ceremonial pomp that reflected, and was representative of, the hierarchical system of Mamluk rule. These architectural qualities were obviously no longer pertinent after the fall of the Mamluks and the secession of the highly charged drama of royal processions. Al-Darb al-Ahmar, however, continued quietly thriving for a further 400 years, albeit with a truncated agenda and modified functions. The buildings added or altered during that long period, though they changed the primary vocation of the street, did not usurp the spatial and formal pre-eminence of the Mamluk monuments. Today, these monuments attest to the outstanding urban and symbolic properties of Mamluk architecture and frame a street that still offers lessons in good architecture. Thus, revitalising al-Darb al-Ahmar and preserving its monuments are not only valuable steps for the reinvigoration of life in the district and the support of cultural tourism, they are also vital to the underscoring of how an historic urban environment can serve as a pedagogical studio for architects and planners.

Recently the documentary film, *Living with the Past* (directed by Maysoon Pachachi and produced by Elizabeth Fernea), was released. By cleverly interweaving short interviews and historic commentaries with extended shots of buildings and people, the film presented a visually stunning narrative of life in present-day Darb al-Ahmar before and during the revitalisation project. But the film had an essentially pedagogical purpose. It was meant as an educational tool for the inhabitants of historic cities, and for students, restorers and planners who work on these historic cities. Furthermore, it was planned as one component of a double-pronged publication. The second component is the current book. It was conceived from the beginning as a complement to the film, to enhance its educational role while addressing a more specialised audience. This book was therefore compiled to provide the intellectual, historic and analytical backbone to the visual and oral accounts of the film. It addresses these aims through a number of essays on all the ancillary subjects indispensable to the understanding of life in an historic Cairene district and to restoring that district. The essays range from the historical to the contemporary and from the practical to the highly theoretical. But both projects, the film and the book, can stand independently, as teaching tools and as significant documents. They can also be combined for maximum effect. This is especially appropriate in an academic setting where the film can be used to introduce the subject and outline its various aspects, whereas the articles of the book can be read as an in-depth examination of the multiple contexts undergirding the narrative presented in the film.

In the end, the book goes a long way to answering the question raised more than 150 years ago when the *Comité de conservation des monuments arabes* was first established. The question was how can Cairo preserve its architectural heritage and also accommodate the needs of its modern inhabitants? The aspiration of the book is no different from that of the programme which was established on the ground by the planners of the Darb al-Ahmar Project: to revitalise the district as a domain of community life and to reintegrate its monuments in the urban fabric as venerated memorials of the past and as repositories of civic, educational and religious activity in the present day.

3 A traveller's account: Nasir-i Khusraw in 5th/11th-century Cairo

Alice C. Hunsberger

When Nasir-i Khusraw arrived in Cairo on 3 August AD 1047, he had been travelling about a year and a half, having left his home in Khurasan on 5 March 1046, accompanied by one of his brothers and an Indian servant. They had traversed northern Persia, Armenia, Syria, the length of the Mediterranean coast, and had also performed the *hajj*. All this, and more, he recorded in his *Safarnama* or *Book of Travels*.[1]

But Nasir's real goal was Cairo, 'the Victorious', resplendent and powerful capital of the Fatimid empire, its Ismaili Shi'i caliph a challenge to both the Sunni caliph in Baghdad and the Byzantine emperor in Constantinople. Nasir would stay there three years, a devotee of the Ismaili branch of Shi'ism, a leading figure in a lively intellectual environment,[2] a trusted envoy of the caliph himself. When he left Cairo, he left with the assignment to spread the Ismaili faith throughout greater Khurasan and Central Asia. His success brought him notoriety and hostility, so that eventually he had to flee, and he lived out his last years in exile in the Pamir mountains of Badakhshan.[3]

Besides his travelogue, Nasir was also the author of many treatises on Ismaili theology, and is celebrated as a major poet of the Persian language. He sings the praises of the Fatimid caliph of his time, al-Mustansir (r. 427–487/1036–1094), and extols the virtues of Ismaili doctrine, such as the superiority of the spoken word over the written, the paramount position of reason and intellect in matters of religion and the need to balance external expressions of faith with a knowledge of their inner meaning.[4]

With the *Safarnama* Nasir does not try to write a geography or a history of the world as others had done, but rather to give a snapshot of his time, his visit. He distinguishes clearly between what he saw and what 'they say'. His work is also unique in that he writes in Persian, specifically for an audience in Khurasan. For example, whilst the Arab geographer Ibn Hawqal describes the Nile as having more water than the Tigris and Euphrates combined,[5] Nasir-i Khusraw says Nile floods are 'twice the size of the Oxus at Tirmidh' (51). Nasir's time, too, was particular. Cairo was a city eighty years old, growing into itself, full of splendour. Yet, even if Nasir did not see the magnificent rebuilding of

walls and gates later in al-Mustansir's reign under the vizier Badr al-Jamali (1074–1094), neither did he witness the catastrophes of drought and famine, the plague of 1063, the clashes between ethnic factions in the Fatimid army, or the looting of the royal treasury (1067–1072).[6] During his visit, the state was strong and vibrant. He observed some of the fault lines,[7] but they did not crack until years after his departure.

The Royal City of al-Qahira

When the Fatimids took control of Egypt in 969, having already subdued the rest of North Africa, they arrived with plans in hand for a new royal city, 'al-Qahira' they eventually called it, to be built near al-Fustat, the economic and military capital established by the early Muslims in 642,[8] at the point on the eastern shore just before the Nile fans out into the channels and islands of the Nile Delta. By Nasir's time, the expanse between al-Fustat and al-Qahira was 'less than a mile,' with an overlap of 'the orchards and suburban buildings of the two cities' (61).

What kind of city would Nasir have seen? On the rectangular layout of the city, Nasir records five gates: Bab al-Nasr and Bab al-Futuh in the north wall looking towards Syria, Bab Zuwayla in the south wall looking towards al-Fustat. The two others, Bab al-Qantara (Gate of the Bridge) and Bab al-Khalij (Gate of the Canal) must both have opened onto the canal which ran along the eastern wall of the city, though maps show three gates facing the canal, and none specifically named 'al-Khalij'.[9] Nasir reports that the city had no fortified wall (59), indicating that the original ramparts of sun-dried brick had crumbled away.[10] But this did not seem to him to be a great problem, because 'the buildings are even stronger and higher than ramparts, and every house and building is itself a fortress'. He adds, 'Most of the buildings are five stories tall, although some are six.' The area surrounding them is laid out in an equally spacious manner: 'All the houses of al-Qahira are built separate from another, so that no one's trees or outbuildings are against anyone else's walls. Thus, whenever anyone wants to, he can open the walls of his house and add on, since it causes no detriment to anyone else.' And, 'in the midst of the houses in the city are gardens

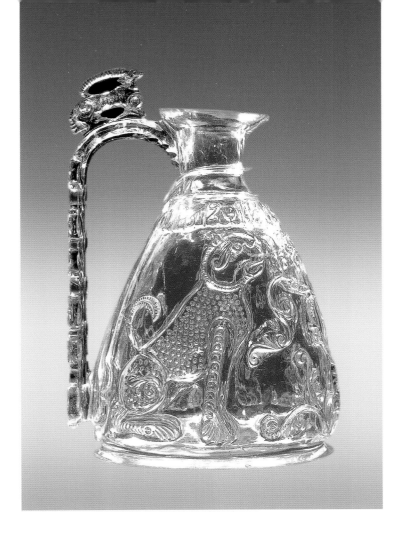

Zuwayla (for North African soldiers from the tribe of Zuwayl, or Zawila), al-Jawdariyya, al-Umara (amirs, or commanders), al-Dayalima (for the Daylamis, from Persia), al-Rum (Greeks, or Byzantines), al-Batiliyya (North Africans), Qasr al-Shawq, Abid al-Shira (purchased slaves, probably Nubians), and al-Masamida (a Nubian people, the Masmudis) (66). This principle of segregation by occupation and ethnic identity persisted in Cairo down the centuries, remaining stable as dynasties came and went, but evolving as occupational shifts occurred.[11]

The Fatimids modelled the palace buildings of al-Qahira on those of their previous capital of Mahdiyya. Inside the city walls, twelve buildings comprised an Eastern and a Western Palace, one on each side of the main thoroughfare which ran through the middle of the rectangle from north to south. A large square between the two served as a royal parade ground. 'The caliph's palace is in the middle of Cairo, encompassed by an open space so that no building abuts it. Engineers who have measured it have found it to be the size of Mayyafariqin' (58), Nasir writes, referring to one of the cities of Syria he had visited some months earlier, which had 'enormous fortifications' made from huge blocks of stone, with great towers every seventy-five feet (9). He explains that because of the open space in Cairo, five hundred mounted watchmen and five hundred on foot 'blow trumpets and beat drums at the time of evening prayer and then patrol till daybreak'. He then makes another comparison to help give a picture of the place. 'Viewed from outside the city, the sultan's palace looks like a mountain because of all the different buildings and the great height. From inside the city, however, one can see nothing at all because the walls are so high.' Indeed, the walls of the palace are of 'rock hewn to look like one piece of stone' (59).

He inquired as to the life inside: 'They say that twelve thousand hired servants work in the palace, in addition to the women and slave girls, whose number no one knows. It is said, nonetheless, that there are thirty thousand individuals in the palace' (58). While those figures come from others, Nasir does also seem to have had first-hand knowledge of the inside of the palace: 'In the sultan's harem are the most beautiful gardens imaginable. Waterwheels have been

and orchards watered by wells.' These are houses 'so magnificent and fine that you would think they were made of jewels, not of plaster, tile and stone!' (60)

We may have a glimpse of the house Nasir and his brother rented, as well as his desire to have one of the rooftop gardens. 'At the time I was there, a house on a lot twenty ells by twelve ells was being rented for fifteen dinars a month. The house was four stories tall, three of which were rented out. The tenant wanted to take the topmost floor also for an additional five dinars, but the landlord would not give it to him, saying that he might want to go there sometimes, although, *during the year we were there, he did not come twice*'(italics added) (60).

One original element in the design of al-Qahira was to house the military along ethnic lines. Nasir identifies ten separate districts, each with its own walls and gates: Barjawan (after a vizier of Caliph al-Hakim),

Rock-crystal ewer inscribed
with the name of the Fatimid
caliph al-'Aziz (r. 975–996)

Heliopolis, Tree of the Holy
Mother, tinted photograph,
circa 1900

constructed to irrigate them. There are trees planted and pleasure parks built, even on the roofs' (60).

In fact, gardens and the cultivation of plants are among Nasir's interests. He described how the Fatimid caliphs maintained the centuries-old gardens of Heliopolis ('Ayn Shams), two leagues outside the city, which were said to have belonged to Pharaoh (65). Located on a high promontory, this garden alone remains dry when all the plain is flooded (61). It is also favoured with a freshwater spring (*'ayn*) from which it takes its name, Nasir says. He particularly records the balsam trees in the garden and how their precious oil was extracted: 'It is said that the ancestors of the present sultan brought the seeds of this tree from the Maghrib and planted them. When it reaches maturity, the branches are scored, and cups attached to catch the sap-like oil that comes out. When the oil is completely drained, the tree dries up, and the gardeners take the wood to town to sell. It has a thick bark that, when stripped, tastes of almond. The next year branches sprout again from the roots, and the process can be repeated.'[12] What he does not mention is the significance of this balsam tree for Christians. The later Mamluk historian, al-Qalqashandi, writes that Christian kings would send presents to the Mamluk sultan, asking in return only the oil of this tree, for they thought it had been made holy during Christ's Flight into Egypt.[13]

The Fatimid state made great use of ceremony to anchor its authority,[14] and Nasir-i Khusraw described in particular detail one of two annual banquets in the palace and the Festival of the Opening of the Canal. He finagled his way into the banquet hall the day before a great feast marking the end of Ramadan in 1049 by explaining that he had seen the great courts of famous sultans in the east and now wanted to see this one. What he saw, he maintains, would make the book far too long were he to try to describe it. He does say, however, that twelve structures had been set up each 100 cubits square and 'each more dazzling than the last'. On one, the dais extended the entire length of the building at a height of six feet. Three sides of the dais were gold, 'with hunting and sporting scenes depicted thereon and also

an inscription in marvellous calligraphy. All the carpets and pillows were of Byzantine brocade and iridescent *buqalamun*, each woven exactly to the measurements of the gold along the sides. There was an indescribable latticework balustrade of gold along the steps' (73). This luxury was equalled in the food. Nasir was told that fifty thousand maunds of sugar, or 175,000 pounds, had been used [15] for, among other things, thousands of little sugar statuettes made for decoration, such as the little orange tree Nasir saw, complete with branches and leaves.

The Opening of the Canal had ancient roots as a festival, testifying to the Nile's centrality to life in Egypt. For millennia its rising and flooding brought fertile silt as well as water to the Nile Valley and pushed back the salt water of the Mediterranean, thus nurturing the land for agriculture. The years it did not rise there was drought and then famine. According to Nasir-i Khusraw, during the weeks of the annual rising, roughly mid-August to the end of October, all the irrigation canals would be closed, including the large canal connecting the Nile to the Red Sea. When it reached the proper height,[16] 'one of the biggest festivals of the year' would begin.

But preparations had already started. For days before, drums and trumpets were sounded throughout the stables to prepare the thousands of horses, camels and donkeys for the noise to come. An ornate tent, large enough for a hundred mounted horsemen to stand underneath it, was set up at the head of the canal.[17] Made of Byzantine brocade spun with gold and studded with gems, this pavilion for the caliph was one of many.

A major feature of the festival was the procession through the city, preceded by trumpets, clarions and drums. Ten thousand horses followed, led by jewel-studded reins and gold bridles, their gold saddles resting on brocade and iridescent saddle cloths embroidered with the name of the caliph. Then came the parade of camels (with howdahs and litters), followed by the armies, arranged in the tens of thousands by their ethnic groups. Nasir adds that there was also a contingent of princes from other lands, as well as 'scholars, literati,

poets and jurisprudents'. At some distance behind these, came the caliph in contrasting simplicity. Mounted on a camel with no gold or silver, he wore a white shirt and a plain coloured cumberbund, but 'the price of this alone is said to be ten thousand dinars'. Beside him, on another camel, rode the royal parasol-bearer, with a bejewelled, gold turban: 'The parasol he holds is extremely ornate and studded with jewels and pearls.' Along each side, people walked carrying incense, filling the air with aromatic smoke. Behind the caliph came the vizier, the chief judge and a large contingent of religious and government officials. They paraded to the head of the canal and the caliph remained mounted for a while inside the pavilion. In Nasir-i Khusraw's time, the caliph would then be handed a spear which he would throw at the dam, officially opening it, after which workers would finish the job with picks and shovels until the water broke through and rushed into the canal (61–65).

It has been pointed out that, of all the historians and chroniclers who wrote descriptions of these processions, Nasir-i Khusraw is the only one who noticed the crowd, a comment that reflects his aim of being the observant guide.[18] 'The custom here is for the people to prostrate themselves and say a prayer as the caliph passes,' he writes (65).

Cairo, crossroads of power and commerce
What the Fatimids had achieved in the establishment of al-Qahira can hardly be underestimated. They controlled the whole of North Africa,

Tiraz textile, cotton
embellished with gold leaf,
Fatimid, 4th/10th century

Sicily, the eastern shore of the Mediterranean, the Red Sea, and the Hijaz, with the two holy cities of Mecca and Medina. They were situated right at the hub of the routes connecting Europe, Byzantium and the Mediterranean with the Red Sea and the sea routes to India and the Far East and down the coast of Africa. Aside from the challenge from the 'Abbasids in Baghdad, the Fatimids needed to establish careful relations with the Byzantine emperors in Constantinople. Nasir-i Khusraw commented on this internationalism several times, as when he visited the ancient city of Alexandria, at the western end of the Delta:

> There is a lighthouse I saw in Alexandria, on top of which used to be an incendiary mirror. Whenever a ship came from Istanbul and approached opposite the mirror, fire would fall from the mirror and burn the ship up. The Byzantines exerted great effort and employed all manner of subterfuge until finally they sent someone who was able to break the mirror. In the days of al-Hakim, a man appeared who was willing to fix the mirror as it had once been, but al-Hakim said it was not necessary, that the situation was would under control, since at the time the Greeks sent gold and goods in tribute and were content for the armies of Egypt not to go near them (54).

But in the eastern part of the Delta on the island of Tanis, where Nasir was very much impressed with the exceptional quality of the textiles produced,[19] there 'is a fully armed garrison stationed as a precaution against attack by Franks and Byzantines'. Tanis itself was a particular object of desire due to the unsurpassed virtuosity of the weavers who produced its precious embroidered and brocaded fabrics, especially the iridescent *buqalamun*: 'I heard that the ruler of Byzantium once sent a message to the caliph of Egypt that he would exchange a hundred cities of his realm for Tanis alone. The caliph did not accept, of course, knowing that what he wanted of this city were its linen and *buqalamun*' (49–50). From the Fatimid side, however, he admitted 'many go on raids to Byzantium', in spite of the dangers of the sea with its 'many gulfs, each of which is two to three hundred leagues wide' (55). The delicate nature

of the balance of power between the two empires would be shown three years after Nasir's departure from Egypt, when the caliph al-Mustansir sent a giraffe and elephant to the Byzantine emperor Constantine IX, most likely in gratitude for grain sent to Egypt in a time of famine.[20]

But in Nasir's time tribute was sent from Sicily, which 'belongs to the caliph of Egypt', a twenty-day journey by ship. Each year a ship would sail from Egypt and come back filled with Sicilian tribute of 'very fine linen and striped fabric, one piece of which is worth ten dinars in Egypt' (55).

Fatimid control of Mecca and Medina carried responsibilities. Nasir witnessed how famine in the Hijaz not only put an end to many pilgrims' plans for the *hajj*, but also sent thousands of refugees streaming into Egypt, where al-Mustansir fed and clothed them (78).

To the south of Egypt, the Fatimids had relations with 'the province of Nubia, which is ruled by another king. The people there are black and their religion is Christianity.' The Fatimids had an extensive trading relationship with Nubia, and many peoples from the south were active in the Egyptian economy at many levels. For example, Nasir mentions the Masmudi province of Nubia, 'which is a land of broad pasture lands, many animals, and heavy-set, strong-limbed, short, black-skinned men; there are many soldiers of this sort in Egypt' (56).

Indeed, Egypt was teeming with people from all over the world. Its own indigenous Jewish and Christian populations held high positions in government and commerce,[21] and traders from India and Africa mixed with their counterparts from Central Asia, Byzantium and Europe. Nasir points out that, at court, the 'ministers of state and servants are all blacks and Greeks' (59), which is what he says about the slaves too (52). Nasir-i Khusraw and his brother were not the only Khurasanis in Cairo, and their servant hardly the only Indian.

Nasir waited until after the great Feast of the Sacrifice to take his leave. On 9 May 1050, he set sail, going upstream ('south' he reminds us) as far as Aswan, from where he crossed the desert by camel caravan to the Red Sea. Years later, in his exile in the mountains of Badakhshan, he would remember Cairo, 'a city whose equal is hardly to be found'.

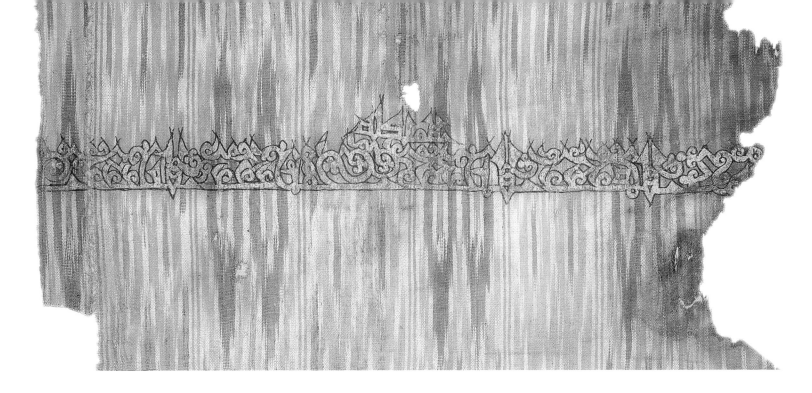

1   *Nasir-i Khusraw's Book of Travels (Safarnama):*
     A Parallel Persian-English Text, ed. and tr. Wheeler
     M. Thackston, Jr. (Costa Mesa, CA, 2001); for Cairo,
     pp. 48–82. Citations from this text will be noted as
     '(page number)'.

2   Farhad Daftary, 'Intellectual Life among the
     Ismailis: An Overview', in Farhad Daftary, ed.,
     Intellectual Traditions in Islam (London, 2000),
     pp. 94–101; Alice C. Hunsberger, 'Nasir Khusraw:
     Fatimid Intellectual', in Daftary, ed., *Intellectual
     Traditions in Islam*, pp. 112–129.

3   Alice C. Hunsberger, *Nasir Khusraw, The Ruby of
     Badakhshan: A Portrait of the Persian Poet, Traveller
     and Philosopher* (London, 2000), especially,
     'The Splendour of Fatimid Cairo', pp. 140–173.

4   For one example of his theology, see Alice
     C. Hunsberger, 'The Esoteric World Vision
     of Nasir Khusraw', *Sacred Web*, 9 (2002),
     pp. 89–100.

5   Ibn Hawqal, *Kitab surat al-ard*, French tr. by
     J. H. Kramer and Gaston Wiet as *Configuration
     de la Terre* (Paris and Beirut, 1964), p. 146.

6   Viktoria Meinecke-Berg, 'Le tresor des califes',
     *Tresors fatimides du Caire: exposition présentée à
     l'Institut du monde arabe du 28 avril au 30 aout 1998*,
     exh. cat. (Paris, 1998), pp. 96–142.

7   Hunsberger, *Ruby*, pp. 150–152, where two
     crises are discussed.

8   Janet L. Abu-Lughod, *Cairo: 1001 Years of the City
     Victorious* (Princeton, NJ, 1971), pp. 3–9.

9   It is remarkable that he does not name any gates
     for the eastern wall, indicating either extreme
     deterioration or added security in having a wall
     with no gates, or an omission in his text. In 1087,
     the new, expanded wall had ten gates.

10   André Raymond, *Cairo*, tr. Willard Wood
     (Cambridge, MA, 2000), p. 37.

11   For example, as the military became a smaller
     proportion of the population; Lughod, *Cairo*,
     pp. 24–25.

12   (S, 66). Ibn Hawqal also mentions this plant and
     its delicious bark, *Configuration de la terre*, p. 159.

13   F. Wüstenfeld, *Die Geographie und Verwaltun von
     Ägypten nach den Arabischen des Abul-'Abbas Ahmed ben
     Ali el-Calcashandi* (Göttingen, 1879), pp. 13–14, in
     Cutler, 'Gifts', p. 257.

14   Paula Sanders, *Ritual, Politics, and the City in Fatimid
     Cairo* (Albany, NY, 1994).

15   *Safarnama*, p. 157. Using three and a half pounds to
     equal one maund.

16   According to Nasir-i Khusraw, the measurement is
     eighteen ells (*Safarnama*, p. 61), but see al-Hakim

     opening the canal at the low level of 14 cubits,
     cited in Sanders, *Ritual, Politics*, p. 103.

17   He also mentions two villas (*kushk*) at 'the head of
     the canal', named Pearl (*lu'lu'*) and Jewel (*jawhara*)
     (60), perhaps analogous to the Pearl Pavilion
     (*manzarat al-lu'lu'*) and Gold House (*dar al-dhahab*)
     facing the canal near the Eastern Palace; see also
     Sanders, *Ritual, Politics*, pp. 104, 112.

18   Sanders, *Ritual, Politics*, p. 186.

19   Tanis is discussed further in Hunsberger, *Ruby*,
     pp. 148–149. Nasir-i Khusraw, *Safarnama*, pp. 49–51.

20   Anthony Cutler, 'Gifts and Gift Exchange as
     Aspects of the Byzantine, Arab, and Related
     Economies', *Dumbarton Oaks Papers,* 55 (2001),
     p. 253, plus citations in note 33.

21   See Nasir's descriptions of the Christian, 'one
     of the most propertied men in all Egypt,' who
     told the grand vizier during a time of drought that
     he had stored enough grain to feed Egypt for six
     years (*Safarnama*, p. 72), and the crisis when the chief
     jewel purchaser for the caliph was murdered by the
     caliph's soldiers, and the Jewish jeweller's relatives
     sought to buy protection for the family, but this
     payment was refused by the caliph, who, instead,
     'compensated them for their loss' (*Safarnama*,
     pp. 74–75).

4 The economy of Historic Cairo: a case study of the markets of Mamluk Cairo

Kassem Abdou Kassem

Cairo, which has been the Egyptian capital for over a thousand years, has passed through many stages in its relatively long history. First, it was intended by its founders, the Fatimids, in 358/969, to be the seat of the Fatimid caliph, his family and entourage. In this early phase of Cairene history we cannot find any historical evidence for an 'economy' of Cairo. This can be explained by the fact that Cairo was purely a political and administrative capital, as it was nearby al-Fustat which was the economic centre of Fatimid Egypt. Cairo maintained its privileged status for the whole of the Fatimid period. The Ayyubid period was a time of transition during which Cairo was transformed into the real, and permanent, capital of Egypt: politically, socially, culturally and economically.

This essay will examine the economy of historic Cairo through the study of the markets of Cairo during the Mamluk period (648–922/ 1250–1517). This case study can be justified partly by the fact that the economy of historic Cairo is too complicated to be examined in a single essay, and partly because urban economy can be studied, to a reasonably satisfying extent, through the markets of any city.

Thus, it is almost impossible to study the economic history of Cairo without examining the development of its markets. The economy of Mamluk Cairo, as viewed through its markets, was urban and contained certain peculiarities because of the military elite's control of the surplus of agricultural production, on one hand, and the sultan's intervention in the activities of the markets on the other.

The story of Cairo markets then, is to some extent the story of the economy of this city. It is a story of growth, maturity and decline. There were, of course, reasons for each part of the story. The historical evidence available on the rise and decline of the Cairene markets makes it possible to reconstruct some aspects of Cairo in the Mamluk period, naturally particularly in the economic and social spheres.

Once the Mamluk regime was established, thanks to the efforts of Sultan Baybars I (658–676/1260–1277), Egypt enjoyed a prosperous phase which continued at least until the beginning of the 9th/15th century. This prosperity can be explained by the fact that the defeat of the Mongols at 'Ayn Jalut (658/1260), the restoration of the 'Abbasid caliphate in Cairo in the following year, and the legitimacy this bestowed on the Mamluk sultanate, all made Egypt attractive to immigrants from the different regions of the Muslim world. Furthermore, the Mongol invasions had provoked a shift from a land route for trade, through Central Asia, to a maritime route through the Indian Ocean, the Arabian Sea and the Red Sea. This shift in the international trade route was an important factor in elevating the importance of the Mamluk state now ruling Egypt and Syria, as well as parts of Iraq and Arabia. International traders used the territories of the Mamluk sultanate as a passage between the Indian Ocean and the Mediterranean. This benefitted both the international traders and the Mamluks.

On the other hand, the Mamluk state under Baybars I proved to be a great regional power. Dominating the Arab world directly and indirectly, it was able to settle the political situation according to its own interests. All these factors made Cairo one of the most famous cosmopolitan cities of the Middle Ages. Piloté de Crête, who visited Egypt at the beginning of the 9th/15th century, said that Cairo was the largest city in his world.[1] Ibn Battuta, a century earlier, was surprised by the vast area the city covered and the huge numbers of people. He described many aspects of the social and economic life of Mamluk Cairo in the first half of the 8th/14th century.[2]

The political, economic and demographic power of Egypt during the first (Bahri) Mamluk state was reflected in the markets of Cairo. These were numerous, and their activity suggests the cosmopolitan nature of the people who used these markets.

But some important points need to be made concerning domestic commerce in Egypt, especially in Cairo. First, the markets in Cairo depended heavily on the military elite, including the sultan himself, to provide the foodstuffs that were sold in them, foodstuffs which came from the countryside. This was because the Egyptian economy had been organised, since the time of Salah al-Din, according to the *iqta'* system, a method of assigning land as a means of payment to the army commanders and other government officials. There were many

Silk Mercer's Bazaar of El-Ghooreeyeh (al-Ghawriyya), colour lithograph, from *Egypt and Nubia* volume 3, David Roberts (1798–1864)

El Moristan Cairo

reasons for the existence of the *iqta'* system in that period,[3] but here we are more concerned with its consequences. The most important of these was that the sultan and his amirs were the only owners of agricultural land in Egypt. Thus, they had a monopoly of agricultural products, especially grain. On the other hand, economic relations between the state and the Egyptian peasantry were governed by a system of tribute. That is to say, surplus agricultural production was extracted by the state through a series of taxes. Once the *iqta'* system was adopted by the Ayyubids (and inherited by the Mamluks), the sultan and the leading amirs came to dominate the urban market for agricultural produce because of their role as the recipients of these taxes, both in cash and most importantly, in kind.[4] This allowed the sultan and the military elite to accumulate considerable reserves of produce. Furthermore, important state officials also received daily supplies of great quantities of foodstuffs, as well as yearly supplies of clothing and of slaughtered animals, not to mention extra supplies during Ramadan and other religious seasons and feasts. The result of all this was to create an economy of patronage in which enormous quantities of agricultural produce remained outside market circulation. This kind of economic system contrasted with the urban economy of Cairo, which was based on commercial exchange.[5] As a result, this 'tribute economy' created many problems during the Mamluk era, affecting the Cairene markets negatively. Second, the markets of Cairo in the Mamluk period were distributed throughout the city according to the kind of goods in which each of them specialised, and not according to the density of population in each district of the city. Markets for foodstuffs, however, were spread all over the city according to the distribution of the Cairene population. Third, in addition to the permanent markets in Mamluk Cairo, some periodical and occasional markets took place, especially on religious occasions and during festivals. Fourth, the Cairo markets reflected various aspects of the economy of the Egyptian capital during the Mamluk period.

In sum, the growth of the Cairo markets during the first phase of the Mamluk era was the result of a considerable rise in the Cairene population and also the shift in world trade towards Egypt because of the Mongol invasions in the first half of the 7th/13th century.

One of the most famous markets in Mamluk Cairo was Suq Bab al-Futuh. According to the chronicler al-Maqrizi it was so prosperous that 'people come to it from everywhere to buy various kinds of meat and vegetables'.[6] Another famous market for foodstuffs was Suq Hara Barjawan, which was used by merchants and sellers of oil, cheese, bread, vegetables and other necessary items of the people's daily fare. One chronicler's description of the various kinds of cheese sold in the Cairo markets during the 9th/15th century reveals the prosperous conditions of these markets in his time.[7] Chickens and other fowls were sold in Suq al-Dajjajin,[8] the central market for these in Mamluk Cairo. Another central Cairene market was Suq al-Tuffah (the apple market) or Dar al-Fakiha (the fruit centre). All the Egyptian production of fruit, whether from the gardens near Cairo, from the provinces, or imported from abroad, was brought to this *suq*, and from this central market fruit was then distributed to shops all over Cairo.[9] The Mamluk chroniclers give the names of and reports about many specialised food markets. These markets were established in residential districts.[10]

As for clothing and accessories, the chroniclers reported the existence of various kinds of such markets: there were some that specialised in selling the official dress (*khila*) the sultans used to bestow on their amirs on various religious and political occasions.[11] The merchants would buy these outfits and uniforms from their makers, or from abroad, and sell them to the *diwan* of the sultan, or directly to the Mamluk amirs. Another market was Suq al-Hawaysiyyan (the market for military belts and bucklers).[12] Specific markets for second-hand clothes also existed, as well as for needles and other items used by tailors.[13] The market for wool imported from Europe was known as Suq al-Jukhiyyin.[14]

In addition to these 'civilian' markets, there were some 'military' markets in Cairo. The armies of the Middle Ages did not have the means to supply their own equipment, their arms, attire and those other necessary items for the soldiers and their horses, so they depended upon civilian craftsmen and merchants. According to the *iqta'* system, every amir was responsible for equipment and supplies for his own soldiers. Such things were available in Suq al-Silah (the market for arms) which was established in the Ayyubid period. Attached to Suq al-Silah was another *suq* specialising in equipment for horses and horsemen, known as Suq al-Muhimiyyin. Linked to these two markets, another market offered the leather equipment necessary for horses and other beasts of burden,[15] such as saddles.[16] This latter market was known as Suq al-Lajmiyyin.

In Mamluk Cairo one particular market was attached to the annual pilgrimage to Mecca and Medina. Its name was Suq al-Marahilin (the market of the travellers), and it specialised in providing camels, then the most popular means of travel by land. In that market so many camels were available for the journey to the Hijaz that the people of Suq al-Marahilin could outfit more than a hundred of them in a single day. These camels were used also in the pilgrimage to Jerusalem which was, and still is, sacred to all Egyptians. A similar market was Suq al-Mahayir in which were sold some objects used particularly during the pilgrimage to the Hijaz. Two similar *suq*s were added later to meet the increasing demands of the pilgrims.[17]

In addition to these specialised markets serving the military and the religious life of the Cairene people, various markets provided for the daily needs of the inhabitants of Cairo and its visitors. The Cairenes brought their furniture from Suq al-Sanadiqiyyin (the market of the box makers). In this *suq* wooden furniture used by ordinary families was made and displayed. One market specialised in perfumes, the Suq al-'Ambariyyin, which was established by the sultan al-Mansur Qalawun on the site of a prison. Egyptians of all classes were fond of ambergris.

Suq al-Shamma'iyyin (the market of the candle-makers) was very important in the everyday life of the Cairenes, since candles were used everywhere on a daily basis. Special ornate candles were used during family celebrations (e.g. marriage, the birth of a child). In certain religious seasons and festivals, larger and more ornate candles were needed, so this market was particularly prosperous during Ramadan (the month of the Muslim fast). Cairenes regularly used this *suq* as a

place to walk and to have a promenade.[18] It was open until after mid-night and the light shining from the many candles made the market a pleasant place.

The markets mentioned in the previous pages were not, of course, the only markets in Cairo during the Mamluk period. But they are representative of the variety of markets. It is not, however, possible to give an accurate figure for the number of these markets because during the Mamluk era they changed in both numbers and activity. The main purpose in this paper is to examine the relationship between the markets and the economy of Mamluk Cairo.

Some markets were demolished, while new ones were established, or prospered, according to the demographic and economic develop-ments that were taking place. Some markets also adopted new names because the craft of their occupants had changed; for example Suq al-Sharakhiyyin (the market of cooks), changed to Suq al-Shawayyin (those who roast meat) in the early 8th/14th century. This same *suq* then took the name Suq al-Magharbilin at the beginning of the next century. Names of markets in Cairo also changed considerably because of various developments in the history of the city itself. And one must note that the names of the Cairene markets were by no means always derived from their activities. The sources, especially those by al-Maqrizi and Ibn Duqmaq, mention many *suq*s whose names were derived from their location,[19] from some foreign group or community,[20] or named for individuals.[21] Some markets even had bizarre names.[22]

According to Ibn Duqmaq and al-Maqrizi, the markets of Cairo usually had gates, and some had their own storehouses. The markets of Cairo were also centres of financial activity because of the presence of those who changed currency in the large markets like the Suq al-Silah.[23]

In addition, wandering peddlers walked up and down the streets of Cairo in the Mamluk period selling everything Egyptian women could need,[24] a practice still common in Cairo and other cities. Other peddlers used to sit in the *suq*s causing trouble for themselves and for the people of the *suq*s.[25] Another entire market was also assigned to these vendors: the Suq al-Qufaisat (the market of little cages) was the market where women went to buy rings, earrings, necklaces and other items of costume jewelry. The *suq* derived its name from the little iron cages on which the costume jewelry favoured by poorer Cairene women was displayed. The sellers of goods in this *suq* paid the supervisor of the hospital built by Sultan al-Mansur Qalawun, Bimaristan al-Mansuri, rent for sitting on the ground in the *suq*. Why? Because this *suq* was a part of the endowment (*waqf*)[26] of the hospital. Furthermore, peasants from rural areas adjacent to Cairo often brought the produce of the countryside there to sell.[27]

Thus a great variety was to be found in the markets of Mamluk Cairo, variety both in goods, activity and location, as can be seen in the examples given above. But the most important issue to consider in the study of these markets is that they were the means by which the urban economy of Cairo was run during the Mamluk age; the Mamluk mili-tary elite controlled the markets for foodstuffs (as mentioned above), and the state supervised and even controlled the activities of the other *suq*s both directly and indirectly.

Many officials were responsible for supervising and controlling the markets;[28] the most important was the *muhtasib*, one of the high-ranking officials of the state. The *muhtasib*'s responsibility was ranked fifth in importance in the *diwan* of religious affairs.[29] One of the *muhtasib*'s duties was to inspect the markets (though he was, also, responsible for other aspects of daily life). The *muhtasib* was considered responsible for everything in the market on the one hand, and on the other he had the authority to punish the merchants (and others) according to his own judgement. His assistants inspected the *suq*s to check weights and measures, prices and the quality of the items of food being sold.[30] However, the status of the *muhtasib* deteriorated dramatically in the last decades of the Mamluk period so that many unqualified persons were assigned to this most important of jobs.[31] This deterioration had, of course, many negative consequences.

Cairene society saw the *muhtasib* as responsible for the markets, especially the price of foodstuffs. If he was successful in controlling the markets and setting prices, people would praise him in every

Tinsmiths working outside
their shop, coloured postcard,
19th century

possible way, but if he failed, they would attack him, even locking him up in his house for long periods of time.[32]

The intervention of the state in the markets was not restricted to inspections by the *muhtasib*; rather it took other forms. Some scholars have called the economy of Egypt during the Mamluk period a tributary economy,[33] while others called it a moral economy;[34] overall, it can be said to have been a mixture of a feudal and a market economy. The most specific feature of the economy was of course the numerous forms of tribute and tax imposed by the state on every aspect of economic life in Egypt, and particularly in Cairo. The great variety of taxes imposed on Cairene markets and merchants demonstrates the extent of the state's intervention in market affairs, as well as the relationship between the state and its subjects. Such taxes were frequently imposed, or cancelled, in what seems an arbitrary fashion, but it is worth noting that these taxes increased in number and kind during the second Mamluk sultanate.[35] As the role of the state was central to the economy of Cairo, the markets were seriously affected by developments in Mamluk politics. The considerable increase in political instability in the second sultanate was a debilitating factor in the economy of Cairo, particularly in the activity of the markets. Conflicts between the sultans and their opponents, or between strong amirs who were rivals for power, frequently resulted in riots on the streets of Cairo, and as a result the markets were closed. Often, these conflicts turned into street fights during which the markets were plundered and the people in them attacked.[36]

This political instability was by no means the only negative factor that affected the markets of Mamluk Cairo. Many other factors contributed to the ultimate overthrow of the Egyptian economy. This is evident in the number of markets that were demolished in Cairo from the first decade of the 9th/15th century onwards. Lamenting that the once prosperous markets of Cairo that had been demolished, al-Maqrizi remarked:

> There were in the city of Cairo and its surroundings a very great number of markets, most of them now vanished. It is enough to take as

evidence for those numerous markets the fact that fifty-five *suq*s were reduced to ruins in the area between Bab al-Luq and Bab al-Bahr, some of which had contained about sixty shops, and I witnessed their prosperity [before the crisis]. This was in the western part of Cairo only. What can one think about the other three areas of the city?[37]

The decline in the markets can be explained, partly, by depopulation, one of the enormous changes in Egyptian society in the aftermath of the Black Death (749/1348). The terrible death-toll following the arrival of the Black Death (the Arab chronicles called it *al-fana' al-kabir*, the Great Annihilation) provoked a sense of overwhelming horror throughout Cairo and all over Egypt. The epidemic seems to have had a catastrophic effect on the population of Cairo, especially the artisans, to judge by al-Maqrizi's remarks:

> All the crafts disappeared. There were no water-carriers, laundrymen or grooms to be found. The wages of a groom reached 80 dirhams a month, having previously been 30 dirhams. It was announced in Cairo that anyone who had a craft should return to it, and some of them were flogged.[38]

The effects of depopulation did not end with the outbreak of 1347–1349. More outbreaks of plague followed, and other factors such as famine conspired to reduce the population still further.[39] The prosperous days of the early 8th/14th century were over.[40] The effects of the epidemics of plague were obvious in the markets which were reduced to miserable remnants of those prosperous markets that the Cairenes had known in the first half of the Mamluk era. Some markets shrank to only a few shops; others were completely ruined.[41]

Other subverting factors contributing to the decline of the *suq*s of Cairo included the chaos caused by the riots and disturbances with which the Julban Mamluks terrorised Cairo and its inhabitants.[42] The Julbans were not subjected to the same strict order to which the Mamluks of the Bahariyya state (who were brought to Egypt in their childhood)

CAIRE
Ferblantiers

were subjected. They were not committed to the relationships honoured by their predecessors, namely the *ustadhiyya* (e.g. lordship) of the sultan, or any other master, and *khusdashiyya* (comradeship) with their fellows in the service of the same master.[43]

The first instance of disorder caused by the Julbans occurred in 877/1472–1473 when they attacked one of the senior officials of the state.[44] Since no power restrained their actions, they continued to offend the great amirs and even the sultans.[45] Their actions often caused markets to be closed for many days, and were accompanied by plundering of the merchandise kept in the *suq*s.[46] This chaos, combined with other factors, contributed to the devastation of the Cairo markets after the second decade of the 9th/15th century. In spite of the decline in the revenues of the Mamluk state and its shrinking economy, the money paid to the Mamluks rose considerably because of the increase in their numbers, the corruption that dominated the Mamluk administration and the decrease in the yields of the *iqta*'s held by the great amirs in the Egyptian countryside.[47] The fact that the sultans could not pay these exorbitant salaries regularly was reason enough to agitate the aggressive nature of the Julbans. The chronicler Ibn Iyas reported many

instances of rioting and aggressive acts by Mamluks during the reign of Sultan Qaytbay and Sultan al-Ashraf Qansuh al-Ghawri.[48] In 907/1502 Sultan Qansuh al-Ghawri confiscated a large amount of property from his subjects and ordered the people of Cairo to pay the rent due on their houses and shops ten months in advance. Ibn Iyas reported on the consequences, remarking, 'As a result, trading in the markets stopped, and most of the shops in Cairo were closed. Everyone was in trouble, the poor as well as the rich.'[49]

In short, in the last decades of its existence the collapsing political system of the Mamluk sultanate was reflected in a deteriorating economy and diminishing markets in the capital. But one final factor was crucial in the history of the Mamluk economy. The monetary system of Egypt in those days was not an invention of the Mamluk state, but rather a continuation of the monetary system known in Egypt since the time of the Umayyads. At the beginning of the Mamluk period, the sultanate had substantial reserves of gold and silver, and for nearly 130 years Egypt did not experience any serious crisis in its currency. But the disappearance of silver dirhams at the end of the 8th/14th century initiated a long process of currency crisis in the last century of the

Mamluk history.[50] The sultans tried to solve this growing crisis by devaluing the silver dirham, but this caused inflation, internal commerce suffered a depression and the prices of goods increased sharply. At the beginning of the 9th/15th century the currency system broke down, and a copper currency of account known as *dirham min al-fulus* replaced the silver dirham as the standard currency. This new currency of account was not stable because it was repeatedly devalued throughout this period. The debasement of currency made life even more difficult for the Cairenes, already suffering from political, economic and social turmoil. The breakdown of the currency system then was an important factor in internal commerce and in the markets of Cairo; many markets were closed or abandoned while others were reduced to a few shops, as we have seen. The purchasing power of the people of Cairo (indeed, of all Egyptians) decreased considerably from the beginning of the 9th/15th century onwards.

In conclusion, the story of the markets of Cairo during the Mamluk period is the story of the economy of this capital city, or even of the Egyptian economy of the time as a whole. We cannot, of course, attribute the prosperity and decline of the markets to a single factor. But the rise of the Mamluk sultanate was accompanied by political stability, military strength, social and demographic growth, and economic power. Those factors created the prosperity which the markets of Cairo reflected up to at least the beginning of the 9th/15th century.

The crisis of the Mamluk state began with the coronation of Sultan al-Zahir Barquq in the last decade of the 8th/14th century. The *iqta'* system, also, in the long run, proved to be a catastrophe for the Egyptian economy. Agricultural production failed to meet the needs of the population. The currency system, which began to break down at the beginning of the 9th/15th century, accelerated the deterioration. Furthermore, political instability, street fighting between opposing Mamluk factions, the corruption of the administration, and the repeated looting of merchandise from the markets created a disastrous situation for markets and merchants. When the Mamluk state came to an end in 922/1517 after only two battles against the Ottomans, the markets of Cairo were virtually ruined. The economy of Cairo waited for the new Ottoman masters to revive it.

1   P. H. Dopp, *L'Égypte au commencement du quinzième siècle* (Cairo, 1930), p. 3.

2   Ibn Battuta, *al-Rihla*, ed. Mahmud Sharqawi (Beirut, 1968), pp. 21–25.

3   For these reasons see Kassem 'Abdou Kassem, *Fi ta'rikh al-Ayyubiyyin wa'l-Mamluk* (Cairo, 2001), pp. 74–80; *Dirasat fi ta'rikh Misr al-ijtima'i 'asr salatin al-mamalik* (Cairo, 1994), pp. 7–21.

4   Adam Sabra, *Poverty and Charity in Medieval Islam: Mamluk Egypt, 1250–1517* (Cambridge, 2000), pp. 135–138. Cf. Boaz Shoshan, 'Grain Riots and the "Moral Economy": Cairo, 1450–1517', *Journal of Interdisciplinary History*, 10 (1980), pp. 462–463.

5   Ibid., p. 136.

6   Al-Maqrizi, *Kitab al-mawa'iz wa'l-i'tibar bi-dhikr al-khitat wa'l-athar* (Cairo, 1270/1853–1854), vol. 2, pp. 93–106.

7   Ibn al-Sayrafi, *Inba' al-hasr bi-abna' al-'asr* (Cairo, 1970), pp. 187–188, 477.

8   Al-Maqrizi, *al-Khitat*, vol. 2, pp. 93–106. This *suq* specialised in selling chicken, ducks, geese and other fowls for food. Suq al-Dajjajin means the market of the chicken-sellers.

9   Al-Maqrizi, *Kitab al-suluk li-ma'rifat duwal al-muluk* (Cairo, 1956–1973), vol. 2, pp. 184ff.; vol. 2, p. 400. This *suq* was founded after the year 740/1339–1340; later some shops were built around it where fruit was sold. Al-Maqrizi, *al-Khitat*, vol. 2, p. 93.

10 See what al-Maqrizi said about Suq Khat Bayn al-Qasrayn and Suq al-Muta'aishin for example, *al-Khitat*, vol. 1, p. 334, vol. 2, pp. 27–28.

11 The particular market for this kind of clothing was Suq al-Sharabishiyyin (e.g. those who sell *sharbush*s). The *sharbush* was a kind of headgear. See al-Maqrizi, *al-Khitat*, vol. 2, pp. 97–98.

12 Al-Maqrizi, *al-Khitat*, vol. 2, pp. 93–106.

13 This *suq* was known as Suq al-Abbarin (i.e., needle sellers [haberdashers?]), though the shopowners sold everything related to tailoring. See al-Maqrizi, *al-Khitat*, vol. 2, pp. 93–106, 34.

14 Kassem 'Abdou Kassem, *Dirasat*, pp. 60–61.

15 Al-Maqrizi, *al-Khitat*, vol. 2, pp. 96–97.

16 Usually, these saddles, especially those which were made for the military elite, were decorated with gold and silver, even with jewels and precious stones. See Maqrizi, *al-Khitat*, vol. 2, pp. 96–97, for more details about the craft of the Saddlers, *al-surujiyyin*.

17 al-Maqrizi, *al-Khitat*, vol. 2, pp. 96–103. The two new *suqs* were established later.

18 Kassem, *Dirasat*, pp. 61–63.

19 For example, Suq Jami' Ibn Tulun (the market of the Ibn Tulun Mosque), Suq Hara Barjawan (the market of the lane of Barjawan), and Suq Bab al-Futuh (after one of Cairo's gates).

20 Suq al-'Iraqiyyin (the market of the Iraqis), Suq al-Magharriba (the market of Moroccans), and Suq al-Yahud (the market of the Jews); the latter was demolished in the time of Ibn Duqmaq during the early 9th/15th century.

21 For example, there were *suqs* attributed to Ibn al-'Ajmiyya, Ma'atuq and Wardan.

22 Suq al-Baraghith (the flea market), Suq Lihar (the blanket market [bedding?]) and Suq al-'Ayatin (the market of those who cry out [their wares?]). See Ibn Duqmaq, *al-Intisar li-wasitat 'iqd al-amsar* (Cairo, 1893–1314/1896–1897), vol. 4, pp. 22, 32–43; al-Maqrizi, *al-Khitat*, vol. 2, p. 106.

23 Al-Maqrizi, *al-Khitat*, vol. 2, pp. 94–96; Ibn Duqmaq, *al-Intisar*, vol. 4, p. 34ff.

24 Ibn al-Hajj, *al-Madkhal* (Cairo, 1960), vol. 1, pp. 102–103; al-Maqrizi, *al-Khitat*, vol. 2, pp. 93–95.

25 Al-Maqrizi, *al-Khitat*, vol. 2, p. 93ff. He says that, periodically, they were expelled by the authorities because of this.

26 This hospital was established by Sultan al-Mansur Qalawun in 683/1284, as part of larger *waqf* complex located in Bayn al-Qasrayn in Cairo which included the sultan's tomb and a *madrasa*. Ibn Habib, *Tadhkirat al-nabih fi ayyam al-Mansur wa banih* (Cairo, 1976–1986), vol. 1, p. 337; see the document of this *waqf* published by Mohammed M. Amin in the appendix of this volume; cf. Sabra, *Poverty and Charity*, chapter. 4, 'Waqf'.

27 Ibn Iyas, *Bada'i' al-zuhur fi waqi'i' al-duhur* (Cairo, 1982–1984), vol. 3, p. 126; vol. 5, p. 67.

28 Al-Maqrizi, *Ighathat al-umma bi-kashf al-ghumma* (Cairo, 1957), p. 28; Ibn Taghribirdi, *al-Nujum al-zahira fi muluk Misr wa'l-Qahira* (Cairo, 1963–1962), vol. 9, pp. 44–46.

29 On *hisba* and *muhstasib* see: Ibn al-Ukhuwwa, *Ma'alim al-qurba fi ahkam al-hisba* (London, 1938), pp. 7ff.; and about its development in Egypt from the Fatimid period up to the Mamluks see al-Qalqashandi, *Subh al-a'sha fi sina'at al-insha* (Cairo, 1331–1338/1913–1920), vol. 5, pp. 451–452; vol. 11, pp. 68–69.

30 Al-Maqrizi, *Kitab al-suluk*.

31 Ibn Taghribirdi, *al-Nujum al-zahira*, vol. 16, p. 153; Ibn Iyas, *Bada'i' al-zuhur*, vol. 3, pp. 165, 233; vol. 5, p. 27; al-Sakhawi, *al-Tibr al-masbuk fi dhayl al-suluk* (Cairo, 1896), p. 268.

32 Al-Maqrizi, *al-Suluk*, vol. 2, p. 239; Ibn al-Furat, *Tarikh al-duwal wa'l-muluk*, vol. 9, p. 435.

33 Sabra, *Poverty and Charity*, pp. 135–137.

34 Shoshan, 'Grain Riots and the "Moral Economy": Cairo 1350–1517', pp. 462–463.

35 Al-Maqrizi, *al-Suluk*, vol. 3, p. 244; Ibn Taghribirdi, *al-Nujum*, vol. 8, p. 46; Sakhawi, *Tibr*, p. 268; Ibn Iyas, *Bada'i'*, vol. 4, pp. 25, 77, 304–305; vol. 5, p. 17. These chroniclers mention various taxes imposed by the authorities on Cairo markets during the last century of the Mamluk era. Some of these taxes were collected monthly. cf. Kassem, *Dirasat*, p. 67.

36 For examples of riots and attacks on the markets see: al-Maqrizi, *al-Suluk*, vol. 3, pp. 352–353, 368; Ibn al-Dawadari, *Kanz al-durar wa jami' al-ghurar* (Cairo, 1960), vol. 8, pp. 372ff.

37 Al-Maqrizi, *al-Khitat*, vol. 2, p. 651.

38 Al-Maqrizi, *al-Suluk*, vol. 2, p. 786, Ibn Taghribirdi, *al-Nujum*, vol. 10, p. 210. It should be noted that this epidemic of the plague continued for almost two years, 748–750/1347–1349.

39 For a list of outbreaks of the plague see, Kassem, *Dirasat*, pp. 167–174; Michael Dols, *The Black Death in the Middle East* (Princeton, NJ, 1977), pp. 305–314.

40 Sabra, *Poverty and Charity*, pp. 122–123.

41 Al-Maqrizi, *al-Khitat*, vol. 2, pp. 93–106; *al-Suluk*, vol. 4, p. 655.

42 The Julban or Ajlab *mamluks*, were the adult slaves who had been brought to Cairo in their youth, or even early manhood, after the sultanate of al-Zahir Barquq in the last decade of the 8th/14th century.

43 Kassem, *Dirasat*, pp. 11–17.

44 Ibn Iyas, *Bada'i'*, vol. 3, p. 82.

45 Ibid., pp. 93–94.

46 Ibn Taghribirdi, *al-Nujum*, vol. 16, p. 98; Ibn Iyas, *Bada'i'*, vol. 3, p. 147; vol. 4, pp. 13, 363; vol. 5. pp. 4–7.

47 Kassem, *Dirasat*, pp. 74–75. In the reign of Sultan al-Mu'ayyad Shaykh the total amount of these salaries (*jamikiyya*) was 11,000 *dinars*; this sum increased under his successor Sultan al-Ashraf Barsbay (825–841/1422–1438) to 18,000 dinars, reaching in the reign of Sultan al-Ashraf Qaytbay (872–901/1468–1496) 46,000 dinars. See Ibn al-Sayrafi, *Inba' al-hasr*, pp. 33–37.

48 Ibn Iyas, *Bada'i'*, pp. 13–18, 29. In 906/1500–1501 Sultan Qansuh al-Ghawri could not pay the salaries of the *mamluks* for three months, so they revolted against him. He protested that the treasury was empty and he had no money and so could not pay any of the factions of the *mamluks*.

49 Ibn Iyas, *Bada'i'*, vol. 4, p. 16.

50 For the story of the Mamluk monetary system, see Kassem, *Dirasat*, pp. 79–83, and for full details of the monetary crisis see, al-Maqrizi, *al-Suluk*, vol. 2, pp. 205–206, 253, 669, 771; vol. 3, pp. 638, 710–712, 805, 851–853, 912; Ibn al-Sayrafi, *Inba' al-hasr*, pp. 133ff; Ibn Iyas, *Bada'i'*, vol. 3, pp. 20–29. Cf. E. Ashtor, *Social and Economic History of the Near East in the Middle Ages* (London, 1976), pp. 291–293.

5 The question of guilds

Pascale Ghazaleh

The study of guilds – groups of artisans or merchants involved in the same activity and more or less loosely organised according to certain explicit or implicit regulations – is central to European economic history. The destruction of the guilds and the creation of a free labour market is seen by most Western historians as an integral part of the birth of capitalism. The question of craft guilds is also central to the study of non-European societies, especially in the Arab countries. Among the latter, Morocco, Syria and Egypt have been the most extensively examined because of the light they shed on different aspects of urban economic, social and political history.

The importance of guilds in the historiography of the Arab and Islamic worlds may be attributed to several factors. First, much of this historiography has been devoted to applying theoretical models elaborated on the basis of the European experience. It is only natural, therefore, that an attempt was made to compare this experience to developments in non-European regions. Second, efforts were made to understand *why* Europe developed differently from many other areas – 'one of the formative questions of classical sociology [was:] why did industrial capitalism first emerge in the West?'[1] This question, in fact, is crucial to social, economic, political and even cultural history. The parameters for the study of non-European guilds, therefore, have usually been dictated by the terms of a comparison with the European experience. Remarkably, the similarities between the two histories are perhaps as great as the differences – but this should not blind us to the fact that they are not precisely alike. One question in particular keeps surfacing: to what extent did Egyptian guilds resemble their European counterparts? It is important to avoid adhering to the notion of the complete specificity of non-European history, but equally important, of course, not to equate the two trajectories. In other words, comparison with Europe may be useful if one is able to avoid the trap of measuring Egypt against the yardstick of European experience.

Is it possible to avoid a rigid framework by resorting to comparison in those specific cases where an abundance of information allows the researcher to determine both the similarities and the points of divergence in various processes, for example, the experiences of craftsmen forced into working in factories in England and Egypt. However, due to restrictions of time and space, I have had to eschew investigations into the role of the guilds in organising production. This would have entailed extensive examination of the urban *iltizam*s in the 19th century, as well as the impact of the system of monopoly devised by Muhammad 'Ali, topics which remain largely uncharted to this day.

The study of guilds and their organisation has often been reduced to an attempt to understand why Egypt or other parts of the Ottoman empire did not follow the same course of economic and political development as Europe, where guilds are perceived to have restricted capitalist development until the invention of new technologies, and the changes in labour organisation that these brought about, were able to break the guild framework and thus pave the way to a free labour market.[2]

The question asked was 'Why did this fail to occur in Egypt?' and the answer almost invariably took one of two forms. Some scholars explained the failure of the Egyptian guilds to undergo the same transformation by the fact that their rigid structure and the monopolies they enjoyed fostered technological stagnation and the absence of any personal initiative and competitiveness. Muhammad 'Ali, from this perspective, was seen as having initiated the industrialisation of Egypt and, thereby, its transformation into a 'modern nation-state'.[3] Others turned in a different direction and argued that the beginnings of capitalist development were in fact evident in both agriculture and urban production at the end of the Ottoman period but were then crushed by the statist policies imposed under Muhammad 'Ali. It is interesting to note that even at this early juncture, these two approaches are merely two sides of the same coin, two opposite answers to the same question. To the assertions of some historians that early industrial development heralded the renaissance of Egypt, its awakening from the slumber of oppression and its liberation from the Ottoman yoke, others have recently responded saying that, far from this being the case, the early 19th century in fact represented the beginning of the end. To those who cried, 'national development', a new generation of scholars replied, 'centralisation'; where their professors had seen stagnation, they discovered dynamic capitalist roots. They suggested that Muhammad 'Ali, first seen as a liberator, may have suppressed the very dynamic he was said to have fostered. In fact, it sometimes appears as though they took the theory of the Oriental despot, long applied to studies of Egyptian society, economy, culture and politics under Ottoman rule, and simply shifted it forward a few years, having made the necessary modifications.

Questions as to why capitalist development did not occur in Egypt led many scholars to adopt the concept of the Asiatic mode of production,[4] which held that Oriental societies were essentially fragmented and stagnant, ruled by despots who forbade the accumulation of wealth that could have led to capitalist take-off.[5] This concept was later rejected; few attempts, however, have been made to develop the theory beyond Marx's summary remarks, which were based on his limited knowledge of India. Instead it was applied, often simplistically, to diverse areas, with the result of much obfuscating of historical reality and the retarding of genuine investigation.

While the work of Orientalists and Arab historians alike relied on extensive knowledge of languages and extant sources for early periods, until the 1970s few Western scholars used indigenous sources in the study of the Ottoman era and the 19th century, largely because it was thought that the idea of the 'Asiatic mode of production'[6] sufficed to both describe and analyse the situation in the Arab lands during this period.[7] However, in contrast, this was not necessarily the case with certain Egyptian scholars;[8] but, due to the circumstances prevailing at the time that these scholars wrote, they were often apt to view the Ottoman period as one of darkness and stagnation, breaking into dawn and dynamism only with Muhammad 'Ali's accession to power. Since the 1970s, however, a wealth of sources relating to both the Ottoman and the Muhammad 'Ali period has been uncovered. The considerable use which has so far been made of these sources does not, however, even scratch the surface of the body of information they

may yet reveal. Due to the sheer volume of documents available, it will take several decades at least for even a summary acquaintance to be made with the archives.

In the case of Egyptian guilds in particular, the two landmark works are by Baer (1968) and Raymond (1973–1974). In the twenty-odd years since these were published, most work specifically dealing with Egyptian guilds has been confined to the repetition of past findings. Sometimes new archival material has been adduced, but the framework for enquiry has remained the same: either descriptions of what is thought to have been the state of Egyptian guilds in the Ottoman era or the 19th century, or attempts to explain the presumed decline, destruction or disappearance of the guilds. To my knowledge, no analytical work on the guilds during the long 18th century (to adapt Braudel's phrase)[9] – the period from 1750 to 1850 – has yet appeared and, more importantly, no efforts have been made even to apply new methodological approaches to well-known primary sources. If we are to understand what was happening at that time, we must make an effort to develop a different methodology and, therefore, to understand how and why people formed or joined guilds in Cairo during this era.

In examining the question of guild organisation, it is necessary to touch on many issues which seem at first indirectly related, but which shed light on several difficult points. First, while Cairo was, and remains, the largest urban centre in Egypt, the site of the most intense economic activity, and the hub of production and distribution, information pertaining to the provinces is useful, either in attempting to rectify lacunae or for the sake of comparison. Secondly, one must extend one's analyses chronologically to both before and after any arbitrarily determined cut-off dates, such as 1750 or 1859. The work of most historians is heavily dependent on the sources available; one of the central questions is: Why are certain documents found until the beginning of the 19th century and not beyond? In an effort to answer this question, I turned to the Ottoman-era archives, seeking to understand where continuities or breaks seemed to occur, and in order to compare this period with that immediately following it. Further,

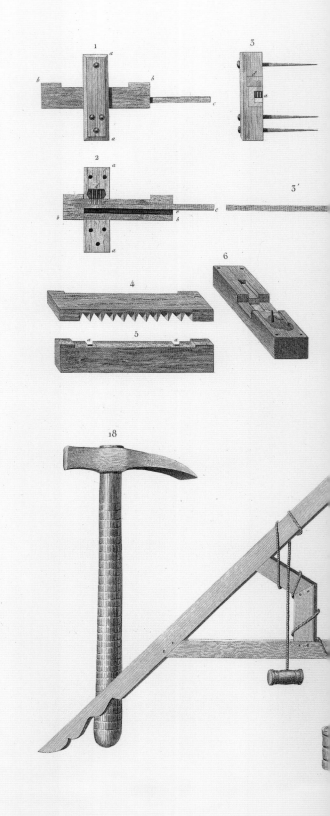

Workmen's tools, engraving,
La Description de l'Egypte,
1809–1822

although I looked principally at questions of internal organisation, the question of guild–state relations is also crucial. In fact, it would have been impossible, or at best a sterile academic exercise, to deal with the question of internal guild organisation in a vacuum, as if the guild set-up was autonomous and cut off the sphere of the state influence and intervention. An important issue is that the dynamic of guild–state interaction in all its variations – from guild to guild, and over time – was a crucial determinant of guild organisation and the forms it took. Finally, one must critique secondary sources. This new reading, whilst it may not provide answers to old dilemmas, may at least open doors to new questions and therefore constitute a contribution to an ongoing debate.

A Quiet Death?

As a reinterpretation of some of the dominant views about guilds,[10] I have tried to test existing theories against a sample of primary sources covering a period of time between the early years of Ottoman rule and the early 19th century,[11] some of which are unpublished and, to my knowledge, heretofore unexamined court cases.

Guilds have been the object of much debate, involving deeply entrenched preconceived notions about Islamic, and particularly Ottoman, society as a whole, and also about the modernisation of Egypt (and Europe) – however one defines 'modernisation' – in the 19th century. The Egyptian guilds have been seen in vastly different ways, so that even the most rudimentary information about guild organisation or their role viz-a-viz the state and society is presented in completely opposing ways.

According to some scholars, the guilds were almost entirely autonomous from the government. This first school of thought lays emphasis on the existence of a (despotic) Ottoman state, and tends to represent guilds as the only manifestation of civic and civil life in an authoritarian environment. This framework[12] permitted reinforcement of the idea that Islamic society remained unchanged between the 8th and 19th centuries, and that it was void of what might be called

The Imperial Fez-maker's
workshop, Istanbul,
19th century

a civic spirit or a municipal life.[13] Medieval Islamic cities were seen as presenting illusions of prosperity that, however, had no basis in solid economics – rising for an instant, they soon decayed in what was an essentially stagnant context. This view represented the guilds as the only manifestation of popular will in a society characterised by isolation and profound rifts between the despotic ruler and the unproductive populace.[14]

This view was not incompatible with the ideas of Louis Massignon,[15] who had presented the guilds as the extension of the Qaramita, Akhi and Futuwwa movements,[16] and was essentially interested in their esoteric ceremonial life. The guilds, he argued, combined revolutionary potential, mysticism, forms of 'heresy', secret initiation rites and a code of chivalry, as well as professional traditions and ethics.[17]

The second school holds that the guilds were in fact created and imposed from above by a government keen to control the urban population. The organisation of the urban economy into guilds was ascribed to the state's need for general control and supervision.[18] The guilds performed a variety of functions for the state: administration, taxation, quality control, the fixing of prices and wages, the supply of services and labour, the supply and distribution of goods, judicial functions (arbitration and mutual assistance), mutual financial help and social functions such as parades on the occasion of a birth or circumcision in the ruling family. The guilds, from this perspective, were largely an instrument in the hands of the government; guild members had only limited control over their own affairs.

These views paved the way for a dirigiste explanation of the evolution of the Ottoman economy, both in Istanbul and in the provinces. Such a framework assumed a strict control of government over the guilds, which, it was presumed, prevented the development of free competition among craftsmen and the adoption of new techniques of production.[19] Other scholars, however, while opposed to the dirigiste view as a whole, agreed that there was a mediocrity in both quality

and quantity of produce, as well as total indifference to the needs and requirements of the consumer, which led to technical stagnation – and therefore, one may extrapolate, to the penetration of (superior) Western goods.[20] The theme of poor quality is a pervasive one; to this day it continues to inform many analyses which attempt to understand the 'ultimate triumph' of Western capitalism.[21]

The implications of this view are twofold. On one hand, the 'decline' and ultimate collapse of the economy is explained purely by reference to perceived internal weaknesses: technological innovation was impossible in a stagnant, rigid system.[22] On the other, the guilds eventually withered away in the face of superior Western technology and through the virtues of the market's invisible hand. Only by ignoring the reality of resistance and adaptation – the strategies adopted by Egyptian artisans and merchants, as well as by their European counterparts – is it possible to say that, by the early 1900s, 'not many of the guilds seem to have survived. Most of them had died quietly and nothing is known about the exact year of their passing away; nor is the fact of their death mentioned in any of our sources.'[23]

Bernard Lewis, Louis Massignon and Gabriel Baer are by no means the only scholars to have written on guilds, Egyptian or otherwise. Yet the central arguments they present are representative of much scholarship on this subject and I have dwelt briefly on their ideas with a view to suggesting the tendencies of the most influential scholars in the field.[24] While there are many points on which the two main groups diverge, both may be viewed essentially as variants of the overarching framework of Oriental despotism. Within the two main groups, many variants exist and disagreements abound on tangential points. Still, the main classification holds true for most scholarship on Egyptian guilds.

Thus, I believe it is time to reassess these classifications in the light of newly available sources. New questions need to be raised about what Egyptian guilds actually did, and how they adapted and changed in response not only the government, but to the needs of their members. The fact that builders in Cairo still refer to themselves as belonging to *ta'ifat al-mi'mar* (the Master Mason's guild) is surely an indication the guild has not completely disappeared. The institution lives on, perhaps in another form. The need for more research is clearly indicated.

1   Bryan Turner, *Orientalism, Postmodernism and Globalism* (London and New York, 1994), p. 22.

2   Peter Gran phrases his analysis of the origins of this view with customary incisiveness: 'the original French writers [of the *Description de l'Egypte*] served to further contribute to the mystification of the Egyptian commercial industrial economy by subordinating it in their accounts, thereby perpetuating in subsequent historical literature, the image that it was traditional and fading like the old Egyptian state itself and of no importance to Europe. The result was that the Egyptian merchant, artisan and nomad appeared to be stuck in some rut and to have no relation to modern capitalism[,] which was mainly to be found in far-off Europe.' Peter Gran,

'Late 18th-Century – Early 19th Century Egypt: Merchant Capitalism or Modern Capitalism?', in *L'Egypte au XIXe Siècle* (Paris, 1982), p. 268.

3   This retrospective nationalist sentiment is characteristic of the work of many Egyptian scholars, especially among the post-1952 generation as well as those trained in the early nationalist school of the 1920s. For a presentation of Muhammad 'Ali as the founder of modern industry and the modern Egyptian state, see Afaf Lutfi al-Sayyid Marsot, *Egypt in the Reign of Muhammad 'Ali* (Cambridge, 1984), especially pp. 21 and 162–195.

4   Whilst the concept of the Asiatic mode of production is primarily a tool of Marxist analysis, it may also be considered an expression of the 19th-

century European worldview. Huri Islamoglu-Inan, 'Introduction: Oriental Despotism in World-System Perspective', in Islamoglu-Inan, ed., *The Ottoman Empire and the World Economy* (Cambridge, 1987), pp. 1–2. While the validity of the theory of the Asiatic mode of production has been hotly debated, even within Marxist schools of thought, its premises, assumptions and conclusions continue to enjoy widespread legitimacy.

5   This view is an extremely pervasive and self-perpetuating one. For a thoroughly crystallised version, see Perry Anderson, *Lineages of the Absolutist State* (London, 1979), pp. 503–504: [T]he economic magnitude or opulence of … Islamic cities was not accompanied by any municipal

autonomy or civic order. Towns had no corporate political identity; their merchants little collective social power ... [I]ndividual merchants could rise to the highest political positions in the counsel of dynasties, but their personal success was invariably exposed to intrigue or hazard, while the wealth of their houses could always be confiscated by military rulers. While Anderson is here referring to 'Islamic cities' before the 15th century, in the Oriental despot/Asiatic mode of production perspective, time is of little consequence. See Bernard Lewis's view, below, for the same theory, in almost the same words, applied to the Ottoman period and the 19th (and 20th) centuries.

6 '[T]he AMP embodies the central assumption of "Oriental despotism" – that of the existence of a gap between a mammoth state and an unintegrated social structure. Hence, in Marx and Engels' formulations of the AMP, the defining feature of Asian society was the absence of intermediary structures of classes between the hydraulic state and the undifferentiated agrarian base.' Islamoglu-Inan, p. 3. It may be added that this perspective was also applied in the study of the urban economy.

7 Again, for the theory of the Asiatic mode of production, see Anderson, p. 504. 'Just as no mercantile or professional guilds organised the body of the propertied, no artisan guilds protected or regulated the activity of the small craftsmen in the great Arab cities.'

8 'Ali al-Jiritli, *Ta'rikh al-sina'a fi Misr fi'l-nisf al-awwal min al-qarn al-tasi' 'ashr* (Cairo, 1952), p. 10; and Ahmad al-Hitta, *Ta'rikh Misr al-iqtisadi fi'l-qarn al-tasi''ashr* (Cairo, 1955), pp. 1, 10–14.

9 'The long sixteenth century', which Braudel defines as running from 1451 to 1650. Fernand Braudel, *Civilisation Matérielle, Economie et Capitalisme,*
XVè-XVIIIè Siècle, vol. 1, *Les Structures du Quotidien* (Paris, 1979), p. 39.

10 This section is based partially on my article 'The Guilds Between Tradition and Modernity', in Nelly Hanna, ed., *The State and its Servants: Administration in Egypt from Ottoman Times to the Present* (Cairo, 1995). See the section on 'The Oriental Despot Framework'.

11 Useful compilations of material from the registers of the *mahakim shar'iyya* are Galal El-Nahal's *Judicial Administration of Ottoman Egypt in the Seventeenth Century* (Minneapolis, MN, 1979) which provides a valuable commentary; and 'Abdul Rahim 'Abdul Rahman Abdul Rahim's edited compilations of the records relating to the Maghribi community of Cairo. For a brief overview of rural administration, the latter's 'The Documents of the Egyptian Religious Courts (*al-mahakim al-shar'iyya*) as a Source for the Study of Ottoman Provincial Administration in Egypt (923/1517–1213/1798)', *Journal of the Economic and Social History of the Orient*, 34, pp. 88–97, is also interesting.

12 See most notably Bernard Lewis, 'The Islamic Guilds', *Economic History Review*, 8 (1936–1938), pp. 20–37.

13 Lewis, p. 20. See also the magnum opus of Raymond, whose view was surprising considering his extensive work on the very urban institutions which he stated did not exist: '[L'] *organisation spontanée de l''espace économique urbaine, en dehors de toute coordination, et même de toute intervention, de la part des autorités, était la seule que fut concevable dans une ville ou n'existait aucune institution proprement urbaine.'* André Raymond, *Artisan et Commerçants au Caire au XVIIIè Siècle* (Damascus, 1973,) p. 372. Raymond subsequently revised his views on the topic. See 'The Role of the Communities (*Tawa'if*) in the Administration of Cairo in the Ottoman
Period', in Hanna, ed., *The State and Its Servants*.

14 Lewis's article on Egyptian guilds, although brief, was influential and is often cited to this day. Yet he seemed interested not so much in the guilds *per se* as in an entirely different type of organisation. Following Louis Massignon, he argued (albeit on the penultimate page of his article) that, in the 19th and 20th centuries, the guilds were 'transformed into trade unions of the European type. Those of Tunisia, Syria and Dutch Indonesia have affiliated themselves to the Communist Trade Union International. Others are still in a state of transition.' He also referred to the guilds as espousing an anti-authoritarian feeling. It does not seem overly paranoid to suggest that Lewis's article was intended more for US policy-makers than for the ivory-tower academic audience he seemed to be addressing.

15 Louis Massignon, 'Sinf', *EI2*.

16 For brief remarks on the *futuwwa* in Baghdad, the 'Ikhyan Rum' in Anatolia, and the Qaramita, see Muhammad 'Abd al-Sattar 'Uthman *al-Madina al-Islamiyya* (Kuwait, 1988), pp. 362–363.

17 Lewis, pp. 21, 25, Interestingly, neither Lewis nor Massignon made any direct reference to what the guilds actually did – what purpose they served, which trades were organised in guilds, their economic significance. Nor did they allude to regional variations between, say, Cairo and Istanbul.

18 Gabriel Baer, *Egyptian Guilds in Modern Times* (Jerusalem, 1964), p. 18. 'A guild or corporation in 19th century Egypt may be defined ... as a group of town people engaged in the same occupation and headed by a shaykh.' For Baer's views on the guilds, see also: *Fellah and Townsman in the Middle East: Studies in Social History* (London, 1982), p. 149; 'Guilds in Middle Eastern History', in M. A. Cook,

ed., *Studies in the Economic History of the Middle East From the Rise of Islam to the Present Day* (London, 1970), pp. 11–30. Baer was essentially interested in the guild's functions from the government's point of view, although he did not make this interest explicit.

19 R. Mantran found that the guilds' 'spirit of monopoly' made it easier for the rulers to control them, but also made innovation virtually impossible: their monopoly over the sale and purchase of goods proved, 'through a narrow conservatism, an obstacle to all expansion, all progress'. This view implies that the internal regulations of the guilds remained the same from the Middle Ages to the 17th century, and that neither technological nor material evolution, nor even a simple change in the quality and conditions of work, occurred. See Robert Mantran, *Istanbul dans la Seconde Moitié du XVIIè Siècle: Essai d'Histoire Institutionnelle, Economique et Sociale* (Paris, 1962), pp. 358, 388. Raymond expresses similar views on this matter. Raymond, *Artisans*, pp. 584–585.

20 André Raymond, who has written the most influential and well-researched work on Cairo artisans and merchants to date, argues that poor quality was a common characteristic of workmanship within the guild system. '*L'histoire d' Abu Qir résume assez bien … toutes les critiques que les contemporains pouvaient addresser au systeme corporatif: caractère héréditaire de la maîtrise, dont étaient exclus les individus venant de l'extérieur, - monopole exercé par la corporation et ses maîtres sur une activité professionnelle, - exploitation du consommateur, - totale indifférence des maîtres de métier à toute idée de progrès et en conséquence stagnation technique*', Raymond, *Artisans*, p. 585. Of course, Raymond does not state the story of Abu Sir and Abu Qir literally. Still, the tale (which concerns a dyer who refused to work in any colour but blue, and which, incidentally, vaunts the superiority of

the Egyptian dyer, who knows how to dye cloth in a plethora of colours), along with the reports drawn up by Western consuls (merchants and commercial representatives eager to advertise their products at the expense of locally made goods) provide the bulk of the material on which Raymond bases this assessment. Ironically in light of the Abu Qir story, Jomard states explicitly that 'at the largest dyeworks in Cairo, called "the Sultan's dyeworks" [*masbaghat al-sultan*], woollens and silks and (cotton) cloths, etc., are dyed in green, blue, black, red, yellow, and in every colour.' Jomard, *Wasf madinat al-Qahir*, p. 261.

21 For a few examples in Raymond, see also *Artisans*, p. 207 (for the 'rustic' quality of Egyptian craft production in comparison with the skillful work of the Mamluk period), p. 214 (for the 'limited character of craft production', the 'absence of a veritable market' and the 'lack of capital' which hampered the division between production and sale considered essential to capitalist development), p. 230 (for the 'drop in quality' of Egyptian textiles, resulting from European competition, which kept prices low), and p. 235 (for the 'mediocrity' of the metal and iron workers). Henri Laurens, who has studied the roots of French Orientalism extensively, nevertheless relies almost exclusively on Raymond for his assessments of Egyptian social reality during the 18th century, and refers to the guilds as 'veritable sanctuaries of conservatism', Cf. Henri Laurens et al., *L'Expédition d'Egypte* (Paris, 1989) p. 64. Raymond's article placing penetration of Western commodities and the beginning of peripheralisation around 1750 is also a good example of this type of analysis. See André Raymond, 'L'Impact de la Pénétration Européenne sur l'Economie de l'Egypte au XVIIIè Siècle', *Annales Islamologiques*, 18 (1982), pp. 217–

235. The 'internal crisis' which led to European domination of coffee, sugar and textile commerce was apparently due to technological stagnation, which led to the production of poor-quality goods at high prices, and the eventual replacement of 'indigenous' goods by the products of European competitors. It remains unclear, however, why this 'penetration' should have undermined the crafts in Egypt when Egypt had always been part of the world economy. Two questions remain: first, did a trade deficit represent decline? Secondly, to what extent may we rely on the opinions of European consuls on 'indigenous' goods to determine their quality?

22 Some historians today place the beginning of Western penetration around 1750 (Raymond, 'L'impact'). This date also marks 'the starting point of Europe's realisation of its material superiority over other cultural areas.' (Laurens, p. 16). Until further research is carried out to modify or confirm the consuls' conclusions, it may be possible to suggest that 1750 simply marked the beginning of Europe's adoption of modern military techniques, accompanied by assumptions of moral and racial superiority, and a propaganda campaign promoting European products. It is also possible that Egypt's peripheralisation was delayed by attempts to centralise economic activity, and actually took place much later than that of the rest of the Ottoman empire: after the mid-19th century.

23 Baer, *Egyptian Guilds*, p. 146.

24 Their influence, incidentally, continues to this day, with the dependence of many Arab scholars on the products of Western academia. For an almost verbatim translation of Baer's views, and those of Gibb and Bowen, see Salah Haridi, *al-Hidraf wa'l-sina'at fi 'ahd Muhammad 'Ali* (Cairo, 1985).

6 | Regulating medieval Cairo

Kristen Stilt

In the film *Living with the Past*, al-Darb al-Ahmar is a densely-populated centre of activity. Sellers of bread and *ful* hawk their goods side by side with shoemakers and textile embroiderers, who share narrow streets with mosques, schools and houses. Cairo in the Mamluk period (1250–1517) experienced demographic growth and urbanisation, and the people of al-the Darb al-Ahmar faced practical questions not unlike those of today:

[1] What should be done when a merchant extends his stall into the street, blocking the passage of donkey carts? How should one deal with a shop owner who sweeps his rubbish into the public right-of-way? How to determine if a greengrocer is giving customers less than they paid for? And how does a consumer ensure that the local baker is not adulterating dough with sawdust?

In the Mamluk era a state official, the *muhtasib*, was responsible for these types of concerns.[2] Armed with a legal manual explaining the laws that he was to enforce – ranging from ensuring that a merchant's scales worked properly to preventing men from loitering outside the women's bathhouse – the *muhtasib* would patrol public areas and enforce these laws wherever he saw a violation.[3] Functioning under the Islamic legal principle of *hisba* – commanding the right and forbidding the wrong – the work of the *muhtasib* was an important aspect of the law in society.[4]

A manual from the Mamluk period written to guide the *muhtasib* in his work, entitled *Ma'alim al-qurba fa' ahkam al-hisba*, provides descriptive and detailed information about the kinds of matters under the jurisdiction of the *muhtasib*.[5] The purported author is Diya' al-Din Muhammad b. Muhammad b. Ahmad al-Qurashi al-Shafi'i, known as Ibn al-Ukhuwwa (d. 729/1329). Very little is known about Ibn al-Ukhuwwa as a person, though his focus in the manual on specifically Egyptian issues – such as water from the Nile or the coins used in Egypt – has led scholars to the conclusion that he wrote for the benefit of *muhtasibs* in Cairo and that he himself was most likely an Egyptian.[6]

This essay translates and paraphrases extracts from *Ma'alim al-qurba fa' ahkam al-hisba* that indicate how issues affecting residents

and consumers of Cairo were to be treated in the medieval period.[7] While the manual is vivid and colourful, giving the reader the impression that its author was closely connected to the commercial and social activities discussed, it does have certain limitations. Most importantly, the manual tells the *muhtasib* what *he* should do in instructing people as to how *they* should behave. It is for today's readers to consider the manual in conjunction with other kinds of source material, such as historical chronicles, to better understand how the *muhtasib* was able to enforce the manual's provisions and the difficulties he may have encountered in trying to do so.[8]

Ma'alim al-qurba fa' ahkam al-hisba consists of seventy chapters, but the focus in this essay is on a few topics closely connected to daily life in Cairo. Including regulations on food and clothing, bathing, education, religious practice and the managing of space in a crowded area, this essay brings to light the ways in which the *muhtasib* was supposed to serve the people living and working in the very same streets that appear in *Living with the Past*. While the provisions of the manual are best understood in their own historical context, the underlying issues, concerns and challenges of urban life, as reflected in the manual, will readily resonate with today's readers.

Bread and bakers

The medieval Cairene's basic food was bread.[9] Most typically made from wheat, European travellers in Egypt found it preferable to their own dark bread.[10] Since preservatives were not used in bread, people tried to buy bread daily from local bakeries.[11] Chapter 12 of the manual regulates production of this essential food.

Bakers must not knead the dough with their feet, knees, or elbows, because not only is this disrespectful to food, but also sweat from his body or armpits may fall into the dough. He must wear a tight smock and a face mask, since he might sneeze or talk and some of his saliva might fall into the dough. He must shave the hair on his arms to prevent it from contaminating the dough. If he is working in the day, someone should stand next to him with a fly swatter to keep away the flies.

Cairo contemporary scene, a shop selling scales

The *muhtasib* should pay particular attention to the ways in which bread can be adulterated; there are bakers who mix chickpeas and beans into the dough, for example. Bread should not be baked until the dough has risen, because unleavened bread is heavy on both the scales and the stomach. If the dough does not contain enough salt, then healthy spices such as caraway, sesame and aniseed should be sprinkled on the top of the bread. The baker should not remove the bread from the oven until it is thoroughly baked, but he must do so before it is burnt. It is in the public interest for the *muhtasib* to assign to each bakery the amount of bread to be baked there each day, so that people do not suffer from a shortage of bread.

Butchers

Meat may not have been daily fare for the poor of medieval Cairo, but at least on holidays, and 'Id al-Adha (the Feast of the Sacrifice) in particular, many a sheep would be consumed, and the extensive Islamic laws concerning slaughter made butchers an important and carefully regulated profession.[12] Chapter 16 summarises the legal requirements for slaughter, then goes on to deal with practical issues for butchers.

The *muhtasib* should prevent butchers from slaughtering animals at the doors of their shops because it pollutes the streets with blood and dung, and this constricts the public area of the street and harms people by spraying them with impurities. Rather, they should slaughter in the slaughterhouse. They are not permitted to hang their meat beyond the line of benches outside their shops because if they do so the meat will brush against the clothes of passers-by. Butchers must hang the meat of goat and lamb separately and not mix them. Goat's meat should be marked with saffron to distinguish it from others, and the tail of the goat should be left hanging on the carcass until all of the meat on it is sold.

When the butcher has finished his work for the day, he should sprinkle salt on the cutting board to protect against maggots in the hot season. He should then cover the board with a palm leaf mat held in place by a jar full of stones so as to prevent dogs licking the board and insects crawling on it. In the public interest butchers should not cooperate on fixing a single price for their meat.

Weavers

For their clothing, the people of medieval Cairo would probably have purchased cloth from a weaver, or taken yarn to a weaver to have it woven into cloth. That cloth would then have been taken to a tailor to have it made into clothes if the customer was unble to sew at home.[13] While the manual refers to the weaver and tailor with the male pronoun, many women in the Mamluk period also participated in the textile and clothing industry, mainly working from home.[14] Regulations for weavers are found in Chapter 30 of the manual, and those for tailors in Chapter 31.

The *muhtasib* should order the weavers to weave the cloth tightly. They must not sprinkle flour or plaster on the cloth when weaving it, because these conceal the cloth's coarseness and makes it appear closely textured, and this is dishonest behaviour. If a weaver takes yarn from a person to weave it into material, the weaver should first weigh the yarn. After the weaver makes the cloth, he weighs it again when returning it to the customer, so that the customer knows that he or she received the full amount of cloth due.

If the customer alleges that the weaver used a different yarn, and the customer has a sample of the yarn he brought and the weaver accepts that this was indeed the kind of yarn he received, then they should go to a person experienced in matters of yarn and cloth, who should decide whether the cloth was made from that kind of yarn. If the customer does not have a sample of the yarn, then the weaver can repudiate the allegation by taking an oath that the cloth is indeed made from the customer's yarn. Weavers may not spread out their cloth in the passageways used by people because this impedes passers-by.

Tailors

They are ordered to cut the cloth well, shape the collar properly, make both sleeves the same length and sew the hem evenly. It is best that the needle is fine and the thread in the needle short, because if it is long it will fray and weaken. Valuable material such as silk and brocade must be weighed upon receipt, and then the garment weighed upon presentation to the customer so it will be known if the tailor tried to retain any of the material. There are tailors who, when working with cloth such as silk, will seek to increase its weight with saltwater to equal the weight of the material they want to keep from themselves.

The *muhtasib* should prohibit tailors from keeping people waiting for their finished garments and inconveniencing them by making them return repeatedly to the tailor's shop. They should not keep people's goods for more than one week, unless it was made clear to the customer at the beginning that the job would take longer.

Shoemakers

As with the production of garments, so with shoes which were made by individual shoemakers. Chapter 39 governs production of shoes:

Only well-tanned leather is to be used in making shoes, not untreated hides. For stitching, the heart of the flax should be used, and the length of the thread should not exceed one *dhira'*[15] because otherwise it will fray. The needle should be fine and pig's bristles should never be used because it is impure according to the Shafi'i school. The shoemaker should not delay in giving a customer his or her finished shoes, unless they have given the customer a specific deadline in advance. This is because people suffer from having their goods withheld and having to return repeatedly to the shoemaker.

Water

An adequate supply of water is crucial for a city's well-being: for drinking, washing, cleaning, and production of food and goods. In 1311 the Mamluk sultan al-Nasir Muhammad constructed an aqueduct that ran from the Nile; Sultan al-Ghawri extended it to the Citadel in 1507.[16] For areas not served by the aqueduct, water had to be carried from the Nile and then it was dispensed freely from water fountains (*sabils*) or sold.[17] Chapter 70 includes regulations for water providers and carriers.

Portal of a bathhouse in
Cairo built by the Mamluk
amir Bashtak in 742/1341

As for providing water in clay jugs, the water merchant should be ordered to keep clean the large clay vats in which water is stored, covering them and frequently washing out the dirt that accumulates in them. They should also clean the small clay jars used for drinking, washing them with potsherds and potash every day, and disinfecting them because they get contaminated by people's mouths and breath. The small jars should be hung up so that they can be cooled by the breeze. Covers for the large vats should be made from palm fronds, and no one should drink from the ladle used to convey water from the vat to the jars, nor should anyone put a dirty hand into the vat. The water merchant should take pains to keep his shop, body and clothing clean.

The *muhtasib* should make unannounced inspection visits by day and night, and if he finds an uncovered vat or dirty drinking jar, or finds that well water has been mixed with fresh, then he should punish the merchant, pour away his water, and close the shop as a warning to others. Wise men who have travelled to other lands and drunk from the waters in those places agree that the best and sweetest water is that of the Nile.

The *muhtasib* should order water-carriers to enter the river at a point that is sufficiently far from dirty areas and they are not permitted to fill their water skins near a watering spot for animals or the drain of a bathhouse. If a water-carrier acquires a new water skin, for the first few days he should only transport water in it destined for the tanks of mills and presses, or for making clay. During this time, he may not sell water for purposes of drinking because the taste, colour and smell of the water carried in the new skin is affected by the tanning. When the new water skin no longer changes the water, then the *muhtasib* permits him to use it to transport drinking water.

Bathhouses

Cairo's bathhouses were also great consumers of water. Some homes had their own bathing facilities, but since this required quantities of water and fuel beyond the means of most people, the city's bathhouses provided an important service to the population.[18] Both men and women went to the bath, separately of course, either to the same bathhouse at different days or times, or to separate bathhouses. The *muhtasib* was also responsible for the baths, as discussed in Chapter 42 of the manual.

The *muhtasib* should order the bath attendants to sweep and wash the bathhouse and clean it thoroughly with clean water several times a day. The tiles should be scrubbed with a rough material to remove any leaves of the lotus tree or marshmallow, because people can slip on them. The bath attendant should have a number of wraps to hire out to people, and for men these should be big enough to cover the area between the navel and the knees. For women, they should be long and loose, covering most of the body. Baths should be opened at dawn because people need to wash before the prayer. The warden of the bathhouse must watch over people's clothing while they are bathing and if anything is lost, he is held responsible. A large clay vat of drinking water should be kept in the bath, especially when the weather is hot, and there should be lotus leaves and depilatory paste available in the bath because people may need them but be unable to leave the bathhouse to get them. It would be good if a seller of lotus leaves was always outside the bathhouse selling leaves and other bathing accoutrements.

Instructors of boys

In the Mamluk period, education was typically provided in elementary Qur'anic schools (sing. *kuttab*), after which students might then proceed to the *madrasa*. These venues of instruction were almost entirely the domain of males. While women in the Mamluk period were benefactors of educational institutions, girls typically did not attend them nor did women teach in them.[19] Some women, however, did receive education, as there were notable female scholars in the Mamluk period. Girls seem to have been taught in less formal settings, such as teaching circles in mosques and private homes.[20] Chapter 46 of the manual regulates instructors of boys.

Writing should not be taught in mosques, because the Prophet ordered that boys and the insane be kept out of mosques because they write on the walls and dirty the floor with urine and other impurities.

Rather, teachers should be instructed to hold lessons in open areas on the edges of the market. Likewise, they may not teach in their homes.

Teaching is the noblest profession, according to a saying of the Prophet. A teacher must be pious, virtuous and trustworthy, have memorised the Qur'an, and be possessed of a good hand and knowledge of arithmetic. It is best if the teacher is married, and no bachelor may open a school for the instruction of boys unless he is a respected elder (shaykh), distinguished in religion and virtue.

The teacher should be gentle with young boys and first teach them the alphabet, then the short verses of the Qur'an, and then subjects such as arithmetic and letter writing. When boys are seven years old, the teacher should instruct them in how to pray with the congregation, as per the Prophetic tradition. The teacher should order them to honour their parents and obey their commands.

If the boys are bad mannered, use obscenities in their speech, or do other things which are not permitted, the teacher should beat them as a punishment. The teacher should not use a thick stick that can break bones nor a thin one that will not be felt, rather it should be medium in size.

The teacher should not use any of the students for errands that would bring shame on the family of the boy, such as moving dirt or manure, or carrying stones.

Mosque attendants and muezzins

The mosque was an important centre of religious life. Chapter 47 is dedicated to the care of mosques and the religious activities that take place inside them.

The *muhtasib* is charged with supervising all the mosques and ordering their attendants to sweep and clean them every day, shake the dust from the floor mats, clean the walls and wash the candle-sticks. Candles should be lit every evening. The doors of the mosques should be closed after the prayer time and the mosques should generally be protected from boys, the insane and anyone who eats, sleeps, per-forms his craft, or sells goods in the mosque. Likewise, searching for stray animals in the mosque, or sitting and talking about worldly affairs in it, is forbidden. The *muhtasib* should also exhort the people living in the local area to be diligent in attending Friday prayers at the mosque.

As for the call to prayer, only a reliable, trustworthy and honourable man who knows the times of prayer may make the call to prayer from the minaret. The *muhtasib* should test the muezzins for their knowledge of the prayer times, because if someone does not know when to make the call to prayer, he may do so at the wrong time, causing people to pray too early, in which case their prayers would not be valid. It is preferable for the muezzin to have a good voice, and the *muhtasib* should prohibit him from excessively stretching out the voice or singing the call to prayer. The muezzin should lower his gaze when ascending the minaret and avoid looking at women or into people's homes.

Use of space

One significant issue for a crowded city is the use of space, and by the Mamluk era Cairo was already replete with both people and buildings. The mosque complex of Qijmas al-Ishaqi, for example, built in 1480–1481, 'is situated on a triangular piece of land at the intersection of two streets, and provides an excellent example of the ingenious way in which architects of the late Mamluk period adjusted the parts of the building to the available site.'[21] The area had already been developed such that the builders had to devise a creative way of fitting the complex into the existing space, constructing the mosque's *sabil-kuttab* on the other side of a narrow passageway and connecting the two by a raised walkway.[22] Chapter 8 of the manual deals with the physical space of public areas:

The streets are common property, and no one may appropriate them for personal use. No merchant may sit in the narrow streets of the market nor extend shop benches into passageways beyond the line of pillars supporting the roof of the market, because this is bother-some to pedestrians. Tethering animals in the streets of the market is forbidden except when required for alighting and mounting. Throw-ing refuse into the middle of the streets, scattering melon rinds and spraying water, are all forbidden because these actions may result in someone slipping or falling. Expelling water from spouts that extend into narrow streets is forbidden because it soils the clothes of passers-by and constricts the streets.

The *muhtasib* should order carriers of firewood, straw, paving stones and the like, to unload their goods from their pack animals when they stop in courtyards. If they keep the animals standing with these loads, the animal will be injured and the Prophet forbade inflicting pain on animals other than at the moment of slaughtering.

No one may peer into a neighbour's home from a roof or window, nor may men sit in the path of women without specific need.

The above excerpts are only a few of the regulations contained in the seventy chapters of Ibn al-Ukhuwwa's manual. Other topics include regulation of fryers of fish, druggists and makers of other medicinal products, milkmen, brokers, silk weavers, money changers, goldsmiths, veterinarians, physicians, oculists and surgeons, as well as means of punishment at the *muhtasib*'s disposal. Ibn al-Ukhuwwa's manual is undoubtedly of use since it is a wonderful source of information about the social and economic life of Mamluk Cairo, and the relationship between law and society more generally, and thus it awaits further study.

1   For a discussion of the development of Cairo in the Mamluk period, see André Raymond, Cairo, tr. Willard Wood (Cambridge, MA, 2000), pp. 111–191.

2   For a fuller description of the position of *muhtasib*, see 'Hisba', *EI2*; Emile Tyan, *Histoire de l'organisation judiciaire en pays d'Islam* (Paris, 1943), vol. 2, pp. 436–484; al-Mawardi, *al-Ahkam al-sultaniyya wa'l-wilayat al-diniyya*, tr. Wafaa Wahba as *The Ordinances of Government* (Reading, 1996), pp. 260–280.

3   See, for example, Chapter 53 of the *muhtasib* manual cited in note 5, which provides that the *muhtasib* 'should be closely connected to the markets, going through them at all times and circulating amongst the traders and sellers. He should investigate shops and streets, inspect weights and measures, and inspect their products and foods and that which they adulterate. He should do this by day and night at different times and when they are not expecting it.' Levy ed., p. 219.

4   For an extensive discussion of the concept of *hisba*, see Michael Cook, *Commanding Right and Forbidding Wrong in Islamic Thought* (Cambridge, 2000).

5   *The Ma'alim al-Qurba fi Ahkam al-Hisba of Diya' al-Din Muhammad Ibn Muhammad al-Qurashi al-Shafi'i*, ed. with partial trans. Reuben Levy (London, 1938); Muhammad b. Muhammad b. Ahmad al-Qurashi, *Kitab ma'alim al-qurba fi ahkam al-hisba* (Cairo, 1976). A manual from the later Mamluk period, Muhammad b. Ahmad b. Bassam (d. before 1440), *Nihayat al-rutba fi talab al-hisba*, ed. Husam al-Din Samarra'i (Baghdad, 1968), bears enough resemblance to Ibn al-Ukhuwwa's text to suggest that Ibn Bassam was aware of it and drew from it. Another possible explanation is that both Ibn al-Ukhuwwa and Ibn Bassam relied upon an earlier, Ayyubid, manual, 'Abd al-Rahman b. Nasr al-Shayzari's *Nihayat al-rutba fi talab al-hisba* (Cairo, 1946), which is shorter but could have been the original source for each of these two later authors. Al-Shayzari's text has been translated by R. P. Buckley as *The Book of the Islamic Market Inspector* (Oxford, 1999).

6   Levy ed., p. xvii. There is also a manuscript of a text very similar to that of Ibn al-Ukhuwwa attributed to Ibn al-Rif'a (d. 1310), who was a *muhtasib* in Fustat and a well-known legal scholar. A copy of the manual, *al-Rutba fi talab al-hisba*, is preserved in the Arab League Manuscript Institute in Cairo as film 25, *Siyasa*. What is important is that the evidence indicates that the text was written, and copied, in Cairo in the Mamluk period, regardless of whether the author was Ibn al-Ukhuwwa or Ibn al-Rif'a.

7   To make this essay accessible to a wide range of readers, I paraphrase in English certain portions of the chapters cited. The discussion is not a translation of the text, in whole or in part.

8   Huda Lutfi faced a similar issue in 'Manners and Customs of Fourteenth-Century Cairene Women: Female Anarchy versus Male Shar'i Order in Muslim Prescriptive Treatises', in Nikki R. Keddie and Beth Baron, ed., *Women in Middle Eastern History* (New Haven, CT, 1991). She deals with the 'gap between prescriptive literature and the existing reality of women's everyday life.' p. 117.

9   For the importance of bread in the daily diet, see Adam Sabra, *Poverty and Charity in Medieval Islam* (Cambridge, 2000), p. 113; Boaz Shoshan, 'Grain Riots and the "Moral Economy": Cairo, 1350–1517', *Journal of Interdisciplinary History* (1980), pp. 459–478.

10 Sabra, p. 113.

11 Ibid.

12 See Sabra, pp. 114–115.

13 As Sabra notes, we have very little information about the clothing of the poor of medieval Cairo, while the ceremonial garb of the elite is fairly well described. Ibid., p. 109.

14 See Yossef Rapoport, 'Marriage and Divorce in the Muslim Near East, 1250–1517' (PhD, Princeton University, 2002), pp. 67–79.

15 Equal to about .58 of a metre.

16 Caroline Williams, *Islamic Monuments in Cairo: A Practical Guide* (5th ed., Cairo, 2002), p. 40.

17 For the significance of providing water, see 'Sabil', *EI2*. *Sabils,* drinking fountains, have been replaced by piped water, but several beautiful ones remain as monuments, such as the *sabil-kuttab* of Ruqayya Dudu (1761). See Williams, p. 85. A *sabil* was often built with a Qur'anic school (*kuttab*) attached. Williams, p. 22.

18 For a discussion of the history of the bathhouse, see 'Hammam', *EI2*.

19 Jonathan Berkey, 'Women and Islamic Education in the Mamluk Period', in Nikki R. Keddie and Beth Baron, ed., *Women in Middle Eastern History* (New Haven, CN, 1991), pp. 144–145.

20 Ibid, p. 146.

21 Williams, p. 91.

22 Ibid.

7 Women and family life in the darb

Amira Sonbol

What was a typical Cairene household like in the past and how can relationships between its various members be defined? More specifically, can we talk about a 'typical' Cairene family and is such a family any different from ones in existence in other areas of Egypt, the Arab world, the Islamic world, or in similar societies throughout the world during the same time period? In other words, is there anything unique about the concept of the 'family' when it pertains to the Arab world and does the phrase 'Islamic family', which is consistently used by Islamists today, help define intra-family and inter-family relations?

This paper is about women in Cairo's popular quarters during the Ottoman period, and takes the approach that a family is loosely defined as a kinship unit organised within a household. Nicholas Hopkins defines it as 'an economic unit of production or consumption ...[with] kinship values and norms strengthen[ing] a pattern of interaction ... provid[ing] the ideological basis for the teamwork that is required to make this small group successful in social terms.'[1] A family living in Ottoman Cairo could be extended, nuclear or some transitional structure between the two. Couples could start off living within the larger family, could remain permanently within the extended household or eventually move on to their own home. A wife's power within the family would be tied to the family's composition and size. The variations of family structures found in Ottoman Cairo belie the idea that a particular model for an Islamic, or Arab, or Cairene family existed; economic and other particular conditions played an important role in defining kin relations.

Today it has become usual among Islamist writers to call upon society to re-establish the 'Islamic' family model (al-usrat al-muslima) which, according to their discourse, has been supplanted or 'deformed' by modern un-Islamic, presumably Western, structures. According to these writers the family – formed of father, mother and children – is the social unit preferred and chosen by God for men, 'it is the essential unit in building society. The holy shari'a gave family particular attention and importance befitting its proper position so as to lead towards greater horizons'.[2] The Islamic family then becomes a unit which is aimed at obeying God and following his rules, in which the primary job of the father and mother is to raise the children and teach them their religion, the love of God and high morals. Islamists also use reciprocal rights defined by God to determine relations between husband and wife; amongst these are a husband's respect and financial support for the wife and the absolute obedience of the wife to the wishes of her husband. The wife is also expected to act honorably, keeping herself and her husband's property safe. A girl has to consent to being married, she must marry her social equal and her husband has to treat her well. In this understanding marriage and family are the only honoured relationships in Islam.[3]

It is important to point out that a fundamental diversity in the shape of the family (nuclear, extended or transitional forms) has been a constant in Islamic society and still is today. The shape and function of the household has changed, as have basic kin relations, so that the 'kin that count',[4] to use Marilee Meriwether's perceptive phrase in her description of inter-family relations in Syria, have become a tighter and more immediate group today. The group is tighter than that which existed before the institutions of the nation-state assumed many of the functions that connected members of large families to each other and to the guild to which the family's main provider belonged. In a hara or darb of pre-modern Cairo, people depended on each other, helped each other out and often sued together for common causes. Although members of a family quarrelled together, they were expected to present a united front against outsiders and they could be expected to help each other financially; after all they often shared ownership of property, or lived in the same building, worked together or were beneficiaries of waqfs set up by common forebears. This was to change in the modern state when the law recognised the nuclear family as a legal unit with the husband as the patriarchal head. The state then dealt with the legal unit, the family, through its male head; it was he who carried a family identity card listing his wife or wives, his minor sons and unmarried daughters, with the dates of birth, sex and other information. That was not the case in pre-modern Cairo; then the legal unit was the individual, and the courts dealt with the individual and their rights and responsibilities rather than with the head of a family, even when the case involved communal action undertaken by a quarter or a guild with a shaykh representing the group; the records make that clear. As for family litigation, the records included the name of each member involved in the litigation. The head of the family had the right of 'force' (*wilayat al-ijbar*) with regard to under-age children,[5] but this right could be held by the mother and did not have to go to a male *wali*.[6]

This paper will focus on the life of a woman living in the *darb* as she moves from her family's home to that of her husband; her life in the extended family and in the *hara*, and then her move to form her own nuclear family. The intention is to show how the family functioned, how various forms of family existed together and how the dynamics of life dictated variations in social norms and gender relations.

Marrying into an extended family
All sources dealing with marriage in Islam generally agree that a girl's consent is necessary for a marriage to be legal. But in practice girls could be forced into marriage without much of an attempt made to ascertain if they consented. A girl could also be married when she remained silent; this is seen as agreement; perhaps shyness or modesty prevented her from showing any enthusiasm for marital relations. In contrast, today's laws not only require the girl's consent but set a minimum age for marriage; for girls it is sixteen and for boys eighteen. Today, of course, minimum age requirements are quite often bypassed, particularly in villages and poorer urban quarters. Things were not much different in pre-modern Cairo.

Ottoman Cairo tended to follow the Shafi'i *fiqh* (jurisprudence) and so its inhabitants in popular and middle-class quarters, like al-Darb al-Ahmar, adhered to the Shafi'i *madhhab* (legal school), although the Hanafi school was the school followed by the Ottoman state and members of the military class and was the *madhhab* of the chief *qadi* appointed by Istanbul. However, immigrants to Cairo from the Egyptian South or from North Africa preferred the Maliki legal school, while travellers from Turkey or Syria went before the Hanafi judge. Some courts, at least officially, specialised in certain types of legal case at the beginning of the Ottoman occupation, but court records illustrate that these divisions were hardly followed in practice. So while the rules required that litigation dealing with women and orphans had to be taken to the *qisma 'arabiyya* court, in practice such litigation was brought before all of Egypt's various courts. Marriage records in these courts indicate that it was standard practice for under-age girls and boys was to be married by the father, grandfather or mother through *wilayat al-ijbar*. Consent was apparently not required by the courts – or at least such consent was not indicated in the records. Even if the girl had reached majority by reaching puberty (*bulugh*) and *rushd* (rationality), a young bride (we will call her 'Husna' here for simplicity) could still be coerced into marriage if, as was likely in Cairo, her family was Shafi'i. If the family followed the Maliki *madhhab*, she could be coerced unless she had previously been married. The logic of the Shafi'is and the Malikis is that experience of married life allowed the girl to make the right decisions when choosing a husband; if she had lived with a husband for a year she was considered a *thayb* (woman) even if the marriage had not been consummated. Only the Hanafi *madhhab* allowed an adult, hitherto unmarried, girl to choose her own husband, but at the same time it limited her power to act by giving her father the right to have the marriage annulled if he did not consider her husband her social equal.

But a girl such as Husna was not stuck in the marriage if she discovered that it was not to her liking. Her parents might have placed conditions in the marriage contract which would allow her to divorce if things did not suit her, for example if there was bad treatment by her husband or his family, or if he were to take a second wife. The *madhhab* also allowed Husna to sue for and receive a divorce once she reached majority and decided that she did not want to stay married to this man. If Husna's husband was a cousin or the son of close friends or associates, it was expected that the marriage would work and that

The daughters of Suleyman Pasha,
Cairo, detail, from the *Utazási
Album* by Count Iván Forray,
Pest, 1857

which can house the head of the family with his young unmarried children'.[7] When one of the children married, the house was sometimes altered to make separate quarters for the new couple. This was sometimes arranged automatically, but as Hanna points out, it often took action by the court to push the husband to make a separate house for the wife or to alter the living conditions in the old home. Court records show that wives often sued for a separate entrance so as not to use the same courtyard as the rest of the family, or for a wall to be built between the general, larger, family quarters and the private quarters in which the couple lived. This is understandable given the fact that in most houses, particularly in the popular quarters, the *qa'a* in which people lived and ate during the day was turned into sleeping quarters at night, not allowing for much privacy.

Husna's life changed perceptibly on her marriage. Where once she played in the *hara* with children of her own age and went to the *kuttab* of the local mosque in order to learn how to read and to memorise the Qur'an, she was now a young wife with domestic responsibilities and children. If, even though the marital contract was signed, she was not old enough for the marriage to be consummated, she could continue to live in her father's home until the dowry was paid in full or until she reached *bulugh*, a requirement for consummation. Her father could demand compensation for the cost of her support while she remained in his home, or her husband might prefer that she come and live with his family until it was time to the consummate the marriage rather than pay for her upkeep at her father's. In the husband's home, she would have begun to help with the housework, cleaning and cooking, and in general followed the orders of his mother or the oldest woman of the household. Perhaps Husna was a second wife, and in that case had to serve, and follow the dictates of, an older wife as well. She might also have been born into a family that followed a particular craft, like weaving or tanning, and then married into the same craft. She would have then have taken part in the family business. She might also have had her own business, such as a small shop or a coffee house that she had inherited from her father or managed in partnership with another

Husna would easily fit into the husband's wider family. Quite often in such marriages the couple were engaged as small children and knew that they would eventually marry. If it was not that sort of relationship, or if Husna came from outside the *darb*, life in the wider family would not always be pleasant for her, especially in the early years of the marriage since she could be living in the same household as her mother-in-law, sisters-in-law, and possibly the wives of her brothers-in-law. As she grew older and became more established, Husna probably found her own place and things went smoothly, and if not she either divorced her husband or tried to ensure she and her husband moved out.

The household lived closely together. In her excellent study about life in Ottoman Cairo, *Habiter au Caire*, Nelly Hanna describes a typical middle-class home, Bayt al-Islambouli, as containing 'a large *qa'a* (sitting room), wide corridor, two toilets and three small rooms, all of member of her own family.[8] If Husna's husband was well off, she would not have been expected to do any particular work apart from what was expected of the all the women of the household. If not, she might have had to look after an elderly mother or father and take over important functions in the running of the household.

Life in the hara

Generally speaking, social life in Egypt's alleys consisted mostly of visiting neighbours and family. Gossip, like everywhere in the world, was a favourite pastime, for women as they sipped coffee at home and for men in the local coffee house, or, in the afternoons, sitting on the

wood or brick 'sofa' (*mastaba*) or wooden bench (*dikka*) that could be found just outside the front door. Views on politics, cultural matters and the common gossip of the street were exchanged and people knew most of what went on in the houses of their neighbours. The Prophet's birthday (*mawlid al-nabi*) and the feasts following Ramadan and the *hajj* were special. As a child, and like her children later, on these occasions Husna would have worn colourful clothes, often new, and would have gone out to play on the swings watched over by the adults, men and women. Food was important and vendors of all types sold cooked food in Cairo's streets. Special items for the feasts, like raw-sugar dolls and knights symbolising the beautiful girl (*sitt al-husn*) and her courageous saviour on horseback (*al-shatir hassan*) have been favourites of children on feast days (*mawalid*) since Mamluk times. During Ramadan, colourful lanterns lit by candles (*fawanis ramadan*) were used by children playing hide and seek and other games in the evening.

Men enjoyed listening to tales of valour like those about Abu Za'id al-Hilali or 'Antar b. Shadad told by *rawis* (storytellers) in the city squares and coffee houses. Women liked to go out in groups, walking by the Nile or taking boat rides to enjoy the river. They enjoyed singing and dancing together and going shopping. In fact, shopping was one of the reasons for divorce most commonly cited by husbands suing a wife through the courts to obey him and stay at home. There were also public celebrations like the departure to the Hijaz of the *mahmal* (gold-embroidered cloth woven in Egypt to cover the Ka'ba), or Sham al-Nissim, celebrating the arrival of Spring, or the festival of the Nile flood. These brought out the general population of Cairo to play and celebrate. Husna would also go to the cemetery to visit her deceased relatives. If a member of the family died, she was expected to meet guests coming to pay condolences, and to provide unsweetened coffee and food for the closest relatives or those who had travelled from the country to pay their respects. In turn, she was expected to pay her condolences when a relative or acquaintance died, and was expected to observe the requirements for such events such as wearing black as a sign of mourning. Traditions regarding death were the same for all

Woman carrying food
to cotton-workers,
City of the Dead, Cairo,
Henri Cartier-Bresson, 1950

Egyptians; no matter whether Muslim or Copt, women went to the cemetery every Thursday, except the fourth, then marked the fortieth day after the death when the soul is said to have finally left the body. These rites are said to date from Ancient Egyptian times and had little to do with Islam or Christianity except for the prayers recited and the men performing the ceremony.

Visiting the graves of the *awliya'* (lit. friends of God) was very important to Egyptians, and Husna probably went with another woman from her family, particularly when one of them had a special need or desire, such as supplicating God for a child, or the safe return of a beloved son or husband. Sometimes the prayers concerned getting rid of a rival wife. If Husna lived in al-Darb al-Ahmar, in the heart of Cairo, it would be easy for her to visit the tombs of the most important *awliya'*. To the north of the *darb* was Fatimid Cairo which is where the Husayn Mosque, the most popular mosque in Egypt to which thousands flocked each year, was located. To the south was the *qarafa* (cemetary) with the mosque of Sayyida 'Aysha just outside the cemetery and the mosque of al-Imam al-Shafi'i. All were popular places of pilgrimage and prayer. Women and sometimes men, went to them, prayed and made their supplications either silently, or out loud; many cried out in their grief and some brought perfume to clean the tomb of the saint. Like others of her community, Husna would have had a strong belief in the power of these saints, including lesser ones like Sayyidna al-Khidr, related to the Prophet, who had the ability to fly and to perform miracles for those who asked. Husna would probably have used fortune-tellers who could discover what was hidden: or gone to witches for amulets (*hariz*) to win back her husband's love, to help her to have more children, or to resolve household problems. Sometimes the amulet was sought in order to break the evil eye or a spell she thought had been laid upon her, her husband or a member of their family, if mischief befell them for no apparent reason. Men also resorted to fortune-tellers and witches, and believed strongly in the power of envy (*hasad*) and its possible effects on their health and their affairs.

76   al-Darb al-Ahmar in Egyptian history

Many homes did not have kitchens, and cooked food was bought in the market or brought to the door by vendors. But a rich house would have a large kitchen and would often have provided food for the poor. Certainly if Husna belonged to such a household, she would help distribute the meat of the sheep or bull slaughtered on the Feast of Sacrifice after the pilgrimage ('Id al-adha). Whilst this was a *sunna* (tradition following the Prophet's example) expected of Muslims, only the rich could afford to perform it and ordinary people expected rich members of the community to perform the sacrifice and distribute the meat. Only choice parts of the slaughtered animal, like the liver, were kept for the rich man's family. The rich were also expected to provide a table of food in God's name (*sufrat al-Rahman*) so that poor people could break their fast during Ramadan. Meat was a favourite in Egypt, but was not affordable for most of the population, hence the great value placed on this type of philanthropy, that is, slaughtering and offering fresh meat or providing a table of food. Fish was another favourite and the Nile gave a plentiful supply, so fish was affordable. Fish was cooked in many ways which are still popular with ordinary Egyptians. For example, very small fish, no larger than a finger, were eaten fried or grilled and known in this form as *besariya*, when salted known as *muluha*.[9] Other favourites, of Egyptians of all classes, included broad beans (*ful madami*), still regarded as the national dish; porridge (*balila*), and farmer's cheese (*jibna qarish*).

If she had money of her own or had married into a well-to-do family, Husna would probably have stayed inside the house on most days doing nothing. But for the majority of women, home was where they returned after a long day's work, or the place where they undertook various crafts in order to make some money. Husna might have taken in wool or linen to weave, or have gone out to work as a weaver of cloth or of carpets in one of the many workshops found in quarters like al-Judariyya near al-Azhar or Bab al-Khalq.[10] At home, if she had a courtyard or garden, Husna could have kept chickens or ducks and sold eggs. If her husband sold cooked food in the market, she might well have been involved in its preparation and delivery. She could

perhaps even have been a water-carrier (*saqqa'*), though this job is thought to have been exclusively male. While most of the tailors that are known of were men, it is established that women took in sewing and hired themselves out by the day to sew in people's homes. Husna could also have been in the entertainment business as a dancer, a singer, or a fortune-teller. She could have been trained in the art of medicine, for instance, to perform circumcisions or to act as midwife, or doctor.[11] If Husna was involved in any of these professions then she probably came from a family that specialised in it and would have been apprenticed to her brother, mother or uncle. As a midwife, she would have enjoyed the respect of her neighbours and the local community, and would probably have been expected to be an expert witness in court cases involving women, such as rape or other types of violence.[12]

Generally speaking, the *hara* was a safe place for its inhabitants. It was usually shut at night with gates. The *hara* was watched over by young men who were careful of the conduct and the welfare of the women of their quarter and who would not restrain their anger if one of the women, or men for that matter, was ill-treated by the inhabitants of some other quarter of the city. So Husna could generally go about her business assured of her safety; still, women mostly went out in groups or accompanied by a male of the family. The frequency of rape cases in the court records indicates that despite the general security of the city and the vigilantism in the various quarters, rapes did take place; the usual victim was a poorer woman or a young boy. Sometimes rape took place in the household, probably an act of violence against a domestic servant. If Husna came from a poor family and had to work as domestic help, as many women did, she probably went home at night because she was married, but we know little about the subject of married women and domestic labour during the Ottoman period. Usually, unmarried girls from villages or slave girls bought in the market were the domestic help and in the case of the latter, they could be bought with concubinage in mind as part of the girl's duties. Over all however, life in the *hara* was safe. Girls and their families could bring cases of violence committed against them to court without any sense of shame; and they could expect the courts to deal very severely with the perpetrator once rape was proved. Intent was not then taken into consideration by the judge as in modern law; this can permit leniency towards perpetrators of violent crimes.

This paper about the life of women in Ottoman Cairo has been an attempt to illustrate the diversity of family structure and relationships in pre-modern Egypt. The court records of other towns in Egypt have been used to demonstrate that the realities of urban life were similar during particular periods, and also that context and class played a very important role in determining social and gender relations. In contrast to the normative view of an Arab and Islamic family in which women played a specific subservient and secluded role, the evidence from the past demonstrates that there were many models and variations on the family, and that women were an important part of the dynamics of life, and of the shaping of family and society.

1   Nicholas Hopkins, 'Introduction', in *The New Arab Family, Cairo Papers in Social Science*, ed., Nicholas Hopkins, 24 (2001), p. 3.

2   'Abd al-Hakam 'Abd al-Latif al-Sa'idi, *al-Usra al-muslima: usus wa mabadi'* (Cairo, 1992), pp. 9–10.

3   Muhammad al-Biltagi, *Fi ahkam al-usra: dirasa muqarina, al-zawaj wa'l-furqa* (Cairo, 2001), pp. 115–120.

4   Margaret L. Meriwether, *The Kin who Count: Family and Society in Ottoman Aleppo, 1770–1840* (Austin, TX, 1999).

5   Cairo, Dar al-Watha'iq al-Qawmiyya, Sijillat Mahakim Shar'iyya, Dumyat, Ishhadat 975 [1568], 8:54–28; 1011–1015 [1601–1605], 43:11–26, 48–182, 84–182; 999 [1592], 30:9–30; Isna, Ishhadat, 1191–1192 [1777–1778], 29:20–47; Manfalut, Sijillat 1228 [1812], 5:47–167; Alexandria, Da'awai 1273–1281 [1856–1864]), 1:3–8 & 11; 1:14–36.

6   Dishna, Ishhadat 1908, 166:9–20, 10–22, 13–30, 15–33, 15–34, 16–35, 20–74; Dumyat, Ishhadat 999 [1592], 30:10–33; 1011–1015 [1601–1605], 43:84–182

7   Nelly Hanna, *Habiter au Caire: La Maison moyenne et ses habitants aux XVIIe et XVIIIe siècles* (Cairo, 1991), p. 151.

8   Alexandria Shari'a Court (1130), 65:141–247.

9   'Ali al-Sayyid 'Ali, 'al-Nazihun ila al-Qahira fi al-'asr al-Mamluki', in Nasir Ibrahim, ed., *al-Tawa'if al-mihaniyya wa al-ijtima'iyya fi al-'asr al-'Uthmani* (Cairo, 2003), pp. 42–43.

10 Ibid., p. 42.

11 'Abd al-Hamid Sulayman, 'Muqata'at al-khurda wa tawabi'uha: dirasat al-tanzim al-mali wa al-daribi li'l-hiraf al-hamishiyya wa al-basita fi Misr al-'Uthmaniyya', in Nasir Ibrahim, ed., *al-Tawa'if al-mihaniyya*, pp. 74–128.

12 Egypt, al-Bab al-'Ali (1152), 221:283–429.

8 Learning and science in Historic Cairo

Heinz Halm

The oldest Arab-Islamic metropolis of Egypt, al-Fustat (or Fustat Misr), was originally – like Kufa and Basra in Iraq or Qayrawan in Tunisia – a military camp which the Muslims had established in the course of their conquests in the year AD 643. As an Islamic and Arabic-speaking island in a country inhabited by Copts, the city with its large mosque, the 'Amr Mosque, which still exists today, was from the very beginning the intellectual centre of the land of the Nile. Eminent founding fathers of the Arab-Islamic civilisation lived and worked here. For example, Muhammad ibn Idris al-Shafi'i (767–820), the great jurist and founder of one of the four Sunni schools of law, found asylum here after a conflict with opponents of his views in Baghdad. Each morning, he would gather his pupils around him to lecture to them in the court-yard of the 'Amr Mosque. This led to his most important work, the 'Fundamental Book' (*Kitab al-umm*), as well as to the 'Treatise' (*al-Risala*), which forms the foundation of Islamic legal theory. Al-Imam al-Shafi'i's tomb is, even today, visited by the inhabitants of Cairo as a place of pilgrimage and al-Imam al-Shafi'i is honoured as a saint.

From Baghdad, too, came al-Mas'udi (893–956), one of the great writers of Arabic prose literature (*adab*). In 943 he wrote his most cele-brated work here, the voluminous 'Golden Meadows' (*Muruj al-dhahab*), a compendium of cosmography, geography and history, the like of which the Islamic world had never known before.

In the year 969, following the difficulties of internal unrest, famine and epidemic, Egypt surrendered without a fight to Jawhar, the viceroy of the Fatimid caliph, al-Mu'izz (953–975), who then, fol-lowing the orders of his lord, laid out a new military camp north-east of al-Fustat for his future residence, thus inaugurating a new era of intellectual life in Egypt. This city of palaces, called 'the Victorious' (*al-qahira*), was, to begin with, reserved for the caliph's court and his army and civil servants. Its centre was the palace, in the vicinity of which a new mosque was built, 'the Radiant One' (*al-azhar*), which was soon to vie with the 'Old Mosque' (*al-masjid al-'atiq*) as a centre for study and teaching. Since in early Islam teaching, studying and science were private matters and there were no public institutions set aside for

them, the mosques with their vast halls and large courtyards served as suitable places in which those who possessed any kind of knowledge could gather students and listeners in a circle (*halqa*) around them. In Islam knowledge was not the privilege of the few, but in principle was accessible to anyone.

In June 973, the Fatimid caliph al-Mu'izz made his entry into Cairo. Thus the metropolis of the Nile province became the capital of an empire which extended from the Atlas mountains to the Euphrates and could vie with Baghdad and Christian Constantinople. The Shi'i Ismaili faith of the Fatimid dynasty lent the new regime its special character: the Fatimid ruler was not only the successor (*khalifa*) of the Prophet Muhammad, but also – from the Ismaili point of view – the religious leader (*imam*) of all Muslims. The Ismaili doctrine, which was as deeply imbued with Islamic tradition as it was with the philo-sophical ideas of the period, was now disseminated in regular teaching sessions, which were called 'sessions of wisdom' (*majalis al-hikma*). These were held on certain days – especially Thursdays – in a room of the caliph's palace by the 'supreme missionary' (*da'i al-du'at*) in the name of the imam. Although only the initiated were admitted to these sessions, the initiation itself was open to everyone and was apparently highly sought-after, for it is known that it sometimes led to a most dangerous crush of people in front of the conference hall. The texts that were read out at these teaching sessions were then copied and distributed. A major part of this *majalis* literature has come down to us in manuscripts and is partly accessible in modern print.

In addition, there were public lectures held on the subject of Ismaili jurisprudence after the Friday prayers in al-Azhar Mosque nearby, to announce the new legal system to the population. The vizier Ya'qub ibn Killis wrote a handbook on law, though this could by no means assert itself against the great legal treatise prepared by al-Qadi al-Nu'man (d. 974), the 'Pillars of Islam' (*Da'a'im al-Islam*). The latter work is still the standard text on law for Ismailis all over the world.

The vizier Ibn Killis (930–991) was, meanwhile, much more suc-cessful with another measure he adopted:

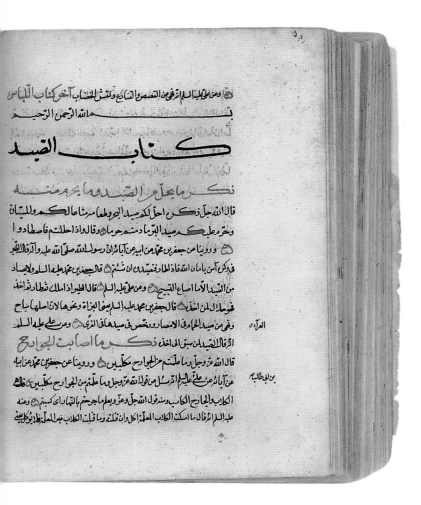

In the year 378/988, the vizier Abu'l-Faraj Ya'qub ibn Killis asked
the caliph al-'Aziz bi'llah to specify the salaries for a few of the jurists.
Thereupon, the caliph bestowed on each of them an adequate salary.
He ordered a piece of land to be bought and a house to be built next
to al-Azhar Mosque. Each Friday they assembled in the mosque and
formed circles after the [midday] prayer until the time of the afternoon
prayer. They also received a certain sum each year out of the vizier's
own fortune. There were thirty-five of them; on the feast of breaking
the fast, al-'Aziz presented them with robes of honour and let them
ride through the city on mules.

Ibn Killis thus inaugurated a tradition of teaching and study at
al-Azhar Mosque that has lasted over a thousand years. It is true, however,
that teaching at al-Azhar was often interrupted and that after the end
of the Fatimid dynasty it ceased altogether for almost a hundred years.

In addition to mosques as centres of teaching and studying, 'sessions'
(*majalis*) also played an important part in the academic life of the
period. These were regularly held by high-ranking and wealthy patrons
seeking social prestige. Here, too, the vizier Ya'qub ibn Killis played
a leading part.

Ya'qub valued men of science and gathered scholars around himself.
Each Thursday evening, he personally assembled an audience (*majlis*)
attended by judges, jurists, Qur'an reciters, philologists and all kinds
of dignitaries, the highest legal officials as well as experts on tradition,
and read to his guests from his own works. When the session ended, the
poets rose to recite panegyrics about him. There were people in his house
who copied the Venerable Qur'an; others copied works of traditional
science, jurisprudence and even light fiction and medicine, during
which work they compared manuscripts, vocalised and punctuated.

'Salons' of this type were all the more important for scientific
studies since there did not as yet exist any institutions for research
into medicine and the natural sciences. Science and research were
a matter of private initiative. Private scholars communicated their
knowledge and their discoveries to their own sons or their students.
The initiative, described below, that was taken by al-Hakim (996–1021),

the son and successor of the caliph al-'Aziz, on 24 March 1005 was therefore a pioneering venture.

On that day the so-called Dar al-'Ilm (House of Knowledge) in Cairo was inaugurated. The jurists took up residence there, and the books from the palace libraries were moved into it. People could visit it, and whoever wanted to copy something that interested him could do so; the same was true of anyone who wanted to read any of the material kept in it. After the building had been furnished and decorated, and after all the doors and corridors had been provided with curtains, lectures were held there by Qur'an readers, astronomers, grammarians and philologists, as well as physicians. Guardians, servants, domestics and others were hired to serve there.

In this building they placed all the books that the Commander of the Faithful, al-Hakim bi-Amr Allah, had ordered to be brought there, that is, manuscripts in all the domains of science and culture, in a way and a degree that had never been done before by a prince. He allowed people from all walks of life access to all this, whether they wanted to read books thoroughly or dip into them. One of the blessings already mentioned, the like of which had never been heard, was that he also granted substantial salaries to all those who were appointed by him to do service there – jurists and others. People from all walks of life visited it; some came to read books, others to copy them, and yet others to study. He also donated things people needed: ink, writing reeds, paper and inkstands. The house had been owned formerly by the Slav Mukhtar.

We know from descriptions of the city that this house stood on the north-west corner of the great esplanade in front of the caliph's palace (almost opposite the present Aqmar Mosque). As an institution, the Dar al-'Ilm was as new as it was unique in the Islamic world. The caliph al-Ma'mun in Baghdad (813–833) had already established a 'Cabinet of Wisdom' (*Bayt al-Hikma*) in one of the buildings of his palace, but this was no msore than a library, which moreover does not appear to have survived its founder; a similar institute had been founded by the Persian vizier Abu Nasr Sabur in 991 or 993 in a suburb of Baghdad.

In al-Hakim's Dar al-'Ilm however, scientific research itself was institutionalised and actively promoted, at least during the reign of its founder.

From the Dar al-'Ilm a number of mathematicians, logicians and jurists, as well as several physicians, were summoned by al-Hakim; the representatives of each discipline appeared before him separately, in order to argue in his presence; thereupon he presented all of them with robes of honour and gifts.

Astrolabe, made by
'Abd al-Karim al-Misri,
Egypt, 7th/13th century

The researchers working at the Dar al-'Ilm were, to begin with, paid fixed salaries, but in the year 1010, the caliph safeguarded his foundation by means of an extensive bequest (*waqf*), so that not only the salaries, but also the material stock, the maintenance and equipment appeared to be permanently secured. Unfortunately however, this state of affairs did not last.

Along with the religious scholars and jurists – whose functions, at the time, were often identical – as well as the poets, grammarians and philologists, the Arabic texts of the period constantly mention doctors, mathematicians and astronomers. The latter, above all, whose skills were not only required for astrological speculation, but also for the calendar, needed special and often expensive instruments and places particularly suitable for observing the sky. Observatories therefore were a vital part of life in the Islamic world, and to them we owe our system of numbers and calculation with decimals. But they were expensive and so rare. The caliph al-Ma'mun had had an observatory built near the Shammasiyya Gate in Baghdad and another on Jabal Qasyun near Damascus. In 1012, the caliph al-Hakim told his supreme judge, Malik ibn Sa'id to build an observatory (*rasad*) on one of the foothills of the Muqattam Mountains south-east of Cairo. For the time being, however, this remained a project. Not until much later was the matter taken up again by the *amir al-juyush* al-Afdal ibn Badr al-Jamali (1094–1121), but this time, in 1119, the plan fell through because it was too technically ambitious: the casting of the bronze hoop that would be about 7 yards in diameter and 21 yards in circumference could not be carried out, because the gigantic device would buckle under its own weight. But even without such enormous instruments, the sky could be precisely observed. It was thanks to al-Hakim's initiative that the 'Hakim Table' (*al-zij al-Hakimi*) was developed, a chart for comparing astronomical data, which the astronomer Ibn Yunus al-Shami al-Hakimi constructed for the caliph. This chart, which replaced the older one of the 'Abbasid caliph al-Ma'mun, was to be the standard work of Arab astronomy for several centuries.

As for medicine, the place for teaching and studying it was naturally the hospital. Its model was an institution of ancient Persia, the Medical University of Gundeshapur in the province of Khuzistan in south-western Persia, founded by the Great King Khusraw Anushirwan in the year 555. Here, too, the caliphs of Baghdad adopted the Persian tradition: Harun al-Rashid (786–809) established a similar institution in the south-west suburb of Baghdad, and the amir of Egypt, Ahmad ibn Tulun (868–884), followed his example in al-Fustat. No wonder, then, that the Persian name for hospital, *bimaristan* (shortened to *maristan*) has been preserved as a loan-word in Arabic.

The hospital of Ibn Tulun was the only one in Egypt for a long time. It was not until the reign of the Fatimid caliph al-'Aziz (975–996) that a lunatic asylum was built, in the vicinity of al-Azhar Mosque. It consisted of a single large ward with the walls embellished with Qur'anic verses. In the year 1024 the caliph al-Zahir, accompanied by some of his household, visited the hospital and had the patients presented to him. He endowed the hospital with running water, assumed the costs for drugs and the care of the patients and gave each of them 50 silver dirhams; the director was given 500. A third hospital was established in Cairo after the end of the Fatimid dynasty (1171) by Sultan Salah al-Din on the site of the Fatimid Western Palace. This was followed in 1284 by the *maristan* of the Mamluk sultan Qalawun.

In Cairo there was no state-controlled training of physicians and no supervision of their activity. This was bitterly lamented by the physician Ibn Ridwan (998–1061), who practised in Cairo. The son of a baker from Giza, he rose to become the personal physician of the caliph al-Mustansir (1036–1094). In his book, he said that physicians should be trained by the state: 'The king ought to take care of them, so that no one can use this art to earn their living unless they be qualified, and he should honour the best of them so that the others might emulate him.'

But there could be no question of that in Cairo. Ibn Ridwan swore against the quacks who made trouble in the city and led poor people by the nose with all kinds of hocus-pocus. He himself was of course, trained at the hand of the ancient authors, Hippocrates and Galen, for

the Arabic translations of their writings were obviously familiar to erudite physicians like himself, while the quacks acted according to the motto: 'Whoever has to resort to a book is a poor beggar.'

Books as the basis of all knowledge and every science were omnipresent in Cairo; the library was an evident part of the palace. Thus we hear astonishing things about the library of the Fatimids: in the reign of the caliph al-'Aziz (975–996), it contained no less than 20 copies of Tabari's (d. 923) vast *Chronicle*, which runs to 13 thick volumes in modern print; of the lexicon by the grammarian Khalil there were 30 copies, of the main work of the philologist Ibn Durayd (837–933) there were as many as a hundred copies. In the year 1068, when this library was plundered by a band of Turkish mercenaries, it filled 40 rooms. At that time, a major part of the stock must have been lost. But the Cairo library was soon re-established. It had been stored in a building of the (smaller) Western Palace – the one in which Sultan Salah al-Din later installed a hospital. When the caliph visited the library, he rode over from the Eastern Palace and dismounted onto a platform that had been specially built for him. He remained seated on this platform, and the librarian brought him the book that he desired.

This library contained a great many bookshelves set all around the enormous hall; the shelves were divided into compartments by vertical partitions; each compartment was secured by a hinged door with a padlock. There were more than 200,000 books and a few without bindings: jurisprudence according to different schools, grammar and philology, books about the traditions of the prophets, history, biographies of rulers, astronomy, spiritual knowledge and alchemy – on each discipline the [relevant] manuscripts, among them also ones that had not been completed. All this was written on a label attached to the door of each compartment. The manuscripts of the Venerable Qur'an were preserved in a higher place. Whenever the caliph wanted to pause, he walked around for a while and looked at the shelves. There were two copyists; apart from them, two servants: the man with the ladder and another.

The contents of the library were reported to amount to fantastic figures; mention is made of 1,600,000 volumes; another author speaks of 200,000; closest to the truth is probably the lowest of the numbers referred to, 'more than 120,000', according to the chronicler Ibn Wasil. When Salah al-Din overthrew the Ismaili Fatimids in the year 1171 and reintroduced Sunni Islam as the official religion of Egypt, he got rid of the library and converted the building into a hospital. He had some of the books destroyed – probably whatever was connected with the doctrine of the Ismailis; he sold others, and the remaining 100,000 books, he donated to his friend and adviser, the erudite Qadi al-Fadil, who presented them to the college he had founded, al-Madrasa al-Fadiliyya.

This marked the beginning of the last chapter of traditional Islamic teaching: the era of the *madrasa*s.

The Arabic term *madrasa* means 'centre of learning' (or else: of teaching), so it can simply be translated as 'school'. But it means school in the sense of a centre of higher learning, a university or college, and one in which religious Islamic sciences are taught, above all jurisprudence. The institution of the *madrasa* originated in eastern Iran. The oldest known school of this type was destroyed by a conflagration in Bukhara in 937. Having started as a private institution founded by private scholars for the purpose of lecturing in their own fields, the *madrasa* became the object of the attention of high-ranking personalities during the Saljuk period (post 1055): kings, viziers, important officials and military men, as well as noblewomen. One man above all was responsible for the furtherance of the *madrasa* and its popularisation and spread: the vizier Nizam al-Mulk (1018–1092), who served as minister to several Saljuk sultans. In 1067, he founded the first Nizamiyya

madrasa in Baghdad with an endowment (*waqf*) from his private fortune, dedicating it to the teaching of Sunni (Shafi'i) jurisprudence. Further Nizamiyyas followed in Central Asia, Iran and Iraq.

The great vizier's example was soon followed by numerous minor potentates. The Zanjids brought the idea of the *madrasa* from Mosul, on the Euphrates, to Syria; from there, Sultan Salah al-Din transplanted it to Egypt. Although it is known that two schools were already established in Alexandria under the last Fatimids, it was in Cairo that the *madrasa* was properly introduced for the first time under Salah al-Din: he and his officers founded no less than nine *madrasa*s in the city. Under his first three successors, seven more were added. And now, there was no end to the building of these colleges; together with the mosques, they continued to shape the cityscape of Cairo's historical nucleus. Initially, each of these *madrasa*s was dedicated to one of the four main Sunni legal schools (*madhahib*; sing. *madhhab*), and the *mudarris* (professor) appointed by the donor had to belong to it. But

soon *madrasa*s were added for two school traditions or even for all four legal schools. The type of building imported from Iran, the 'four-iwan structure', was well adapted to the purpose: around a rectangular inner courtyard were – usually on two floors – the living units which had to be divided among several students, and on each side of the courtyard there opened up a large, vaulted hall (*iwan*). Depending on the weather, this all offered protection from the sun or the rain, and could accommodate a circle of listeners around the teacher. The most splendid example of this kind of four-*madhhab madrasa* in Cairo is the foundation of the Mamluk sultan al-Hasan, which lies at the foot of the Citadel, and was built between 1356 and 1363.

Teaching at the *madrasa* continued in the traditional fashion until around the end of the 19th century: the professors taught what they themselves knew; there was no established curriculum. When a student had, in his professor's opinion, attained a level of knowledge which enabled him to teach, then he was granted a diploma, literally the 'permission' (*ijaza*) to work as a teacher. Despite their promotion by rulers, prominent civil servants or army officers, the *madrasa*s continued to be private foundations, for according to Islamic law, a pious endowment (or *waqf*) could only issue from private property (*milk*). Hence al-Azhar, which was abandoned after the end of the Fatimid dynasty and became dilapidated, was rebuilt for teaching in 1266 through the private endowment of a Mamluk officer, and newly organised in accordance with Sunni Shafi'i doctrine. This marked the beginning of the second period of continuous teaching activity at the venerable al-Azhar Mosque, which still continues today. In 1876, al-Azhar had more than 10,000 students and 361 professors. But it was only to become a university in the modern sense when the ruler of Egypt, Khedive Isma'il, introduced a series of reforms in 1872, the first one being the issuing of a standard final diploma. The great reformer Muhammad 'Abduh (1849–1905) then modernised the hitherto predominantly religious and legal approach of the college by introducing subjects such as mathematics and geography, in their modern understanding, and by restructuring the teaching staff, as well as the entire curriculum.

9 Coptic Christians: faith and practice in Egyptian contexts

Febe Armanios

Long before al-Darb al-Ahmar became a busy district of Cairo as it is today, filled with minarets and bazaars, the Christians of Egypt were in attendance at the church of the Virgin Mary (also know as the 'Lady of Perpetual Help'[1]). The church, which is seen in its more modern state in the film *Living with the Past*, is located at the end of a path off Sukkariyya Street at the edge of al-Darb al-Ahmar and Harat al-Rum (the 'Greek Quarter') in Cairo. The exact date of construction is unknown, but some believe that it might have roots in Antiquity.[2] Other sources state that the church was founded in the 10th century AD and was demolished and rebuilt several times.[3] The most recent renovation project, which began in the 1980s, is the latest in a series of restoration endeavours that have occurred throughout its history.

One of the most significant sources for the status of this church during the Mamluk era in Egypt (1250–1517) is the work of the 14th-century chronicler known as Abu Salih 'the Armenian', who paints a dynamic picture of the history of the church of the Virgin. Abu Salih asserts that this 'large and ancient church' had belonged to the Armenian community until local Coptic Christians came to claim it as their own after the number of Armenians in Egypt declined during the 12th century. The chronicler provides details of ceremonies that the Copts performed in order to make this church 'theirs', and he also mentions the new paintings that were commissioned for the church at that time.[4]

Today, the church complex, as shown in *Living with the Past*, houses two important historic churches: the church of the Virgin Mary, below ground, and the church of Saint George, which is above ground. These churches possess a significant collection of iconographic works, many of which date from the 17th and 18th centuries, a period of iconographic revival in the Coptic Church. The complex served as the patriarchal headquarters of the Coptic Church between 1660 and 1799, after which it moved to another district in Cairo (Azbakiyya).[5] After it ceased to be a centre for the patriarchate, the church of the Virgin Mary fell into ruin and has only recently been restored. With specific consideration given to this church and to its place in Coptic life, this article will address the subject of Coptic faith and practice in the context of medieval and modern Egyptian history. The historical and cultural background to be provided in this essay will help explain the present popularity of the church of the Virgin at al-Harat al-Rum, which is now the focus of one of the most important annual Coptic festivals, that of Saint Marina.

From its unpredictable status during the lively heyday of medieval Cairo to its well-established political presence today, the Coptic Orthodox Church has always occupied a central place in the daily life of most Christians in Egypt.[6] On both popular and theological levels, the Church exalts in a tradition of struggle and sacrifice, embodied in its assertion that it is founded upon the 'blood of martyrs'.[7] Its calendar derives from the reign of the Roman emperor Diocletian (AD 284–305), a time when many Christians in Egypt were killed for upholding their faith. Tales of these brutal killings have been passed down as part of the communal heritage and constitute some of the central texts of the Coptic Church (the *Synaxarion*[8] is one such book). The Church also prides itself on having established the institution of monasticism.[9] This monastic heritage has continued within the Coptic Church leadership, with the patriarch (referred to as 'pope') and the bishops traditionally emerging from Egypt's ancient desert monasteries.

Coptic Christianity is a distinctive brand of Orthodox Christianity, one that is shared with the Armenian, Syrian and Ethiopian Orthodox Churches and requires explanation here. At the Council of Chalcedon in 451, the Copts, as well as other groups, were singled out as supporters of what is called the monophysite doctrine, and because they were in opposition to the majority they were branded as heretics. The dispute at Chalcedon concerned the nature of Christ: Orthodox Christians argued that Jesus had two distinct natures, one divine and one human. The Monophysites rejected this position, believing that Jesus had only one nature, that his divinity enclosed his humanity.[10] Thus the Copts liberated their Church from Byzantine spiritual domination. In the centuries after the Islamic conquest of Egypt (641), the divisions among Egyptian Christians, some of who still held to Byzantine doctrine, led to what one historian has referred to as a divided community 'in a state of constant transition'.[11]

Interior of the church of the Virgin Mary, al-Darb al-Ahmar, still from the documentary *Living with the Past*

Lustre-ware bowl showing a Coptic monk or priest with a censer, Fatimid, second half of the 5th/11th century

The Four Gospels, the opening
page of St Matthew's Gospel,
Bi-lingual Coptic and Arabic
(the Arabic to the right of and
below the Coptic text), Nitria,
Egypt, 707–708/1308

While today it is known that the Copts are one of the Middle East's oldest and most numerous Christian communities and that they comprise approximately 10 per cent of the population of Egypt,[12] it is less well known that, up until the 14th century, they constituted a much larger percentage of Egypt's population. However, following a period of turbulent events, from sporadic persecution to the selective enforcement of legal prohibitions by Muslim authorities against Christians and Jews, this situation changed rapidly. The conversion of numerous Copts by the mid 14th century reduced this Christian group to a small minority.[13] Moreover, due to periodic clashes and violence between Muslims and Christians, Muslim chronicles reported that by the mid 15th century most churches in Egypt had been defiled or destroyed.[14] Despite these outbreaks of violence and the mass conversions, both of which reduced the numbers of Copts in Egypt, the surviving community was able to maintain a number of churches, including the church of the Virgin at Harat al-Rum.

Notwithstanding a relationship which sometimes bordered on hostility, and in the face of fundamental religious differences, Christians and Muslims in Egypt have historically shared numerous rituals and practices. The Coptic faith, as practised in the medieval period and up until modern times, is profoundly ritualistic,[15] and these rituals have often permeated Muslim practices. Medieval Muslim chroniclers report that one of the Coptic sacraments, baptism, was performed by both Christians and Muslims, who believed that submerging their children in cold water would bestow upon them a lifelong immunity from disease.[16] Today, the attendance by Muslims at the festivals of Coptic saints and vice versa, clearly illustrates this overlap on a popular level between the practices of the two communities. One can argue that, in this kind of community religious practice, the differences between what constitutes official and unofficial Christianity,[17] or what defines Muslim or Christian practice, have often been blurred.

As an example, in the context of the medieval period, one of the best known celebrations among Copts and Muslims was the 'Festival of the Martyr'. Huda Lutfi's study of Coptic festivals in the Mamluk

era indicates that until the 14th century, this ancient annual spring festival was observed on the banks of the Nile and was one of the most important celebrations of Cairene life. During the festival, the finger of a male Coptic martyr, symbol of an ancient sacrificial gift, was thrown into the river to assure the Nile's prosperity. The rituals behind the Festival of the Martyr are described in detail by the famous chronicler al-Maqrizi:

> On this day, Copts come from all the villages to watch the ceremony. They ride horses and perform acrobatics on top of them. Residents of al-Qahira [Cairo] and al-Fustat from all classes proceed to the banks and islands of the Nile to pitch their tents. All male and female singers, entertainers, prostitutes, effeminate males and reprobates of all types eagerly participate in the festival. Infinite numbers of people congregate, only the Creator can estimate them. Countless sums of money are spent, and numerous sins are performed in excess. Chaos erupts and some people get killed. Over one hundred thousand silver dirhams worth of wine is sold on this day, of which five thousand gold dinars are appropriated as tax. One merchant sold twelve thousand silver dirhams worth of wine. The congregation of festivities always takes place in Shubra, one of the districts of al-Qahira. Thus the peasants of Shubra pay their *kharaj* tax to the state from the revenue which they procure from the sale of wine on the feast of the martyr.[18]

As the description indicates, all the 'residents of al-Qahira' participated in this festival. However, through a degree of resentment against what was seen as lewd behaviour, official Muslim clerical elements later urged a willing government to put an end to this tradition. The festival came to an end in 1355 when Mamluk officials had the finger of the martyr burnt and the ashes thrown into the Nile.

Both Copts and Muslims in medieval Egypt also participated in many other public rituals, not only religious festivals. For instance, at celebrations welcoming the return of Mamluk sultans to Cairo after a

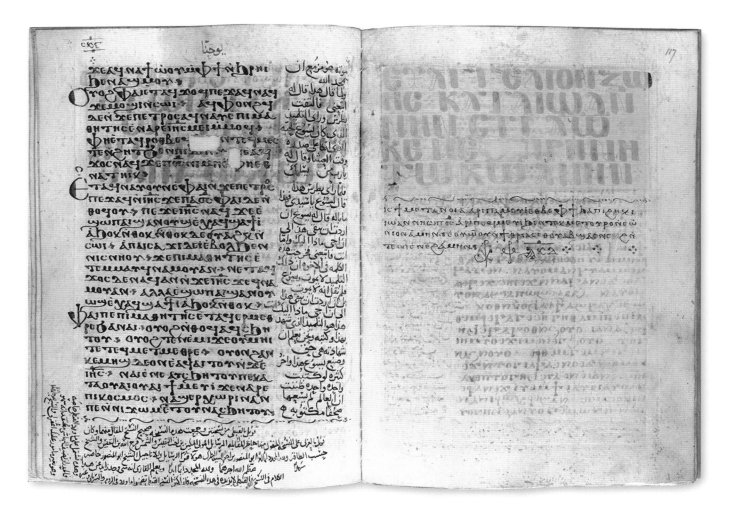

long absence, Copts alongside Muslims decorated their shops, their streets and the markets. Indeed these narrow streets, the shops and the markets are evoked in the images of al-Darb al-Ahmar in *Living with the Past*. According to Muslim chroniclers, Christians would fill the streets on these occasions, holding Bibles and lighted candles to honour the return of the sultan.[19] While these symbols evoked religiosity, the celebration was not religious in nature.

Ultimately, within the Coptic community, the outlawing of certain popular festivals did not discourage all of them. Festivals continued to take place with the blessing of Church authorities. Throughout the past centuries, many popular traditions evolved at a local, grassroot level, but it can be added that historically the Coptic clergy nurtured these activities among the faithful. By keeping alive their memory, the veneration of saints has strengthened the Church's time-honoured assertion that it was founded upon the blood of martyrs. Pilgrimage

has fostered the ties between believers and their local churches, shrines and sanctuaries. While it has denounced some popular customs as 'heretical' or contrary to official doctrine, for the most part, the Church has either turned a blind eye to these practices or has sought, with various degrees of success, to legitimise them so that they take place under the auspices of local church leaders. The Coptic Church established a particular presence or control at the festivals of saints by including a more structured or 'liturgical' element, which was determined by the ecclesiastical authorities. For instance it was, and still is, common to have a reading of a homily about the saint, written by an esteemed father of the Church, and which includes a narrative of the saint's sufferings and a description of the miracles performed at their shrine.[20] Today, as will be discussed below, this type of festival takes place at the church of the Virgin at Harat al-Rum, under the auspices of Church leaders, in celebration of Saint Marina.

Throughout the past and up to the present, Coptic believers have visited shrines as a regular part of their religious life. A holy place (*mazar*), such as the church of the Virgin at Harat al-Rum, which is associated with a saint (the Virgin Mary and Saint Marina) or a particular miraculous icon (the Church has many historic and sacred icons) is a popular source of worship. In *Living with the Past*, we witness such scenes of veneration, as Coptic believers stand before icons, light candles and offer up their pleas to the Divine. Some of the most well-known shrines are associated with the Holy Family's visit to Egypt.[21] Local lore says that the Holy Family (Mary, Joseph and the infant Jesus) stopped briefly at the church of the Virgin in a district close to Harat al-Rum (Hara Zuwayla), and this has been traditionally a major pilgrimage site in Cairo.[22] Since the early days of Christianity in Egypt (2nd century AD), believers actively participated in pilgrimages as a form of devotion to deceased saints and revered martyrs, or sought out famous holy figures, usually monks, in order to receive remedies, miracles or fatherly guidance from them.

Considering the significant place of saints, their veneration and their festivals in Coptic life, it is surprising that historically there have been only a few Coptic saints with active cults. The extent of activity is marked by a believer's recurrent visits to a shrine, attendance at the annual feast of the saint (*mawlid*)[23], the offering of appropriate restitution for sins – whether in spiritual or financial terms – and the invocation stating belief in the miraculous powers of a saint. Of the dozens of names commemorated in the *Synaxarion*, the work in which most of the stories about Coptic martyrs and saints are recorded, only a handful, led by the most revered of them all, the Virgin Mary, have had churches, shrines and monasteries founded in their name.[24] Ultimately, what seems to be of importance to most of the Coptic faithful is not the number of saints venerated but the belief in their supernatural abilities and in the effectiveness of their powers of intercession. Through prayer and also through the act of *nadr* or vow-making, believers hope that the most powerful of these saints, such as the Virgin Mary and Saint George, will be persuaded to intercede with God on their behalf and help them in their time of need.

As can be seen in the film *Living with the Past*, icons depicting figures of saints are a focus for prayer and ritual in the Coptic Church. Likewise, in Coptic homes depictions of saints, in the form of amulets or small icons, are extensively displayed. In these homes, saints are regarded as 'members of the extended family'. The multiplicity of their images in a single home is considered a sort of *baraka* or blessing for believers. The extent to which these saints are deemed central to the daily life of Coptic believers can be seen in the widespread occurrences of apparitions and visions. In Egypt, visions play a major role in the religious life of both Muslims and Copts.[25] According to Valerie Hoffman, it is common for 'spiritually sensitive Copts' to have visions of deceased saints, supernatural apparitions, bursts of light, or to have encountered the supernatural manifestations of religious icons, which 'speak, heal, weep, bleed, or emit light'.[26]

It is in the wider context of festivals, the veneration of saints and traditions shared between Egypt's Muslims and Christians, that we must understand the popular festival which takes place nowadays at the church of the Virgin at Harat al-Rum. The annual festival, for which the church of the Virgin is most renowned, takes place on 30 July (Coptic date: 23 Abib) and celebrates the martyrdom of Saint Marina of Antioch, a saint who is shared between several Eastern Orthodox churches. Although the Coptic *Synaxarion* is vague about when Marina was martyred, non-Coptic traditions relate that she was killed during the reign of the infamous Diocletian (3rd or 4th century AD). They also relate that Marina's body was subsequently buried in Antioch, until her remains were reportedly moved to Italy. Oral traditions at the church of the Virgin in Harat al-Rum report that the relics[27] of a young woman, buried at the church, were discovered sometime in the 1920s by a foreign visitor. The visitor became paralysed after touching the remains, and remained so until the Coptic patriarch of the time healed him. Subsequently the mysterious relics were placed in a small container and kept in a shrine at the church. Soon afterward, they were referred to as the body of 'Saint Marina'. Local lore further asserts 'Marina's relics' had been transferred from Italy to Cairo, several centuries earlier, when they were taken to the adjoining Coptic convent of Saint Tadrus (Theodore).

While these claims are unverifiable, it matters little to the thousands of Coptic and Muslim believers who attend this annual festival. They come hoping for miraculous cures or for the chance to see the 'hand' of Saint Marina, which is brought out by the local clergy and displayed to the public only at the time of the festival. It is said that the hand of the saint has not suffered any physical decay (corruption) and that her fingernails continue to grow. Moreover, while many Copts seeking miraculous cures are healed merely by coming to the festival or by touching the tube containing Saint Marina's relics, others are healed when touched or prayed over by a Coptic clergyman.

Ultimately, it is unclear why this cult has emerged in relatively recent times: however, locals and perhaps the church authorities may have been attempting to restore the prestige formerly associated with the seat of the patriarch by promoting this cult. In this sense, Saint Marina's festival (and many more like it throughout Egypt) embodies the ways in which the Coptic clergy and the mass of believers come together to develop local lore and traditions, eventually defining Coptic beliefs and practices. The participation of Muslims and Copts, side by side, has been and continues generally to be a hallmark of Egyptian popular religious practice. Ultimately, this festival has contributed to the centrality of the church of the Virgin to both Christian and Muslim Egyptians, not only those living in the district of Harat al-Rum and in the neighbouring al-Darb al-Ahmar but throughout Cairo and Egypt.

1 It is known in Arabic as 'al-'Adhra' al-Mughitha'.

2 Alfred Butler, *The Ancient Coptic Churches of Egypt* (Oxford, 1884), vol. 2, p. 283.

3 Otto Meinardus, *Christian Egypt: Ancient and Modern* (Cairo, 1977), p. 304.

4 'This church became a [Coptic] patriarchal church, and the liturgy was conducted henceforth by the priests of the church of the Lady in the Harat al-Rum. Abu Sa'id ibn al-Zayyat provided for the painting of the apse of the church, which was executed by Abu'l-Fath ibn al-Akmas, known as Ibn al-Haufi the painter; and this work was finished in the month of Amshir, in the year 892 of the Blameless Martyrs [Jan-Feb, AD 1177].' Abu Salih the Armenian, *The Churches & Monasteries of Egypt and Some Neighbouring Countries*, tr. B. T. A. Evett (2nd. ed., Oxford, 1969), pp. 9–10.

5 In the mid 17th century, the Coptic patriarch Mittawus IV (1660–1675) decided to move the patriarchal headquarters from nearby Harat Zuwayla to this church complex in Harat al-Rum. Eventually, his successor, Patriarch Yuhanna XVI

(1676–1718) furnished a new patriarchal residence there, where the headquarters stayed until the 19th century. See Iris Habib al-Masri, 'Harit al-Rum', in Aziz S. Atiya, ed, *The Coptic Encyclopedia*, vol. 4, pp. 63 and 77.

6 The conception of Copts as a separate 'ethnic' group has come into being since the late 19th century, when a number of them began to adopt the Protestant or Catholic faiths. Since then, Coptic Christians have come to identify with one another not because of a shared Orthodox Christian creed, but presumably by reason of a mutual 'ethnic' identity.

7 This is a general reference to the 'age of martyrdom' in the Coptic Church, which lasted from late Antiquity roughly until the Islamic conquest of Egypt in AD 641, during which Copts struggled to keep their creed against the policies of the Byzantine emperors.

8 'Synaxarion' is the Coptic and Greek form of the Latin 'synaxarium' and it indicates the compilation of the lives of saints, martyrs, religious events

and heroic stories in the Coptic Church. See Aziz S. Atiya, ed., *The Coptic Encyclopedia* (New York, 1991), s.v., René-Georges Coquin, 'Synaxarion, Copto-Arabic'.

9 The founder of monasticism is generally held to be St Anthony, an Egyptian hermit who lived in the Red Sea desert in the 3rd and 4th centuries and who founded the first monastic communities.

10 Theodore Hall Partrick, *Traditional Egyptian Christianity* (Greensboro, NC, 1996), pp. 39–40. For more on Coptic sentiment and the Chalcedonian council see W. H. C. Frend, 'Nationalism and Anti Chalcedonian Feeling in Egypt', in Stuart Mews, ed., *Religion and National Identity* (Oxford, 1982). Copts, like other opponents of Chalcedon, define the nature of Jesus as composite, rather than singular. For this reason, they reject the label 'monophysite', preferring 'non-Chalcedonian' instead.

11 Terry G. Wilfong, 'The Non-Muslim Communities: Christian Communities', in Carl Petry, ed., *The Cambridge History of Egypt* (Cambridge, 1998), p. 175.

12 Note the wide variation in these numbers. As reported in a recent study, estimates by various scholars have ranged from 3,200,000 and 8,000,000. See Andrea Pacini, ed., *Christian Communities in the Arab Middle East* (Oxford, 1998), p. 317.

13 Donald P. Little, 'Coptic Converts of Islam during the Bahri Mamluk Period', in Michael Gervers and Ramzi Jibran Bikazi, ed., *Conversion and Continuity* (Toronto, 1991), p. 263.

14 Aziz S. Atiya, 'Mamluks and the Copts', *The Coptic Encyclopedia*.

15 At the core of Coptic 'official' customs are seven sacraments (baptism, chrismation [anointing with holy oil], communion [the Eucharist], confession, marriage, ordination and the anointing of the sick), a rich liturgical heritage, and the strict, nearly vegan, fasts that believers are obliged to follow.

16 See references in Qasim Qasim, 'al-Wad' al-ijtima'i li'l-aqbat fi 'asr salatin al-Mamalik', in *al-Tarikh wa'l-mustaqbal* (Minya, 1990), p. 165.

17 As Tony Watling notes in the case of Catholicism in the Netherlands, a church's 'official' recognition of dubious 'unofficial' practices might be a way to 'revitalise the church' and that 'not doing so may lead to' the decline of the institution. See '"Official" Doctrine and "Unofficial" Practices: The Negotiation of Catholicism in a Netherlands Community', *Journal for the Scientific Study of Religion*, 40 (2001), p. 574.

18 Al-Maqrizi, *al-Khitat*, vol. 1, p. 69, as cited and translated by Huda Lutfi, 'Coptic Festivals of the Nile', in Thomas Philipp and Ulrich Haarmann, ed., *The Mamluks in Egyptian Politics and Society* (Cambridge, 1998), p. 265.

19 Qasim, 'al-Wad' al-ijtima'i', pp. 152–153.

20 De Lacy O'Leary, *The Saints of Egypt* (London, 1937), p. 32.

21 The historical memory of the Holy Family's (Mary, Joseph and Jesus) time in Egypt, which tradition relates lasted over three years, became a vivid element in Coptic ritual, literature and art, despite the fact that the Bible is silent on the details. See Stephen Davis, 'Ancient Sources for the Coptic Tradition', in Gawdat Gabra, ed., *Be Thou There: The Holy Family's Journey in Egypt* (Cairo, 2001), p. 153.

22 C. Hulsman, 'Tracing the Route of the Holy Family Today', in Gabra, ed., *Be Thou There*, p. 65.

23 The term *mulid* (*mawlid* in formal Arabic) means 'birthday'. Among Copts, a *mulid* celebrates a saint rejoining with God, i.e. it is the anniversary of a saint's death or martyrdom.

24 Even fewer have annual festivals which are celebrated. As Otto Meinardus writes, about the contemporary Church, 'the Copts depend for their religious life only upon very few saints', Meinardus, *Christian Egypt*, pp. 147–148.

25 Valerie Hoffman states that 'miracles and supernatural interventions are readily accepted by the Orthodox Church establishment, in contrast to the contemporary Islamic establishment.' Valerie Hoffman, *Sufism, Mystics, and Saints in Modern Egypt* (Columbia, SC, 1995), p. 335.

26 Ibid.

27 In the context of Christian history, relics range from the entire physical remains of a saint or martyr, to fragments of their bodies, clothing, or possessions deemed holy and miraculous.

10 The Jewish presence in medieval Cairo

Norman A. Stillman

Little is known about the Jewish community of Egypt at the time of the Islamic conquest, which began in December AH 18/AD 639. There had been a continual Jewish presence in Egypt since Achaemenid times, and Egypt had always been the leading centre of Hellenistic Jewry in Antiquity. However, by the time of the Muslim takeover, the number of Egyptian Jews had been considerably reduced in the suppression of Jewish uprisings during the first two centuries of the Common Era and later as a result of Byzantine Christian persecution. Still, the Jewish population was large enough to impress the Muslim conquerors, for according to the early chronicler Ibn 'Abd al-Hakam, 40,000 Jews lived in Alexandria alone when the city fell to the Muslims in 642.[1] The Jews are listed among the marvels of the city along with 4,000 gardens, 4,000 bathhouses, and 400 royal places of amusement.

As members of one of the scriptural religions recognised in the Qur'an, or *ahl al-kitab* (People of the Book), the Jews of Egypt were required to pay a tribute, or *jizya*, to the Islamic state in return for their protection. However the *jizya* was probably not a great new hardship since Egyptian Jews were already paying a poll tax and other fiscal impositions to the Byzantine authorities. The Muslim conquest in all likelihood brought them some relief since their legal position in the Byzantine empire had been declining for more than a century, and the years immediately preceding the Muslim takeover had been marked by a policy of outright persecution under the Emperor Heraclius. This was because of the Jews' collaboration with the Persians during the recent round of wars between the two rival empires, which had ended with a Byzantine victory and the expulsion of the Persians from Syria, Palestine and Egypt in 6–7/628.

The occupying Arab forces established themselves in their own camp town, which was the new military and administrative centre, al-Fustat, founded near the Byzantine fortress town called Babylon. Whether any Jews lived among the Copts and Greeks there is unknown, and indeed unlikely. At the time of the conquest most Egyptian Jews lived in Alexandria and the major towns of the Nile Delta. Cairo, of course, was not to be founded until three centuries later when the Fatimids took over the country. But for all intents and purposes, the history of the Jewish presence in Cairo may be considered to begin with the establishment of al-Fustat; a separate urban entity for centuries, it eventually became known as Misr al-qadima or Misr al-'atiqa; that is, Old Cairo.

Like other garrison towns, al-Fustat originally housed only the Muslim conquerors, but early on Christian and Jewish retainers who had accompanied the Arabs from Syria, and other native providers of goods and services, began to settle in it as well; like Qayrawan in Tunisia and Kufa in Iraq, al-Fustat progressively developed into an urban metropolis inhabited by Muslims and non-Muslims alike. During the first century of its development, it had an organised Jewish community. Already by 151–152/750, a certain Abu 'Ali Hasan al-Baghdadi is referred to in a Jewish document as Rosh ha-Qahal, or 'Head of the Congregation' in al-Fustat.[2] As everywhere within the Islamic Empire, Jews, together with other Peoples of the Book, were protégés, or *ahl al-dhimma*, of the ruling Muslims, and in exchange for their submission, tribute and a humble status, received the protection of the state, general religious tolerance, a considerable measure of freedom of economic endeavour and a good deal of internal communal autonomy, with their own leaders and institutions. Except for the chance mention of a congregational leader and an occasional note, no account is found of the evolution of the Fustati Jewish community in the first two centuries of the Islamic era. The Arabic sources have relatively little to say about the non-Muslim population, while the Jews themselves wrote hardly anything on any subject, least of all their own history, during these two crucial centuries of far-reaching political, social and economic change for all the Middle East and its inhabitants, including the Jews. But even though the specific course of events remains shrouded in darkness, the outcome is clear. During this time, the transformation of the Jews into a primarily urban people, a process which had already begun in late Antiquity, was completed. The Babylonian Talmud was disseminated from Iraq throughout the Jewish world and became the constitutional framework of medieval and later Judaism. Jews, along with other peoples in the Caliphate, began to take part in the burgeoning commercial revolution that followed the 'Abbasid rise to power. Considerable numbers of Jews began migrating to Egypt from the Islamic East, particularly after political upheavals in the second half of the 9th century shook Iraq and Persia. This was also the time when Egypt first became a semi-independent province under Ahmad b. Tulun. Ibn Tulun, who was a Central Asian Turkish outsider, was not averse to having non-Muslims in his entourage, which included a Jewish physician. During Ibn Tulun's rule, the Jewish community purchased a church in al-Fustat from the Coptic patriarch Michael in order to convert it into a synagogue (much to the chagrin of the later Christian chronicler, Abu Salih the Armenian). The building was probably acquired to provide an adequate house of worship for the growing congregation of Jewish immigrants from Iraq and Persia.[3]

Even as the Jewish community in al-Fustat and in other towns of Egypt was growing in size and prosperity, the leading spiritual centres of Jewish life were still in Iraq and Palestine with their great Talmudic academies, or *yeshivot*, headed by officials known as the *gaon*. The veteran Egyptian Jews officially looked to the Palestinian *yeshiva* for ultimate spiritual and legal authority; though Iraqi and Persian Jewish immigrants and their descendants who followed the Babylonian rite turned to the Babylonian *yeshivot* of Sura and Pumbeditha for spiritual and legal guidance. The two main congregations in al-Fustat were Palestinian, *kanisat al-Shamiyyin*, and Babylonian, called *kanisat al-'Iraqiyyin*. Many other larger Egyptian Jewish communities had two similar congregations, but not the smaller ones. All in all, over ninety names of cities, towns and villages with Jewish populations are documented historically.[4]

In addition to the mainstream Palestinians and Babylonians of the so-called Rabbanite Jewish community, the Karaites formed a distinct communal group. A schism founded in Baghdad during the mid 8th century by 'Anan b. David, the Karaites only became a major sect during the 9th century. The Karaites rejected the Rabbinic traditions of Talmudic Judaism and accepted the Bible as the sole source of religious law (hence their name in Hebrew, *qara'im*, which means 'Scripturalists').

Just when the Karaites first became established in Egypt is not known, but they were probably numerous by the 10th century, although they always constituted a minority within the Jewish community. Many Karaites at the time belonged to the wealthy elite of merchants and government officials. Despite theological and ritual differences between Rabbanite and Karaite sects which were a source of constant friction elsewhere in the Middle East, in Egypt they formed a more or less a single Jewish community which could act in concert in times of emergency and for charitable fundraising. Intermarriage between Rabbanites and Karaites occurred frequently in Egypt at this time, although it was always rare elsewhere and became less common in Egypt towards the end of the Middle Ages. Nevertheless, the Karaites remained an integral part of the Cairene Jewish scene until the dissolution of Egyptian Jewry in the mid 20th century; even today there are Karaites among the handful of Jews who have remained in the country. In many respects, the Karaites were the most Egyptian of all Egyptian Jews, as one modern Egyptian Karaite writer states:

> By birth, the Karaite is an Egyptian. Most, if not all, his ancestors were born in Egypt. He is Egyptian by virtue of his physical characteristics, the way he talks, acts, and even the way he dresses.[5]

A Samaritan community also existed in medieval Egypt and was considered part of the Jewish subject population by the Islamic governmental authorities during the later Middle Ages, though it had seceded from the main body of Jewry more than a millennium earlier and neither considered itself, nor was considered by other Jews, to be part of the greater Jewish community.

Jewish Egypt must have had some higher educational facilities during this period. The great theologian, exegete and translator of the Hebrew Bible into Arabic, Sa'adya b. Joseph Gaon (882–942), was born in Dilaz in the Fayyum district of Upper Egypt. That he remained in his native land until the age of twenty-three before emigrating to Tiberias in Palestine to further his studies, indicates that a person

could get the foundation of a good rabbinic education in Egypt.
He composed his *Sefer ha-Agron*, a Hebrew rhyming dictionary and
grammatical treatise three years before departing for Palestine, which
indicates that the new Hebrew linguistic and philological studies,
inspired by the Arabic language studies (*fiqh al-lugha*) of Muslim
scholars, were already cultivated among Egyptian Jews at that time.
The great Jewish philosopher and physician, Isaac Israeli (*circa* 855–955),
who spent the second half of his prodigiously long life in Qayrawan
and who, through the Latin translations of his works, came to be known
in medieval and Renaissance Europe as *Eximius Monarcha Medicinae*,
was also born, raised and educated in Egypt. Like his younger contemporary, Sa'adya, he too sought renown outside his homeland in a more
flourishing Jewish cultural centre.[6]

Only after the Fatimid conquest of Egypt and the establishment of
the caliphal seat of government in the newly founded city of Cairo in
972 did Egypt become a prominent centre of Jewry, even as it became
a political, economic and cultural centre of the Islamic world. Many
Jews were attracted to Cairo, as they had been earlier in the century to
Qayrawan and al-Mahdiyya in Ifriqiya, by both the laissez-faire economic
policies of the Fatimids and by the chance for service in the Fatimid
bureaucracy. With the exception of persecutions between 1007 and
1021, when many churches and synagogues were closed or demolished
and the sumptuary laws of *ghiyar* (differentiation) were vigorously
enforced, the Ismaili Fatimids showed more tolerance towards their
non-Muslim subjects than most Islamic rulers. They did not normally
enforce the requirement for *dhimmi*s to wear distinguishing clothing,
nor did they impose the discriminatory tariffs for *dhimmi* merchants
found in certain forms of Muslim jurisprudence. They had even fewer
qualms than other sovereigns in employing 'non-believers' in the civil
service, even up to the ranks of the *ashab al-khil'a* or 'those who wear
the robe of honour' – that is, members of the royal entourage. Jews and
Christians entered the elite class through service on the royal medical
staff, as purveyors of supplies and luxury goods to the court, or offering secretarial and administrative skills.[7]

Under the Fatimids, Fustat-Cairo became the hub of a great trading network that extended from North Africa and Islamic Spain in the West to India and China in the East. This global nexus was established by the Fatimids during their reign in al-Mahdiyya, Ifriqiya. Many Maghribi merchants migrated to Egypt with the Fatimids, and from the evidence of the Geniza documents, these merchants included Jews. Together with the *ashab al-khil'a* and the scholars, the great merchants formed part of the elite echelons of Cairene Jewry, though most of the Jews of medieval Fustat-Cairo were modest artisans and tradesmen.[8]

By the year 1000, Egypt had a very sizable Jewish community, and this continued to be the case until the 13th century when the population of Egypt was decimated by plague and famine. Al-Fustat had a Rabbanite community of 3,600 souls, plus a Karaite community and a small congregation in nearby Cairo, bringing the total Jewish population in the capital to well over 4,000.[9] Alexandria's Jewish community was probably about half as large.

We know more about the Jews of Fustat-Cairo, and of Egypt generally, during this period than about any other medieval Jewish community anywhere, thanks to the rich documentation that has survived in the so-called Cairo Geniza. The Geniza was a vast repository of discarded written materials – sacred and secular, literary and documentary – attached to the Ben Ezra Synagogue in al-Fustat. Discovered by Europeans in the late 19th century, the Geniza contained over a quarter of a million manuscripts and fragments, dating back to the mid 8th century. The greatest share of material, however, was from the 10th to the 13th century, from the Fatimid, Ayyubid and early Mamluk periods.[10]

No Jewish quarters existed in the major cities and towns of Egypt during this period, except perhaps in al-Mahalla al-Kubra, where a specific quarter (*hara*) is identified in an early 13th-century document.[11] Rather, Jews were concentrated in a few neighbourhoods. One was al-Qasr al-Sham', the old Byzantine fortified area (also known as al-Qasr al-Rum) around which the Islamic garrison town had evolved. This had been inhabited by Jews and Christians before the Muslim conquest. Within this section was an area known as Suwayqat al-Yahud (The Little Jewish market), but this name was probably due to the presence of a Jewish abattoir (Majzarat al-Yahud) there, and not because it was a centre of Jewish commercial activity.[12] There was also a lane, Zuqaq al-Yahud, on which both the Palestinian and the Babylonian synagogues were located. But Jews also lived in other sections of the city, including al-Raya quarter, named for those who had borne the standard of the Muslim army and which was the site or the original area of Muslim settlement near the mosque of 'Amr. Nearly half a millennium after the Arab conquest, the neighbourhood had become predominantly Christian, but was being bought up by Jews. The pattern of Jewish settlement began to change during the Fatimid period when, between 1026 and 1107, most of the Jews moved from Old to New Cairo.[13]

Little is known about either the structural organisation of Egyptian Jewry or the mechanism of its administrative relationship with the Islamic state before the Fatimid period. Until the middle of the 11th century, no single Egyptian Jewish official was recognised by the government as leader and authoritative representative of the community.[14]

In the early years of Fatimid rule, the state authorities recognised the *gaon* of the Palestinian Yeshiva as having supreme communal authority over all the Jews in the empire. This, however, did not prevent Jews of the Babylonian rite from sending legal queries and donations to their diocesan authorities, the *gaon*s of the Iraqi academies. The Egyptian capital was in fact the great transfer point for donations and queries sent to both Palestinian and Babylonian *yeshivot* by Jews from all over the Islamic Mediterranean and for the return to them of gaonic responsa, religious books and treatises, and other forms of international Jewish communal correspondence. (It is for this reason that the Geniza has proved to be a source of information of such tremendous value for the entire Islamic world and not just for Egypt.) During the last decades of the 10th and the first three decades of the 11th century, the official intermediaries in charge of facilitating this flow of letters, documents and funds were the merchant princes, Abu Yusuf Ya'qub b. 'Awkal and his son Abu'l-Faraj Yusuf.[15]

The highest local Jewish leader in Egypt at this time was the representative of the Palestinian Yeshiva. He was called the *rav rosh*, or chief scholar, and resided in al-Fustat. He functioned not unlike a *mufti* in the Muslim system. His primacy of place was recognised by both the Palestinian and Babylonian congregations. Throughout the first quarter of the 11th century, the position of *rav rosh* was occupied successively by a father and a son, Shemarya b. Elhanan (d. *circa* 1012) and Elhanan b. Shemarya (d. *circa* 1025). The father established a school of higher Jewish learning in al-Fustat, and his son had access to the caliphal presence and often received favours from the ruler.[16]

After Elhanan b. Shemarya's death, the office of *rav rosh* seemed to fall into desuetude and the chief *dayyan*s, or judges, of the Palestinian Jews acted as communal leaders for all the Rabbanite Jews of Egypt. Their function was somewhat parallel to that of the *qadi*s in Islam. Still, each of the Rabbanite congregations had its own leaders, and each looked to the *gaon*s in either Jerusalem or Baghdad as the ultimate authorities in Jewish legal, ritual or exegetical matters. The head of the Palestinian congregation usually bore the title of *haver*, or 'Member of the Academy', and the head of the Babylonians that of *alluf*, or 'Distinguished Member'. Despite some dissension between Jewish leaders in al-Fustat, the Rabbanite Jews had a sense of being a single community, and this feeling extended somewhat to the Karaites.

Each Egyptian Jewish community had a common chest for the social services of the community which included philanthropy, the upkeep and maintenance of the houses of worship and communal properties, and the salaries of communal officials. This was in keeping with both the longstanding Jewish tradition of providing for one's own and with the Islamic social system, under which charity and social service were the responsibility not of the state, but of each confessional group. Thus the Jews, like the Muslims and Christians, had their own pious foundations which they often referred to by the Arabic designations of *waqf* or *habs*, as well as by the Hebrew terms *heqdesh* or *qodesh*. The *ahbas al-yahud* were administered by the *dayyan*s of the Jewish court and were legally recognised as *waqf* properties by the

state, an important guarantee against arbitrary sequestration. During the first half of the 11th century, about 140 Jewish households in al-Fustat received regular allotments of bread from the community chest. This indicates that more than 10 per cent of the urban Jewish population was poor.[17]

Around the year 1065 the Fatimid government created a single Jewish authority, the Ra'is al-Yahud (Head of the Jews) for all Egyptian Jewry. In Hebrew he was referred to as *nagid* (prince), a title used earlier in the Maghrib and Spain. This new post was established when the Palestinian gaonate was in decline, weakened by internal rivalries. The loss of Palestine to the Saljuk Turks in 1071, together with other factors, caused the Fatimids to turn increasingly Egyptocentric. Thus a Jewish community under local leadership was desirable. Furthermore, administrative independence from the Palestinian gaonate probably began to look attractive at this time to the Jews of Egypt themselves, as the Palestinian *yeshiva* and its leadership became increasingly tarnished by unseemly and divisive squabbles. The function of the Ra'is al-Yahud evolved slowly over the next two hundred years under the Fatimids and Ayyubids. By Mamluk times, the powers and responsibilities of this official were well defined and spelled out in such administrative handbooks as al-'Umari's *al-Ta'rif* and al-Qalqashandi's *Subh al-a'sha,* where it clearly states that:

It is incumbent upon him [i.e., the Ra'is al-Yahud] to unite his community and to gather their various elements in obedience to him. He is to judge them in accordance with the principles of his religion and the customary usages of its religious leaders. He must see to it that their persons are protected by their being humble and lowly and by their bowing their heads in submissiveness to the followers of the faith of Islam, by their giving way to Muslims in the streets and when they are intermingled with them in the bathhouse. He is responsible for appointing the various offices of rank among his coreligionists from the rabbis on down, according to their degree of merit and in accordance with their agreement. He has the final say in matters pertaining to all of their synagogues.[18]

In other words, the Ra'is al-Yahud eventually became the supreme Jewish authority within Egypt with unprecedented powers over every aspect of Jewish communal life in addition to being the sole representative of his religious community, including the sectarian Karaites, before the Islamic state. Mark Cohen has hypothesised that the office of Head of the Jews developed along with changes in the Coptic patriarchate at that time. In Cohen's view, the recognition extended to the Ra'is al-Yahud by the Fatimid government probably came as part of a conscious policy of centralisation instituted by the military strongman, Badr al-Jamali. This hypothesis makes good sense, but unfortunately, the details of the development of the office are still not clear.[19]

Like many of the top communal offices in the medieval Islamic world, the position of Ra'is al-Yahud in Egypt tended from its very inception to be dominated by a single family. Three of the first four occupants of the office were members of a family of physicians who served at the royal court – Judah b. Sa'adya (*circa* 1064–1078), his brother, Mevorakh (*circa* 1078–1082 and again 1094–1114), and the latter's son, Moses (1112–*circa* 1126). Their combined rule of more than half a century was interrupted for a little over a decade, between 1082 and 1094, when David b. Daniel, an ambitious member of the Davidic House and a disappointed aspirant to the Palestinian gaonate, usurped the office. From the late 12th to the early 15th century, the position was passed on in true dynastic succession from the great Moses Maimonides (d. 1207) through his descendants right up to the time of the Ottoman conquest. The office then passed to appointees from Constantinople, but was terminated around 1560 after local objections to the outsiders.

In addition to the Ra'is al-Yahud, many other officials in the Egyptian Jewish community were connected with government, and although Muslims always constituted the majority of civil servants, non-Muslims were represented in the bureaucracy out of all proportion to their numbers in the general population. This was due, in part, to the tolerance of the Fatimid and Ayyubid regimes, but may also be attributed to the fact that careers in government were fraught with danger and, therefore, were not attractive to the majority of people. Furthermore, unlike many pious Muslims, Jews considered government service to be a highly honourable calling.[20] The highest offices of the realm were of course reserved for Muslims; there were notable exceptions, Christians who wielded the power of vizier, sometimes bearing the title and sometimes not. But individuals of Jewish birth who achieved this exalted office, such as Ya'qub b. Killis (d. 991), Hasan b. Ibrahim al-Tustari (d. 1064), and Sadaqa b. Yusuf al-Fallahi (d. 1048), all converted to Islam before becoming vizier.[21]

The one Jewish courtier who rose to the very pinnacles of power in Fatimid Egypt during the third and fourth decades of the 11th century was Abu Sa'd Ibrahim b. Sahl al-Tustari, the scion of a wealthy Karaite mercantile and banking house of Persian origin that was established in Egypt during the reign of al-Hakim. According to al-Maqrizi,[22] Abu Sa'd became purveyor of luxury goods to the caliph al-Zahir, and his star rose still higher when a black slave girl he had sold to the royal harem became Queen Mother and acted as regent for her son, the young caliph al-Mustansir, who succeeded in 1036 upon the death of his father. The dowager-regent relied upon her former master to be her advisor and confidant. After the death of the vizier al-Jarjara'i in 1044, Abu Sa'd became the power behind the throne with the ability to make or break viziers – something that he actually did. However, he was murdered at the height of his career in a plot involving the Turkish troops and the apostate Jewish vizier, Ibn al-Fallahi. As was frequently the case when a non-Muslim rose so high and became conspicuous in the affairs of state in the Islamic world, Abu Sa'd's downfall was preceded by anti-*dhimmi* agitation, and a popular satiric verse written by the poet Rida b. Thawb prior to his death ran:

The Jews of this time have attained their utmost hopes
and have come to rule. Honour is theirs, wealth is theirs too,
and from them come the counsellor and ruler.
People of Egypt, I have good advice for you –
Turn Jew, for heaven itself has become Jewish![23]

Tiraz texile bearing the name
of the Fatimid vizier Ya'qub
ibn Killis, made in 371/981

Abu Sa'd's brother and business partner, Abu Nasr Harun, and Abu Sa'd's son Abu 'Ali Hasan, were granted protection by the caliph following the murder. Abu Nasr himself entered government service shortly thereafter, but his career was brief. His property was confiscated and he died in prison under torture in 1048. Abu Sa'd's son survived, converted to Islam at some point and became al-Mustansir's vizier in 1064.[24]

The fall of the Tustaris did not mean an end to the presence of Jews in Fatimid government service. A certain Abu'l-Munajja b. Sha'ya served under the vizier al-Afdal as fiscal inspector of the province of Damietta and was responsible for the excavation of a large irrigation canal which was named after him (khalij Abi Munajja). Another Jewish official, Ibn Abi Dimm, served as a secretary in the chancery under the caliph al-Amir.[25]

Jews continued to serve in the government bureaucracy under the Ayyubids, but in lesser numbers and in less conspicuous positions than under the Fatimids. In fact the eighty years of Ayyubid rule marked a period of transition for the Jews of Egypt, as they did for the country as a whole. The Sunni Ayyubids began their reign with a wave of anti-dimmi fervour born of their resistance to the Crusaders. However, members of the dimmi upper class were often still able to evade the requirement to wear a distinguishing mark, which was considered a mark of humiliation (dhull) and differentiation (ghiyar). Periodic decrees by the Ayyubids – like other Muslim rulers in various times and places – reminded the upper-class non-believers that they should pay for their exemption, which they readily did.

The Egyptian Jewish population declined in the Ayyubid period in the wake of the disastrous famine and epidemic of 1201–1202 and the lesser epidemics of 1217, and 1235–1236. A Geniza letter from 1217 specifically invokes a prayer 'May God spare the people of Israel from the Plague' then ravaging al-Fustat.[26]

The demographic decline of the Egyptian Jewish community followed its economic decline. The laissez-faire commercial policies of the Fatimids seem to have given way to a Middle Eastern brand of feudalism. High tariffs, debased coinage, the formation of restrictive guilds and the allocation of agricultural lands as *iqta'* for the military elite – all contributed not only to declining prosperity, but to the marginalisation of the non-Muslims in the economy.

Although the Ayyubid period marks a steady downward spiral in Egyptian Jewish prosperity, it was also the time when the greatest scholar of post-Talmudic Jewish history lived in Egypt. Moses Maimonides (1138–1204) came to Egypt from the Islamic West in 1165, where he served as physician to the *qadi* al-Fadil and later to the Ayyubid sultan, al-Malik al-Afdal. He also served as Ra'is al-Yahud. It was in Egypt that Maimonides produced an enormous body of responsa and his two greatest works, his great law code, the *Mishneh Torah*, his only work in the Hebrew language, and his philosophic chef d'oeuvre, 'The Guide to the Perplexed' (*Dalalat al-ha'irin*). His son, Abraham, who succeeded him as court physician and as Head of the Jews, founded a pietist circle inspired by Sufi practices, whose members were called *hasidim*. He also wrote an important guide to mystical piety, *Kifayat al-'abidin* ('The Complete Guide for Worshippers'). Both Maimonides and his son introduced various reforms and tried, to no avail, to shore up the morale of the Egyptian Jewish community which was becoming increasingly despairing during these years.[27]

The general state of Egyptian Jewry deteriorated even more under the Mamluks. The sumptuary laws were enforced with ever-increasing vigour. Since the Mamluks did not allow native Arabs to dress like Mamluks or ride horses, they were not going to permit non-believers to dress like Muslims. As of 1301, '*dhimmis* were so-to-speak colour coded by their outer garments'. Yellow became the identifying colour for Jews, blue for Christians and red for Samaritans.[28] The decree of the sultan al-Malik al-Salih in 1354 went even further. Christians and Jews were limited in the size of their turbans. Non-Muslim men were to wear a metal neck ring when visiting the public baths, so that even undressed they could not be mistaken for Muslims. Jewish and Christian women were barred altogether from bathing with Muslim women.[29]

During the first century and a half of Mamluk rule, a humiliating Jew's oath for Jews appearing before a Muslim court was reintroduced after a five-hundred year moratorium on such oaths. This degrading, ludicrously worded adjuration is reminiscent of the notorious oath *More Judaico* in Christian Europe.[30]

One truly unusual anti-*dhimmi* decree was made by Sultan Chaqmaq in 1448. This edict banned Jewish and Christian physicians from treating Muslim patients, a momentous reversal of the longstanding non-confessional nature of the medical profession in the Islamic world. In the two centuries that immediately preceded Chaqmaq's ban, a number of polemical treatises had appeared containing horror stories about the malevolence of *dhimmi* doctors towards their Muslim patients.[31]

European Jewish travellers, such as Friar Felix Fabri, who passed through Egypt during the second half of the 15th century testify to the serious demographic and social decline of local Jewry, and European Christian travellers describe a similarly gloomy picture for their Egyptian coreligionists during this period. Obadiah da Bertinoro, who passed through Egypt in 1487 on his way to the Holy Land, mentions Jewish officials selling off ritual ornaments, Torah scrolls and codices from the synagogues of Cairo and Jerusalem to foreigners, including Gentiles. In one instance related by Obadiah, the beadle of al-Fustat's Ben Ezra Synagogue sold off a Torah scroll and promptly converted to Islam to avoid prosecution. He also notes widespread poverty and an appalling lack of charity towards the Jewish poor (a startling reversal from the highly organised social services of earlier periods). His contemporary, Meshullam da Volterra, testifies to the serious decline in the Jewish population of a number of Jewish communities. He mentions, inter alia, that the Jewish community in Alexandria had dwindled to only sixty families at the time of his visit in 1481.[32]

The Mamluk period marks the nadir of medieval Egyptian Jewry. The community would recover somewhat with the arrival of Iberian exiles at the end of the 15th and the beginning of the 16th century and with the new prosperity that came in the wake of the Ottoman conquest. However, not until the second half of the 19th and the first half of the 20th century did Egyptian Jewry recover, for a limited time, the wealth and influence it had known under Fatimid rule.

1   Ibn 'Abd al-Hakm, *Futuh Misr*, ed. Charles
    C. Torrey (New Haven, CT, 1922), p. 82.

2   Taylor-Schechter 16. 79, 1. 3. The document is
    published with a facsimile, by Israel Abrahams,
    'An Eighth-Century Genizah Document',
    Jewish Quarterly Review, 17 (1905), pp. 426–430.

3   Abu Salih, *The Churches and Monasteries of Egypt.
    Anecdota Oxoniensia* VII, tr. B. T. A. Evetts (Oxford,
    1885), p. 136; S. D. Goitein, *A Mediterranean Society*
    (Berkeley, CA, 1967), vol. 1, p. 18.

4   See Norman Golb, 'The Topography of the Jews
    of Medieval Egypt', *Journal of Near Eastern Studies*,
    24 (1965), pp. 252–270 and 3 (1974), pp. 116–149.

5   Mourad El-Kodsi, *The Karaite Jews of Egypt, 1882–1986*
    (Lyons, NY, 1987), p. 21.

6   For extensive biographies of each of these two
    figures, see Henry Malter, *Saadia Gaon: His Life and
    Works* (Philadelphia, PA, 1921), and Alexander
    Altmann and Samuel M. Stern, *Isaac Israeli: A
    Neoplatonic Philosopher of the Early Eleventh Century*
    (London, 1958).

7   See Norman A. Stillman, *The Jews of Arab Lands:
    A History and Source Book* (Philadelphia, PA, 1979),
    pp. 43–44 and 52.

8   For a survey of the economic life of medieval
    Egyptian Jewry, see Goitein, *A Mediterranean Society*,
    vol. 1; for intimate views of the mercantile life, see
    Goitein, *Letters of Medieval Jewish Traders* (Princeton,
    NJ, 1973).

9   This estimate is based on Goitein's calculations,
    for which see Goitein, *A Mediterranean Society*, vol. 2,
    pp. 139–140. This figure is considerably higher than
    Ashtor's estimate of only 1,500, which is probably
    closer to the mark for the 13th century, although
    Ashtor argues for the validity of his calculations
    for the earlier period as well. See Eliyahu Ashtor,
    'Prolegomena to the Medieval History of Oriental
    Jewry', *Jewish Quarterly Review*, 50 (1959), pp. 56–57;
    and Eliyahu Ashtor, 'Some Features of the Jewish

    Communities of Medieval Egypt', *Zion*, 30, 1–2
    (1965), pp. 63–64 [Hebrew]. Both Goitein's and
    Ashtor's estimates are less than that of the late
    12th-century traveller, Benjamin of Tudela, who
    reports that 7,000 Jews were living in Fustat-Cairo
    at the time of his visit there. See Marcus Nathan
    Adler, ed. and tr., *The Itinerary of Benjamin of Tudela*
    (London, 1907; repr., New York, n.d.), p. 98
    (Hebrew text), pp. 60–70 (English trans.).
    However, the numbers in the manuscripts, and
    indeed the manuscript tradition of Benjamin's
    travelogue itself, are highly problematic.

10 For a general introduction to the Geniza and a
    magisterial survey of the social and economic life
    of medieval Egyptian Jewry based upon its contents,
    see Goitein, *A Mediterranean Society*. For the history
    of the discovery of the Geniza, a survey of its contents
    and the establishment of the largest single collection
    of documents, which reads almost like a detective
    novel, see Stefan C. Reif, *A Jewish Archive From Old
    Cairo: The History of Cambridge University's Genizah
    Collection* (Richmond, Surrey, 2000).

11 Taylor-Schechter 12.166 (dated 1202).

12 See Paul Casanova, 'Essai de Reconstitution
    topographique do la ville d'Al Foustat ou Misr',
    *Mémoires de l'Institut Français d'Archéologie Orientale
    du Caire*, 35 (1913), pp. 18–19; and also E. J. Worman,
    'Notes on the Jews in Fustât', *Jewish Quarterly
    Review*, 18 (1905), pp. 28 and 30.

13 For the Lane of the Jews, see Goitein, *A Mediterranean
    Society*, vol. 2, p. 291 and the sources cited there,
    p. 589, n. 7. Concerning al-Raya, see Norman
    A. Stillman, 'The Jew in the Medieval Islamic City',
    in Daniel Frank, ed., *The Jews of Medieval Islam:
    Community, Society, and Identity* (Leiden, 1995), p. 5.
    On the population shift to New Cairo, see Goitein,
    A Mediterranean Society, vol. 2, p. 128.

14 The view long held by many scholars, that the
    Fatimid government set up the office of *nagid*, or as

    he was commonly called in Arabic, Ra'is al-Yahud,
    in order to provide a substitute for Jewish loyalties
    previously given to the Exilarch, the Jewish official
    at the rival 'Abbasid caliphal court in Baghdad, has
    been shown to be completely erroneous. Goitein,
    A Mediterranean Society, vol. 2, pp. 23–40. Goitein's
    conclusions have been corroborated and expanded
    upon by Mark R. Cohen, *Jewish Self-Government in
    Medieval Egypt: The Origins of the Office of Head of the
    Jews, ca. 1065–1126* (Princeton, NJ, 1980).

15 See Norman A. Stillman, 'Quelques renseignements
    biographiques sur Yosef Ibn 'Awkal, médiateur
    entre les communautés juives du Maghreb et les
    Académies d'Irak', *Revue des Études Juives*, 132 (1973),
    pp. 529–542; and Norman A. Stillman, 'The
    Eleventh-Century Merchant House of Ibn 'Awkal
    (A Geniza Study)', *Journal of the Economic and Social
    History of the Orient*, 16 (1973), pp. 15–88.

16 For biographical data on these two individuals, see
    Jacob Mann, *The Jews in Egypt and in Palestine under
    the Fatimid Caliphs*, Preface and Reader's Guide by
    S. D. Goitein (New York, 1970); Shraga Abramson,
    Ba-Merkazim uva-Tefusot bitqufat ha-Ge'onim
    (Jerusalem, 1965), pp. 105–173; S. D. Goitein,
    'Shemarya b. Elhanan: With Two New Autographs',
    Tarbiz, 32 (1963), pp. 266–272 [Hebrew with
    English summary]; and S. D. Goitein, 'Elhanan
    b. Shemarya as Communal Leader', in Sidney
    B. Hoenig and Leon D. Stitskin, ed., *Joshua Finkel
    Jubilee Volume* (New York, 1974), pp. 117–137 [Hebrew].
    See also the important doctoral dissertation of
    Elinoar Bareket, *The Leaders of the Jews in Fustat
    during the First Half of the Eleventh Century* (Tel Aviv,
    1987) [Hebrew with English abstract].

17 For a detailed picture of the Jewish social services,
    see Goitein, *A Mediterranean Society*, vol. 2, pp. 91–143
    and 413–510; and Moshe Gil, *Documents of the Jewish
    Pious Foundations from the Cairo Geniza* (Leiden,
    1976). Cf. also Norman A. Stillman, 'Charity and

Social Service in Medieval Islam', *Societas*, 5 (1975), pp. 105–115.

18 Al-Qalqashandi, *Sub al-a'sha* (Cairo, 1913–1919), vol. 11, pp. 390–391, trans. in Stillman, *The Jews of Arab Lands*, pp. 269–270.

19 Cohen, *Jewish Self-Government in Medieval Egypt*.

20 For a comparison of attitudes towards government in Islam and Judaism, see S. D. Goitein, *Studies in Islamic History and Institutions* (Leiden, 1966), pp. 197–213; and Norman A. Stillman, 'Subordinance and Dominance: Non-Muslim Minorities and the Traditional Islamic State as Perceived from Above and Below', in Farhad Kazemi and R. D. McChesney, ed., *A Way Prepared: Essays on Islamic Culture in Honor of Richard Bayly Winder* (New York and London, 1988), pp. 132–141.

21 For the career of Ibn Killis, see Walter J. Fischel, *Jews in the Economic and Political Life of Mediaeval Islam* (rev. ed., New York, 1969), pp. 45–68; for Hasan al-Tustari, see Ibn Muyassar, *Ta'rikh Misr*, ed.

Henri Massé (Cairo, 1919), p. 32; and also Moshe Gil, *The Tustaris: Family and Sect* (Tel Aviv, 1981), p. 58; for Ibn al-Fallahi, see al-Suyuti, *Husn al-muhadara fi ta'rikh Misr wa'l-Qahira* (Cairo, 1968), vol. 2, p. 201.

22 Al-Maqrizi, *al-Khitat* (Bulaq, 1270/1853; repr. Baghdad, n.d.), vol. 1, pp. 424–425. In addition, see Fischel, *Jews in the Economic and Political Life*, pp. 68–69 and the sources cited there.

23 Ibn Muyassar, *Ta'rikh Misr*, pp. 61–62; al-Suyuti. *Husn al-muhadara*, vol. 2, p. 201. Goitein, *A Mediterranean Society*, vol. 2, p. 374, has pointed out that the last verse may contain a punning allusion to Abu Sa'd.

24 Fischel, *Jews in the Economic and Political Life*, pp. 86–87 and the sources cited there.

25 For Ibn Munajja, see al-Maqrizi, *al-Khitat*, vol. 1, pp. 72, 477, and 487–488; and for Ibn Abi Dimm, see Ibn Muyassar, *Ta'rikh Misr*, p. 74.

26 Taylor-Schechter 16.305v, 1. 26. See also, Michael

W. Dols, *The Black Death in the Middle East* (Princeton, NJ, 1977), pp. 33–34.

27 For succinct surveys of the life and work of the Maimonides father and son, see the articles 'Maimonides, Moses', *Encyclopaedia Judaica*, vol. 11, cols. 754–781; and 'Abraham Ben Moses Ben Maimon', *ibid.*, vol. 2, cols. 150–152. See also now S. D. Goitein's moving portrait of Abrahamx in *A Mediterranean Society*, vol. 5, pp. 474–496.

28 Yedida Kalfon Stillman, *Arab Dress: A Short History From the Dawn of Islam to Modern Times* (Leiden, 2000), p. 111.

29 This decree is translated in Stillman, *The Jews of Arab Lands*, pp. 273–274.

30 The text of the oath from al-'Umari's *al-Ta'rif* is translated in Stillman, *The Jews of Arab Lands*, pp. 267–268.

31 Ibid., pp. 71–72.

32 Ibid., pp. 74–75.

11 | Faith and practice: Muslims in Historic Cairo

Roy Mottahedeh

The main body of this essay is devoted to a discussion of the Muslim liturgical year, the annual cycle of public religious observance. This will involve the private and public devotional lives of Muslims. In addition, some of the changes in religious observances over the years will be discussed, and those observances described in both past and present.

The Islamic Revelation sees itself as Adamic, since God's kindness has provided man with spiritual guidance from the time of the first man. This recurrent revelation was monotheistic from the start but became more dramatically so from the time of the Prophet Abraham, who smashed idols and openly defied polytheism. With the coming of Islam, revelation is perfected for mankind. This perfected revelation is largely or entirely contained in the Qur'an, the full body of the formal revelations received by the Prophet Muhammad. The great majority of Muslims accept the Qur'an as the stable centre of their belief. In time, the behaviour of the Prophet, presumably because he was the best qualified to understand the revelation, became a supplement to the Qur'an as a source of correct Islamic behaviour. The general word for correct behaviour became *shari'a*, or 'way', which included many precepts concerning reward or punishment not in this world but in the next.

Before turning to Muslim devotional life, its possible and actual relations to its legitimating sources should be mentioned. The broad agreement on the centrality of the Qur'an left many questions unresolved. Does it correspond to the 'Guarded Tablet' referred to in the Qur'an, apparently an archetype of perfect revelation that exists in heaven? If this archetype is something beyond any specific language, does the interpretation of it into a specific human language such as Arabic deprive it of some of its clarity? Such disputes, with their various strategies intended to interpret scripture, are characteristic of great scriptural traditions. To make an analogy, in the study of the United States' Constitution, for example, we see those who regard the historically determined specific intent of the framers as the paramount criterion for interpretation, and also those who believe that the widely expressed intent of the framers is 'justice' as the paramount criterion.

For the latter group provisions should be interpreted in a sense most likely to result in the doing of justice.

In a broad sense two streams of interpretation exist in the Islamic tradition, a scholastic tradition and an anti-scholastic tradition. Both would agree that it is sometimes important to know the specific circumstances of revelation; is a passage in the Qur'an addressed to a limited group, or to an individual, or to all mankind or to all Creation? Both would also agree that it is important to recover the lexical and grammatical world of the time of revelation. But the anti-scholastic would feel that at this point he or she could immediately apprehend the meaning and implication of revelation, whereas the scholastic would have many more questions: is the language metamorphic, hortatory, etc.

In any case, in pre-modern times the general Muslim understanding of religion was continuous and it has enveloped such figures so important to Christians as Jesus, Mary and John the Baptist. This places Muslims in the mainstream of the Abrahamic tradition of Jews and Christians that sees the creation as the beginning of things and judgement leading to heaven or hell as the end of things. Many modern believers, in all three Abrahamic faiths, have tried to reinterpret these beliefs. Islam shared with other Abrahamic monotheisms the dilemmas that seem to be created by belief in an almighty God: is there free will or predestination; could God's omnipotence create objects beyond His control, and the like. The radical monotheism of the Qur'an, as generally understood, made some of these problems easier and some harder to resolve. Rejection of the Trinity removed the Christian problem of the status of Jesus as an intermediary but posed a dramatic problem regarding how to know God, since many Muslims felt that God was only describable by His entire difference from worldly things. A rich literature of Muslim devotional works makes clear that such philosophical problems did not affect the devotional life. The extraordinary presence and influence of Sufism, the mystical orientation among Muslims, from the 12th to the 21st century show that the individual's striving to find the divine within themselves remained a vital part of the life of many Muslims.

For all the different interpretative and theological strategies of Muslims, the vast majority agreed on the basic forms of worship expected of them. As a well-known maxim states: 'People who pray to the Qibla [i.e., in the direction of the house Abraham constructed in Mecca and the focus of Muslim pilgrimage] do not call each other unbelievers.' When asked to define Islam, many Muslims will quote the saying ascribed to the Prophet in which he sets out the five principal duties of Muslims: to perform the daily prayers, to give alms, to fast in the month of Ramadan, to perform the Pilgrimage to Mecca, and to bear witness that there is no god save God and that Muhammad is the Messenger of God. All of these fundamentals of religion are acts, even though the last act is a testimony to a belief. This essay describes these acts and the way in which they explain the life of the believer. It should be remembered that Muslims use a lunar calendar of twelve months, which is approximately eleven days shorter than the solar year, and therefore 'annual' events in this lunar calendar move over time through all four seasons.

The obligatory prayers are said five times a day, once at dawn, once at noon, once halfway to sunset, once at sunset and once when night has closed in. As can be seen, these times are determined by observation; the time for the mid-afternoon prayer is the moment when a stick casts a shadow half its length. The act of obligatory prayer consists mainly of a prescribed number of 'bowings', which include recitation both of the Qur'an and of pious formulas, as well as movements which include the worshipper placing his hands, nose and forehead on the ground. Such prostration is understood to engender humility before God. A saying ascribed to the Prophet ends: 'I accept the Worship only of him who humbles himself before My Greatness and does not exalt himself over Me, and feeds the needy for the sake of [the vision] My Face.' [1] Worship in the obligatory prayers is an aspect of *dhikr*, 'mindfulness', of God, frequently mentioned in the Qur'an and with the implication that one should both keep God present in the mind and make mention of God.

On Fridays (except among certain Shi'is) an extra congregational prayer of two 'bowings' replaces the usual noonday prayer. All Muslims who are able should attend, hence specific mosques (literally, *masjid*, place of prostration) like the Cairene mosque of 'Amr b. al-'As, founded by this conqueror of Egypt, are given the appellation *masjid jami'* or 'congregational mosque'. In these mosques, after the Friday prayer has been said a sermon is preached. (Some Muslims reverse the order and put the sermon before the prayer.) The preacher customarily stands on a high place; hence the beautiful pulpits that adorn most Cairo mosques. The sermon consists of two parts with a brief pause between, and it was an established element of the second part to offer a prayer on behalf of the Muslims. It became customary to mention the ruler's name in the sermon, an important act recognising a claim to sovereignty. When the Fatimid general Jawhar entered Egypt in 969, he immediately went to the mosque of 'Amr and had the Friday sermon preached in the name of the Fatimid caliph, then still in Ifriqiya. [2]

Alongside this daily and weekly schedule of obligatory prayers there are the prayers at the festivals and the non-obligatory or supererogatory prayers which are so prominent in the life of Muslims. The liturgical year of feast and fasts, especially among Egyptians who have grown so fond of the birthdays of their 'saints', is as full of solemnity and celebration for the Muslim as one could desire.

The tenth day of Muharram, the first month of the year, was a voluntary day of fasting, and celebrated as such by the Sunni Muslims. For Shi'i Muslims, however, it is the day of the martyrdom of Husayn, the grandson of the Prophet, whose killing is seen by Shi'is as history's blackest betrayal of a saintly figure, one who was the rightful and divinely guided leader of the Muslims. The tragic events leading up to and following Husayn's martyrdom make all of the first twelve days of Muharram occasions for mourning. In Fatimid times the head of Husayn was transferred to Cairo, where a special section of the caliphal palace was devoted to it. Although Egyptians have for centuries been Sunnis and no longer have public mourning ceremonies like the Shi'is on Ashura, anyone who has visited the mosque of 'our Master' Husayn knows the intensity of emotion that surrounds it. Its importance as a congregational mosque is such that overflowing crowds are

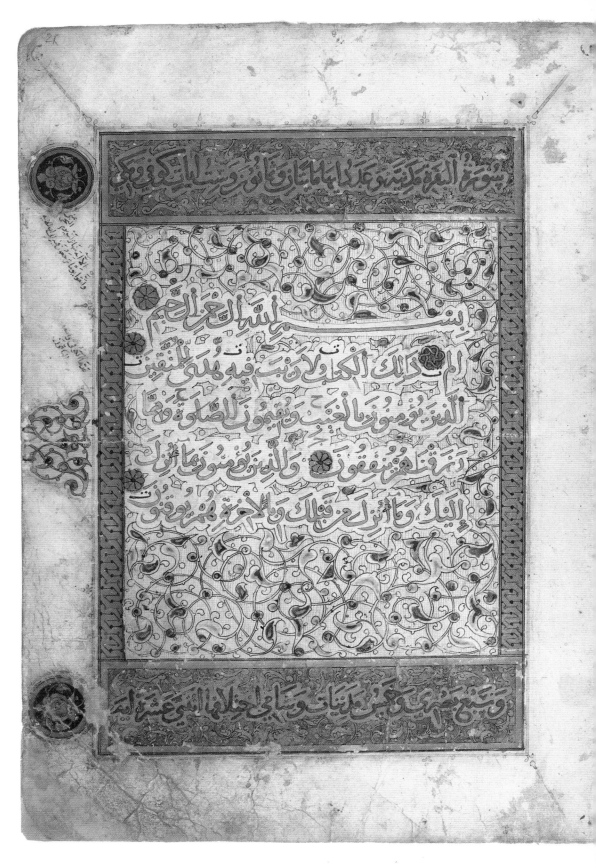

al-Darb al-Ahmar in Egyptian history

A Mamluk Qur'an,
the *Fatiha* and the opening
verses of *Surat al-Baqara*, in
muhaqqaq and *thulth* script,
mid 8th/14th century

to be found on adjacent streets praying on mats and rugs every Friday at noon. Even today the highest officials, including the President, come to it to pray on the days of the great festivals.

The twelfth day of the third month, Rabi' I, is the great *mawlid al-Nabi*, the celebration of the Prophet's birthday, and is in some ways the model for the 'birthdays' of holy men and women that fill the Egyptian religious calendar. In Cairo the popular celebration of this birthday dates back at least to the 13th century.[3]

The great English scholar E. W. Lane, describing the Prophet's Birthday in 1834, tells of the enormous tents erected, mostly for the Sufis, the devotees of the mystical interpretation of Islam, whose ceremonies are called *dhikr*, the mindfulness and mention of God discussed above. Many lanterns, some of them in fanciful shapes, illuminated the festival which went on night and day for nine days. Swings for children, rope dancers, sweet sellers, storytellers, all add to the semi-carnival atmosphere that surrounds this and many lesser *mawlid*s. Professional reciters sing poems that use the language of love as an expression of religious longing. For many years, on the actual day the master of the Sa'di Sufis rode his horse over the backs of devotees, but legal scholars disliked this public 'miracle' and it has long been abandoned. Similarly there were ecstatic Sufi-inspired women dancers, whose presence in public was sometimes tolerated and sometimes not.[4]

The emergence of the Prophet's Birthday as a major festival reflected an increasing interest in personal devotion to the Prophet. Most learned Muslims accept accounts of the Prophet which emphasise his claim to be a man like other men, principally distinguished by His Mission to receive and transmit revelation, and hence called 'The Messenger' (*rasul*). The greatest (some would say only) 'miracle' he performed was to pass on the Qur'an to humankind. Yet, in time, most popular and even some learned believers openly identified the 'light of Muhammad' with the 'principal light' which was the first thing created. To tell stories of the Prophet or sing poems in his honour came to be meritorious acts in themselves, and were the model of much other literature not of the high tradition. And yet the antagonism of those

who believed in a more austere version of Islam and rejected these celebrations never died away. Occasionally, governments even supported this austere view.

The next month, Rabi' II, is witness to what used to be the second most celebrated *mawlid* in Egypt, named after 'the two Hasans', Hasan and Husayn, the grandsons of the Prophet, of whom Husayn is by far the more important, in part because of his martyrdom referred to above. This *mawlid* was widely celebrated in and around al-Darb al-Ahmar district, so close to the mosque of Our Master Husayn, and where many shops stayed open all night. The day after the event Qur'an readers could still be seen in the area, for many visitors paid for the entire Qur'an to be recited (or, more accurately, to be cantillated), which would take four reciters, relieving each other at intervals, about nine hours. The actual recital of the revealed book, itself a miracle in part because of the unique beauty of its language, is a pious act whether performed in private or in public; and the proper cantillation of the text by professional reciters can have variations that delight the listener and enhance what is seen to be the majesty of the text.

The festival of Sayyida Zaynab, the sister of Husayn and the granddaughter of the Prophet, which takes place in the middle of the seventh month, or Rajab, is one of several festivals commemorating a saintly woman. It is a measure of the intensity of popular feeling that her mosque is the only mosque other than that of Husayn at which non-Muslims are not welcome. At those times when women visitors are numerous in the inner sanctuary it is considered out of bounds to men.

The night of 27 Rajab commemorates the *mi'raj*, the Prophet's miraculous ascension to Heaven, usually understood to be the topic of the Qur'anic verse: 'Glory be to He who has carried His servant by night from the sacred mosque to the *masjid al-Aqsa* (the farthest mosque) which We have surrounded by blessings (or "whose enclosure We have blessed"), in order that We might show him certain of our signs; He is the all-hearing, the all-seeing' (XVII:50). That such an event was an occasion for story and legend is no surprise. On the night of the *mi'raj* the Cairene Sufis until recently carried out the same variety of ceremonies as they had at the *mawlid al-Nabi*. Storytelling was strongly associated with this festival, especially stories of the Prophet's Night Journey. These stories grew in popular telling to encompass a sometimes glamorous journey through the seven heavens with descriptions of all parts of the cosmos. For the pious, the Night Journey became symbolic of the journey of the deceased to the presence of the Throne of the Divine judge. For Sufis it was also the archetype of the journey of the soul from its attachment to the physical world to its release into the world of pure consciousness of God.[5]

The *mawlid* of the very great jurist, al-Shafi'i, (d. 820), is commemorated near the beginning of the eighth month, Sha'ban. This descendant of the Prophet's tribe, Quraysh, was born in Askalon and died in Cairo at the age of forty-seven. A brilliant student of Islamic learning, he gave system to the young science of Islamic law and in the process may have helped the legal disciplines to gain precedence over theology. After two centuries of rule by the Shi'i Fatimids, the Sunni dynasty of Saladin, which had conquered Egypt in 1171, sought to make the tomb of al-Shafi'i, an intellectual hero of the Sunnis, as popular as the Holy Shrines of the Shi'is, such as the mosque of Husayn. Al-Shafi'i's resting-place is the largest freestanding mausoleum in Egypt, built in Cairo in 1211. The shrine is not only filled at the time of the *mawlid* but also daily by many visitors, including the ill, who are borne in litters around the cenotaph. For those who seek Shafi'i's spiritual guidance and/or intercession there is even a place to post letters to him.

Two weeks later comes the night of the middle of Sha'ban, which has some of the character of a New Year's Day in that it is felt to be the turning point of the year. It is often called the night of the *bara'a*, the Absolution. A special prayer is recited after the evening prayer and the 36th chapter of the Qur'an, *Surat al-Yasin*, is recited, after which the Believers offer their personal prayers. In Egypt this night is associated with the *sidrat al-muntaha*, the lote tree that sits at that point which is the closest a person can come to God and beyond which no one can pass. Legend has claimed that this tree has as many leaves as there are people. The tree is shaken on this night and the leaves inscribed with the names of those destined to die in the coming year fall off. The awe felt at the boundary between divine knowledge and human knowledge (which is limited by ignorance of the time of one's end) made this popular story a favourite theme of Muslim poets.

With the sighting of the new moon at the end of Sha'ban, the ninth month, Ramadan, begins. (Muslim days and dates run from sunset to sunset.) In this month, believers fast from sunrise to sunset. Many Egyptians who observe the daily prayers indifferently feel the Fast to be an iron obligation. The ill, the infirm, pregnant or nursing women and children are exempt, as are travellers who make a journey of more than three days, but these latter must make up the fast days missed at some other time of the year.

For most Muslims this is a time of heroism and inner purification. This month of fasting is not seen as a hardship (although when it falls in summer it is a considerable feat). Yet anyone who has fasted knows the sense of surprise that one feels afterwards when one allows oneself to drink or eat. And the denial of other sensual pleasures, including sex, during the daytime gives the one who fasts the sense of mastery over the 'lower self'. The Prophet is reported to have said that in this way fasting becomes the 'gateway to divine service'. It is also one of the main duties of Muslims, the fulfillment of which is visible to God alone.[6]

The great Sunni theologian al-Ghazzali explains that there is a higher stage of observance of the Fast since the Prophet is reported to have said five things annul it: lying, backbiting, slander, a false oath and a 'glance of passion'. Concentration on the name of God and recitation of the Qur'an is the fast of the tongue; refraining from listening to evil the fast of the ears. But at its highest level, 'The fruit of hunger is contemplation of God, of which the forerunner is mortification. Contemplation is the battlefield of humans, whereas mortification is the playground of children.'[7]

For the ordinary Muslims of Cairo, however, the Ramadan fast has the excitement of a world half turned upside down. In Cairo, families eat a glorious pre-dawn brunch which may include specialities prescribed in family tradition. After the dawn prayer, work and even

Interior of the Amir Khayrbak
complex, built 908/1502
and later, after restoration
works by the Historic Cities
Programme

schools begin earlier to accommodate the early start of daily life. By the noon prayer some of the festive spirit of the pre-dawn brunch has worn thin. The working day ceases for most Muslims in the early afternoon and, by late afternoon many Muslims are at home resting (which often turns into sleep). Immediately after sunset the believer prays, then eats lightly, smokes if so inclined, then sits down to a serious meal, which includes meat for those who can afford it.

This schedule implies a shift of emphasis from day to night, when the most emotionally resonant events take place. The pious spend much of the night in supererogatory prayers called *tarawih*, in which many of the 'bowings' that are the essential units of the obligatory prayers are performed. These may be interspersed or followed by readings from the Qur'an, and the larger mosques are open all night for prayer. In Cairo many go home to sleep a few hours before the early brunch preceding the 'daybreak prayer'. But many also go to coffee shops or to the numerous tents put up for the month, both to meet friends and to listen to the musicians and, especially, the reciters of tales who come into their own more on these nights than on other occasions. In shops nowadays, which are often gaudily strung with 'Christmas tree' lights, and where thin, newly baked pastries with a pleasing but never filling taste of honey are served, reciters tell the exploits of figures such as 'Antara. This son of a black slave girl, who in history and in legend was already a hero before the Prophet appeared in the 7th century, lives on for several centuries among the storytellers to fight for the good, even dealing the Crusaders heavy blows in the 11th century. It is no surprise that older texts of the 'Thousand and One Nights' seem to be prompt texts for reciters of this ingenious collection of stories. As the Ramadan fast obliges the believer to feel that normal daytime pleasures are not to be taken for granted, Cairene Ramadan nights give a sense of the wondrous world that ordinary nights of sleep so lack.

The crown of Ramadan is the night of the twenty-seventh, called *laylat al-qadr*, 'The Night of Power (or Destiny or Decree)'. This night is discussed in the Qur'an, where it is declared 'better than a thousand

months. The Angels and the Spirit descended with the permission of their Lord to regulate everything. It is Peace until the rising of the dawn', (xcvii: 3–5). It is understood that the 'Angels' and 'the Spirit' are free from their usual charges and engaged in blessing mankind. Moreover, tradition relates, as the gates of heaven have been opened, prayer enters freely and is more certain of success; and many Muslims pray fervently on this night. It is said that on this night all animal and vegetable kind bow down to God in adoration, thereby assuring the universal peace that envelops creation on this occasion.

The first day of the next month, Shawwal, is one of the two days properly designated 'festival' ('*id*) in the Islamic liturgical calendar. It is called the 'Festival of Breaking the Fast', or, simply, 'the Lesser Festival'. While giving alms is an important part of the preceding month of fasting, this Lesser Festival is above all about alms-giving. It is felt fitting that after a month of restraint and self-purification, those believers able to do so should give whatever they might still owe morally to others in order to complete the 'change' that the Fast has effected. After a special prayer of two 'bowings', a sermon, and spontaneous prayer, the congregants, usually dressed in their finest, visit their friends, warmly greeting even remote acquaintances, affirming the ties strengthened by the Fast. On this festival, which continues for a few days, Cairenes go out to the City of the Dead at Qarafa carrying branches of palm and sweet basil to put on the tombs. While women were the majority of visitors to the dead a century ago, such visits are (now) occasions when men and women associate with each other fairly freely, as they do in the *mawlid*s.[8]

Egyptian control of the Hijaz, the province that contains Mecca, Medina and all the places essential to the Pilgrimage proper, was effective during much of the Fatimid (969–1171), Ayyubid (1171–1250), and Mamluk (1250–1517) periods. Egyptian domination meant that the Pilgrimage caravan from Egypt with its government-appointed 'Commander of the Pilgrimage' had precedence over other caravans. At some time in this period Egypt acquired the honour of providing the 'covering' (*kiswa*) for the Ka'ba, the rectangular structure called 'the house of God', built first by Adam and rebuilt by Abraham, which pilgrims must circumambulate. For most of the past eight hundred years the 'covering' has been designed and constructed in Egypt, and it was long the custom for the 'covering' to be put on display on the sixth day of Shawwal in the mosque of Husayn until the departure of the Pilgrimage. In 1834 Lane, witnessing the parade of military bands and Sufi dervishes that accompanied the 'covering' to its place of display, mentions a mounted man 'fantastically dressed in sheepskins' and wearing 'a high skin cap and a grotesque false beard' who occasionally pretended to write legal opinions with a stick.[9] Clearly an element of mockery of high authority, not only of great legal authorities but of the sultan himself, made a sly appearance in some of these great public events.

In the latter part of Shawwal the principal officials of the Pilgrimage used to pass from the Citadel, which dominates the city visually, along a procession route, accompanied by the *mahmal*, which is a square frame of wood covered with richly embroidered panels and silver crescents that is carried on the back of a tall camel. On one of the front panels is a representation of the enclosure of the Ka'ba together with the sultan's cartouche. Until 1952 the *mahmal* was a symbol both of the holy and communal nature of the Pilgrimage and of the sultanic authority that supervised and patronised the Pilgrimage caravan.

It seems not at all inappropriate that in the Islamic tradition, usually so opposed to physical representations of divine things, the 'clothing' of the most holy building and of the beast that accompanied the pilgrims in their journey to this most holy place, should be a focus of such loving care. To walk in procession to see off and then to welcome home this caravan, (for the *mahmal* returned), was one way in which Cairene Muslims as a community indirectly participated in the Pilgrimage.

The twelfth and final month of the year is literally called the 'Month of the Pilgrimage (to Mecca)'. Pious tradition makes the site of the Ka'ba the first place devoted to the One God, and the Black Stone, embedded in the walls of the Ka'ba, the object which holds the covenant between man and God. It is moreover of cosmological significance, as it was and sometimes still is seen as the spiritual axis of the world, the most central place on the earth, the first spot at which dry land appeared over the waters and the place at which the upper and lower worlds communicate. It is, in terms of place, what *laylat al-qadr* or the Night of Power is in terms of time.

The pilgrim approaching the Hijaz must at certain set points put him or herself in a state of *ihram*, 'consecration', which is not only a state of ritual cleanliness but also of dress in a simple cloak-like garment. Like the Fast, a state of consecration will be broken by certain acts such as sexual relations, and Muslim thinkers notice and speculate on the similarity.[10]

Throughout the Pilgrimage the pilgrim must form the 'intention' to do an act before performance of the act. Many Muslims feel this pattern should fill their lives, for God judges humankind by intentions and not acts; circumstance can intervene in all sorts of ways that prevent the fulfillment of a sincere intention.

The actual rites of the Pilgrimage are rather complicated and groups of pilgrims generally have a guide. On the tenth day of the month the pilgrim (or group of pilgrims) must slaughter a sheep, goat, a bovine or a camel in commemoration of God's substitution of an animal for Abraham's son (identified as Isma'il, Ishmael, by most contemporary Muslims, but as Isaac in the Old Testament). At present, great care is taken that this food be given to the poor. This festival is celebrated on the same day by Muslims everywhere in the world and is called the Great Festival or the Festival of Sacrifice. In discussing this sacrifice, the Qur'an specifically discusses the relation between ritual and belief: 'For every religious community we have established a rite (or, "place to perform a rite")' (XXII:34); and: 'Neither their flesh or their blood will ever reach to God; but the reverential fear/piety from you will reach Him' (XXII:37). Just as the repeated refrain in the obligatory prayer is: 'God is Great', so the repeated refrain of the pilgrim is *labbayka*, 'I heed Thy call, I am at Thy service'.

According to a popular etymology a much used word for sacrifice, *qurban*, reflects the effort to grow close to God; and indeed the repeated explanation of much pious behaviour is that it is 'seeking closeness to God'. The longing for the Beatific Vision, seeing the Face of God, is an honourable goal in the eyes of most Muslims (even if some hold that, strictly speaking, God is 'unseeable'). The Sufi mystics see Abraham's willingness to sacrifice his son as an understanding that obedience to God will slay the 'lower self', which is the true sacrifice at the Great Festival.

The great periodic celebrations of the Muslim community described above by no means include the full devotional life of the believer.[11] It is hard to imagine a Muslim community that celebrated more *mawlid*s than Egypt. The growing acceptance of the *mawlid* or Birthday of the Prophet led to increasing numbers of yearly *mawlid*s honouring 'saints', often leading Sufis but sometimes persons adopted as saints by Sufis, and sometimes persons of a sanctity more diffusely defined. In Egypt in the past there were more *mawlid*s than days in the year; *mawlid*s are still so numerous that there is a category of people, *mawlidiyya*, who travel throughout the year from *mawlid* to *mawlid* selling 'sugar dollies' (a speciality of *mawlid*s) or accommodation in tents with bedding and the like. Some advocates of an austere form of Islam detest these *mawlid*s altogether; others dislike only the entertainments that accompany them: the feasting and shopping at the fairs that spring up at most *mawlid*s, the sword-swallowing and glass-eating 'miracle' workers, etc.

Rituals are multivalent, capable of encompassing several different types of significance at the same time. Feasting is as often a companion to piety as is fasting. One reason is that feasting is communal. Many of the lesser *mawlid*s in some sense constitute the largest possible versions of the face-to-face communities to which villagers and inhabitants of small towns could belong. And this sense of belonging, particularly in the period before the modern system of universal elementary education (and sometimes even now) provided a possible path by which to bring talented local people into the wider community. The village teacher would send his promising student to continue his religious education at the local town of the *mawlid*, and the teacher

there would send students on to the city. In the *mawlid* town and the city were pious endowments that would give a modest living to students who had been recommended. Since such schools were once the only means of education except for private tutoring, some students would leave the system at some middle level and work for the government. Others, of modest ability, would be sent back to be teachers in their original *mawlid* district. Others with more learning (and, possibly, more political skill) would pass to the top of the ladder as well-paid judges, professors at *madrasa*s (colleges), etc. The local *mawlid* not only defines a community, but also defines ways to enter the wider community of Egypt.

The emphasis in this essay on communitarian religious rituals should not obscure the importance of more private rituals. Some of these more private practices coincide with public rituals. For example, the practice of *i'tikaf*, a vow to retreat to the mosque and more or less withdraw from society in order to fast and recite the Qur'an can be observed for any number of days at almost any time of the year. Yet it is most observed for the last ten days of Ramadan, in part because the exact day of the Night of Power is uncertain but must surely fall in these ten days and the one who withdraws for this period is therefore constantly spiritually ready to participate in the blessings of this wondrous night.

Many other practices of private piety exist, from saying the rosary (older in the Muslim than in the Christian world) to observing the many supererogatory fasts recommended for the truly devout. Yet even in Muslim ritual matters, which were usually public, a strong emphasis on the privacy of the home meant that a Muslim might absent him or herself from public ceremony or even flout such private duties as fasting. A much-repeated story is told of the second caliph, 'Umar, who scaled the walls of a house and saw the owner in a reprehensible state. When 'Umar reproved him, he replied, 'If I have sinned once, you have sinned three times.' 'How so?' asked 'Umar. 'The Qur'an says "Do not spy" and you have done so. The Qur'an says "Come into houses through their doors" and you have entered over the roof. And the

133 CAIRO. — PROCESSION OF THE HOLY CARPET.

CAIRE
Fête du Prophète

Qur'an says "Do not enter the houses of others until you have made yourself known and greeted the inhabitants", and you have not greeted me.' Totally out-lawyered, 'Umar retreated.[12]

Some of the rituals already discussed helped to create a larger community in a different way. The Coptic Christian holiday (possibly of Pharaonic origin), 'Smelling the Breeze', is celebrated on the Monday after Easter by virtually all Egyptians. A fair number of *mawlid*s are interconfessional; in Upper Egypt Christian *mawlid*s are very popular with Muslims. The *mawlid* of a Jewish saint, Abu Hasira, in the Delta province of Bahaira still attracts both Muslim and Jewish devotees. In 1940 an astute observer of *mawlid*s wrote that the Feast of Saint Teresa, celebrated by the comparatively small Catholic community of Egypt, was attended by many Muslims and Jews.[13]

Rites de passage, like supererogatory piety, do not fit into the formal liturgical year, as people are not born, married or buried according to schedule. Women can play special functions at these occasions. Egyptian women use the high-pitched trill, called 'ululation' (*zagharit*) at the emotional climax of such rituals, even the burial of a distinguished man of learning.[14] More surprising (and often condemned) is the appearance of the *ghaziyya*, 'dancing women', at weddings and other events, including the *mawlid*s. Popularly believed to be from a tribe of gypsies, their numbers probably included non-gypsies who adopted the gypsy style. Some say their performances inspired the Western belief (to which Egyptians have adapted) that Egypt was the home of an established type of dance called the 'belly dance'.

Egyptian festivals such as the 'Smelling of the Breeze' mentioned above, and the Inundation of the Nile, have no overt connection with the Muslim liturgical year. But this last festival was and is a major event that all Egyptians celebrate. Like many other festivals, it was also an occasion for the caliph or sultan to participate in a *mawkib*, a procession or cavalcade. In the time of the Fatimid caliphs (969–1171) the caliph, surrounded by finely dressed soldiers and courtiers, and heralded by drums and trumpets, would set out from the palace to the place of the festival or ritual. The procession would move to the point where the canal which ran through Cairo was cut open to the flooding Nile.[15] The presence of Qur'an readers at this ceremony shows that no one ever felt that a Jeffersonian high wall should separate civic and religious ceremonies. The caliph (and later the sultan) would also lead processions to the great gatherings where prayer was conducted on the two *'id*s.

The Shi'i Fatimid caliphs led a major procession on the great festival of al-Ghadir on 18 Dhu'l-Hijja. This procession ceased to take place with the fall of the Fatimids. Such a festival gives us some understanding of the ruler's motives for participating in selected rituals and festivals of the capital. The ruler could foster a ritual which reinforced the ideological and emotional claims of the dynasty, as did the festival of al-Ghadir when Shi'is commemorate the occasion on which the Prophet publicly designated 'Ali as his successor. On Muslim festivals already established, the ruler could show that he commanded not only the final source of coercive power but also decided at what time and at what places ceremonies began. Some degree of acceptance of the ruler was shown by the popular and learned participation in these events.

The position of the ruler in ritual reminds us how futile it is to import the modern Anglican Church concepts of 'high' and 'low' into the analysis of pre-modern Muslim Egypt. 'High church' implies a ritual-prone, priestly-oriented church as contrasted with 'low church', which minimises these things in favour of a looser organisation of liturgical patterns and a declared intent to focus on the message of Christianity rather than its external forms. In contrast, a Muslim learned man opposed to *mawlid*s might well be an enthusiastic devotee of a Sufi *dhikr*. Designations like 'high' and 'low' culture also do not fit well on the medieval Egyptian versions of Islamic culture. The court and the circles of learned men might be considered the focuses of high cultural life (and courtiers did indeed help to define 'elegance'). But if one asks who did or did not believe in the efficacy of magic squares, no 'high' and 'low' distinctions emerge.

The appearance of the ruler at two kinds of rituals, one based on the solar and the other based on the Muslim lunar year, created a dissonance.

Urban rents were often fixed against the lunar calendar; agricultural rents were fixed against the solar calendar. Living through a year calculated two ways does cause some confusion. But it also puts the more religious nature of the liturgical year in the foreground. One is obeying God whether the Fast be in December or July. There is both wonder at the change of circumstances and fascination in one's ability to obey regardless of the length or the harshness of the climate.

In all discussions of the ritual year there are important distinctions that the learned consider but others may not. Since *dhikr*, 'mindfulness/mention' is so important, a great emphasis is put on speaking or reading out loud. Of course one can read the Qur'an silently, but it is more common to read it out loud. There are obligatory and prohibited acts in Islamic legal thinking, but there are also recommended, not recommended and morally neutral acts. In the case of worship, there are obligatory things but also acts of common usage in worship, such as saying 'Amen'. And, as mentioned above, in performing the obligatory elements in worship, an act can only be properly performed if the believer has first formed the intention to perform the act. How well people adhered to these prescriptions of the schoolmen is another question.

Was there a consciously constituted category of religious rituals? The ceremonies of the Pilgrimage are called *manasik*, a term which may at first have referred to the place of sacrifice. The day of sacrifice and the day of the end of the fast are called *'id*, which comes close in meaning to 'festival'. A *du'a* is a calling upon God, sometimes required as in the Pilgrimage, sometimes spontaneous. Many other terms are used for specific 'rituals'. 'Ritual' is a useful category, but it does not seem to have existed as an overt category in pre-modern Muslim Egypt.

One key to understanding the category that these and similar words might constitute is given in a saying ascribed to the Prophet: 'Whoever performs a prayer in congregation has filled his chest with divine service' (*'ibada*). The category of 'divine services' (*'ibadat*) is well known to every student of Islamic law but covers a wider category than the words 'rituals', 'ceremonies', 'prayers' and so forth. It covers all

things that 'express the relationship and attitude' of an individual to God.[16] Therefore, vows might be part of a book on *'ibadat*.

This understanding of ritual as a part of the direct interaction of a single person with God is shaped in the eyes of the learned by the radical monotheism of Islam. According to a frequently repeated story 'Umar said, when he kissed the Black Stone, 'By God, I know that you are only a stone, and had I not seen the Messenger of God kiss you, I would not kiss you.'[17] It is God who chooses to sacralise the Black Stone and the Ka'ba in Mecca. Nothing is sacred in its own right: it becomes sacred only through God's designation. Of course, to many Muslims living near a shrine associated with the local *mawlid*, the sanctity of the shrine may have seemed stronger than a spot with some revocable license.

If, however, Divine license is so important for the learned, then the specific moment that God granted that license becomes significant. In this sense Divine history becomes an anchor for the believer's understanding of rituals. Adam, Abraham and Muhammad created the Pilgrimage to Mecca at God's behest. (The widespread agreement among Muslims as to how to perform the Pilgrimage argues that this and many similar rituals do genuinely go back to the time of the Prophet.) Rituals can also offer the possibility of re-enacting events of sacred history. The theme of the re-enactment of the sacrifice of Abraham is very strongly present in the Festival of Sacrifice, but commemoration, as in the *mawlids*, is more often a theme than is re-enactment. Yet as the case of the *mawlids* shows, for many Muslims the book of ritual possibilities was not shut at the death of the Prophet. The distinguished scholar-jurist, al-Suyuti, said that there was no evidence that early Muslims celebrated the Prophet's Birthday, but that this festival is a 'praiseworthy innovation' (*bid'a hasana*).[18]

Rituals force us to think about the relation between what people do in a ritual, what they say (or are supposed to say or think) while performing it, and what they think or say afterwards as to what happened in the ritual. Let me first suggest that too much difference has been created between thinking and doing; thinking is a physiological activity which is 'action', while 'doing', such as speaking in the context of supplication in prayer, may be a means to formulate a 'thought', such as the form in which God may answer the prayer. Some scholars speak of the 'meaning' of ritual: for example, as we have said above, it creates community, whether at the local *mawlid* or, among all Egyptians, at the rising of the Nile. Yet it is unlikely that this interpretation of the 'meaning' of these rituals would be held by many of the participants. Moreover, Islam is necessarily a flexible religion, in that it encourages congregation, especially for rituals, yet admits the possibility of a person stranded on a desert island living a morally perfect life and being saved.

It is misleading to speak about the 'meanings' of ritual since there is nothing approaching the lexical correspondence between 'word' or 'utterance' and 'definition' or 'meaning'. Perhaps we can only search for the various forms of 'significance' of ritual, a word that better comprehends implied or unstated meanings. The term 'significance' also allows for unintended meanings and meanings of which the participants are not fully aware. Moreover, the significance of ritual can shift.

The significance of ritual often includes the affirmation of continuity, not only because of the largely fixed order in which they are carried out but also because of the language, often the same in different rituals. This makes the worshippers sense that they are related to each other. One powerful way in which rituals in the Egyptian context are significant is that they unite the seen world and the unseen world (and in the Qur'an God is frequently called 'the Knower of the Unseen World', e.g. VI:73). The significance of the ritual will almost always be modified both by context and by that inward configuration (based on prior experience or disposition) of the worshipper that leads him or her to interpret context.

This very brief list of aspects of the significance of ritual omits one element of ritual that is very often present. In the Abrahamic faiths, ritual signifies doing and saying things because one believes. It may never be possible completely to deconstruct 'belief'. The believer acts for the sake of 'God's Face'. We have mentioned the claim that Muslims disagree over theology more than over certain central religious practices. The other side of this coin is the inner freedom of the believers to weave interpretation into their rituals, for who can pretend to say definitively to another what is the 'Face of God'?

1   E. E. Calverley, *Worship in Islam, Being a Translation with Commentary and Introduction of al-Ghazzali* (Cairo, 1957), p. 55.

2   Paula Sanders, *Ritual, Politics and the City in Fatimid Cairo* (Albany, NY, 1994), p. 44.

3   H. Fuchs and F. de Jong, 'Mawlid', EI2, vol. 6, p. 895.

4   E.W. Lane, *An Account of the Manners and Customs of Modern Egyptians* (New York, 1973), pp. 442ff.

5   B. Schrieke, et al., 'Mi'radj', EI2, vol. 7, p. 97.

6   G. E. von Grunebaum, *Muhammadan Festivals* (Ottawa, 1976), p. 57.

7   Ibid., pp. 58–59.

8   Lane, *An Account of the Manners and Customs of Modern Egyptians*, p. 480; see also Louis Massignon, *Opera Minora*, vol. 3 (Beirut, 1963), p. 237.

9   Lane, *An Account of the Manners and Customs of Modern Egyptians*, p. 483.

10 Von Grunebaum, *Muhammadan Festivals*, p. 27.

11 'Periodic' is the term used by William A. Graham in his brilliant essay, 'Islam in the Mirror of Ritual', in Richard G. Hovannisian and Speros Vyronis Jr., ed., *Islam's Understanding of Itself* (Malibu, CA, 1983), p. 62.

12 See R. Mottahedeh, and K. Stilt, 'Public and Private as Viewed Through the Work of the *Muhtasib*', *Social Research*, 70, 3 (2003), pp. 735–748.

13 J.W. McPherson, *The Mowlids of Egypt (Egyptian Saints-Days)* (Cairo, 1941), p. 322.

14 Lane, *An Account of the Manners and Customs of Modern Egyptians*, p. 517.

15 Sanders, *Ritual Politics and the City in Fatimid Cairo*, pp. 114–117.

16 Calverley, *Worship in Islam*, p. 37 (a saying of the Prophet), p. 3 on *'ibadat*.

17 Graham, 'Islam in the Mirror of Ritual', p. 67.

18 Von Grunebaum, *Muhammadan Festivals*, p. 76.

12 The architectural heritage of al-Darb al-Ahmar

Caroline Williams

Al-Darb al-Ahmar begins at the Bab Zuwayla and extends in a south-easterly direction towards the Citadel. Like many streets in Cairo it has several names (al-Darb al-Ahmar, Shari'a Tabbana, Bab al-Wazir, Shari'at al-Mahgar) that fuse to make up collectively al-Darb al-Ahmar, the Red Alley. Its length is no more than a kilometre but its chronology stretches from the 11th to the 19th century AD: from the Fatimids, Cairo's founding dynasty, to Muhammad 'Ali Pasha, the formal initiator of Egypt's modern history. Fourteen major monuments are located along al-Darb al-Ahmar. They offer examples of the variety of Cairo's architectural heritage, and they also attest to the relationship between the architecture and the community it serves. The buildings show how this architecture served specific military, religious, educational, ceremonial, commercial and residential needs; how it reflected major themes of Islamic civilisation such as *waqf, hajj* and urban planning, and how the contemporary concern of an integrated and diversified context has been an intuitive part of the Islamic urban setting for a very long time. This is the street that is the setting for the film *Living with the Past*.[1]

Three major historical periods are represented along this street. For the Fatimid/Ayyubid years of the 12th and 13th centuries the remaining monuments are primarily fortifications, defensive enclosures that defined urban boundaries. Under the Mamluks (AD 1260–1517), al-Darb al-Ahmar was developed as a connecting artery and as a ceremonial route between the Fatimid city of al-Qahira and the Ayyubid citadel. The architecture that survives is primarily that of mosques and *madrasa*s built by high-ranking amirs. During the era of the Ottomans and then the house of Muhammad 'Ali (1517–1890), the architecture along this street reflected Cairo's new status as a provincial capital and economic centre for trade. Many buildings were reused for buying and selling. In the 19th century the Citadel again became an important administrative centre, and the street became dotted with residences that are still part of its fabric.

The Fatimids (969–1171)/The Ayyubids (1171–1250)
The oldest monument on al-Darb al-Ahmar, its beginning both in time and space, is the Bab Zuwayla, the Gate of the Zuwayl tribe. This was the

main gate on the southern wall of the royal-administrative-residential centre of al-Qahira founded in 969 by the Fatimid dynasty who came from Ifriqiya and conquered Egypt. In 1087 the all-powerful vizier Badr al-Jamali imported skilled Armenian stone masons to refortify the gate. The minarets were added more than 300 years later, and they give a sense of drama to the massive structure below. But the gate was never required for defensive purposes and, instead, under the Mamluks, it acquired important ceremonial functions. Drum rolls from the central platform would announce the entry of the sultan and important amirs to the city, and the sultan would sit on this gate to watch the *hajj* caravan depart.

The mosque of al-Salih Tala'i', the oldest mosque on al-Darb al-Ahmar, was built in 1160 just before the Fatimid dynasty came to an end. Its plan is one that was developed early in Islam, the so-called hypostyle, congregational, or Arab plan. It is a simple square or rectangle, in which an open courtyard is framed on all four sides with arcades. The arcades are deepest on the sanctuary side, the side of Mecca, towards which the congregation faces when it prays.

An interesting part of this mosque is the row of shops that lies below the main and side facades. These are the oldest surviving expressions in Cairo's architecture of an Islamic institution that goes back to the time of the Prophet himself. This is the *waqf* system in its religious and architectural form. The term *waqf* (literally 'stop') refers to non-perishable property dedicated to God such as land and buildings the income of which is designated for charitable purposes. In the case of al-Salih Tala'i', the rent from these lower level shops contributed to the upkeep of the mosque and the salaries of its personnel, such as the imam, the teachers, the preachers and the custodial staff. Thus, in addition to its religious and spiritual ties, the mosque was linked economically to the community. This independent source of funding also meant that religious leaders and teachers held social and political positions economically independent of the ruling class.

In 1303 a terrible earthquake rocked Cairo. Many mosques were damaged, including that of al-Salih Tala'i'. Sultan al-Nasir Muhammad (see below) ordered his superintendent of buildings to make repairs. The fine *mashrabiyya* or turned wood lattice screen that fronts the porch and the handsome metal door through which one enters are part of these early 14th-century donations, as is the handsome *minbar* in the sanctuary. Although these activities do not constitute conservation per se, they manifest a regard for the value of the building as a whole and are examples of the continuing concern for monuments that has been part of Cairo's architectural history.

At the other end of al-Darb al-Ahmar, near the Citadel, three hundred metres of 12th-century Ayyubid Wall have recently been excavated. When Salah al-Din ibn Ayyub, the great Muslim counter-Crusader, came to power in Cairo in 1171, he built the Citadel as a fortification against both external and internal threats. The walls were part of his plan to join the Fatimid city with the Citadel, which was the new dynasty's base. The gates, towers, interior chambers and galleries along these walls are handsome examples of the defensive architecture of the period.

The Mamluks (1250–1517)
The real glory of the street begins with the reign of al-Nasir Muhammad ibn Qalawun, who at the age of eight in December 1293 became the ninth Mamluk sultan. It was not until 1310 however, and after he had twice been deposed, that his third and most glorious reign began, lasting thirty-one years. During this time he built extensively on the site of the Citadel. Al-Darb al-Ahmar developed as a way to connect the Fatimid city, still an important centre of activity, with the new political-administrative-military residence that the Mamluks were building for themselves in this fortified enclosure. The majority of the monuments along this route are thus from the Mamluk period.

Under the Mamluks, the area outside the Bab Zuwayla became associated with the annual pilgrimage to Mecca, the *hajj*. It was from Bab Zuwayla that the *mahmal* procession began its journey south to the Holy Cities of Arabia during the pilgrimage season.[2] The *mahmal*, literally 'that which is carried' or 'the litter', was a camel palanquin that came to symbolise the Mamluk regime's political protection of the Hijaz. After the Mongols had devastated Baghdad, the caliphal capital of the 'Abbasids, in 1258, the Mongols were in turn defeated and prevented from reaching Egypt by the Mamluks. Sultan Baybars, the first real Mamluk ruler, established the 'Abbasid caliphate in Cairo. The *mahmal* was first sent in 1262 when the pilgrimage route via Suez, Aqaba and the east coast of the Red Sea, closed during the Crusades, was reopened. In this way Baybars symbolically demonstrated his role as protector of the Holy Places and of the 'Abbasid caliphate. The practice of sending the *mahmal* to Mecca from Cairo continued until 1952.

One of the oldest mosques on al-Darb al-Ahmar is the mosque of Ahmad al-Mihmandar, 1324–1325, built by a Mamluk who was chief

of protocol, one of the great court dignitaries in the reign of al-Nasir Muhammad. As *mihmandar*, he received visitors and guests at the sultan's court. He was also *amir al-hajj*, the official in charge of the annual pilgrimage to Mecca. This position was created when the 'Abbasid caliphate was brought to Cairo after 1262 and it was a post given only to amirs or military commanders of the highest rank since it entailed great responsibilities. The *amir al-hajj* was in charge of pilgrimage logistics: the organisation of supplies, the travel arrangements, the protection of merchants, the sick and the poor, policing the camp of the pilgrimage caravan and the application of penalties to any convicted wrongdoers.

The facade of the mosque is a good example of the Mamluk style whose elements, once established, continued to epitomise Cairene style after the Mamluk period had ended. The facade begins below a cornice crowned with merlins in the form of a fleur-de-lys design. This creates visual interest along the horizontal line of the roof. Five recesses divide the facade – three are topped with stalactite hoods while the other two are treated differently: the one with the keel-shaped arch above a circular window indicates that it is the external marker of the *mihrab* niche, while the last, much deeper and marked by stalactites and a hood studded with stars, is the entrance. The whole facade is divided horizontally by a great *tiraz* or inscription band, which begins with Qur'an 2:255, the *Ayat al-Kursi* or Throne verse:

> God, there is no god but He, the Living, the Everlasting. Slumber seizes Him not, neither sleep; to Him belongs all that is in the heavens and the earth. Who is there that shall intercede with Him save by His leave: He knows what lies before them and what is after them, and they comprehend not anything of His knowledge save such as He wills. His Throne comprises the heavens and earth; the preserving of them oppresses Him not; He is the All-high, the All-glorious.

and continues:

The erection of this mausoleum and the blessed mosque has been ordered of his own pure wealth from that which God has given him, and been endowed for all Muslims by the slave needy of God – exalted be He – Ahmad the Mihmandar, Chief Syndic [*naqib*] of the victorious armies of al-Malik al-Nasir.

When the mosque was restored in the name of the Ottoman sultan Ahmed III in 1722–1723 the interior lost its Mamluk decorations.

At the architectural level, al-Nasir's patronage resulted in the revival of the hypostyle or Arab mosque plan, which had fallen into disuse. The sultan himself built three hypostyle mosques and his example was followed by many amirs who built Friday mosques within the city along major roads which were then being developed. The mosque of the amir Altunbugha al-Maridani, 1339–1340, further down al-Darb al-Ahmar is one such example. Documented references attest to Sultan al-Nasir's great interest in building, not only in his own foundations, witness his frequent exhortations to his amirs to build fine monuments. He made available to them official contributions of various kinds: materials such as marble and wood, and workmen, builders or architects. For the mosque of al-Maridani the sultan provided marble and wood out of the royal purse, and as a special mark of favour sent the chief court architect, Mu'allim ibn al-Suyufi to plan the mosque. Al-Maridani was not only a favourite amir but the sultan's son-in-law, a closeness made apparent by giving the mosque a dome in front of the *mihrab*, a feature indicative of exalted rank, similar to that in al-Nasir Muhammad's mosque outside the Citadel.

In the arrangement of the mosque of al-Maridani, the congregational plan has been adapted to the location on the street and within the urban fabric. Since the beginning of the 12th century, mosque plans in Cairo had had to deal with two considerations: the alignment of the exterior walls along the street where they were located, and the proper interior south-east orientation of the mosque towards Mecca. The mosque of al-Maridani offers a fine illustration of how these

View of the mausoleum and minaret of the Khayrbak complex during restoration works, Historic Cities Programme, 2001

Prayer hall of the restored
Khayrbak complex with the
minbar and new lamps,
Historic Cities Programme,
2006

urban considerations were adapted. Inside everything looks regular, but outside the discrepancy between the orientation towards Mecca and the street alignment is taken up by the stair-step arrangement of the facade. The minaret sits over the entrance, setting the style for subsequent Mamluk minarets. From now on the graceful finial over an open, arched canopy becomes standard. When approaching from the direction of Bab Zuwayla the purpose of the minaret as a beacon of religion becomes obvious. As one walks down the street it is constantly in view. Inside, the *qibla* arcade is separated from the rest of the mosque by a superb *mashrabiyya* screen. This screen dates from the earliest period for this kind of work. In Cairo, because good wood was scarce and therefore prized, it was used primarily for decoration or for special accents.

Just after al-Darb al-Ahmar changes its name to Shari'a Tabbana stands the *madrasa*-mosque complex of Umm al-Sultan Sha'ban, built in 1368. She was the concubine of a son of al-Nasir Muhammad, and rose to power when her son Sha'ban ascended the throne at the age of ten. Sultan Sha'ban began the structure for his mother, Khawand Baraka while she was making the pilgrimage. This structure is the only royal foundation, and the only one honouring a woman, situated on this main artery leading from the Bab Zuwayla towards the Citadel.

The third reign of al-Nasir Muhammad (1310–1341) was a period of peace and prosperity for the empire. The Crusader and the Mongol threats had been resolved and, as an indication of the security of the regime, it became safer to make the Pilgrimage. The sultan himself, unlike any previous Egyptian sultan, went three times: in 1313, 1320 and 1332. The *hajj* was a way of giving thanks, and was also one of the feasts in which the court women played an active role and received many honours. Princess Tughay, the beloved wife of al-Nasir Muhammad, was the first to do so. She went in 1322 in thanksgiving for the birth of her son, Anuk. She went again in 1338. In her entourage was Sitt Hadaq, the stewardess in charge of the affairs of the harem. Lady Hadaq commemorated her visit to the Holy Cities by building a mosque in another part of medieval Cairo. Khawand Baraka continued this tradition among ladies of the Mamluk elite of going on pilgrimage.

The lady's *hajj* added to the sultan's religious aura. During the Mamluk period, building *madrasas* was a popular act of piety for women and the *madrasa* of Umm Sha'ban is the most prominent one to bear a woman's name.

The arrangement of the *madrasa* is based on the Persian mosque plan: four vaulted recesses (*iwans*) opening off a central court – a plan admirably suited for a building in which to teach the four schools of Sunni law. In the case of this *madrasa* however it is the *qibla iwan* and the opposite *iwan* that are defined, because here only the Shafi'i and Hanafi legal interpretations were taught. The plan of this *madrasa*-mosque also shows the conflicting problems of creating regular facades on the street and the proper orientation for the *qibla*. The complex has two mausoleums: one in which Khawand Baraka and her daughter are buried, and the other where Sultan Ashraf is interred.

Continuing towards the Citadel, the next mosque is that of Amir Shams al-Din Aqsunqur, 1346–1347. He was al-Nasir Muhammad's master of the hunt, and another son-in-law. He was one of the most important amirs at court, especially under the short-lived successors of Sultan al-Nasir. His mosque is another example of a courtyard mosque, and again the amir's closeness to the sultan is advertised by having a dome over the sanctuary.

In 1652–1654, however, the mosque was usurped by Ibrahim Agha Mustahfizan, a prominent commander of the Ottoman Janissary corps. He added the beautiful Ottoman blue and white tiles on the *qibla* wall for which the mosque is now famous and which give it its popular name, the Blue Mosque. A combination of light indigo and turquoise is the characteristic colour scheme, while the designs show growing plants or cut flowers: cypress trees, carnations, tulips, bluebells, peach blossom and long serrated leaves. The tiles use the patterns of Iznik, a famous Ottoman ceramic centre, but they were probably made in Damascus. The tiles on the *qibla* wall and in the tomb chamber are the most lavish use of Ottoman tiles in Cairo.

In the late 14th century a new group of Mamluks came to power. They were of Circassian origin, from barracks in the Citadel rather

Detail of the exterior of
the Khayrbak mausoleum,
Historic Cities Programme,
2007

than those on the island of Rawda in the Nile, and they are referred to as the Burji (Citadel) Mamluks. The mosque of Aytmish al-Bajazi, 1383, at the Citadel end of the street, was built by an amir who was regent for the young Faraq ibn Barquq, son of the first Burji sultan. The monument can be recognised by its stone dome decorated with slanting ribs, an example of the experimentation in dome design during the middle to late 14th century.

On al-Darb al-Ahmar are two other mosques which belong to the Burji, or late Mamluk period. The first is the mosque-complex of Qijmas al-Ishaqi, built between 1480 and 1481, placed to the north of and not far from the mosque of al-Mihmandar. The amir Sayf al-Din Qijmas occupied several posts during the reign of Sultan Qaytbay. He was master of horse and *amir al-hajj*. The position of his mosque on al-Darb al-Ahmar, between the scene of pilgrimage activities at one end, and the stables and the horse market of the Citadel at the other, indicates his diverse responsibilities.

The mosque of Qijmas al-Ishaqi is an excellent example of the development of Islamic architecture in Cairo up to the end of the 15th century. Its plan and surface arrangement differ from those of earlier mosques and *madrasa*s on al-Darb al-Ahmar. The structures built at the end of the Mamluk period moved away from single purpose buildings (i.e. a mosque, a school) towards complexes that were designed for many different functions. In addition to the mosque, the Qijmas structure includes a tomb, a *sabil-kuttab*, or water fountain and Qur'anic school. Qijmas died and was buried in Damascus, but since 1852 his tomb chamber has been occupied by the body of a holy man, Abu Hurayba, and the mosque is sometimes known by the saint's name. The *sabil-kuttab*, which is also part of the mosque ensemble, provided the neighbourhood with drinking water, and taught its children the Qur'an. The mosque is built over shops that run continuously around the exterior walls. These shops are part of the *waqf* for the mosque. Hisham, seen in the film *Living with the Past*, is the current proprietor of the shoe shop first rented by his grandfather. Another interesting aspect of this mosque, and a characteristic of other mosques of this period in other parts of the historic city, is that its arrangement and plan have been affected by subsequent urban development in Cairo. In the late 15th century, sufficient space for building rectangular congregational mosques was less available. Qijmas's site is triangular, and the master builder or engineer has fitted the various parts of this complex most skillfully and ingeniously on to the available land. Finally, the plan of this mosque, part Arab mosque and part Persian *madrasa*, has evolved into a new distinctly Cairene plan, the *qa'a* plan. Here, the scale of the main chamber is more intimate; the inner courtyard has been minimised and covered with a lantern ceiling, and the lateral vaults of the *madrasa* have been reduced, so as to render the internal shape rectangular rather than cruciform.

This mosque is also a fine example of the architectural style of the Qaytbay period. Sultan Qaytbay's reign which lasted almost thirty years (1468–1496) at the end of the Mamluk period balanced that of Sultan al-Nasir Muhammad's at the beginning. Qaytbay was also a great builder and patron of architecture. Both outside and in, the mosque of Qijmas al-Ishaqi shows a high standard of skill in the various crafts employed in its decoration, such as in the colour harmonies of the marble paneling, the fine stone carving of the walls, and the splendid, beautifully decorated and gilded wood ceilings.

At the other end of al-Darb al-Ahmar, just beyond the Blue Mosque, and within sight of the Ayyubid Walls, is the complex of the amir Khayrbak, 1502–1520, one of the chief amirs in the last years of the Mamluk empire. Sultan al-Ghawri appointed him viceroy of Aleppo, but he was rapacious and cruel, and his ambition led him to intrigue with the Ottoman Turks. He betrayed Sultan al-Ghawri at the battle of Marj Dabiq near Aleppo in 1516. The Ottomans routed the Mamluk army and the door to the conquest of Egypt was opened. As a reward, the 'Traitor Khayrbak', as he was subsequently called, was made the first Ottoman viceroy of Egypt.

Khayrbak's monument is interesting because it was built in two stages. As a rising amir, Khayrbak annexed the palace of an amir from the early Mamluk period. Next to it Khayrbak built his mausoleum in

1502, to which later, when he was made viceroy of Egypt, he attached a mosque and a *sabil*. At the entrance a block of pharaonic stone bearing hieroglyphic inscriptions and the figure of the mummified Osiris was used as the sill. This may have been deliberately placed there so that all those entering this religious establishment would tread the pagan gods incised on it underfoot. There are other examples of the use of pharaonic stones in the Islamic architecture of Cairo.

It is when coming from the Citadel end of al-Darb al-Ahmar that the best view of this building is obtained. One sees the wonderful way in which the prime elements of a Mamluk building – rectangular facade, spherical dome and vertical minaret – are arranged for optimum visual effect. The contemplation of the dome, with its triangular shoulder support system and the richly carved tapestry of interlacing leaves and hearts, creates another excuse for a pause along the way.

Ottoman Period (1517–1798)
Under Ottoman control (1517–1798) Egypt became a province exploited by a distant power. The Janissaries, the new army or crack militia, had the responsibility of guarding the city and the Citadel. They were a powerful element in the governing of the city between their arrival in the 16th century and their downfall at the end of the 18th century. Ibrahim Agha Mustahfizan was a forceful leader of the Janissary corps in the middle of the 17th century. From 1632 to 1657 (for 25 years) he was an active developer of buildings along al-Darb al-Ahmar. For about 250 metres, from the mosque of Khayrbak to the mosque of al-Aqsunqur (which he retiled and in which he built his mausoleum), Ibrahim's buildings lined both sides of the street. They were primarily income-producing investments and included public and commercial monuments such as a watering trough for animals, a fountain, house-*waqf*s or rental houses, and *rab'*s, blocks of apartments rented by middle and working-class tenants. Unfortunately, only small parts of these holdings remain, but their existence is known of through the *waqf* documents.

Further up the street, almost adjacent to the mosque of al-Mihmandar, is a *sabil-kuttab*, all that is left of what was a much larger economic unit. It was built by Muhammad Katkhuda Mustahfizan, chief of the Janissary corps, in 1677. We know from the *waqf* for this fountain that it was attached to a *wikala*, a commercial depot in which goods were stored and traded, over which was located a *rab'*, and some shops. This property was later bought as an investment by Yusuf Kizlar Agha, chief of the black eunuchs in charge of the imperial harem in Istanbul. To the buildings of Muhammad Katkhuda, Yusuf Kizlar Agha added more shops on the same side of the street and on the opposite side, eight shops, a coffee house and second floor apartments, all today replaced by modern buildings.

Next to the *madrasa* of Umm Sha'ban is the entrance to the mansion of Ahmad Katkhuda al-Razzaz, another officer of the Janissary corps. Examples of grand domestic architecture are rare in Cairo because they were not protected by religious interests or endowment deeds. This residence is in fact two establishments in one. The entrance on al-Darb al-Ahmar is part of a *rab'* or commercial tenement built by Sultan Qaytbay in the late 15th century, hinting thus at the direction buildings on the street would take. Behind what remains of Qaytbay's establishment is an entrance on a parallel street, Suq al-Silah, to the house that Ahmad al-Razzaz built in the late 18th century (1776). In the early 19th century the two houses were joined. In this double residence over 190 rooms were arranged around two courtyards and housed an extended family with its complicated hierarchies of gender, family relationship, servants and employees.

Muhammad 'Ali

During the 19th century the Citadel became the main residence and administrative centre of Muhammad 'Ali Pasha, an Albanian officer appointed by the Ottoman sultan in Istanbul as viceroy of Egypt. He ruled Egypt from 1805 to 1848, and founded a dynasty that lasted until 1952. Muhammad 'Ali initiated the processes of modernisation and Westernisation which were continued in the 19th and 20th centuries by his successors. Many of the 19th-century survivors along al-Darb al-Ahmar are houses that were built for government functionaries and administrators who worked in the Citadel. One can pick them out by looking at the *mashrabiyya*s overhanging the street, or by a carved doorway at street level. One example is the cluster of 19th-century houses around Bayt al-Sukkar that is featured in *Living with the Past*, directly opposite the mosque of Aytmish. Another lies behind and to the side of the *madrasa* of Umm al-Sultan Sha'ban. Here, a decorated

doorway marks the entrance to the house of Muhammad Mazhar who went to France in the early 19th century to acquire a Western education. He returned as an engineer, and worked on the Nile barrages, built to regulate the depth of the water in canals flowing from the Nile. These modest houses are not registered monuments but they are part of the historic fabric of the area.

In the first half of the 20th century, the focus of restoration and preservation was on individual monuments along al-Darb al-Ahmar. After 1952, the revolutionary government of Egypt, preoccupied by a new internal order and overwhelming regional problems, was unable to deal with the area's increasingly overcrowded, deteriorating infrastructure, makeshift living facilities and the natural disasters which assailed it. Now, at the beginning of the 21st century, there is a new change of direction, a realisation that this area is part of an urban heritage which has a social and historic value that should be preserved as part of the collective life of the community and the country. These monuments, with their domes, minarets, calligraphic inscriptions, wooden lattice grills and ghostly whispers of a proud past, are the background against which the voices of the neighbourhood vibrate, laundry flutters as it dries and spicy aromas permeate the air. The monuments along al-Darb al-Ahmar are the 'past' from which the living contemporary community derives the symbiotic relationship highlighted in *Living with the Past*.[3]

1   *Living with the Past*, produced by Elizabeth W. Fernea (2001).

2   The *mahmal* procession is described in E. W. Lane, *The Manners and Customs of the Modern Egyptians*

(London, 1908), pp. 444–448, 488–493.

3   In October 2007 the Aga Khan Trust for Culture (AKTC) completed the restoration of the *madrasa-*mosque complex of Umm al-Sultan Sha'ban and

the complex of Amir Khayrbak among several buildings it is restoring in the southern section of al-Darb al-Ahmar.

Prayer hall of the Khayrbak
complex before restoration,
Historic Cities Programme,
2003

13 From shards to bards: pottery-making in Historic Cairo

Fahmida Suleman

Ma t'ayyatush 'ala fukhkarkum da luh 'umr zay a'markum
Do not cry over your [broken] pottery, you have the same destiny.
An Egyptian proverb.[1]

The cultural anthropologist, Nessim Henry Henein, collected one hundred and forty-nine contemporary proverbs related to earthenware pottery from several pottery-making regions in Egypt. Many of the proverbs she cites are ironic in tone, such as *Ma fi'l-fakhura mithlu-hu* (There isn't a match for him in the potter's kiln), which is said of someone of low regard. While another, *Lau la al-kasura ma kanat al-fakhura* (If it doesn't break, it isn't pottery), is said to console someone who has broken something.[2] By recording these adages, Henein is writing history from the point of view of the people who make the pottery and use it. In this way, pottery is given social relevance as a metaphor of life. Is it justified to assume that material artefacts – specifically pottery – held a similar importance in the lives of their makers and users in earlier periods of Cairo's history? Historical texts from the Fatimid, Ayyubid and Mamluk eras were rarely, if ever, written from the point of view of the potter, artisan or merchant.[3] Court-commissioned histories and travellers' accounts may mention artefacts of a precious and costly nature, however, these seldom included a description of locally made ceramic wares. It remains one of the preoccupations of historians of Islamic art and archeology to try and understand the material arts in the context in which and for which they were made: in order to understand their relevance to the people who made them, the merchants who sold them and the clients who commissioned and/or purchased them. To do this, the historian searches for references within the written sources, however minute they may be, that refer to these contexts.

We will attempt to offer some insights into the use, and perception, of various types of pottery made in Historic Cairo and al-Fustat during the Fatimid and early Ayyubid periods (between the 10th and 12th centuries AD).[4] We will also attempt to contextualise this pottery, placing it in the day-to-day lives of the citizens of al-Fustat as well as in the lives of those living in and around the Fatimid court at al-Qahira.[5]

Various Arabic terms were employed in this period to designate 'pottery', 'ceramics' and 'porcelain'.[6] One of the most commonly used terms in the literature is *sini* (pl. *sawani*), which is derived from the Arabic word for the country of China – *al-Sin*.[7] The reason for this derivation is obvious: Chinese porcelain was considered by both the potters and the consumers of the medieval Muslim world as the pottery *par excellence* in terms of its whiteness, translucency, the strength of the porcelain and the elegance of its shapes. The 11th-century author, al-Tha'alibi (d. 1037), explains the history of this derivation and describes the best type of Chinese porcelain in his *Book of Curious and Entertaining Information*:

> The Arabs used to call every delicately or curiously-made vessel and such like, whatever its real origin, 'Chinese' (*siniyya*), because finely made things are a speciality of China. The designation 'china' has remained in use till this day for the celebrated type of dishes (*sawani*). [The Chinese] also have fine, translucent pottery, used for cooking purposes; a piece of this may be used equally for boiling things, for frying or simply as a dish for eating from. The best of these are the delicate, evenly-pigmented, clearly-resounding apricot-coloured wares, and after that, the cream-coloured wares with similar characteristics.[8]

Various types of Chinese ceramics were imported into the Islamic world certainly by the early 9th century, and archeological evidence confirms the widespread demand for them since shards of Chinese pottery have been found in numerous excavations of Islamic sites from Spain to Iran.[9] Results from excavations at al-Fustat reveal that the importation of Chinese ceramics into Egypt was at its peak between the 11th and 14th centuries, probably due to the shift of international trade routes from the Persian Gulf to the more direct Red Sea route which occurred at this time.[10] According to George T. Scanlon, the Director of the American excavations at Fustat, '[Certain types of] Chinese wares were highly valued by the [medieval] citizens of Cairo,

Lustre-ware bowl with
a groom and giraffe, Egypt,
480/1087

Lustre-ware fragment with the
face of a lion, Egypt, 4th–5th/
10th–11th century

for quite a few shards had been pierced for wiring, no doubt to hold the pieces together if the vessel became broken.'[11]

The impact of these Eastern wares was also immediately felt in the local pottery-making industries. The importation of Chinese porcelain spurred medieval potters to develop their own techniques in striving to imitate the whiteness and translucency of the Chinese models, in addition to copying their refined shapes.[12] However, the imitation could never be a complete technical success since clays in the Middle East lacked kaolin, which was a key component of the fine white Chinese clays that allowed a slow firing of the vessels at very high temperatures, resulting in a thin but strong ceramic body. To compensate for this, the potters of the Islamic lands used specially made glazes to cover their earthenware pottery that fired to an opaque creamy-white finish.[13] Furthermore, Egyptian potters began experimenting with clay recipes around the 12th century by adding varied amounts of crushed quartz in order to create a hard white clay body.[14]

In addition to the term *sini*, which appears to have designated both Chinese ceramics and the local Chinese-inspired glazed wares, medieval sources use the terms *fukhkhar* and *ghadar*, both of which indicate various types of glazed and unglazed pottery. For example, the term *fukhkhar* is generally understood to mean baked pottery or baked vessels of clay, as opposed to *khazaf*, which can designate un-fired vessels.[15] This is confirmed by some sources which describe a person called a *fakhkhar*, *fakhuri*, or *fakhurani*, as one who manufactures and installs clay pipes and fittings used in buildings.[16] In another source, by contrast, vessels made of *fukhkhar matliyya* indicate deluxe gilt or gold lustre wares.[17] Similarly, the term *ghadar* on its own may denote clay that is cohesive and of a dark or ashy dusty hue.[18] Yet, the phrase *al-ghadar al-shifaf al-sini* designates fine translucent Chinese porcelain, and a *ghada'iri* is one who manufactures porcelain-like dishes.[19] The word, *ghadara*, also derived from *ghadar*, came to designate a type of large dish or bowl, and is used in this way in the phrase *ghadara min ghada'ir al-khazaf al-ahmar*, which means 'a bowl from among the red earthenware bowls'.[20] The last phrase contextualises the term *khazaf* to mean

'terracotta pottery', and not simply un-fired clay vessels. The Arabic terms, therefore, encompass a range of meanings to designate various types and qualities of glazed and unglazed pottery.

The available evidence suggests that the pottery for everyday use in the homes of the medieval Egyptians was the same or similar in all religious communities, unless it was an item that played a specific religious or ceremonial role. We are fortunate to have the Cairo Geniza papers as a rich and unique source of information on aspects of the day-to-day, official and private correspondence, and transactions taking place in medieval Fustat. Although the information in these documents is particular to certain Jewish communities,[21] there is a substantial portion of material that incorporates evidence of the activities and lives of Muslims and Christians of al-Fustat.[22] In S. D. Goitein's invaluable edition of the Geniza documents, in the volume entitled 'Daily Life', he shows how in the home, drinking water brought from the Nile was kept in large earthenware jars with copper covers. For the table, water was kept in porous clay jugs covered with beautifully embroidered cloths, which naturally cooled the water inside whilst keeping it clean and fresh.[23]

This description of clay jugs used specifically to cool and dispense water brings to mind the numerous earthenware vessels with built-in filters that have been retrieved during the excavations at al-Fustat.[24] These vessels (Ar. *qulla*) by their material and design were meant to serve a purely utilitarian purpose. The pierced filters served to deter the entry of insects and other unwanted materials into the liquids intended for human consumption, while the unglazed bodies would keep the water cool and fresh. The Egyptian potters, however, transformed these functional vessels into objects to be admired. While they decorated them lightly on the outside, the potters concentrated their attentions on the pierced filters. The pierced decoration spanned from intricate floral and geometric patterns resembling lacework, to figural designs including people, animals of all sorts, and fantastical beasts.[25] Epigraphic decoration was also included in the repertoire with timeless words of wisdom imprinted on these objects such as, 'Forgive [others]

and you will be forgiven [by God]', and 'Be happy with a little and you will have a lot'.[26] Like the proverbs collected by Henein, these vessels were also references to human sensibilities and imperfections.

According to the Geniza documents, other indispensable household items were the *kuz zayt*, a small jug with a pouring spout for dispensing the various oils used for filling lamps and cooking meals, and the *zabdiyya*, a deep bowl which came in different sizes and materials and was used for various purposes.[27] The Geniza documents offer us information on household pottery, based on several sources, primarily bridal trousseau lists and merchant's letters. The information from bridal lists is often limited because the bride would not necessarily enumerate all the pottery she brought with her as it was breakable, and hence, an insubstantial commodity.[28] According to the Geniza documents, it was usually the husband who provided the home, and the wife who provided its furnishings among the middle classes of al-Fustat. As Goitein says,

> In addition to her jewellery and clothing a bride brought in sitting and sleeping facilities, draperies, hangings, and decorative covers of furnishings, inlaid or plain chests and trunks [serving as cupboards and wardrobes], objects used for lighting, deodorising, washing, and cleaning, and, of course, kitchen utensils [i.e. copper

goods] and sometimes tableware. However under certain circumstances, the objects brought in by the wife had to be returned to her at the termination of the marriage. Consequently, they had to be of durable material. It excluded, for instance, china and other pottery, glass vessels, and mats, all of which were commonly used in daily life but occur only rarely in trousseau lists.[29]

To be sure, these trousseau lists do not represent a full inventory of household items or of ceramic wares. Nevertheless, the ceramic items that are mentioned in these lists are all the more significant. For example, there are bridal lists that include five or six *zabdiyya*s made of fine glazed pottery (*sini*),[30] although a more expensive *zabdiyya* made of silver was also included in a trousseau list with a value of ten *dinar*s.[31] Another example from the dowry list of an affluent bride, dated AD 1140, includes an entry for a locally made jewelry box (*qimatra*) of porcelain (*sini*) and embellished with silver (*muhallah bi-fidda*), with a value of twenty *dinar*s.[32] Though locally made (i.e. not Chinese porcelain), this was still a prized item of considerable value if one compares the price of her silver water container with a cover, goblet and ladle, priced at fifteen *dinar*s, and her enamelled gold bracelet worth twenty-five *dinar*s.[33] Perhaps it was the size of the box in addition to its silver decoration that increased the value of this particular ceramic piece.[34]

The other source of pottery information in the Cairo Geniza is the records of business transactions which sometimes mention the type and quantity of *ghadar*, or fine glazed pottery, being ordered during that period. For example, a letter from Aden, dated 1135 reads, 'I asked him to buy [in Fustat] a basket of *ghadar*: bowls, platters and cups.' While another letter from Alexandria included an order for fifty *zabdiyya*s and ten platters 'with decorations in colour' from Cairo.[35] This gives the impression that whole sets of crockery might have been ordered as matching 'dinner services'.[36] That one's fine pottery was a thing to be proud of is attested from the author of a letter who boasts, 'I happened to get here [Fustat or Alexandria] carnelian-red *ghadar* and everyone envied me for this.'[37] Another Adenese client writing to his contact in al-Fustat, again around the year 1135, had very specific requirements when placing his order: 'Please buy me six painted platters, made in Misr. They should be of middle size, neither very large nor very small; and twenty [regular] bowls and forty small ones. All should be painted, and their figures and colours should be different.'[38]

What can be made of these descriptions of the various bowls and platters being ordered and shipped across the Red Sea around the mid 12th century? The first order placed for a basket of 'bowls, platters and cups' made in al-Fustat may be referring to sgraffiato[39] wares, some of which were direct imitations of lightly incised Chinese wares, and have been found in abundance in the excavations there. In all shapes and size, these wares were glazed in a variety of colours, such as green, turquoise, cobalt blue, honey-brown and manganese purple.[40] Another type of pottery that was also made in Egypt was polychrome glazed ware. Colourful lead glazes were applied in a radial design over the entire earthenware bowl in mixed hues including greens, blues, ochre, black and white, which were often fixed under a transparent glaze. This type of pottery could have easily been ordered with specific colours in mind and would have been perfectly suitable for purchase in larger quantities for everyday use in the home.

The description of the 'carnelian-red *ghadar*' is very interesting since this is an instance where the written sources are not entirely validated by the extant material evidence. Thus far, the excavations at Fustat have not revealed this kind of pottery. However, the closest parallel one can make is with the exceedingly rare ruby-lustre pottery that is dated to the 9th century, a century before the founding of Cairo, and ascribed to the potters of 'Abbasid Iraq. Excavations at the 'Abbasid capital of Samarra north of Baghdad have unearthed examples of a yellow-bodied pottery that is first covered in an opaque white glaze, followed by a decoration of ruby-red and gold lustre on the front and reverse of the vessel, using copper-oxide pigments.[41] Due to the paucity of material finds for this ware, it has been assumed that this type of lustre pottery had a very short production span which began and ended in 9th-century Iraq. In the absence of any material evidence from the 11th and 12th centuries, one can only postulate that the medieval Egyptian potters may have produced red-glazed pottery similar to ruby-lustre.[42]

Finally, the painted wares of various sizes 'with different colours and figures' described in the third letter from the Geniza, may be referring to the types of pottery excavated at Fustat with figural decoration executed in various techniques of over- and under-glaze painting using manganese-black pigments.[43] They could, however, refer to lustre ceramics decorated with a variety of figural subjects that appear to have been produced in abundance in Egypt throughout the Fatimid period. The colours of the lustre ranged from golden-yellow and copper-brown to olive-green, which were usually painted over an opaque-white glazed clay body.[44] It was however, the lustrous silvery and golden sheen on this pottery that made it so popular.

Lustre pottery was an innovation of the potters of 'Abbasid Iraq and its international appeal is attested by the appearance of Iraqi lustre shards at excavations in Spain, North Africa, Egypt, Syria, Pakistan, Iran and Thailand.[45] Lustre pigments, made of silver and copper-oxides, were painted in a variety of designs on the surface of an already glazed vessel, which was then re-fired under special conditions. The results of a successful re-firing created a ceramic ware with a painted decoration that gleamed like gold or silver. Unlike its Iraqi counterpart, lustre

pottery produced in Egypt appears to have had a more limited geographic distribution to the areas within Fatimid domains and to regions where the Fatimids had Mediterranean trading partners.[46]

The craftsmen of Fustat used the lustre technique on both glass and pottery[47] and several medieval Islamic sources mention these wares in both urban and royal contexts, suggesting a broad range of quality. For example, in his *Safarnama* ('Book of Travels'), the Persian *da'i*, Nasir Khusraw (d. after 1073), offered his impression of lustre painted objects in the markets of al-Fustat during his visit to Fatimid Egypt in the mid 11th century: 'In Old Cairo they make all types of pottery they make cups, bowls, plates and so forth, and paint them to resemble the *buqalamun* [textile] so that different hues show depending on how the article is held.'[48]

In another passage he explains: 'In this city of Tinnis they weave [a type of cloth called] *buqalamun*, which is found nowhere else in the world. It is an iridescent cloth that appears to be of different hues at different times of the day.'[49]

Additionally, Arab writers likened the effects of *buqalamun* to peacock feathers,[50] and the Geniza documents also mention iridescent textiles designated as *ta'usi* or 'like a peacock'.[51] Thus, it is highly plausible that the peacock-eye motif that often surrounds the principal image of lustre bowls, such as on the famous giraffe lustre bowl, was a deliberately self-referential symbol.[52] The unrestricted use of the peacock-eye motif as a background pattern may have symbolised the wondrous effect of light and the play of colour seen on peacock's feathers, the *buqalamun* textile, and on lustre-painted objects.[53]

Nasir Khusraw's account confirms that lustre pottery was easily attainable in the Egyptian markets as affordable luxury ceramics, and the Geniza documents confirm that people ordered this ware from pottery workshops. According to one letter, earthenware goblets with gold lustre (*saghara fukhkhar matliyya*) were ordered in al-Fustat.[54] Furthermore, the 11th-century *Book of Gifts and Rarities* firmly locates lustre ceramics in a royal context as part of the items stored in the Fatimid palace treasuries alongside costly Chinese porcelains:

There were found vaults (*khaza'in*) full of all kinds of Chinaware (*sini*) [commonly] used by people. Six of them contained large and small porcelain basins (*ajajin*) resting on three legs (*arjul*) in the form of lions, people and animals. Each basin was worth a thousand dinars. They were made for washing laundry. There were found [other] vaults full of all kinds of trays painted [or embellished – *madhuna*] with gold. Each was ten spans or less wide, so that one accommodated the second smaller one [and so on], ending with one [tray] whose size was less than that of a dirham.[55]

It appears that members of the Fatimid court already used lustre ceramics in their palaces in North Africa, before the establishment of the Fatimid state in Cairo. An early 10th-century account by the North African Fatimid *da'i*,[56] Ibn al-Haytham, describes a lavish meal in the palace at Raqqada:

As I entered [Abu'l-'Abbas] commanded Sulayman to remove my boots. Sulayman took off the boots, folded the *taylasan* and turban, and brought out the washing water in a silver vessel. He then brought out a new gilded dining table [*sufra jadida mudhahhaba*], and another table [*ma'ida*] carried by two servants was brought in, over which was a bamboo cover that concealed all of it. A servant removed the covering revealing an array of food in gilded Chinese [i.e. China] bowls [*bi-sakarij mudhahhaba siniyya*]. There followed a continuous succession of hot food of marvellous concoction.[57]

Lustre-painted trays stored in the Fatimid treasuries may have been on public display during the Nile inundation ceremonies held in Fatimid Egypt in 1123, according to the account of the Mamluk historian, al-Maqrizi (d. 1442): 'In 517/1123 (gold or lustre?) trays (*al-sawani al-dhahab*) filled with human and animal figurines were brought in addition to the wall hangings and carpets. There were elephants, giraffes, lions and other beasts made of gold, silver, and amber, all ornamented with pearls, sapphires and chrysolite.'[58]

Public celebrations held at the time of the Nile inundation and the two Great Festivals,[59] were occasions that allowed the inhabitants of Cairo and Fustat to participate in the ceremonies of the court. The Fatimid caliphs al-'Aziz (975–996), al-Hakim (996–1021), and al-Zahir (1021–1036), rode with full regalia in grand processions through Cairo accompanied by their troops, courtiers and bedecked elephants and giraffes.[60] We have already mentioned the famous lustre bowl depicting a groom leading a caparisoned giraffe, and although we do not know who the owner of this bowl was, it has been confirmed that it was painted by the artist, Muslim b. al-Dahhan.[61] Not much is known about Muslim[62] except that he was certainly active as a lustre potter during the reign of the Fatimid caliph, al-Hakim bi-Amr Allah.[63] There is, therefore, a strong case to argue that Muslim, or artists from his atelier, witnessed these processions during the reign of al-Hakim, or that of his son and heir al-Zahir, and that the image on this bowl refers precisely to these events. It must be pointed out that the groom leading the bedecked giraffe on the lustre bowl is depicted in attire decorated with *tiraz* bands, which further suggests the context of a royal procession.[64]

A recent study by Viktoria Meinecke-Berg has established that there are perhaps four other 'giraffe bowls' in existence very similar to the bowl under discussion.[65] This implies that Muslim and members of his atelier were commissioned to produce several lustre bowls depicting an adorned giraffe and running groom. These bowls may have served a commemorative purpose following such grand occasions during the reign of al-Hakim or al-Zahir. The bowls, as commemorative gifts, could have served as a means of celebrating these ceremonies after the event, and for disseminating a message of political stability amongst a wider audience.[66] A striking parallel to this lustre bowl was produced as a French porcelain dish in the 19th century – eight centuries after the Egyptian piece was made. This porcelain dish, depicting a bridled giraffe with her Arab groom, was commissioned on the occasion of the presentation of a Masai giraffe in 1826 to the French King, Charles X, by Muhammad 'Ali, the Ottoman viceroy of Egypt.[67]

Medieval Egyptian ceramics represent a period of experimentation and innovation design, clay recipes, glazes and techniques of decoration. These developments in Egyptian ceramics influenced the pottery industries of Syria, Iran and beyond. During a period of active maritime trade, al-Fustat and Cairo attracted people from faraway lands who brought with them their ideas, skills, tastes and artistic wares, all of which influenced the local production of pottery. The sheer variety of lively figural, vegetal and epigraphic designs on Egyptian pottery established the medieval potters as artisans of exceptional creativity and skill, who drew inspiration from their past and present. At a deeper level, everyday vessels functioned as metaphors of life. John Lewis Burckhardt's collection of Egyptian proverbs from the early 19th century attests to the longevity of the material found in Henein's present-day study. The adage, *hisab al-quwwar 'ala al-duwwar* (The [broken] pots are charged to the one who carries them about on his head), refers to those who are rich but make the poor pay for their mishaps. A *duwwar*'s profession is to sell pots by carrying them about on his head, and though he gives most of the proceeds to the potter, he is held accountable for any breakages.[68] A more philosophical message from the famous Persian poet and scholar, 'Umar Khayyam (*circa* 1048–1123), recalls a sentiment similar to the contemporary Egyptian proverb, 'Do not cry over your [broken] pottery, you have the same destiny':

Last night I dropped and smashed my porcelain bowl,
A clumsy folly in a bout of drinking.
The shattered bowl in dumb appeal cried out,
'I was like you, you too will be like me!'[69]

Sitting one evening in the potter's store,
I watched the potter as he spun his wheel;
Deftly he shaped a handle and a lid
From a pauper's hand and from a monarch's head.[70]

1 From Nessim Henry Henein, *Poteries et proverbes d'Égypte* (Cairo, 1992), p. 66, no. 140. Henein collected these proverbs in the early 1990s. I would like to thank Dr Zeina Khouri-Klink and Dr Jeremy Johns for their helpful comments in the preparation of this paper. The subject of this paper is explored further in the chapter 'Pottery in the Written Sources', in Fahmida Suleman, *The Lion, the Hare and Lustre Ware: Studies in the Iconography of Lustre Ceramics from Fatimid Egypt (969–1171 CE)*, D.Phil. thesis (University of Oxford, 2004), pp. 35–61.

2 Henein, *Poteries et proverbes*, p. 65, nos 138–139.

3 Exceptions to this are the *hisba* manuals, guidebooks for the *muhtasib* (market inspector), which have come down to us from the Mamluk period. See for example Ibn al-Ukhuwwa, *The Ma'alim al-qurba fi ahkam al-hisba of Diya' al-Din Muhammad ibn Muhammad al-Qurashi al-Shafi'i known as Ibn al-Ukhuwwa (d.729/1329)*, ed. and tr. Reuben Levy (Cambridge, 1938), pp. 89, 223–224.

4 For an excellent study of the manufacture, trade and use of ceramics in the Ayyubid and Mamluk periods see Marcus Milwright, 'Pottery in the Written Sources of the Ayyubid-Mamluk Period (ca. 567–923/1171–1517)', *BSOAS*, 62 (1999), pp. 504–518.

5 Fustat was the commercial and industrial city, just south of Cairo, where the majority of the urban population lived in the Fatimid period. Al-Qahira (short for, 'Al-Qahira al-Mu'izziyya', 'the victorious city of al-Mu'izz'), is the Arabic name from which 'Cairo' is derived and the city was founded by the Fatimids in 969 (though named by al-Mu'izz in 973) as their royal and administrative capital. I shall use Cairo throughout.

6 The English word 'pottery' generally denotes earthenware vessels made of baked clay, which may be glazed or unglazed. Whereas, the term 'ceramics' often connotes glazed vessels made of both coarser earthenware clays and those that have hardening or whitening additives such as sand or quartz. 'Porcelain' or 'china' are more specific terms denoting a hard, white, translucent ceramic made of fine white clay, which is glazed and fired at high temperatures.

7 For this etymology see E. W. Lane, *An Arabic-English Lexicon*, Book 1, Part 4 (London, 1863), p. 1757.

8 Abu Mansur al-Tha'alibi, *The Book of Curious and Entertaining Information, the Lata'if al-ma'arif of al-Tha'alibi*, tr. C. E. Bosworth (Edinburgh, 1968), p. 141. For the Arabic see idem, *Kitab lata'if al-ma'arif*, ed. P. de Jong (Leiden, 1867), p. 127.

9 For a general survey of archeological sites where Chinese pottery has been found see Basil Gray, 'The Export of Chinese Porcelain to the Islamic World: Some Reflections on its Significance for Islamic Art, Before 1400', *Transactions of the Oriental Ceramic Society*, 41 (1975–1977), pp. 231–261. For a more recent survey of Islamic excavation sites in the Levant see Marcus Milwright, 'Gazetteer of Archaeological Sites in the Levant Reporting Pottery of the Middle Islamic Period (ca. 1100–1600)', *Islamic Art*, 5 (2001), pp. 3–39.

10 George T. Scanlon, 'Egypt and China: Trade and Imitation', in D. S. Richards, ed., *Islam and the Trade of Asia* (Oxford, 1970), p. 85.

11 Scanlon, 'Egypt and China', p. 88. Scanlon's excavation reports for Fustat have been published in several volumes of the *Journal of the American Research Center in Egypt*. For a complete bibliography see George T. Scanlon and W. B. Kubiak, *Fustat Expedition Final Report: Volume Two, Fustat-C*. (Lake Winona, IN, 1988).

12 Several studies have been carried out on the trade of Chinese ceramics and its impact on the pottery of the Islamic world through the ages. In addition to the articles by Scanlon, 'Egypt and China' and Gray, 'The Export of Chinese Porcelain', already cited, others include: Yolande Crowe, 'Early Islamic Pottery and China', *Transactions of the Oriental Ceramic Society*, 41 (1975–1977), pp. 263–278; Lisa Golombek et al., *Tamerlane's Tableware: A New Approach to Chinoiserie Ceramics of Fifteenth- and Sixteenth-Century Iran* (California, 1996); and Jessica Hallett, *Trade and Innovation: The Rise of a Pottery Industry in Abbasid Basra*, D.Phil. thesis (University of Oxford, 2000).

13 Tin-opacified glaze results as opaque white after firing because of the presence of numerous particles of tin oxide. This type of glaze (which also included lead) was developed by Iraqi potters in the 8th century and does not appear to have been produced before the Islamic period. See Sheila R. Canby, 'Islamic Lustreware', in Ian Freestone and David Gaimster, ed., *Pottery in the Making: World Ceramic Traditions* (London, 1997), p. 111. Since tin was an expensive imported metal a cheaper opacifying method, also employed by potters of the Islamic world, was the use of alkaline glazes. See Jonathan Bloom and Sheila Blair, *Islamic Arts* (London, 1997), pp. 107–108.

14 The addition of enough ground quartz to the clay (a ratio of roughly 10:1) ultimately resulted in a new ceramic body which modern scholars variably term 'stone-paste' or 'fritware'. Scholarly debate continues on the origins of 'true stone-paste' wares in the Islamic world. For the argument in favour of Egypt's role in this development as opposed to Iran's see Oliver Watson, 'Fritware: Fatimid Egypt or Saljuq Iran?', in Marianne Barrucand, ed., *L'Égypte Fatimide: son art et son histoire* (Paris, 1999), p. 302.

15 Lane, *Arab-English Lexicon*, Book 1, Part 6 (London, 1877), p. 2350. See also Jean Sauvaget's study of these terms in his, 'Introduction à l'étude de la céramique musulmane', *Revue des Études Islamiques*, 33 (1965), pp. 44–50.

16 The *fakhkhar* thus had a different profession from a *qaddar*, a maker of pots and other receptacles, and a *kuzi*, a maker of narrow-necked water jugs without spouts. See S. D. Goitein, *A Mediterranean Society: The Jewish Communities of the Arab World as Portrayed in the Documents of the Cairo Geniza*, vol. 1: 'Economic Foundations' (Berkeley and Los Angeles, CA, 1967), pp. 110–111.

17 *Mediterranean Society*, vol. 4: 'Daily Life', p. 148 and note 77. Further discussion of this pottery and others mentioned in this section follows later.

18 Lane, *Arab-English Lexicon*, Book 1, Part 6, p. 2266. It is also found vocalised as *ghudar*. See Sauvaget, 'Introduction', p. 45.

19 *Mediterranean Society*, vol. 4: 'Daily Life', p. 146 and note 52, and for *ghada'iri* see, *Mediterranean Society*, vol. 1: 'Economic Foundations', p. 111.

20 See J. G. Hava, *ghadara* – plural, *ghada'ir* meaning, 'large dish, bowl', *al-Fara'id Arabic-English Dictionary* (Beirut, 1982). For this phrase see al-Tha'alibi, *Curious and Entertaining Information*, p. 112 and idem, *Lata'if al-Ma'arif*, p. 87.

21 The documents that have come down to us were stored in a synagogue of one of the three Jewish groups in Fustat, that is the Palestinian Jews. Hence the Iraqi (Babylonian) and the Karaite Jews of Fustat, as well as the Jews of Cairo and other Egyptian cities, must have had their own genizas in which to store their documents, which have not come down to us. See Paul E. Walker, *Exploring an Islamic Empire: Fatimid History and its Sources* (London, 2002), pp. 128–130, for a discussion of the limitations of this material as an historical source for the Fatimid period.

22 This cache of documents dating from the 10th to the 13th century was discovered in 1890 and S. D. Goitein's (1900–1985) remarkable study of this material has been published in six volumes and several articles.

23 *Mediterranean Society*, vol. 4: 'Daily Life', p. 142.

24 The clay filter and jar were formed separately, and then the filter was joined to the inside of the neck of the receptacle before firing. See George T. Scanlon, *Fustat Expedition Final Report: Volume One, Catalogue of Filters*, A.R.C.E Reports 8 (Lake Winona, IN, 1986).

25 See the Paris catalogue of Fatimid art, *Trésors Fatimides du Caire* (Paris, 1998), cat. nos 134–145, pp. 181–183, for examples.

26 Paris, *Trésors Fatimides,* cat. nos 128–133, p. 181. These filters have been variously dated from the 10th to the 12th centuries. Baked-clay water jugs are still used in present-day Egypt and are also called *qulla* (pronounced √olla in colloquial Egyptian) or *mashrabiyya*, 'lattice-work', which probably refers to the filter decoration, though none appear to be as elaborate as the medieval filters. See Henein, *Poteries et proverbes*, p. 20 for modern examples.

27 *Mediterranean Society*, vol. 4: 'Daily Life', pp. 142–143, 145. For a typology of medieval vessel shapes and their uses see Sauvaget, 'Introduction', pp. 51ff.

28 According to the bridal trousseau lists in the Geniza, gold jewellery and textile items ranked the highest in both monetary and social value.

29 *Mediterranean Society*, vol. 4: 'Daily Life', pp. 105–106, and see also p. 146.

30 Ibid., pp. 145–146. Goitein has translated the term *sini* in this case as fine earthenware and emphasises that it should not be read as Chinese porcelain, and if 'it is described as translucent, or is included in a luxurious trousseau, [then] it might have been porcelain'. He does not give the value of these bowls.

31 *Mediterranean Society*, vol. 4: 'Daily Life', p. 145.

32 Ibid., p. 322, no. 28.

33 Ibid., p. 322, nos 10, 24.

34 Goitein has translated this as a porcelain box with silver lustre. The term *muhalla* generally means to ornament, decorate or embellish. The verb *h*

alla (*bi-dhahab*) could mean to gild, so perhaps *muhalla bi-fidda* might mean silver gilt or silver lustre. Ghada al-Qaddumi translates *muhalla* as 'embellished and bedecked'. See *Book of Gifts and Rarities (Kitab al-hadaya wa'l-tuhaf): Selections Compiled in the Fifteenth Century from an Eleventh-Century Manuscript on Gifts and Treasures*, tr. Ghada al-Qaddumi (Cambridge, MA, 1996), pp. 80, 86, 103. For the Arabic see *Kitab al-dhakha'ir wa'l-tuhaf li'l-Qadi al-Rashid b. al-Zubair*, ed. Muhammad Hamid Allah (Kuwait, 1959), pp. 31, 41, 67. See also Hava, *halla bi-dhahab* 'to gild a thing' in *al-Fara'id*. See *muhallan* as 'decorated, embellished' in Hans Wehr, *A Dictionary of Modern Written Arabic* (3rd ed., New York, 1976).

35 *Mediterranean Society*, vol. 4: 'Daily Life', p. 145.

36 Ibid., p. 146.

37 Ibid., p. 146. The term used to describe the colour was *'aqiq*.

38 Ibid., p. 146.

39 Scanlon, 'Egypt and China', p. 88. Sgraffiato comes from the Italian *sgraffire*, 'to scratch', and refers to the decorative technique of incising a design into the body of a vessel before applying a glaze.

40 George T. Scanlon, 'Fustat Fatimid Sgraffiato: Less Than Lustre', in Barrucand, ed., *L'Égypte Fatimide*, p. 265.

41 See Ernst J. Grube, ed., *Cobalt and Lustre: The First Centuries of Islamic Pottery. The Nasser D. Khalili Collection of Islamic Art*, vol. IX (London, 1994), cat. no. 19, p.27, for an image of a ruby-lustre bowl and for further bibliography.

42 Excavations by Scanlon at Fustat have uncovered ruby lustre although it has been dated to the Tulunid period. See George T. Scanlon, '1965 – Fustat Expedition Preliminary Report', *Journal of the American Research Center in Egypt*, 8 (1966), p. 89.

43 For examples of lead glazed wares with figures

painted in green and manganese-black see Helen Philon, *Early Islamic Ceramics: Ninth to Late Twelfth Centuries*, Athens Benaki Museum Collection (London, 1980), pp. 55–57, figs. 117–121 and colour plate IV. For examples of manganese-black painted wares in over- and under-glaze techniques using clear and turquoise glazes see Philon, *Early Islamic Ceramics*, pp. 260–261.

44 For examples of turquoise-glazed lustre bowls see the Paris catalogue, *Trésors Fatimides*, cat. nos 41 and 120, pp. 115, 177.

45 Archeological evidence attests that the technique of lustre decoration originated in Egypt and Syria on glass, possibly as early as the 4th–5th century, although the earliest dated piece of lustre glass originates from Egypt, (dated 773). See Scanlon, '1965 – Fustat Expedition', pp. 83–112. However, 9th-century Iraqi potters invented the technique of lustre decoration on a ceramic body. For the history and technique of lustre pottery through the ages, see Alan Caiger-Smith, *Lustre Pottery: Technique, Tradition and Innovation in Islam and the Western World* (London, 1985).

46 Lustre distribution in Fatimid domains included Egypt, Palestine and the areas down the Red Sea coast into Yemen, and in the Mediterranean regions such as Italy where the Fatimids had trading partners. Evidence of the latter are the *bacini*, which were lustre and other types of ceramic bowls that were used to decorate the façades of medieval Italian churches. See G. Berti and L. Tongiorgi, *I bacini ceramici medievali delle chiese di Pisa* (Rome, 1981).

47 It has been suggested that the similarities of the designs and production methods of both lustre-painted glass and lustre pottery point to a common workshop for these ateliers. See Anna Contadini, *Fatimid Art at the Victoria and Albert Museum* (London, 1998), p. 96 and note 61.

48 Nasir Khusraw, *Safarnama (Book of Travels)*, tr. W. M. Thackston Jr. (New York, 1986), p. 54.

49 Ibid., p. 39.

50 Ibn al-Haytham (d. 1040), a scientist and mathematician of the Fatimid period, likens the textile *abu qalamun* to peacock feathers as they both 'appear to change their appearance at different times of the day according to the different lights shining upon them'. Ibn al-Haytham, *The Optics of Ibn al-Haytham*, tr. A. I. Sabra, vol. 1 (London, 1989), 1:4:25.

51 *Mediterranean Society*, vol. 1: 'Economic Foundations', pp. 106 and 419, note 41.

52 This bowl depicting a groom leading a giraffe, from the Benaki Museum, Athens (acc.no. 749), is dated to the first quarter of the 11th century.

53 One could argue that the reverse decoration on lustre bowls comprising concentric circles and dashes also refers to the large iridescent 'eyes' and fine feathers of peacocks' tails. See Suleman, *The Lion, the Hare*, pp. 46–49.

54 *Mediterranean Society*, vol. 4: 'Daily Life', p. 148 and note 77. The term *saghara* is derived from the Persian loanword, *saghar*, 'goblet', and the term *matliyya* from *tala* (*bi-dhahab*) carries the meaning 'to gild a thing', and probably refers to lustre decoration. See Hava, *al-Fara'id*, under the verb *tala*. *Matliyya* (*bi al-dhahab*) also occurs in the *Book of Gifts and Rarities*, which al-Qaddumi translates as 'overlaid or over-coated with gold', p. 99.

55 *Book of Gifts*, pp. 34–35. The complete Arabic phrase is *al-sawani al-madhuna al-mudhahhaba*, which al-Qaddumi translates as, 'trays painted with gold', although it could equally be translated as 'ceramics (*i.e. sawani*) painted or embellished in gold'. For the Arabic text see *Kitab al-Dhakha'ir*, p. 256.

56 I would like to thank Dr Jeremy Johns for the reference to this account, which was written by Ibn al-Haytham between 909 and 910. See

below for full reference information.

57 *Sakarij* (sing. *sukurruja, sukruja*) denotes bowls, platters or plates. Ibn al-Haytham, *The Advent of the Fatimids: A Contemporary Shi'i Witness (An Edition and English Translation of Ibn al-Haytham's Kitab al-Munazarat)*, ed. and tr. Wilferd Madelung and Paul E. Walker (London, 2000), p. 107 (Arabic text), p. 153 (English translation). Lustre ceramics were also produced in North Africa since Iraqi lustre tiles and a skilled lustre potter were sent by the 'Abbasid caliph to Qayrawan in *circa* 862–863 to decorate the Great Mosque there. Lustre production in Ifriqiya is also attested in the account of the traveller, Ibn Hawqal (*circa* 950). See Georges Marçais, *Les Faïences à réflets métalliques de la Grande Mosquée de Kairouan* (Paris, 1928), pp. 9–11.

58 Paula Sanders, *Ritual, Politics, and the City in Fatimid Cairo* (New York, 1994), pp. 105–106. Al-Maqrizi, *Kitab al-mawa'iz wa'l-i'tibar bi-dhikr al-khitat wa'l-athar* (Bulaq, 1853), vol. 1, p. 472. The term *siniyya'* appears in the Geniza documents and is translated as 'a round tray', often made of copper or brass. However, the word *sawani*, which is the plural of *sini* (i.e. porcelain, ceramics), is also given by Hava as a possible plural for *siniyya*, 'in the Syrian dialect', though this is not given in Lane's dictionary, or in Goitein's study of the Geniza documents. Hence, the phrase *al-sawani al-dhahab* could mean 'lustre pottery wares', or possibly 'round trays made of gold'. The latter meaning may be more likely in this instance. See *Mediterranean Society*, vol. 4: 'Daily Life', pp. 145–146. See Hava, *sini – sawani*, in *al-Fara'id*.

59 These are the two Muslim festivals of *'Id al-fitr* (Festival of Fast-breaking) and *'Id al-nahr*, also known as *'Id al-adha* (Festival of Abraham's Sacrifice).

60 For these accounts see al-Musabbih, (d. 1029), *Akhbar Misr* (Chapter 40, AH 414–415): vol. 1, *Partie*

Historique, ed. A. F. Sayyid and T. Bianquis (Cairo, 1978), pp. 65ff., 80–81, 451. See also al-Maqrizi, *Khitat,* vol. 1, p. 451. See idem, *Itti'az al-hunafa' bi-akhbar al-a'imma al-Fatimiyyin al-khulafa',* ed. Jamal al-Din al-Shayyal and M. H. M. Ahmad (Cairo, 1967–1973), vol. 1, p. 279 and vol. 2, p. 58. See also Viktoria Meinecke-Berg, 'Das Giraffenbild des fatimidischen Keramikmalers Muslim', *Damaszener Mitteilungen,* 11 (1999), p. 335.

61 His name literally means, 'Muslim, the son of the Painter'. The evidence for Muslim, or his atelier, producing this bowl is convincingly presented by Viktoria Meinecke-Berg in 'Fatimid Painting on Tradition and Style: The Workshop of Muslim', in M. Barrucand, ed., *L'Égypte Fatimide,* pp. 349–358.

62 See 'Abd al-Ra'uf 'Ali Yusuf, *'Khazzafun min al-'asr al-Fatimi wa asalibuhum al-fanniyya'* (Potters of the Fatimid Period and Their Artistic Styles), *Bulletin of the Faculty of Arts, University of Cairo,* 20 (1962),

pp. 173–223 and plates. See also Marilyn Jenkins, 'Safid: Content and Context', in P. Soucek, ed., *Content and Context of Visual Arts in the Islamic World* (Pennsylvania and London, 1988), pp. 67–75.

63 We know this because Muslim signed another bowl which included the name of his patron, who was one of al-Hakim's associates, [Abu?] al-Hasan Iqbal al-Hakimi. See Marilyn Jenkins, 'Muslim: An Early Fatimid Ceramist', *Bulletin of the Metropolitan Museum of Art,* 26 (New York, 1968), pp. 359–369.

64 *Tiraz* is defined as linen textiles with inscribed or decorative bands, often, though not always associated with the court. For an explanation of the production and use of *tiraz* fabrics in the Fatimid period see Contadini, *Fatimid Art,* pp. 39–58. For a discussion on the iconography of this bowl see Suleman, *The Lion, the Hare*, pp. 131–155.

65 Meinecke-Berg, 'Fatimid Painting', pp. 354–355 and idem, 'Das Giraffenbild', p. 333 and note 8.

66 For an interpretation of Fatimid ceremonial and the purposes behind some of them see Sanders, *Ritual, Politics, and the City,* pp. 66–67.

67 An account of this giraffe's journey from Ethiopia to France is given by Michael Allin in *Zarafa* (London, 1999).

68 Burckhardt comments that many of these proverbs were formerly collected by an 18th-century shaykh. John Lewis Burckhardt, tr., *Arabic Proverbs; or the Manners and Customs of the Modern Egyptians, Illustrated from their Proverbial Sayings Current at Cairo,* ed. William Ouseley (London, 1830), p. 71, no. 224.

69 'Umar Khayyam, see Dashti, Ali, *In Search of Omar Khayyam,* tr. L. P. Elwell-Sutton (London, 1971), quatrain no. 40, p. 194.

70 Khayyam, *In Search of Omar Khayyam,* quatrain no. 39, p. 193.

Jonathan H. Shannon

Cairo, *Umm al-Dunya*, the Mother of the World – and the Mother sings. Walk through her streets today and you are presented with a richly textured tapestry of sounds: from the legendary Umm Kulthum holding forth from a crackling radio in the back of an old cafe, to the latest 'Amru Diab hit blasting from a passing car, to the call to prayer floating melodiously above the veritable cacophony of voices, shouts and sounds that constitutes the modern Cairo soundscape. Moving back in time, one would find a similarly rich musical culture in the city going back many centuries, for Cairo has been an important centre, if not *the* centre, for music in the Arab East for many generations. From the current plethora of pop stars singing from the Nile to the Big Three of 20th-century Arab music – Muhammad 'Abd al-Wahab, 'Abd al-Halim Hafiz and of course, the greatest, Umm Kulthum – and back in time to the great masters of the late 19th and early 20th century – 'Abduh Hamuli, Salama Higazi and Sayyid Darwish – some of the greatest music the Arab world has known has come from Egypt and in particular from Cairo, which has drawn the best and brightest talents from around the Arab world to its cosmopolitan cultural scene.

The roots of music in Historic Cairo go back many generations before 'Abd al-Wahab and Umm Kulthum appeared on the scene. These stars drank from a deep well of musical inspiration: religious chant, folk music, Andalusian song and urban art music are only some of the diverse forms of the musical culture of Historic Cairo. Although we have no recordings or accurate records of the kind of music performed in the earliest years of Cairo's existence (beginning at the end of the 10th century), a little sonic archeology will allow us to 'listen' to what the sounds may have been like in times past.

What follows is a brief sonic excavation of the City Victorious through six 'layers' of sound, beginning (in reverse chronology) with the founding of the city in the 10th century and ending with the present. Excavation brings to light the social and political contexts in each layer, and allows us to listen for the major styles of music and song, and the primary instruments, artists and forms of technology employed in music-making.

LAYER I *Fatimid Cairo, 10th–12th Century*

Cairo (*al-Qahira*, 'The Victorious') was founded in AH 358/AD 969 by the Fatimid dynasty, near the site of the ancient Pharaonic capital of Memphis and the early Islamic city of al-Fustat. The Fatimids were a Shi'i Ismaili Muslim dynasty who came to Egypt from North Africa, ushering in an era of cultural efflorescence and religious tolerance. We have little information about the performance of music in Cairo during its early years, but there can be little doubt that the city's musical culture partook of the richness of Fatimid cultural and intellectual life, which brought together influences from North Africa, medieval Europe, the Sudan and the Levant. The music of Fatimid Cairo would have mirrored in splendour, and possibly in style and form, the intricate ornamentation of its mosques and palaces. The harmony and beauty of Islamic art, architecture and calligraphy in Fatimid Cairo[1] suggests that there must have been a unified aural-visual aesthetic, and it is perhaps no coincidence that Egypt was the first Muslim land to embrace the melodious recitation of the Qur'an (an art form known as *tajwid*) and call to prayer (*adhan*). The sound of the recitation of the Qur'an was heard in mosques and homes around the Fatimid city and formed a component of a genre of Islamic chant known as *inshad*.[2]

There was a rich urban musical tradition as well. By the time the Fatimids founded Cairo, Muslim musical theorists and philosophers such as al-Kindi, al-Farabi and the Ikhwan al-Safa' had developed sophisticated theories of music that strove to understand music in terms of its relationship to the fields of mathematics, astronomy, geography, ethics and, last but not least, philosophy. Musical melodies and modes were thought to correspond to specific times of day, cosmological configurations and the bodily humours and dispositions.[3] This early Muslim music would have been performed in the Fatimid courts and the palaces, using such instruments as the '*ud* (a short-necked lute), and possibly a psaltery similar to the modern-day *qanun*. Frame drums, flutes and poet-vocalists would have rounded out the ensembles.

al-Andalus – such as the Jewish scholar and physician, Maimonides, and the Muslim mystic, Ibn al-'Arabi – as well as refugees from the Christian advances in the Iberian peninsula, brought with them to Cairo their rich artistic legacies, including the art of the *muwashshah* (pl. *muwash-shahat*), a poetic-musical genre developed from earlier Arabian and Iberian song styles in the fertile cradle of Andalusian culture.[4] Egyptians began to sing and compose their own *muwashshahat* as early as the 12th century, as the collection *Dar al-Tiraz* by Ibn Sana' al-Mulk indicates.[5] At the same time, the Sufi orders of mystics became widespread in the Muslim lands, enriching the practices of *inshad* with the *dhikr*, a ritual remembrance of God based on chanting and ecstatic dance. Many of the *muwashshahat* that made their way from al-Andalus were of a religious or Sufi nature, and these became the staple of ritual life in Cairene mosques, Qur'anic schools (*kuttab*s) and Sufi lodges (*zawiya*s).

In addition to the elite and scholarly genres of music performed at the Fatimid court, music in Cairo during this period no doubt drew extensively on the rich folk music traditions of the Nile Valley. These would have been performed on instruments such as the *rabab*, a two-stringed spike-fiddle, drums such as the *tabl*, and wind and reed instruments such as the *salamiyya* and *mizmar*.

LAYER II *Ayyubid and Mamluk Cairo, 12th–15th Century*
The next level in this sonic excavation takes us into 12th-century Cairo, where we find that the Fatimids have lost control of Cairo to the Ayyubids, led by Salah al-Din al-Ayyubi ('Saladin'). By the middle of the 13th century, the Mamluks, the elite cavalry corps of the Ayyubid army, had taken control of Cairo and the empire of Egypt and Syria from the Ayyubids, thus initiating a regime which lasted nearly three centuries.

During this tumultuous time of Crusades and internal dissent, the musical culture of the city retained its Fatimid flavour but was enriched by influences coming from Muslim Spain (al-Andalus), Anatolia and Persia. Travelling scholars and religious authorities from

LAYER III *Ottoman Cairo – 16th–20th Century*
Moving forward, sonic excavation reveals one of the richest periods in the development of Cairo's musical culture: the era of Ottoman rule. The defeat of the Mamluk sultan al-Ghawri in 1516 ushered in the era of Ottoman domination in Egypt and the Levant. In addition to the rich panoply of architectural monuments from this period – exquisite mosques and palaces, ornate *sabil*s (fountains), tombs and the impressive development of the Citadel – the Ottoman period also saw the establishment of a rich tradition of courtly music in Istanbul, its imperial capital, and in also Cairo, Aleppo and other regional centres. This tradition was a mixture of the musical cultures of the previous eras, especially the Mamluk-era *muwashshahat*, and the cyclical song forms of what developed into the Turkish *fasil* and Levantine *wasla*, as well as vocal and instrumental styles from Persia and the Balkans.[6]

19TH-CENTURY CAIRO
Sonic excavations in 17th and 18th-century Cairo reveal the growth of an increasingly complex Ottoman musical culture. As we enter the 19th century, however, the soundscape becomes even more complex

and rich than in previous generations. By the 19th century, Cairo was one of the most important centres for musical life in the Levant along with Aleppo. The roots of modern Arabian song are to be found in 19th-century Cairo, an important centre of Arab modernity beginning with the reforms initiated by Muhammad 'Ali Pasha in the early 1800s.

As Cairo was transformed by Muhammad 'Ali and his successors from the capital of an Ottoman province into a cosmopolitan independent capital, there arose a style of music notable for its emotional tenor and complex song forms. Its most famous exponent in the 19th century was the great 'Abduh al-Hamuli (1847–1901), who led a musical renaissance that borrowed from Egyptian, Turkish, Syrian and Persian musical elements to forge a unique style sometimes called 'Khedival', referring to the khedive or Ottoman vicegerent of Egypt, and an indication that this was music performed for the elite.[7] Other well-known artists of this period who performed in Cairo included the great vocalists and composers Yusuf al-Manyalawi (1847–1911), Salama Higazi (1852–1917), Muhammad 'Uthman (*circa* 1855–1900), the Syrian Ahmad Abu Khalil al-Qabbani (1842–1904), 'Abd al-Hay Hilmi (1857–1912) and others.[8] Called shuyukh (sing. shaykh), the prominent singers of this era had often had training in the art of Islamic chant (*inshad*).[9] Musicians from more conservative Damascus also emigrated to Cairo and contributed to the development of its growing artistic scene, the most prominent of these being Abu Khalil al-Qabbani, a founder of the musical theatre, and Sami al-Shawwa (1889–1965), 'Prince of the Violin'.

These male vocalists would perform for mostly male audiences consisting of the Khedive and elite classes, and, by the late 19th century, in Cairo's new theatres, salons and in the tents (*saradiq*) of the Azbakiyya Gardens, scene of a cosmopolitan nightlife in the late 19th century. By the 1880s there had appeared in Cairo the first professional musical theatre groups, which performed sketches and plays, sometimes adapted from European repertoires. For example, in 1890 Salama Higazi played the role of Romeo in an adaptation of Shakespeare's *Romeo and Juliet*.[10] This would form the basis for important developments in 20th-century Cairene music and song.

Although we know more about the male singers, the so-called *shuyukh* or *mashayikh*, women singers, musicians and dancers were also an important part of Cairene musical life in the 19th century, as they had been throughout the Islamic world for many centuries. Known as *'alima*s and *usta*s, professional female performers sang, danced and played instruments at weddings and other private celebrations, often from behind a screen in order to maintain a sense of decorum.[11] By the late 19th century they were taking to the stage alongside their male counterparts in the musical theatre, as well as performing in more public settings such as cafes, salons and the infamous cabarets of the Azbakiyya. Munira al-Mahdiyya (1884–1965), known later as the 'Sultana of Song', began her career as an *'alima* in the famous 'Eldorado' cabaret. By 1914 she was singing and acting on the public stage, and is often regarded as the first Muslim woman to have performed on the public stage before a male audience.[12]

An important musical development in 19th-century Cairo was the consolidation of a performance genre known as the *wasla*.[13] The *wasla* is a cycle or suite of vocal and improvisational genres that includes instrumental preludes (*sama'i, bashraf* and *tahmila*), the *muwashshah*, the *qasida* (a classical Arabic poem sung to an improvised melody), the *layyali* (the melodious repetition of the words *ya layl* and *ya 'ayn*, 'Oh Night, Oh Eye'), the *mawwal* (a poem in colloquial Arabic sung to an improvised melody), the *taqsim* (instrumental improvisations), and the *dawr* (a complex, multi-part song in colloquial Arabic for a soloist and choir). While the other genres could be heard around the Levant at this time, it was the *dawr* that arose as a unique product of Cairo's artistic renaissance. The great composer and singer Muhammad 'Uthman is usually recognised as the originator and chief proponent of the *dawr*, which remains a staple of *wasla* performances in Cairo to this day. The *dawr* not only constituted a new genre of music, it also promoted a new style of solo singing, indeed a new category of singer or instrumentalist: the *mutrib*, literally 'one who produces *tarab*', a heightened emotional state, akin to ecstasy, produced in audiences by skilled performers.[14] Whereas the shaykh was associated with an older style of singing, closely related to Qur'anic chant, the *mutrib*, while influenced by the older styles, was more freely able to express his personal emotions through song. The *dawr* features sections of *ahat* in which the solo singer demonstrates his vocal and improvisatory skills by rendering the sigh 'Ah' in rich, melismatic phrases, while in the final section (known as the *hank*) the *mutrib* and chorus (*madhhabgiyya*) alternate in a call-and-response fashion.[15]

This music was performed by what we know today as the traditional *takht* ensemble consisting of '*ud*, *qanun* (a plucked zither), *rabab* (replaced in the latter decades of the 19th century by the European violin), the *nay* flute, drums such as the *diff*, *tar*, *darbukka* and *naqus*, and the vocalist. Prior to the 20th century the Ottoman *tanbur* (a long-necked, fretted lute) would supplement and sometimes replace the '*ud* in these contexts, and instruments from folk music genres such as the single-reed *arghul* were sometimes utilised as well.[16]

In addition, the various folk music traditions of the Nile Valley remained important components of the musical culture of Cairo, especially as musicians from rural areas increasingly began to migrate to the new cosmopolitan city, and as urban artists began to compose new songs influenced by the spirit of folk song and dance.

LAYER IV *Early Modern Cairo*

In the 19th century Cairo saw the rise of what is often known today as classical Arabic music, especially the genres of the *wasla*. Turning our excavations to early 20th-century Cairo, we find the gradual rise of a modern Arabic musical tradition. A number of social and cultural transformations proved decisive in the rise of modern Arab music. The most important of these were a result of Cairo status as a cosmopolitan urban centre, drawing increasing numbers of migrants from rural areas as well as from other Arab countries in search of employment as well as opportunities for performance. Beginning in the late 19th century, Cairo was an important centre of the Arabic Renaissance (*nahda*), with Syrians and other Arabs leaving their more parochial and conservative home towns and coming to Cairo to establish newspapers and busi-

nesses, and, as has been discussed, to perform in the new public performance spaces for which Cairo was becoming known: the cafes, cabarets and theatres of the Azbakiyya Gardens and 'Imad al-Din district. Borrowing from European genres such as operetta, local folk traditions and 19th-century urban classical music, this cosmopolitan mix of artists created new forms and styles based in musical theatre.[17]

On the new stages of Cairo a new class of performers – Egypt's first professional artists in the modern sense of the term – performed for a new public that, though hybrid and cosmopolitan, celebrated a growing sense of Egyptian national identity. This was especially the case after the 1919 Revolution, in which Egyptian students, teachers, lawyers and labourers rose up against the occupying forces of the British to demand independence. Although it took another thirty-three years before

Egyptian independence was achieved, this movement nonetheless inspired a plethora of nationalistic songs. Among these are the works of the great Alexandrian composer and singer Sayyid Darwish. Darwish, commonly considered the father of the modern Egyptian song, composed for the new musical theatre and sang songs that combined elements from Egyptian folk music and European high culture. He was an inspiration to the major artists who followed in his footsteps, most notably Muhammad 'Abd al-Wahab, the giant of 20th-century Arab music.

One consequence of the rise of Cairo as a great cosmopolitan centre and the concomitant rise of a new ideology of Egyptian national identity was the melding of styles and genres from the 19th century and the formation of a modern, urban musical culture – a sort of second 'heritage' (*turath*) after the 19th-century Khedival heritage.[18] Among the new genres that evolved on the stage of the musical theatre in the 1920s were the *taqtuqa* (a light song in colloquial Arabic of unknown origin[19]), the *ughniya* (song), and the *munuluj* (monologue) and *diuluj* (dialogue). As opposed to the older genres of *muwashshah* and *qasida*, which were for the most part anonymous compositions, the newer genres were composed by a new class of professional composers: Sayyid Darwish, of course, and the great Muhammad al-Qasabji, Abu al-'Ila Muhammad and Zakariya Ahmad were the most prominent Egyptian composers of the first half of the 20th century. Along with 'Abd al-Wahab, Muhammad al-Qasabji and Zakariya Ahmad in particular are the most important of the composers who brought Egyptian music into the modern period by bridging the two kinds of musical heritage outlined above.

Another important factor in promoting the standardisation of a modern Egyptian sound was the development of a theory of Arab music, thus producing the standardisation of its instruments and genres, and the rise of conservatories and clubs for the teaching of this music.[20] We might understand this as the result of a process of 'classicisation' of a diverse set of musical practices with hybrid origins into an Arab urban artistic musical tradition. Perhaps the most important event in this development was the First Congress on Arab Music, held in Cairo in 1932. This congress brought scholars and performers from around the Arab world and Europe to Cairo to discuss the principles of Arab music theory (especially regarding the modes and rhythms that might be called 'Arabian'), to devise a standard Arabic scale and guidelines for the study and instruction of the instruments and genres of 'Arab' music.[21] Following the Cairo Congress, Cairo saw the rise of conservatories and clubs for the instruction and preservation of Arab classical music tradition.

Newer musical genres were often performed alongside the older, classical genres of *qasida, muwashshah, mawwal* and *dawr*. Of these only the *dawr* remained a staple of performance into the 1920s, though it too had declined significantly by the mid 1930s[22]; the others were considered archaic or too long for modern tastes. As an indication of the relative importance of these genres to the repertoire of modern Egyptian performers, the great Umm Kulthum, despite her religious and classical background and training, only recorded two *muwashshah*s among the many hundreds of *qasida*s, *ughniya*s and other genres she performed and recorded over her career. One factor in promoting lighter (and faster) genres of music was the rise of the recording industry in the early 20th century and the rise of a Cairene middle-class public who bought and listened to these recordings. The limitations of early recording technologies had the effect of speeding up and shortening Arab musical genres such as the *qasida*, since the limited amount of time that a wax cylinder or vinyl album could contain on a single side restricted the recording of the longer genres such as the *muwashshah*, which require many sides.[23]

In addition to these major transformations in the styles and substance of Arab music in Cairo in the early 20th century, we note the increasing presence of women performers in public, not only the *'alima*s but *mutriba*s (women vocalists) such as Munira al-Mahdiyya, Ratiba Ahmad, Na'ima al-Misriyya, the young Umm Kulthum, and others. The professionalisation, in the modern sense, of singing for male artists in the late 19th and early 20th century paved the way for the stronger presence of female artists in the public domain of the performing arts.[24] Umm Kulthum, who in her early years performed disguised as a boy, began her ascent to fame after she moved to Cairo in 1928 and began lessons in the urban art tradition that had been established in the first decades of the 20th century.[25] Her success in part built on the earlier success of Munira al-Mahdiyya in the cabarets of the Azbakiyya Gardens.

LAYER V *The Golden Age of Arab Song (1935–1975)*
Moving up in time brings us to what is considered by many Cairenes to be the richest period of musical life in their city: the Golden Age of modern Arabic song as represented by the musical careers of the 'Big Three' of modern Arabic music: Umm Kulthum, Muhammad 'Abd al-Wahab and 'Abd al-Halim Hafiz. In this era, walking through any of Cairo's streets of an evening, one would hear Umm Kulthum's strong voice issuing from a radio at the back of a coffee shop, 'Abd al-Wahab's inventive compositions playing on a turntable or, later, a cassette player, or 'Abd al-Halim crooning from the silver screen of a cinema. For this was not only an era of great singers and composers, but also one that saw of the rise of Egyptian mass media which was a major factor in the development of modern Egyptian – and Arab – music.

The careers of the great performers of this era are already well known: much has been written on the rise of Umm Kulthum from a religious singer in the Egyptian Delta who performed dressed as a boy, to perhaps the most popular and influential singer of the 20th century anywhere[26]; the ascent of Muhammad 'Abd al-Wahab from his early (supposed) apprenticeship to Sayyid Darwish, his tutelage under Ahmad Shawqi (Prince of Poets), to his role ushering in the modern era of Egyptian and Arabic music through his wide-ranging borrowings and innovations; and the place of 'Abd al-Halim Hafiz, the 'Nightingale of the Nile', in the pantheon of great performers of the cinema as well as the stage.

The context for the rise of this rich constellation of talents was the rise of mass media technology and a technologically modern Egyptian nation. After the Revolution of 1952 and the rise to power of Gamal 'Abd al-Nasser, Egypt entered a phase of rapid economic growth which was mirrored by a corresponding political and cultural efflorescence. It was the rise of mass media forms of technology – radio, television and mass-market recordings – that enabled Umm Kulthum, 'Abd al-Wahab, 'Abd al-Halim and others, to form audiences, as well as to appeal to them, and thus their remarkable talents reached out to a far wider audience than any of their predecessors had known. All three of them featured in motion pictures, beginning with 'Abd al-Wahab in 'The White Rose' (1933), and including six films made by Umm Kulthum and dozens by 'Abd al-Halim.[27] It was this basis of technological advances in the recording, transmission and consumption of music that allowed for the development of the modern Arabic song: its orchestration, instrumentation, performance aesthetics and its unique sound. It is this feature of mid 20th-century Cairo that is perhaps its most enduring legacy to the late 20th and 21st century.

LAYER VI *Music in Cairo today*
Indeed, in this final layer – the layer of contemporary Cairo – it is the varied forms of mass media technology themselves more than individual artists that are the most distinctive feature of music in the City Victorious, as is also the case elsewhere in the global cultural economy. Beginning with the 'open door' (*infitah*) policies of Anwar Sadat, the Egyptian music market became host to – some would say was flooded by – a wide range of transnational musical forms and genres, making an already hybrid and modern musical culture an active participant in the formation of global musical aesthetics: from the European and American pop-inspired songs of Ahmad 'Adawiyya's 'Zahma ya Dunya', to the Flamenco rhythms and sounds of 'Amru Diab's 'Habibi Nur' and 'Ayn', to the various genres of techno, house (*dar*), and hip-hop inspired music of Cairo's vibrant club and underground music scenes as heard on cassettes, CDs and computers hooked up to the internet.[28] Cairo, from its origins, has had a remarkable ability to absorb the musical cultures of a wide range of peoples – from North Africa to the Arabian Peninsula, Sub-Saharan Africa, Europe, Persia and beyond. The contemporary history of music in Cairo shows that this ability has not lessened, despite the (inevitable) outcries from Cairo's intelligentsia against the contemporary music and its supposed 'vulgarity'. As this brief sonic archeology has shown, Cairo's music – like its social, cultural, economic and political fortunes – has always been hybrid and vibrant.

1 See Irene Bierman, *Writing Signs: The Fatimid Public Text* (Berkeley, CA, 1998); Paula Sanders, *Ritual, Politics, and the City in Fatimid Cairo* (New York, 1994).

2 See Michael Frishkopf, 'Inshad Dini and Aghani Diniyya in Twentieth Century Egypt: A Review of Styles, Genres, and Available Recordings', *Middle East Studies Association Bulletin*, 33 (2000), pp. 167–183.

3 See Henry George Farmer, *A History of Arabian Music to the XIIIth century* (London, 1929).

4 See Lois Ibsen al-Faruqi, *The Nature of the Musical Art of Islamic Culture* (Ann Arbor, 1975).

5 Although some scholars claim that Egyptians learned the art of the *muwashshah* from the Syrians in the early 17th century, see Ali Jihad Racy, *Musical Change and Commercial Recording in Egypt 1904–1932* (PhD University of Illinois at Urbana Champaign, 1977) p. 60; but this makes little sense given the Egyptian poet Ibn Sana' al-Mulk's work, which was both a collection of *muwashshahat* and a guide to writing them, see al-Faruqi, Ibid., p. 5. While it may have been the case that the art of singing the *muwashshahat* in Egypt was learnt from Syrian and especially Aleppan artists in the 17th century, the fact that the *muwashshah* was a genre of sung poetry from its origins in al-Andalus undermines this claim as well. Nevertheless, it remains true that the *muwashshah* was, and continues to be, more popular among Syrian artists than among Egyptian artists.

6 See Walter Feldman, *Music of the Ottoman Court Makam Composition and the Early Ottoman Musical Repertoire* (Berlin, 1996).

7 F. Lagrange, *Musiques d'Égypte* (Arles, 1996), p. 69.

8 Ibid., pp. 69–107; al-Khula'i, 1993 [1904], pp. 137–175.

9 See Kristen Nelson, *The Art of Reciting the Qur'an* (Austin, TX, 1985); Virginia Danielson, 'Min al-mashayikh: a view of Egyptian musical tradition', *Asian Music*, 22 (1990/1991), pp. 113–127.

10 Lagrange, *Musiques*, p. 81.

11 Ibid., p. 74; E. W. Lane, *The Customs and Manners of the Modern Egyptians* (rpr. Cairo, 1991), p. 367.

12 F. Lagrange, 'Shaykh Sayyid Darwish', *Meditérranéenes*, 8/9 (1996), pp. 155–177; see J-F. Belleface, 'Turat, classicisme et variétés: les avatars de l'orchestre oriental au Caire au début du XXe siècle', *Bulletin d'Études Orientales*, 39/40 (1987/1988), [pp. 39–65], pp. 54–55.

13 A. J. Racy, 'The Waslah: A Compound-Form Principle in Egyptian Music', *Arab Studies Quarterly*, 5, 4 (1983), pp. 396–403.

14 See Racy, *Musical Change* and J. Shannon, 'Emotion, Performance and Temporality in Arab Music: Reflections on Tarab', *Cultural Anthropology*, 18 (2003), pp. 72–98.

15 Lagrange, *Musiques*, pp. 92–93.

16 Ibid., p. 75.

17 See Jacob Landau, *Studies in Arab Theatre and Music* (Philadelphia, 1958); Racy, *Musical Change*, pp. 64–66.

18 See J-F. Belleface, 'Turat, classicisime et variétés'.

19 Some claim that the word *taqtuqa* is an inversion of *qatquta*, which signifies something small, with a connotation of gracefulness. Others argue that it is indicates a fast or coquettish woman; see See J-F. Belleface, 'Turat, classicisime et variétés'; Lagrange, *Musiques*, p. 111, and Racy, *Musical Change*, pp. 53–54.

20 See Abraham Marcus, *The Middle East on the Eve of Modernity* (New York, 1989).

21 Prior to 1932, the music we now call Arab or Arabic was usually referred to as Eastern (*sharqi*). Under the influence of European musicologists and an Egyptian king who wanted an Arab music for an Arab people, the diverse performance practices and genres of music from North Africa, the Levant and Turkey were analysed with the aim of determining a standard Arab tradition. Although the results were not unanimously adopted in all the Arab lands and many considered the Cairo Congress to be a failure, the effort to establish a standard for performance and instrumentation remains a goal of many conservatories and scholars of the music.

22 Racy, *Musical Change*, p. 72.

23 See Racy, *Musical Change*.

24 Karin van Nieuwkerk, *A Trade Like any Other: Female Singers and Dancers in Egypt* (Austin, TX, 1995).

25 Virginia Danielson, *The Voice of Egypt: Um Kulthum, Arabic Song and Egyptian Society in the Twentieth Century* (Chicago, IL, 1997).

26 See Virginia Danielson, *The Voice of Egypt*.

27 See Walter Armbrust, *Mass Culture and Modernism in Egypt* (Cambridge, 1996).

28 Ibid.; see also Danielson *The Voice of Egypt*, video recording (Seattle, WA, 1996); T. Swedenburg, 'Saida Sutlan/Danna International: Transgender Pop and the Polysemiotics of Sex, Nation, and Ethnicity on the Israeli-Egyptian Border', in Walter Armbrust, ed., *Mass Mediations: New Approaches to Popular Culture in the Middle East and Beyond* (Berkeley, CA, 2000), pp. 88–119.

15 The representation of medieval Cairo in modern Arabic literature

Randa Abou-bakr

The tradition of Arabic literature dates back more than a dozen centuries, and its genres vary from the well-established and universally acknowledged, to the local and narrowly recognised. Within each genre, there is a wide spectrum which extends from the anonymous folk to the prestigious canonical. It is thus a highly laborious task to trace any phenomenon through a varied body of literature such as Arabic literature.

I have chosen to discuss the work of two prominent modern novelists in which Old Cairo plays a key role: Naguib Mahfouz, Nobel Prize Laureate in 1988, and Gamal al-Ghitani, who could be described as his disciple. In addition to surveying the role played by place in these two writers' work, this article attempts to trace a line of development in its employment, in addition to, when relevant, a comparative assessment of their use of place. To achieve this end, I have chosen two works by each writer that represent two different years in the life of the city.

Both writers grew up in the heart of Old Cairo (particularly in Gamaliyya), and their non-fiction writings and media interviews speak of their fascination with the old city, and their photographic knowledge of its shops and alleys. The influence of place on their work can be seen in the statements they make about Old Cairo's impact on their imagination. In a statement quoted by al-Ghitani, Mahfouz says,

> At times, a human being complains of 'dryness of the soul'. Such moments are well known to writers. Yet when I walk through that area, images pour into my mind. Most of my novels were conceived of in vivid images while sitting in this area. It seems to me that this sense of commitment to a place or to something is a prerequisite of the eruption of feelings and emotions. For me, Gamiliyya is that very place.[1]

Al-Ghitani devotes a great part of his non-fictional writing to descriptions of the features of places in the heart of Old Cairo. Like Mahfouz, he considers the place a major source of his inspiration, yet, arising from the distance of only a few decades that separates the two writers' Cairos, al-Ghitani, in contrast to Mahfouz, is saddened by the change overcoming the city:

> During Mahfouz's time, Old Cairo was the centre for middle-class merchants and high-ranking civil servants. The alleys of al-Gamaliyya were of a strange social fabric. In the same *hara* one would find a palace with pleasure gardens, an average-size house that belonged to a merchant's family, a huge quarter inhabited by tens of poor families, all next to each other, sharing the same space. Today some alleys have been transformed into social garbage-bins ... How saddened I am today when I see them flooded with sewer water.[2]

Though both writers have written historical novels, and are concerned with depicting the social and political upheavals marking the lives of Egyptians, their overall techniques and modes of representation vary greatly. Whereas Mahfouz, being primarily a realist, depicts the impact of social and political conditions on the lived reality of Egyptians, al-Ghitani's works tend more towards symbolic representation, which enhances the magical dimension that ultimately blurs any facile conception of reality.

Apart from his early works dealing with Pharaonic Egypt, Mahfouz has concerned himself with Egypt from the turn of the 20th century onwards. His major works deal with the changes in the lives of Egyptians during the early decades of the 20th century, when they were engaged in battles on more than one front: a foreign occupation, a corrupt monarchy, an unstable political system and social changes of a nature then unknown. Mahfouz chooses the old part of Cairo as the setting for most of those works. His famous *Cairo Trilogy* deals with the period of time from the early to the mid 20th century. The household of Sayyid Ahmad 'Abdelgawwad lies in the heart of Old Cairo, and therefore most of the principal characters interact in that area. Each part of the *Trilogy* is given a place name as its title: *Bayn al-Qasrayn* (Palace Walk); *Qasr al-Shuq* (Palace of Desire); and *al-Sukkariyya* (Sugar Street).

Place is thus pertinently present in the work. Each part of the *Trilogy* represents a development in time, with place standing as symbolic of the change that occurs. Each new era is, so to speak, represented by a new place. However, these places are not far apart, and so in a way they also stand for the continuity of time and the merging of the old into the new. Along with development in time, place also symbolises the developments experienced by the characters. Change of place is, so to speak, echoed by mutability of character. Gamal al-Ghitani has commented on how the changes that come over the central character of Kamal 'Abdelgawwad (a perplexed, thwarted rebel) in the third part of the *Trilogy* are echoed in the increasing range of his movement, and his occupation of a wider circle of space.[3]

On another level, the movement of the novel away from the heart of Old Cairo into far-off areas such as Giza and Helwan in *Sugar Street* can be seen as a reflection of the actual movement of the middle class (of which 'Abdelgawwad's family is representative) away from the heart of Cairo into newer areas. Place can thus be seen as possessing a social character capable of embodying and representing social and political upheavals. The movement of the middle class away from Old Cairo in reality continued until, by the 1970s, this area had utterly ceased to be the abode of the merchants and civil servants who had formerly made up the Egyptian middle class. With the structural shift that the middle class underwent during the middle of the 20th century, there also came a change of locale. In a way, then, Mahfouz was welding his conception of early to mid 20th-century Egyptian society to his strong sense of place and his representation of the changes that the characters undergo.

Not only the rise of the (new) middle class, but also social changes occurring at the micro-level of the family are inscribed in a given place. As the expansion of place and the movement of characters increase with time, so does the disintegration of 'Abdelgawwad's family.[4] This is again reflected in yet another shift in the technique of the work. The interest in describing minute details of place in the first part, *Palace Walk*, gradually dies out, giving way to a depiction of the wandering of characters through the city. Hence the reader perceives the change from the fixity of place, and of family life, evoked by the description of the alley, seen through the eyes of the good but rarely mobile mother, Amina, in *Palace Walk*, to the fragmentation of place observed in many parts of *Sugar Street*.[5]

Mahfouz's *Yawma Qutila al-Za'im* ('The Day the Leader was Killed') (1989), written three decades later, shows the novelist's continued interest in tracing the relationship between the political and the social. Although there is not much allusion to the particularities of place, a few references lead us to surmise that Mahfouz is still dwelling in the same, albeit expanded, area. In this work, it is significant that the inhabitants assume more prominence than the place they inhabit. Although there is very little to link the *Trilogy* and *The Day the Leader was Killed*, the two works could be seen as representing a kind of sequence in terms of negation rather than affirmation. The setting is no longer the abode of the well-to-do merchants, who formed Egypt's rising middle class at the turn of the 20th century. In *The Day the Leader was Killed*, we follow the fate of the families of Mohtashimi Zayed and Sulayman Mubarak, two middle-class families that belong to the Cairo of the 1970s and 1980s; the novel depicts their socio-economic plight which has been generated by Sadat's economic policies. Here, place helps to accentuate the dismal conditions in which the family lives. The change in the character of the place and its inhabitants from *The Trilogy* to *The Day the Leader was Killed* highlights the distance travelled from the first decades of the 20th century to the early 1980s.

The Day the Leader was Killed could be viewed as a continuation of the movement away from the centre of Old Cairo that the last part of the *Trilogy* depicted, and the tendency to expand the circle of action. This expansion again represents the movement of the middle class away from Old Cairo. The house where the central characters live is slightly removed from the heart of Old Cairo. Viewed as the correlative of the disintegration in society and family, and as a symbol of the dying of an older system in the *Trilogy*, this expansion of place in *The Day the Leader was Killed* leads to chaos. Although characters in the novella voice the need to go back to their roots in the heart of the city, for example, in Muhtashimi's fond reflections on his old house in Khairat Street, [6]and 'Ulwan's constant recourse to Riche Café, especially in times of crisis,[7] they lose their grip on their lives when their relationship to the place weakens. The older characters in the novel, who retain memories of the area in its days of glory, are even more out of place in their fast-moving surroundings. Mahfouz at once highlights the characters' rootedness in the place they inhabit and their bitter sense of alienation as a result of the rapid changes occurring all around them. The small old house, incongruous beside its modernised neighbours, mirrors the inhabitants' inability to adapt to the social and economic changes brought about by Sadat's *infitah* policies, and the steps taken towards normalisation of relations with the state of Israel.

Like most of Mahfouz's other works, the *Trilogy* and *The Day the Leader was Killed* are firmly anchored specific historical moments. Each work deals with a crucial stage in Egyptian history through the representation of an 'extended' middle-class family. Mahfouz, as a novelist, is not so concerned with documentation as with presenting his own reading of historical events, translated into a lively web of relationships, or what Samia Mehrez sees in the context of al-Ghitani's work, as 'narratives of history'.[8] Mahfouz, moreover, is not interested in delving into earlier historical eras, but remains within the recent past, a period of around one hundred years. This allows the writer scope to research his subject and give a sober, in-depth analysis of a complex historical moment.

Gamal al-Ghitani's works, however, are 'narratives of history' in a different sense. The younger writer is interested in a wider range of historical eras than Mahfouz. He writes as comfortably of the places, characters, customs and political system of Mamluk Cairo as he does of contemporary Cairene life. His focus is usually on the political and the social as it bears on the often unstable consciousness of the main characters. In his choice of narrative techniques, varying from, and sometimes combining, stream of consciousness, documentation and mock-historical narration, he deliberately shatters the conventions of traditional realism. His narrative scheme constantly reminds the readers that what they are following is a very personal rendering of history, and that the distance between fact and fiction is constantly shifting.

In this scheme place is focal, and is rendered with elaborate detail. The heart of Old Cairo is the scene of most of al-Ghitani's works, and the eras he conjures up can date several centuries back. Though he reproduces the city with the help of the writer's imagination, he has a thorough knowledge of the place he is writing about, both past and present. Al-Ghitani's lively fascination with Old Cairo is manifest in his non-fictional writings, which are documents of the old city's life. A notable example is a book entitled *Malamat al-Qahira fi alfsana* ('Features of Cairo over a Thousand Years', 1997), which describes Cairo's most characteristic features across ten centuries. Here al-Ghitani is intent on describing the details of the city and the daily life of its inhabitants, everything from different kinds of tobacco to mosques and gates.

For al-Ghitani, place and time are interdependent; as he said in an interview, place 'contains time'.[9] Thus, evoking a certain period in history cannot be successfully accomplished without the concomitant evocation of place. In *Zayni Barakat* (1974), the events of the main plot take place in early 16th-century Cairo, and al-Ghitani is concerned with the issue of excessive desire for power and its bent for oppression. This voyage back in time evokes a place as well, and since that particular place (the heart of Old Cairo) used to be the centre of government, it acquires an added meaning. It is the arena that witnesses the game of power between Barakat, the tax collector and market supervisor, and Zakariyya, the chief of police, and later on between Barakat and Zakariyya on the one hand and the people of Cairo on the other.

In *Zayni Barakat*, al-Ghitani in fact does more than evoke time and place. He summons up the very spirit of place in its minutest detail. His descriptions are functional in the sense that they evoke an atmosphere which is crucial to the rendering of events and the portrayal of characters. The elaborate description of dark narrow alleys, dismal market places and claustrophobic prison dungeons is meant to echo

Naguib Mahfouz
in a Cairo street, 1989

Cover of the English
translation of *The Zafarani Files*
by Gamal al-Ghitani

the darkness and horror rampant in the characters' psyches as much
as to stand for the police regime and political intrigue gripping the city.

Al-Ghitani's minute description of the old city seems at times
indulgent: its alleys, coffee houses, market places, private dwellings
and palaces, the people and their customs in dressing, eating, drinking
and pleasure-making.[10] Passages of such nature in the novel might, at
times, appear superfluous. Yet to fully assess their role, one has to view
them within the writer's overall technique, especially his narrative
scheme. Combining the free association of ideas and documentation,
the narration usually seeks to unveil the seemingly incoherent mechanisms of the characters' unstable minds. The indulgence in minute
details reflects a habit of brooding and mental doodling.

It is obvious that al-Ghitani uses history as a means of commenting on the present. In *Zayni Barakat*, he chooses characters from early
16th-century Cairo who could be viewed as representatives of universal
issues such as the lust for, and abuse of, power, the oppression of the
individual in police states, and the inescapable fragility of every
tyrant. The novel could thus be read as a political allegory, and this is
characteristic of both his novels set in the past and those that are more
contemporary. In *The Zafarani Files* (1985) the setting is much more
limited than that of *Zayni Barakat*. The characters and events of the
novel are confined to the alley and are rarely seen against a wider background. The alley itself, as Nadia Abd al-Latif observes, is 'sick and
divided against itself like its inhabitants'.[11] Thus it projects their
inner and outer ailments and is, in a sense, one of the protagonists.
The impotence inflicted on the people of the alley as a result of Shaykh
'Atiyya's talisman is paralleled by the dryness and barrenness of life
there. The place is lacking in the gaiety and liveliness of a typical
Cairene alley, while the shrinking of movement to the confines of the
narrow alley echoes the inhabitants' imprisonment by the powers of
the shaykh – a spiritual as well as a physical imprisonment.

Here, al-Ghitani does not depend on history for his political allegory
but instead employs the element of magic. Thus the plot is based on
the supernatural, the idea that a curse has been placed on the people

ARABIA

The Zafarani Files
Gamal al-Ghitani

of the alley, and events proceed from the ramifications of this act. The political overtones of such a scheme can hardly be overlooked: the indirect manipulation of the ignorant masses can be effected through the scheming mind of a hypocrite, a mind constantly striving to create a positive image of itself. Shaykh 'Atiyya's curse renders the inhabitants impotent just as oppression creates people lacking both will and productive power.

In both works, al-Ghitani makes place, the heart of Old Cairo that he knows best, a focal setting where the inhabitants' trials and tribulations are enacted; indeed it is virtually another actor on the scene, echoing their thoughts and feelings. Though they deal with historical periods that are far apart, both *Zayni Barakat* and *The Zafarani Files* link the fate of the characters to place through the creation of allegories which transcend the boundaries of time. Though the historian in al-Ghitani rarely surrenders his place, the narrative testifies to the fact that he is a historian of place as much as of times and people.

Talking about the intricate, albeit fascinating relationship between place, time and power, Michel Foucault once remarked, 'A whole history remains to be written of spaces – which would at

the same time be the history of powers – both these terms in the plural – from the great strategies of geopolitics to the little tactics of the habitat.' [12]

Ever since the 1970s and 1980s, the growing interest of literary and cultural theory in spaces and places has underpinned the dynamic character of these concepts. Places are no longer seen as a setting for historical events or the backdrop to cultural, political, economic and social change, but as active participants in the movement of history. In this respect, Foucault lays particular emphasis on the active participation of place in the ever-shifting concept of power, and hence of action itself. It is in this fashion that place appears in modern Arabic literature, particularly narrative works: as a participant and an agent. It has come to be intricately interwoven with the representation of unstable concepts such as memory, personal history and the more problematic issue of identity. In the work of both Mahfouz and al-Ghitani, place (notably the heart of Old Cairo) is a dynamic force in the construction of their 'narratives of history'. Their employment of Old Cairo underpins their conception that history is as much a matter of space as of time

1 Gamal al-Ghitani, *Malamat al-Qahira fi alf sana* (Cairo, 1977), p. 225.

2 Samya Mehrez, *Egyptian Writers Between History and Fiction: Essays on Naguib Mahfouz, Son'allah Ibrahim, and Gamal al-Ghitani* (Cairo, 1994), p. 59.

3 Al-Ghitani, *Malamat al-Qahira fi alf sana*, pp. 265–268.

4 Ibid., p. 268.

5 Naguib Mahfouz, *Palace Walk*, tr. W. M. Hutchins and O. E. Kenny (London, 1990), p. 2; idem, *Sugar Street*, tr. W. M. Hutchins and A. B. Sanaan (London, 1992), pp. 178–181, 199, 233.

6 Naguib Mahfouz, *The Day the Leader was Killed*, tr. M. Hashem (Cairo, 2001), pp. 6–8.

7 Ibid., pp. 53, 90.

8 Mehrez, *Egyptian Writers Between History and Fiction*, p. 61.

9 Ibid., p. 62.

10 al-Ghitani, *Zayni Barakat*, tr. Farouk Abdel Wahab, (London, 1990) pp. 36, 81.

11 Nadia 'Abdul-Latif, 'The Incidents of Za'farani Alley Compared with Animal Farm and Brave New World', in *Proceedings of the Third International Symposium on Comparative Literature* (Cairo, 1994), p. 416.

12 E. Soja, 'Heterotopologies: A Remembrance of Other Spaces in the Citadel-LA', in S. Watson and K. Gibson, ed., *Postmodern Cities and Spaces* (Oxford, 1995), p. 4.

16 | Transition, colonialism, modernisation; living with 'Ali Mubarak Pasha: state and civil society in Egypt

Elizabeth Bishop

'Ali Mubarak Pasha's work, *al-Khitat al-Tawfiqiyya al-Jadida* (1886 to 1889), is often regarded as the blueprint for the late 19th-century modernisation of Egypt, including Cairo. This programme, initiated by the Khedive Isma'il as the power of the Ottoman empire waned, was designed to bring Egypt closer to the prolific achievement that the European West had enjoyed since the inception of the Industrial Revolution. Thus 'Ali Mubarak may be seen as articulating the wishes and hopes of the new Egyptian regime; his life and work are crucial to understanding the development of the city.

'Ali Mubarak's (1823–1893) biography and work can serve as the basis for a general discussion of modernity in 19th-century Egypt, because he held significant jobs in government: minister for *waqf* (Islamic charitable and religious endowments), for education and for public works. He directed the school system, the railways, urban reconstruction and the design of agricultural irrigation.[1] As the minister for public works, 'Ali Mubarak oversaw Mahmud al-Falaky's master plan for modernising Cairo; as minister for *waqf*, the implementation of that plan as well as the contemporary state school system. This essay will direct a general discussion of 19th-century forms of modernity in Egypt into a discussion of his published works, concluding with a return to *Living with the Past*.

What would a view of the Hakim Mosque inspire in the observer, to justify converting the site into a museum for Arab artifacts? A view of the rubble of the Hakim Mosque might bear a comparison with the ruins of the Paris Commune in Rimbaud's verse.[2] After a prolonged construction period, the building which present residents of Cairo are familiar with opened in 1903. The architect Alfonso Manescalo designed symmetrical facades for each of the fronts, using repeating bays with arched windows arranged in pairs to conceal both a division of functions (that the first floor served as museum, the second, as national library) as well as the foundation's awkward triangular shape. A building like this reminds the viewer that optical illusions are part and parcel of the geometric effect of modern cities.[3] The modern city's new buildings were not necessarily technically advanced, nor were the patterns of urbanisation innovative, nor urban living newly comfortable. But those new streets were a public space through which the inhabitants of Cairo walked or rode, past institutions of public authority and displays of goods outside shops.

1. Kitab tariq al-hija wa'l-tamrin 'ala al-qurra fi'l-lughat al-'arabiyya
'Exercises in Reading the Arabic Language' *(1868)*
During the 19th century, the governors of Egypt sent a number of qualified candidates abroad to pursue state-sponsored higher studies. Rifa'a al-Tahtawi (1801–1873) published his observations on Europe under the title *Takhlis al-ibriz fi talkhis Bariz*, 'Gold Spun From a Paris Summary' (1839). In this work he was careful to draw attention to the high status Egyptian visitors enjoyed whilst in France. Egyptians did not mix with crowds of working Europeans; rather, they enjoyed the leisure pastimes of the privileged:

> During our stay, we would go out for a few hours to amuse ourselves in the city and pass the time in certain cafes. French cafes do not serve as meeting grounds for the riff-raff of the city. They are, in fact, gathering places for respectable people and are decorated with costly objects [that] indicate great wealth. Indeed, the prices in these cafes are very high, so that only men of fortune can afford to patronise them.

While Rifa'a al-Tahtawi notes that 'there are other seamy cafes, taverns and hashish dens which the poor frequent', he makes it clear to his reader that he avoided them.[4]

Following Rifa'a al-Tahtawi, 'Ali Mubarak visited France twice. On the first visit, he followed a training programme comparable to that of members of the corps of military engineers, the Corps de Ponts et Chaussées. For this reason, Mubarak was familiar with their work: from surveying and drawing maps visualising the entire country, to the Legrand Star railway system which required travellers to pass through the capital city, and even to the administrative regulations

al-Darb al-Ahmar *circa* 1887

that governed the work of private contractors.[5] His instructors noted his intelligence, industry and 'logical' mind.[6] He was then transferred to the École nationale d'ingenieurs de Metz and after he graduated (697 out of 1205 students), like his classmates, he gave a year's military service to the French state. 'Ali Mubarak returned to Paris for a second time, for a month and a half during the Exposition Universelle of 1867. On his return to Egypt from this second trip, 'Ali Mubarak took on three official responsibilities: for education, public works and *waqf*. He published a grammar and reading book, the *Kitab tariq al-hija wa'l-tamrin 'ala al-qurra fi'l-lughat al-'arabiyya* (1868) which was designed to be used in Egypt's new state schools. Three editions of this textbook were published during his lifetime: in 1868, at some point in the 1880s and in 1886.

This textbook was no larger or more elaborate than McGuffey's Reader, used in the United States of America, and yet it changed the way Egyptians encountered public law. In 1867, despite the increasing numbers of students and the financial resources of al-Azhar school of Islamic jurisprudence, 'Ali Mubarak drafted the organic law (10 Ragab 1284/7 November 1867) which brought *kuttab*s under the same system of inspection as state primary schools, even though they were supported by endowments (*waqf*). Essentially, the new law meant that al-Azhar's system of primary schools, the *kuttab*s, and its resources were now part of the government education system with its modern curriculum for mathematics, natural sciences and Arabic grammar.[7] The *kuttab* Qur'anic curriculum, which had traditionally provided the basis for higher studies including Islamic law, was now bereft of resources. A contextualised reading of the *Kitab tariq al-hija* might expand on the suggestion that, while intimacy with the Divine and refreshment for the soul are fine for the private individual, the people should trust the state to administer public law.[8] Such a reading might further suggest that, as the minister of education, 'Ali Mubarak created the basis for contemporary Egypt's distinction between private confession and public law.

2. *Kitab nukhbat al-fikr fi tadbir Nil Misr*
'A Book of Most Worthwhile Thoughts on Taming Egypt's Nile' (1879)
'Ali Mubarak's second publication, though not intended for children, was similar to the school textbook in that it also advanced the nation-state's claim to modernity. His second book, 'Taming Egypt's Nile', includes a narrative summary of Egyptian history that suggests Egyptians should blame any national decline on foreign intervention, invasion and conquest. The nation's past was the heritage of its people. Destruction or vandalism of Antiquity's material traces was a specific and particularly lamentable symptom of ignorance about the nation's past, resulting from centuries of deterioration and stagnation.[9] A description of the then current agricultural policy and its shortcomings also included the notion that a just ruler would respect and encourage a loyal and competent class of civil servants, not that this was a novel concept in the Islamic world.

The Paris visited by 'Ali Mubarak was an open construction site. About 30 per cent of its present buildings were built during the years between his first and second journeys.[10] Dominique Kalifa notes that in Paris, the construction of buildings to house the institutions of order, the Palais de Justice, the Conciergerie, the Préfecture de Police, accompanied the proliferation of news reports about the city's sinister and dangerous places (2004). Although Rifa'a al-Tahtawi noted the institutions for order and commerce, he did not describe the interiors of sleazy cabarets or gambling dens. The educational missions that followed Rifa'a al-Tahtawi's visit imposed regulations governing student leisure time, designed to keep them out of cabarets and all-night cafes. Of the forty-four students on the 1826 educational mission, one

deserted, one fell ill, one was expelled for contracting debts and three were 'returned on account of unsuitability'.[11] Subsequently, twenty-two rules were specified in order to control the behaviour of Egyptian students in France.[12] Of these rules, about a quarter sought to prevent male students from sexual congress with French women, because affairs with foreign women threatened to divert the loyalty of students from their own country. It is worth noting that, of the twelve medical students sent on the 1828 mission, three married French women.[13]

But the proliferation of new rules was a greater danger than women. In *Hadith 'Isa ibn Hisham* ('The 'Isa ibn Hisham Story') (1898–1902), Muhammad al-Muwaylihi's character observes notables and merchants: 'I've seen the effect of working in the stock exchange with my own eyes: destruction of inhabited houses, squandering of vast wealth and the collapse of lofty pillars.'[14] Even though modern citizens enjoy equal access to the mechanisms of the state, and as al-Muwaylihi writes, 'there is no difference between great and small men, between amir and donkey man',[15] Anshuman Mondal argues that al-Muwaylihi's reference to decaying buildings and the squandering of wealth, reflect the author's own concerns about the law.

> Cut off from access to the law he knew, a citizen now required the intervention of professionals. The exercise of this new legal system was layered, with those who saw no harm at all in charging professional fees for access to the rules and laws that governed the nation-state. Muwaylihi's anxiety lends irony to a humble character's assertion that modern states grant rights universally. New classes of civil servants and other professionals in modern regulation, whether or not they worked for the state directly, intervened with the state on their clients' behalf, compromising that universality of access.

3. *'Alam al-Din* (1882)
A four-volume work of fiction, *'Alam al-Din*, was 'Ali Mubarak's third published work. It is a didactic story told via the conversations of group of travellers. 'Ali Mubarak may have read Théophile Gautier,

who argued 'a modern kind of beauty' required the viewer to 'accept civilisation as it is, with its railways, steamboats, English scientific research, central heating, factory chimneys'.[16] 'Ali Mubarak dealt with these very topics in this prose narrative, which follows the conversations between a shaykh of al-Azhar and a British Egyptologist.

Wadad al-Qadi draws attention to the symbolism of the characters in 'Ali Mubarak's novel, *'Alam al-Din*. The titular character 'Alam al-Din and his son Burhan al-Din are accompanied by an Englishman, the '*rajul Inklizi*', or simply al-Inklizi along with another, secondary character, James.[17] To al-Qadi, they personify opposing principles.

How are these opposed? Clearly, two of the named characters are Muslims, and the two foreign characters are not. Al-Qadi draws attention to the titular character's name, as well as the names assigned to his relatives. 'Alam al-Din means 'he who knows the faith'. As al-Qadi explains: 'One thing is sure, right from the beginning: [the] East has religiosity in its very bones, in its very identity.'[18]

What distinguishes the non-Muslim foreigner? Though not identified by name, the foreigner is notable for the extent of his knowledge of the modern world (the post, navigation, history, the stock market, banks and trade), and of Arab literature (he intends to edit and publish the Arabic equivalent to the Oxford English Dictionary, *Lisan al-'Arab*, and make a profit by so doing).

Al-Qadi suggests a reader might expect the novelist, an Egyptian, to build a nationalist narrative around 'Alam al-Din. It was common in 19th-century fiction to focus the reader's attention on the titular character's development, as in, for example, *Jane Eyre*. Yet al-Qadi

CAIRO - The Blue Mosque

notes this novel does not follow the titular character's personality
and growth of knowledge. Rather, this series of conversations reveals
character's lack of knowledge.

Al-Qadi points out that, even with his education at al-Azhar in
Arabic language, grammar, morphology, Qur'anic exegesis, Prophetic
traditions, Islamic law and its sources, and rhetoric, 'Ali Mubarak's
character 'Alam al-Din is notable for what he does not know. 'Alam
al-Din confesses he does not know the statistics for Egypt's agricultural
production and its population, even though Régny had already published *Statistique de l'Égypte* (1870–1873), Amici the *Essai de statistique
generale de l'Égypte* (1879), and Dor the *Statistique des écoles civiles* (1875).

'Alam al-Din possesses experiential knowledge – he is, after all, an
Egyptian – but the reader learns he lacks the positivistic knowledge
that counts in the modern world.

4. al-Khitat al-Tawfiqiyya al-Jadida
'The New Khedival Overview of Egypt' (1886–1889)
In 'The New Khedival Overview', 'Ali Mubarak provided all the
knowledge 'Alam al-Din could require. The twenty-volume work discusses agriculture, land-tenure, rural trade, tribes, town and village
notables, rural and urban institutions. As sources for this information, 'Ali Mubarak refers to published statistics, title census registers,
deeds, a nation-wide cadastral survey and municipal records. He
interviewed the *'ulama'*, he consulted Egypt's historical and geographical literature widely, including works by 'Abd al-Rahman al-Jabarti
(1754–1825) and Muhammad Ibn 'Umar al-Tunsi, and he consulted the
Description de l'Égypte; indeed, Donald Reid considers 'Ali Mubarak's
overview a nationalist riposte to the foreign catalogue of ancient and
contemporary Egypt.[19] The import of Reid's comment, that the *Khitat*
is of symbolic rather than empirical value, may prove useful.

The major portion of this work consists of an alphabetical list of
Nile Valley settlements. Michael Reimer maintains that 'Ali Mubarak's
Khitat has its origins in al-Maqrizi's (d. 1442) similarly-titled *Khitat*, and
is a reference work that describes Egypt's landscape, highlighting its

Backgammon players
outside a Cairo cafe, coloured
postcard, 19th century

pre-Ottoman greatness and celebrating its renaissance under the government of the Khedives.[20] 'Ali Mubarak's *Khitat* provided its reader with what seems to be an encyclopedic description of every Egyptian town or village. Gabriel Baer identifies inconsistencies; while the 1882 census recorded 3,651 towns and villages, and about 8,600 smaller settlements, 'Ali Mubarak lists only 1,155.[21]

In order to discuss the significance of 'Ali Mubarak's *Khitat*, let me return to one of al-Qadi's observations, following a brief detour. Partha Chatterjee noted a 'moment of departure' in the texts of 'Ali Mubarak's close contemporary, Bankimchandra Chattopadhyay (1838–1894). As Chatterjee notes:

> The theoretical position implied in Bankim's discussion – and this is a position which recurs in much of his writing – involves, then, the following line of reasoning: 1) force or power is the basis of the state; 2) the liberty or subjection of a nation is ultimately a question of force or power; 3) but power is not something that is determined by material (environmental or technological) conditions; 4) power can be acquired by the cultivation of appropriate national-cultural values.[22]

Interestingly al-Qadi presages Chatterjee's description of non-European national identities in an increasingly industrialised world characterised by disparities of power. To take a page from Chatterjee's book, might 'Ali Mubarak's publication of a *khitat* indicate the cultivation of appropriate national-cultural values?

5. al-Mizan fi'l-aqyisa
'The Balance in Measurement' (1892)

Reading the description of al-Azhar Mosque and university, Reimer notes that Mubarak limits its function, shearing it of references to its concentration of legal knowledge, describing it as a shrine, a symbol of religious authority, but nothing else. Indeed, in Reimer's reading, for 'Ali Mubarak, rather than being a centre of legal authority, al-Azhar

is a site for lawlessness. 'Ali Mubarak characterises al-Azhar's students and neighbours by their vice and belligerence; their solidarity is 'aggressive;' they 'often come to blows with one another over trivial issues'. While the spirituality and erudition of al-Azhar are to be praised, its students are ambitious, jealous, pugnacious, undisciplined, immoral, territorial, factionalist, proud and petty. During 'Ali Mubarak's life, the army was twice sent in to the mosque to suppress student protests.

Just as Paris had changed during the years between 'Ali Mubarak's visits, so too had Cairo. Cairo streets were busier; they bustled with the business of government. Reid compares the 900 passenger carriages and wagons on Cairo streets during the 1860s, with the fact that, fifty years before, Isma'il's grandfather Muhammad 'Ali had the only European-style carriage in the city. Robert Hunter suggests that pension dossiers for civil servants, from the Dar al-Mahfuzat administrative registers in the Citadel serve as a parallel index; at Isma'il's accession in 1863, 300 pension claims were documented per year.[23] The increase in vehicular traffic indicates an increase in the number of independent professionals on government salaries, serving as intermediaries between the people of Egypt and a modern legal regime of a kind they were unfamiliar with, but to which they were responsible.

These individuals, whether carters or engineers, printers or physicians, could well have had a common appreciation of the value of measurement. Just as the government schools taught a common curriculum for Arabic grammar to all its students, so also the standardisation of property registration and military conscription placed citizens on an equal basis before the state.[24] So too could common indices of measurement serve all Egyptians. In France, the common metre served to make France 'revenue-rich, militarily potent and easily administered'.[25] As in France, so too in Egypt, a rational unit of measurement would promote a rational citizenry.

It is worth undertaking a simple experiment, in order to test 'Ali Mubarak along the line from the state's subjugation to the individual's acquisition of the national-cultural attributes of power. Perhaps 'Ali Mubarak (as a historical character) and the fictional Englishman of his

novel occupy similar positions. 'Ali Mubarak's biography bears similarities with the unnamed Englishman's personal details. 'Ali Mubarak spent five years in France (1844–1849); the fictional Englishman has spent four years in the Arab world. 'Ali Mubarak translated a work of 19th-century French Orientalism, Louis Amélie Sédillot's *Histoire générale des arabes: leur empire, leur civilisation, leurs écoles philosophiques, scientifiques et littéraires* (1854), which was published after his death. The fictional Englishman's ambitious project, to prepare an English translation of Muhammad ibn Mukarram ibn Manzur's etymological dictionary, *Lisan al-'Arab*, has not been accomplished to date (although an Arabic edition came out of the Egyptian government press at Bulaq the same year that 'Ali Mubarak published his novel). Al-Qadi indicates the Englishman's nationality is a strategic choice; modern, not French. Regardless of the international structures of power, the national-

cultural values of these two individuals can be considered comparable in international hierarchies of knowledge and power.

Conclusion

A public building such as that at Bab al-Khalq, designed to house a museum and library, also raises issues about civil society and the state in 19th-century Egypt. What purpose does a museum of Arab artifacts serve, when water vessels, storage containers and woodwork similar to that on display, are used in the surrounding homes?

First, the museum should be understood as a public building in a modernised Cairo. During the 19th century, newly-designated public spaces were ornamented with monumental sculpture. One finds the museum midway between the new public gardens at Azbakiyya and the equestrian statue of Ibrahim Pasha in Opera Square, and the new

Rifa'i Mosque with its anachronistic facade designed by Max Herz, the Islamic Museum's first director. The film *Living with the Past* allows the viewer to take up Donald Reid's challenge, 'perhaps preservationism, not its inverse, is what cries out for explanation'.[26] Reid suggests in addition that, 'in their rush to modernise, many Egyptians were ready to sacrifice old mosques and artifacts'.

In published notes devoted to 'state and civil society', the Italian philosopher Antonio Gramsci remarks on the difficulty of distinguishing modern civil society from state institutions. The forces of order are not strictly confined to the state, but extend to include 'the totality of forces organised by the state and by private individuals to safeguard the political and economic domination of the ruling classes'.[27] A discussion of the Bab al-Khalq Museum might consider whether the bureaucracy of public institutions reorganised and expanded in the 19th century with the establishment of new educational institutions, had the effect (intended or unintended) of restricting access to the law.

Modern nation-states, such as Egypt, place restrictions on artifacts such as a mosque's endowed resources and protect codified laws from intervention by the private individual, whether that intervention be ignorant or malicious. Contemporary visitors to the Islamic Museum may be unaware that law 40 of 1977, as amended by law 36 of 1979, law 144 of 1980, laws 30 and 156 of 1981, 46 of 1984, 2 of 1987, and 108 of 1992, restricts gatherings in public places without official authorisation. Many visitors to the Islamic museum looking at the collection of artifacts may not realise which of the interior ministry's internal regulations require permission for gatherings of five or more persons.

View of a pavement cafe in
Cairo selling Arabic coffee,
coloured postcard, 1920s

1 Darrell Dykstra, 'Pyramids, Prophets, and
   Progress: Ancient Egypt in the Writings of Ali
   Mubarak', *Journal of the American Oriental Society*,
   114 (1994), pp. 54–65; J. Heyworth-Dunne, *An
   Introduction to the History of Education in Modern Egypt*
   (London, 1968); F. Robert Hunter, *Egypt under the
   Khedives: From Household Government to Modern
   Bureaucracy, 1805–1879* (Pittsburgh, PA, 1984);
   Timothy Mitchell, *Colonising Egypt* (Berkeley,
   CA, 1988).
2 viz. Daryl Lee, 'Rimbaud's Ruin of French Verse:
   Verse Spatiality and the Paris Commune Ruins',
   Nineteenth-century French Studies, 32 (2003–2004),
   p. 70 et passim.
3 David Jordan, 'Haussmann and Haussmannisation: The Legacy for Paris', *French Historical Studies*,
   27 (2004), p. 89; Mitchell, *Colonising Egypt*, passim.
4 Sandra Naddaf, 'Mirrored Images: Rifa'ah al-Tahtawi
   and the West', *Alif* (1986), p. 79.
5 Cecil Smith, 'The Longest Run: Public Engineers
   and Planning in France', *The American Historical
   Review*, 95, 3 (1990), [page numbers?]
6 Ahd Muhammad 'Ali, daftar 5, doc. 6858, cited
   in Hunter, *Egypt under the Khedives*, p. 127.
7 Heyworth-Dunne, *Education in Modern Egypt*,
   pp. 362ff; Mitchell, *Colonising Egypt*, p. 76; Michael
   Reimer, *Colonizing Bridgehead, Government and
   Society in Alexandria 1807–1882* (Boulder, CL, 1997),
   p. 55.
8 See Reimer, *Colonizing Bridgehead*.
9 Cited in Dykstra, 'Pyramids, Prophets, and
   Progress', p. 60.
10 Jordan, *Haussman and Haussmannisation*, p. 103.
11 Heyworth-Dunne, *Education in Modern Egypt*,
   pp. 159–163.
12 Ibid., p. 24; Mitchell, *Colonising Egypt*, p. 72.
13 Heyworth-Dunne, *Education in Modern Egypt*, p. 177.
14 Quoted in Anshuman Mondal, 'Between Turban
   and Tarbush: Modernity and the Anxieties of
   Transition in Hadith 'Isa ibn Hisham', *Alif*, 17
   (1997), p. 207.
15 Quoted in Mondal, 'Between Turban and
   Tarbush', p. 209.
16 Quoted in Reff, 'Manet and the Paris of Haussmann
   and Baudelaire', in William Sharpe and Leonard
   Wallock, ed., *Proceedings of the Heyman Center for the
   Humanities* (New York, 1983), p. 150.
17 Wadad al-Qadi, 'East and West in 'Ali Mubarak's
   'Alamuddin', in Marwan Buheiry, ed., *Intellectual
   Life in the Arab East, 1890–1939* (Beirut, 1981), p. 26.
18 Ibid.
19 Donald Reid, 'Cultural Imperialism and
   Nationalism: the Struggle to Define and Control
   the Heritage of Arab Art in Egypt', *International
   Journal of Middle East Studies*, 24 (1992), p. 65.
20 Reimer, *Colonizing Bridgehead*, p. 53.
21 Gabriel Baer, "Ali Mubarak's Khitat as a Source for
   the History of Modern Egypt', in P. M. Holt, ed.,
   *Political and Social Change in Modern Egypt: Historical
   Studies from the Ottoman Conquest to the United Arab
   Republic* (London, 1968), p. 25.
22 Partha Chatterjee, *Nationalist Thought and the
   Colonial World: A Derivative Discourse* (Minneapolis,
   MN, 1986), pp. 57–58.
23 Robert Hunter, 'The Cairo Archives for the Study
   of Elites in Modern Egypt', *International Journal of
   Middle East Studies*, 4 (1973), p. 483.
24 See Kenneth Cuno, *The Pasha's Peasants: Land,
   Society, and Economy in Lower Egypt, 1740–1858*
   (Cambridge, 1992) and Khaled Fahmy, *All the
   Pasha's Men: Mehmed Ali, his Army, and the Making of
   Modern Egypt* (Cambridge, 1997).
25 James C. Scott, *Seeing Like a State: How Certain
   Schemes to Improve the Human Condition have Failed*
   (New Haven, CT, 1998), pp. 31–32.
26 Donald Reid, 'Cultural Imperialism and
   Nationalism', p. 58.
27 Antonio Gramsci, *Prison Notebooks*, tr. Joseph
   A. Buttigieg (New York, 1992), p. 221.

Part two:
al-Darb al-Ahmar in
the 21st Century

View of the restored
courtyard of the Khayrbak
complex, Historic Cities
Programme, 2006

17 Contemporary observations of al-Darb al-Ahmar

Karim Ibrahim and Seif El-Rashidi

Seif El-Rashidi, a historian, and Karim Ibrahim, an architect, were hired by the Aga Khan Trust for Culture to evaluate al-Darb al-Ahmar. Their first task was a house-to-house survey of the people's needs and concerns. They are both natives of Cairo, but neither had ever been in al-Darb al-Ahmar before. Their impressions follow.

Setting the scene
Our work in al-Darb al-Ahmar began in 1997 as the Aga Khan Trust for Culture put forward a proposal for the creation of a park on a rubbish dump at the eastern periphery of 'Historic Cairo'. The eastern edge of al-Darb al-Ahmar, built against the eastern Ayyubid City Wall, overlooked what was still used as a rubbish tip. Mounds of debris, constituting what were called 'the Darassa Hills', almost completely buried the city wall, and the urban fabric of al-Darb al-Ahmar expanded eastwards onto these mounds in the form of shacks that were, nevertheless, the permanent homes of some of the area's poorest residents.

Despite the proximity of this eastern area of al-Darb al-Ahmar to the constantly bustling al-Azhar Street and the Salah Salem Highway, a walk along the line of the buried city wall revealed glimpses of a community that seemed totally isolated from its immediate surroundings. This was of course, a fallacy; the poor living conditions in the shacks on the Darassa Hills, and the blighted appearance of many of the houses along the city wall misleadingly made the area seem like a forgotten microcosm, disconnected from the street life of nearby Khan al-Khalili. Piles of tin and fabric awaiting recycling, packs of dun-coloured stray dogs were barely visible on top of the mounds of decomposed historic waste, and the overall quiet created an atmosphere not unlike that of a faded 19th-century photograph. In reality, however, al-Darb al-Ahmar was, and still is, a vibrant hub of activity in the centre of Cairo.

Without a map the eastern area of al-Darb al-Ahmar, with its narrow streets leading off into countless cul-de-sacs and alleys, might seem confusing. It is, however, quite straightforward. The topography of the area is shaped by the fact that it constitutes the edge of the walled city; a long road, Darb Shoughlan, running parallel to the city wall, forms an uninterrupted linear connection between north and south. This gives the area a strong sense of identity, creating a single thoroughfare along which smaller residential enclaves lie, helping to reinforce the sense of community.

Despite al-Darb al-Ahmar's long history, very few of its extant buildings predate the late 19th century, and the urban fabric consists primarily of three or four storey houses, some of which still retain stone decoration on the ground floor, reflecting the area's erstwhile prosperity. There are also remnants of even more affluent times: ruined mansions and palaces, often with Italianate painted ceilings and murals, and a few, still older, constructed in the Ottoman style. Among these are set the less successful building projects of the 20th century: grey apartment buildings of the 1970s and 1980s, and from the 1990s very loose interpretations of Islamic architecture, generally facades designed to meet planning requirements for contextually appropriate architecture.

This mix of building types can somehow go unnoticed in al-Darb al-Ahmar, so strong is the sense of urban character. A visitor to the neighbourhood once commented on its similarity to Naples, and it does in fact have the feel of a southern Italian town. The narrow streets, frequently obstructed by craftsmen at work and a range of other activities, make scooters the most efficient means of transport, and warm, usually sunny days ensure that laundry is always hanging out of windows and over balconies to dry.

At first, al-Darb al-Ahmar comes across either as the example, par excellence, of a poor, chronically neglected quarter of Cairo, or, conversely, as a neighbourhood that has been spared the ravages of modernity and its discontents. The area's physical environment plays a large part in conveying these initial, not entirely accurate, images. On one hand, the deterioration infrastructure and poor maintenance often impart a sense of hopelessness. On the other hand, the multitude of small-scale craft-related enterprises can misleadingly portray the area as one where local residents, with few worldly concerns and no ambitions for a different life, contentedly engage in age-old artisanal activities.

As our involvement in al-Darb al-Ahmar has been continuous, and usually on a daily basis since 1997, our first impressions were quite quickly superseded by knowledge acquired through our survey work and site documentation. Our working relationship, spanning five years to date, has led to a deeper understanding of the area's potential and problems.

The project's beginnings
Al-Darb al-Ahmar's gradual but steady decline over the course of several decades was suddenly accelerated by the 1992 Cairo earthquake. Although afterwards most of the houses were still standing, it had been necessary to demolish many of the upper floors, thereby compelling the residents to move elsewhere, often to new government-built residential developments on the outskirts of the city. In 1997, when our work started, the general feeling was that the area had seen better days: it had become much quieter, and local residents were often nostalgic for the busier, pre-earthquake times. Yet, people had also come to terms with the fact that the area had changed for the worse and that there seemed little prospect of any improvement. As studies are commonplace, the sight of surveyors, maps in hand, traversing the area did not immediately indicate the scale of things to come.

The beginning of work on the park site in 1998 quickly brought about the feeling that al-Darb al-Ahmar was going to change. The park project was conceived as a green lung for the residents of central Cairo, including of course the inhabitants of al-Darb al-Ahmar, but it seemed impossible that a rubbish dump could be turned into a community amenity.

The impending change raised concerns about a clause in Egypt's antiquities law permitting, even encouraging, the clearance of buildings constructed within the vicinity of registered monuments – of which the city wall is one. Local residents were well aware of this threat to their existence, yet before there had been any interest in the Darassa site the issue had seemed unimportant.

Articles appeared in the local newspapers, announcing the creation of a ring road encircling Islamic Cairo. With these articles came fears of eviction, of large-scale urban transformation and a great deal of uncertainty. Our neighbourhood surveys, previously perceived as unthreatening, were taken by local residents as the ultimate proof that al-Darb al-Ahmar was to be no more and rumours about the clearance of the area multiplied.

Our relationship with the local residents thus began with a great deal of suspicion about our real agenda, perhaps because residents were well aware that relocation tended to be seen as a cure-all for Cairo's urban problems. Two terms quickly became part of the vocabulary of al-Darb al-Ahmar residents, 'the Project', and 'the Company', the great unknowns, of which we were a daily reminder.

We had lots of explaining to do, as each resident wanted to hear first-hand what the project intended to accomplish, and despite widespread disbelief when presented with the scheme's intentions, the warm welcome we received was astonishing. Having a cup of tea or a soft drink in every house was obligatory. 'The demolition team has arrived', residents would joke as we returned to a house for the third or fourth time, only to let us in so that we could draw ground plans or elevations.

The perceived threat of eviction immediately elicited two standard responses from residents; some seemed happy, repeatedly stressing that the area was beyond hope: 'Take us away from here', they would say. Others stressed their links to the area and their horror of living elsewhere. On a deeper level, most residents shared the same view: they were attached to the area but were aware of its problems. In an ideal world most of them would have opted to live in al-Darb al-Ahmar with better amenities and a higher standard of living. For the most part, those who wished to leave momentarily forgot the most likely alternative: living on the outskirts of Cairo, where facilities were extremely limited. In a few cases, residents whose homes had been destroyed in the earthquake even preferred a dilapidated room in al-Darb al-Ahmar to an entire flat on the outskirts of Cairo. Al-Darb al-Ahmar was more practical; it constituted their social network, and was the site and source of their livelihood.

Artisan, still
from the documentary
Living with the Past

In al-Darb al-Ahmar, social life and work are inseparable. Workshops are often small, and where space is required, as in carpentry, craftsmen work in the street, sharing tools and conversation throughout the day. Craftsmen move around following the shade, and local coffee shops place tables in the street that, in turn, follow the craftsmen wherever they go. The working day starts and ends late. Ten o'clock is considered too early to knock at people's doors, breakfast is close to midday, and by the late afternoon street life is at its peak, hammering and welding competing with blaring music and children playing.

Ties are strong and people know each other, at least on a first name basis, if not by nickname. Questions like 'What's *Batta*'s (Duckie's) real name?' were common when our survey required us to collect information about ownership and tenancy. Often, workers and craftsmen are known only by trade names, a telling indicator of the familiarity that exists among local residents who share public spaces.

Yet living in close quarters, especially when resources are limited, also causes friction between people, and al-Darb al-Ahmar is no exception. In some of the smaller cul-de-sacs especially, a lack of privacy often causes rivalry between neighbours, many of whom are related. News and gossip tends to travel fast, discussions and arguments can easily be overheard, and familiarity permits people to get involved, usually with good intentions.

But, while a general sense of camaraderie prevails, and in times of need people tend to stick up for each other, heated arguments often arise, and conflicts of interest are common. Although there is a sense of common identity in al-Darb al-Ahmar, nonetheless, there can be a considerable discrepancy between people in terms of economic situation and level of education. While in the poorest cases, an entire family can be found living in one or two small dilapidated rooms, at the other end of the scale are families that inhabit large well-furnished apartments where each of the children has their own bedroom. A good indicator of economic status is the existence of a formal sitting room, or *salon*, generally used only when there are guests. These are rare, however, and tend to be found in apartments whose residents look down on the area

and consider themselves to be of a better social class. Even within the same building, differences in standard of living can be startling. Almost always, ground-floor apartments, characteristically small, poorly ventilated, dark and very damp, are inhabited by the poorer families. Wealthier families live on the upper storeys, where apartments are more spacious and large windows allow for good ventilation and lighting.

The notion that al-Darb al-Ahmar is a 'traditional' neighbourhood is questionable. The young generation especially, although still maintaining a strong sense of community is very much in touch with Egyptian pop culture; global awareness is strong. Teenagers, like teenagers everywhere, are fashion conscious, listen to the latest pop music and have posters of pop idols on their walls. Local entertainment can be found in computer arcades and one or two snooker halls. Al-Darb al-Ahmar may be poor, but it is very much an urban environment, with a population comprised predominantly of urbanites, well aware of both national and international events. Immigrants from rural areas are rare, and are often regarded as country bumpkins.

Al-Darb al-Ahmar's commercial base is an integral part of the city-wide business network. In addition to shops and businesses catering to the needs of local residents, a significant portion of the workforce is involved in producing goods for a larger market. The cheaper end of the Cairo furniture market, for example, consumes the work of local carpenters and upholsterers. A few, higher-standard workshops also exist and cater to more discriminating clients. Proximity to the tourist sites of Islamic Cairo makes al-Darb al-Ahmar a logical place for the production of souvenirs. Inlaid boxes, copper trays, lanterns and other stereotypical Egyptian-looking items are made here and eventually find their way to the tourist bazaars just north of the district in Khan al-Khalili and into hotel gift shops across the city.

Tent-making (*khayamiyya*) is one of the area's traditional crafts, and today the industry produces appliqué-work bedspreads, wall-hangings and cushions, most of which will end up abroad.

Al-Darb al-Ahmar's role as part of the Egyptian heritage industry is a tricky one, and perhaps one of its most sensitive issues. The local residents' contribution to the tourist industry is often seen as their main asset. In fact, the inlaid boxes and brass trays designed for the tourist market are seen as the sole justification for the existence of a poor urban community by those who envisage al-Darb al-Ahmar as a medieval backdrop for tourism – the setting for excursions 'back in time' involving well-maintained but unused historic buildings, traditional handicrafts and little else.

On buildings and people
In general, local authorities, especially those dealing with antiquities, have a long-standing tradition of not considering local residents as part of the urban fabric of historic cities. This leads to the fear and mistrust of surveyors that we first experienced during our work in al-Darb al-Ahmar; local residents know that, for the most part, they will be seen as obstacles to the realisation of some ambitious tourist-related scheme, and that their needs and rights to the city are likely to be ignored. The process usually follows the same basic scenario: a distant, sometimes snobbish, intellectual-looking person with a map in his hand appears, often dealing arrogantly with local residents and refusing to answer questions. A period of silence is followed by a demolition order and residents are efficiently moved to a remote area on the outskirts of the city. The procedure is so standardised and predictable that it can almost be summarised as a mathematical formula: intellectual-looking person + map + disrespect + refusal to answer questions = demolition of houses and relocation to a remote area.

Egypt's current policy towards historic buildings is flawed, and having developed in the 19th century has never been reassessed. The idea persists that historic buildings are by definition 'monuments'. This view equates functioning community buildings such as mosques or water-fountains with socially obsolete structures such as Pharonic temples that have long ceased to be used for their original purposes.

The so-called monuments of al-Darb al-Ahmar, are in fact simply community buildings of historic and architectural significance which, almost always, are still playing their original roles as components of

Cairo, contemporary scene
with a water-seller

a dynamic and vibrant urban fabric. The process of treating historic buildings as monuments, and isolating them (both physically and socially) from the community has provoked a domino effect of dilapidation of historic urban areas as well as a deep-rooted sense of mutual distrust between residents and the authorities. Historic buildings when treated as monuments are isolated from the community, which in its turn neglects them – leading local authorities to assume that local residents are by nature hostile to historic buildings and must be kept away from them. Local residents therefore lose faith in the authorities and view them as the enemy.

The initial feeling of distrust that we ourselves experienced was eventually dispelled, thanks to the fact that our offices were located in al-Darb al-Ahmar itself, and not in some distant affluent district of the city.

Despite this, the project's approach towards al-Darb al-Ahmar received strong opposition from public figures and intellectuals. What we were doing was criticised as a waste of money. To demolish the urban fabric, vacate the area and start anew was generally seen as a more sensible approach.

But al-Darb al-Ahmar deserves to be rehabilitated with sustainable schemes, integrating socio-economic activities and a tactful use of appropriate building technology. The area has been left to face a very harsh physical, social and economic environment: pollution, a lack of technical know-how, bureaucracy, corruption, outdated plans and a lack of hope. It has never been given the chance to prove its viability, to demonstrate that with the right approach, rehabilitation can succeed. The houses in al-Darb al-Ahmar have lost neither their social nor their physical functionality; structural intervention and a minor remodelling of the use of certain spaces in buildings can prove a highly effective solution to the problem of how to carry out urban renewal in many ways. Upgrading al-Darb al-Ahmar's urban fabric is still cheaper than the cost of vacating the area and rehousing its residents elsewhere, even if one excludes the social costs and calculates only that of providing new homes.

Of course technical, financial and logistic obstacles in the rehabilitation process have to be tackled. In this instance, widespread ignorance existed about the use of proper technology and materials, not only among people in al-Darb al-Ahmar, but also among professionals. Moreover, most of the residents had been deprived of any proper technical assistance. Our role was therefore to provide the technical assistance which was lacking and which was essential for the physical rehabilitation of the area.

Local residents also have had no access to the financial, banking or mortgage systems that can give them the funds required to repair their houses. As most of their assets are not acknowledged by official institutional establishments, they had to rely on informal means to acquire large sums of money, usually through personal collective agreements (known colloquially as '*gam'eyya*' or *murabha*). At present, the formal financial establishments and informal agreements constitute totally separate means, albeit with the same end. They need to be reconciled, in order to allow local residents to benefit from loans and other financial arrangements that word-of-honour agreements cannot always provide.

Further, complex, inefficient and occasionally corrupt bureaucracy made it nearly impossible for al-Darb al-Ahmar residents to repair their houses. Obtaining a restoration permit is nearly impossible; the request had to be made by the owners of the building, which in many cases could consist of more than twenty people per building. To make matters worse, most buildings generated a monthly revenue of as little as twenty Egyptian pounds, so the owners have no desire to maintain their buildings. In purely financial terms, it would have seemed foolish to endeavour to keep the property intact.

Yet it is the owners who must decide to repair buildings; the residents who have lived there perhaps for decades are helpless. They need to get the approval of at least 75 per cent of the owners, registered ownership papers (which were never seen for any building in al-Darb al-Ahmar), a technical report and a supervision certificate from a registered structural engineer, in addition to many other requirements. For a typical resident of al-Darb al-Ahmar this process would have constituted a lifetime's occupation (and success a memorable accomplishment). It would be interesting to know how many restoration permits have actually been issued for al-Darb al-Ahmar in the last decade or so.

The rehabilitation process is all about giving local residents access to proper technical, financial and logistical assistance. For this to happen though, the perception of an area must change. The link between people and buildings, the fact that an urban fabric without people is meaningless, must be acknowledged. Historic buildings, the most prominent of which have been mistakenly treated as monuments, need to be seen within a broader social context. The valuable urban fabric of al-Darb al-Ahmar, instead of being turned into a collection of underused historic buildings, had to be seen as a potential catalyst for economic and social change, and as a means of improving the community's living standards. In the grand schemes to transform historic areas such as al-Darb al-Ahmar, local residents deserve to have the chance to participate.

18 Remaking Cairo, revisioning al-Darb al-Ahmar

Kamran Asdar 'Ali and Martina Rieker

Introduction

Life in al-Darb al-Ahmar has its own rhythm and pace, or so goes the saying about most popular (*sha'bi*) neighbourhoods in contemporary Cairo. However, the ongoing restoration work and conservation projects linked to a general spatial 'uplifting' that are specific to al-Darb al-Ahmar are part of a longer history of the changes that people of the area have endured. Their social circumstances, hopes and concerns are well documented in the papers that follow. Where colleagues like Mohamed Abdel Hafiz Kotb and Ragui Assaad discuss the socio-economic and labour problems in the district, Dina Shehayeb and Ahmed Sedky concentrate on the element of national heritage that the area contains. This recurring image of a cultural repository has in its turn been the motivation for many preservation projects, especially the one spearheaded by the Aga Khan Trust for Culture. Most of the papers reflect these interventions, which are implemented in the area by experts who retain a high degree of sensitivity to the lived aspect of people's daily practices and experience. This sensitivity is particularly evident in the paper by Karim Ibrahim and Seif El-Rashidi who document the variety of opinions and the ambivalent attitudes that greeted their research team when it was seeking to understand the community's views on the proposed park (al-Azhar Park) to be built nearby. This park, on al-Darassa site, is now complete and the early 21st century has brought yet other 'conservation' projects that seek to reshape life in the community. Whether the park becomes intertwined with popular life in the district or remains largely inaccessible to the community due to its high entry fee is a discussion for another analytical piece on public spaces and the poor in Middle Eastern cities. Here, seeking a framework for debate, this paper pre-empts the contributions that follow and presents a critical discussion on 'preserving and conserving' Fatimid Cairo. In doing so it first provides an historical context for Cairo's rapid spatial and demographic transformation in the past century. After that it focuses on how this ongoing process, entangled as it is in the dynamic of destruction/reconstruction, tends to reshape al-Darb al-Ahmar and how it affects people's lives there.

View of the Citadel with the mounds of the Darassa Hills in the foreground, *circa* 1880–1890

Outside Cairo, oil on canvas,
Cesare Biseo, 1883

Historical trajectories

In 1867, the ruler of Egypt, Khedive Isma'il Pasha, visited the Exposition
Universelle in Paris as a guest of Napoleon III. During his journey,
the ruler, who had earlier lived in Paris as a student, was given extensive
tours of the city by Baron Haussmann, who was Prefect de la Seine.
Haussmann was instrumental in the redesigning of Paris, which resulted
in its broad boulevards, formal parks and famous new sewer system.
This redevelopment of the city so impressed the khedive that Cairo, after
his return, became a site for experimentation in 'haussmannisation'.
New areas west of the old Fatimid–Mamluk city were marked off for
expansion based on designs that created grid-pattern radial streets,
long avenues ending in public squares, and public buildings and monuments situated at the end of long vistas.[1]

The frantic pace at which the city was developed after the khedive's
return from Europe was determined by the date set for the opening
of the Suez Canal. In the two years between 1867 and November 1869,
when the canal was officially inaugurated, Cairo went through a series
of rapid changes in order to make the city as presentable to visitors as
any respectable European capital. The effort to modernise the country,
with expenditure on canals, railways and the telegraph, in addition to
the creation of a modern Western style of city put the Egyptian government even deeper in debt to its European creditors. Isma'il had altered
the public face of Cairo, yet he also lost his country as a result of the
financial pressures exerted by the French and the British, who finally
took over day-to-day control of the country in 1882.

Alongside these changes, as Janet Abu-Lughod has demonstrated,
the population of the country grew by 130 per cent between 1847 and
1897. As Cairo's population increased, land was made available by
incorporating the surrounding districts. Draining canals and ditches
created new areas of land that were developed and settled by the end of
the 19th century.[2] With increasing employment opportunities during
and after World War I, Cairo went through another massive increase
in population. By the late 1920s the city's population had passed the
million mark.[3]

In the middle of the 20th century Gamal Abdel Nasser's (1952–1970) industrialisation policy resulted in the construction of the iron and steel works in Helwan on the southern edge of the city and this was balanced by the expansion of an industrial park in Shubra al-Khaima north of Cairo. This growth drew peasants to Cairo looking for employment and so created pressure on a housing market that could not compete with the growth in population, especially at the lower end. To ease this pressure, the state intervened directly in the management of housing stock and built popular housing that it rented out at very reasonable rates in Cairo and other cities to civil servants on low incomes and industrial labourers. These measures were also taken in order to alleviate the housing shortage that Cairo residents had faced, including an increase in rents, during World War II.

Following this period, Cairo's population grew at an annual rate of more than 4 per cent in the 1960s and by the mid 1970s the population was approximately eight million, up from five million in 1960. However, this growth declined rapidly in the mid 1970s when rural Egyptians began emigrating instead to oil-rich Arab states to seek employment.[4] The open-door economic policies of the Sadat era also created a boom in privately-owned luxury housing in the 1970s, largely concentrated in the affluent districts of Cairo and along the Corniche. Increased prosperity resulting from the emigration to the oil-rich Arab states coupled with high interest rates, inflation, skyrocketing prices for property and increasing building costs made it difficult for the low and middle-income households to own their own houses. At the same time Sadat's removal of the Nasser era's substantial government subsidy on rents meant that new owners were free to charge rents based on what the market would bear. This created a discrepancy between the level of earnings of the majority of Cairenes and their ability even to rent a home.

Given the shortage of affordable housing and population pressure, planners in the 1970s proposed that new communities be established in the desert areas not far from Cairo. These self-sufficient towns were meant to provide both employment and housing, thus decreasing the spatial and social pressures on Cairo. In 1979, the Ministry for Housing and New Communities produced legislation designed to work towards a master plan for new cities that was connected to the regional development of cities like Cairo, Port Said and Isma'iliyya. It was estimated that these satellite cities would contain between half a million to a million inhabitants. In the 1990s, other schemes were developed to encourage people to leave the Nile Valley and establish communities in the desert. The Aswan Dam at the southern end of the country and the Eastern and Western deserts were promoted as areas where people could earn a living through agriculture, fishing, small industries or craft production.[5]

These schemes notwithstanding, owning a house in Cairo remains difficult for most low-income households. Since credit and housing finance in easy installments is difficult to obtain, and with the rising cost of land and construction, renting remains the main solution for most families. Families already living in apartments whose rents are fixed, or frozen, are better off. Young couples who try to get into the renting market now spend over 25 per cent of their salaries, the common standard in a free market economy, on renting a place to live. This skewed accessibility to housing has forced most poor families to pool their resources and create what are commonly known as informal housing areas.[6]

Along with the housing crisis, the decrease in the subsidies on food stuffs has led to increases in prices with the result that expenditure on food for the average household has substantially increased in the last ten to fifteen years. This has led many households, already spending more than 75 per cent of their income on food, to cut their food consumption substantially. People in poor urban neighbourhoods stopped eating meat and their main sources of nutrition became bread and beans. Although it is estimated that the per capita daily calorie intake increased from 2,660 in 1969 to 3,501 in 1986, the poorest 10 per cent of the urban population consumes only 26 per cent of this increase compared to the wealthiest 10 per cent who consume 55 per cent of it. Despite the general increase in per capita income in the 1970s and 1980s, since the mid 1980s the disparity in incomes has become more marked. Based on estimates of the market prices for minimum food consumption, in the early 1990s almost 51 per cent of the urban and 47 per cent of the rural population lived below the poverty line, and 35 per cent of the total population consumed less than 2,000 calories a day.[7]

The social unrest unleashed by the removal of subsidies and the rising rate of unemployment have created constant problems of law and order, and civic management for the Egyptian state. In the last few decades, the state has been made acutely aware of the volatility of the urban population, first through the food riots in 1977, and then in 1986 when its own rurally recruited police force joined in the rampage after the price of bread went up. Skirmishes in the early 1990s with Islamist groups in poor urban localities and in the villages of Upper Egypt, have also sensitised the state to the 'breeding ground' imagery that the popular media uses when describing the origin and sites of these events. Yet the solution proposed is one of law and order rather than distribution and social justice.

The increase in informal housing has, as mentioned, gradually expanded the city's boundaries. Cairo has spread outwards through the incorporation of agricultural land and the surrounding desert. In densely populated areas building space has been increased by adding additional floors to already-existing residential or commercial structures. Area surveys, however, indicate that the inner city is losing population as a result of changes in land use, through forcible eviction of tenants by both private landlords and the state. In contrast the outlying northern, southern and western edges of the city have a very high growth rate and communities there have doubled or tripled in size in the last twenty years.[8] The widening of existing roads, the reorganising of sewage facilities, the removal of what are described as 'illegal encroachments', the collapse of old buildings and ongoing efforts at making the inner city of Cairo into what we might call a 'museum space' for tourists, have all resulted in the eviction of people from the more populated districts of the city. Within this configuration of urban life and the new schemes to reorganise urban space in contemporary Egypt, we discuss, in what follows, the impact of these changes on a particular Fatimid neighbourhood of Cairo.

The 'Museumification' of Cairo's medieval districts

> The geographies of exclusion which mark so much urban space are not only geographically delineated but are imaginaries linking the social and the psychic, placing [difference] at the centre of the cityscape.
> Westwood/Williams, *Imagining Cities* (1997)[9]

Municipal, national and international concern for the medieval city's architecture has been the subject of public debate since the earthquake of 1992. Five years after this earthquake the Egyptian government formally launched its plan to restore Islamic Cairo and transform the city's remaining medieval districts into an 'Open Air Museum' or as it has also been termed, 'a tunnel through time'. The project, its progress and plans have since featured prominently in the city's print and visual media. For instance, the completion of twenty-two months of restoration work at the mosque of al-Azhar in July of 1998 was the occasion for the Minister for Culture to remind the public that the Azhar renovation project was the first step in a comprehensive plan to restore Islamic Cairo. On 21 December 1998 the front page of the newspaper *Al-Ahram*, featured an announcement by the Minister for Housing, Muhammad Ibrahim Soliman, with the headline 'al-Azhar and al-Husayn, an Open Islamic Museum'. For the readers of *Al-Ahram,* his announcement that 'studies to develop the area have been completed' and that 'the area linking al-Husayn and al-Azhar will be closed to cars and transformed into a pedestrian zone and a tourist market to serve both pedestrians and religious tourism' was not particularly newsworthy. Yet for the more alert reader, attuned to the history of modern housing policies in the city, the fact that the announcement was made by the Minister for Housing as opposed to a Minister for Tourism, Culture or Antiquities was a cause for reflection.

The lengthy and ongoing process of restructuring the Egyptian economy has had a significant impact on the socialised spaces of the city. Sadat's new economic policy, as mentioned above, initiated the displacement of a good proportion of the population of the working-class district of Bulaq between 1979 and 1981, to make room for the development of modern banking, hotel and commercial complexes along the river front.[10] The 1992 earthquake was another significant event in the politics of Cairo's housing problem. Whereas previously, overcrowding and lack of affordable housing had been steadily pushing the urban poor into the fast growing peri-urban areas, the earthquake now set in motion the systematic displacement of the poor from the inner city. Poor areas of the city that had been damaged by the earthquake were rarely rebuilt; instead the residents were resettled in the remote peri-urban spaces on the edge of the desert. A growing corpus of sociological literature attests to the devastating economic and social consequences of this resettlement on families. Since then, an aggressive municipal policy has proceeded to modernise and 'clean up' large portions of the inner city. Plans for a 'museumification' of Egyptian urban (Cairo and Alexandria) and village spaces (Esna, Edfu, Qurna in Upper Egypt), constituted a new phase in the spatial history of both city and country.[11]

Stepping outside the specifics of Cairene politics for a minute, contemporary 'museumification' policies draw on numerous historical precedents.[12] Firstly, if Haussmann proverbially tore down all of Paris in order to create the modern city, the Khedive Isma'il's interventions were more limited in scope. As Abu Lughod has shown, the area of the new city that he built was quite small, yet, significantly for our argument here, the medieval quarters were hidden behind a facade.[13] These local visions of the modern city and its other (the medieval city), we suggest, mark a particular trajectory in the conception of modern Cairo. Secondly, ideologies of 'museumification' are produced within and draw on Egypt's imbrication in the global tourist industry. Thirdly, the Islamic heritage industry is part of the larger global trend towards the 'museumification' and 'monumentalisation' of the past(s) over the

al-Darb al-Ahmar in the 21st Century

View of the Citadel
from al-Azhar Park, 2005

last decade, whilst also being a response to the shifting religious sensibilities in Southern Mediterranean and Middle Eastern cultures.

In this scenario, the Islamic heritage industry sits awkwardly beside an international tourist industry enthralled by the sites of Antiquity, yet somewhat hesitant in its enthusiasm for things Islamic. It must also negotiate with local audiences that are variously baffled at or uncomfortable with the international tourist industry's focus on a distant past at the expense of what most people in the Southern Mediterranean regard as their continuing personal history. This is especially pronounced in a country like Egypt, where millions have been spent on the on-going restoration process for Pharaonic antiquities whilst Fatimid mosques, for instance, were left to fend for themselves.

The increase in tourist consumption, and the challenges the city faces in developing a more extensive urban tourism, lie at the heart of the 'Open Air Museum' project. The medieval city centre is clustered around the university mosque of al-Azhar. West of al-Azhar and to the south of al-Husayn Mosque lies the medieval Khan al-Khalili market, which now caters almost exclusively to tourists. Variously renovated over past decades the market has parking spaces for buses. The Egyptian tourist industry is overwhelmingly structured around group tourism, consequently the availability of parking for buses dictates the limited selection of sites in the city that tourists can visit. An afternoon of shopping in Khan al-Khalili is the only non-guided event in most tour packages. The mosque of al-Husayn is not accessible to non-Muslims and al-Azhar is generally not included in the official tour packages. Consequently, the Housing Minister's reference to these two sites, including the remarks about religious tourism and the construction of a new tourist market on its doorstep in the same sentence is undoubtedly indicative of the various political agendas and sensibilities with which the Egyptian tourist industry is trying to negotiate. However, it also indicates the ways in which the renovation of medieval Islamic structures is now being presented within the context of a global heritage industry, an industry driven by the late modern nostalgia for an uncontextualised 'other time'.[14]

The municipality solicited international aid to restore collapsing mosques and dilapidated medieval houses and homes in preparation for their display as part of the 'Open Air Museum'. Based on a United Nations Development Programme Study, the plan was to reclaim and renovate historical monuments, relocate 'polluting and noisy' workshops, and rehouse families in alternative sites in the city's peri-urban areas. The network of districts that comprise Islamic Cairo is home to a quarter of a million people (including 30,000 squatters) whose lives and worlds have been consistently represented in the local print media as constituting a parasitic relationship with the monuments.

Across a busy street from Khan al-Khalili, the neighbourhood to the south remains slightly at a distance from the bustle of the tourist industry. In the Bab al-Zuwayla district the markets continue to cater primarily to what is still a poor neighbourhood. As the southern gateway into the medieval city, though, the area is presented as an integral part of the municipality's 'Open Air Museum'. The neighbourhood is abuzz with the expectation of the wealth coming from the Khan side, combined with anxieties about the place of human beings in this exhibition of Egypt's past. Al-Khayyamiyya (the tent-makers), constitute the district's best established and most prosperous business community. A well-established part of the city's economy, their command of a historic craft makes them confident supporters of the municipal project. Confident, therefore, of their role in the 'Open Air Museum', the tent-makers are also quite vocal about who will not fit into the re-scripting of heritage:

> People here are talking about the fact that the government is going to force some people to change their trade, especially because some of these professions are very dangerous for the monuments here, such as this chicken shop. They use water and it threatens the monuments. Some people have already changed their previous trade, becoming tent-makers.[15]

The late 20th-century shoe cart selling plastic slippers, as well as the age-old urban chicken seller, disturb the newly emerging social

Darb Shoughlan with a view
of the Aslam Mosque, 2002

geography of the Egyptian museum. Conflicts between shopkeepers
and informal street sellers are nothing new. But now these tensions
have been legitimised by a new vocabulary. The 'museumification' of
Islamic Cairo is not only a contest over space between the municipality
and the urban poor, but it is giving rise to the use of an equally controversial new spatial grammar in the districts themselves.

Our point here is not to reiterate the debates on the gentrification
of poor urban districts, nor to outline the strategies by which diverse
state-controlled projects implement urban renewal. Rather, we wish
to point towards ways in which older nationalist discourses about the
sha'b ('the folk' as an object of post-colonial people-making projects)
are being transformed by the new heritage industries.

We began this paper by suggesting ways in which a certain vision
of belonging has informed the various means of making sense of the
city's spatiality. The complex historical traces this vision has left, and
its contemporary dismemberment, can be discerned in the local discussion about subjectivity and the national heritage. As we argued
earlier, this discussion has been woven into the experiences of the
working poor and the middle classes in the course of the city's housing
and employment crises during recent decades. Two kinds of tension
in this discussion, in particular, are of interest to our argument here.
One of them concerns the above-mentioned division between the tent-
makers as producers of items connected with the notion of national
heritage and the rest of the community. As one elderly carpet seller
put it, nothing will happen to the tent-makers 'since the government
supports them'. The rumours about the moving of street sellers to
commercially suspect areas such as Salih Salim Street (in the words of
a vegetable seller, a street for cars rather than a 'rural neighbourhood'
such as al-Darb al-Ahmar), fears about how limited skills can, or
cannot, be transformed into new means of making a living (the young
man re-filling lighters, the woman from Fayyum who sells eggs, the
man selling milk), and the overall discrepancies between the rights of
those who have government permits and/or leasing arrangements
with the *awqaf* (religious and charitable endowments) authorities and

those who do not, are creating circumstances in which local debates and conversations define a new set of social divisions.

This climate of insecurity and the contrasting hope of new jobs (for some) is creating powerful narratives about what defines the both community and outsiders. Living in the district as opposed to commuting from other parts of the city (Darassa, Manshiet Nasser, Dar al-Salam) or from villages (Fayyum) outside Cairo, is now becoming a spatial metaphor by which current social position and previous notions of attachment to the neighbourhood and to the nation are being reassessed. As a middle-class shopkeeper with a degree who commutes from the fairly affluent suburb of Maadi to work in his family's shoe business in the area, put it:

> The problem is that the people do not understand the benefits of the project, in addition they do not look at the long term benefits of the project. They are not aware of the importance of the monuments, they do not know that they live in a treasure-box. This *sabil* was restored recently. It was opened by Suzanne Mubarak, now you find all the pavement sellers standing there with their donkey carts as if (they were) in medieval times. They pour water on the monuments and do not pay any attention to the history and value of such things.

The pavement sellers, those whose claims to space within the area have the least legal standing, are now in the rhetoric of middle-class shop owners like our educated informant central targets in the revisioning of the area. Overcrowding in the wider al-Darb al-Ahmar area, amongst other things, began forcing expanding businesses out of their rented shops into the streets in the 1950s. These extensions of shop fronts have been particularly singled out by the municipality as obstacles to the display of the medieval shop fronts. Upper Egyptian migrants, who came into the area and either purchased shops, or shop fronts in the 1950s and 1960s, are universally blamed for this situation. In other words, it is outsiders that have undermined the authenticity of the district. Commenting on being evicted from her stall, a middle-

aged woman selling vegetables in front of Dehisha Mosque argued likewise that it is a new breed of villagers who have taken over their old 'legal' spots that are causing the problems. As she put it, 'These women are not from the neighbourhood, so no one dares to tell them to leave.' A galabiyya seller in northern Bab al-Zuwalya graphically describes an instance of the problems the outsider causes for the district:

> Most of the shops are rented from the *awqaf*, and they have permission; the problem is the people who come and start building a kiosk in the street. These people were removed several times, but the they built the kiosks again because it does not cost them anything, just some pieces of wood and that's it. They started doing this next to al-Ghawri Mosque. First they started building wooden kiosks, then step by step they started to remove the stones under the mosque to have more space inside and that is why the minaret of that mosque collapsed during the earthquake in 1992. The building became very weak because of all that these people did to it. Now they have removed them and they are renovating the building.

The tensions and social divisions in popular urban markets and districts have their own complex histories. Putting in operation the new heritage discourses and the rearticulation of notions of *sha'b* within the neo-liberal Egyptian present, are having various sorts of impact on the texture of such local communities. In particular, they confirm and give fresh meaning to the fault lines within particular districts. These on-going processes authorise and empower new social geographies of exclusion and inclusion. As the poor are, once again, accused of ruralising the city and making Cairo a city of peasants, the image of disorder and chaos is not dissimilar to that in late 19th-century descriptions of unruly *fallahin* in Cairo. These are old divisions that the elite have used to their advantage numerous times before. However, the modern Egyptian state, under pressure from international lenders and pursuing a free-market policy, is no longer prepared to incorporate in society by means of housing and civic reform those who have been left on the margins. Cairo is the main space in which the various visions of Egypt's modernisation have taken shape. Starting in the mid 19th century, the city's inhabitants have lived through many of these visions and changes. It is now the central site where the negotiations of the new 'Egyptian museum' are being expressed; a museum that is bound to redefine the ordinary people's relationship with the city. Within this context, it is also site where a fresh 'hausmannisation' is taking place, the effects of which on the lives of the poor and the marginalised is a story that remains largely untold.

1   See Zeynip Celik, *Displaying the Orient* (Berkeley, CA, 1992), p. 35 and Abu-Lughod, Janet, *Cairo* (Princeton, NJ, 1971), p. 105.

2   In the first decade of the 20th century the High Dam was built almost 500 miles south of Cairo at Aswan. The Nile waters became tamed enough for the expansion of the city across the river onto its western bank.

3   With Egypt's population reaching 60 million today, Cairo accounts for almost a quarter of the total population whereas in 1897 it did not have even a tenth of the country's population. This also reverses a trend of Egypt as a primarily rural country. In 1907, 81 per cent of the population lived in villages, whilst currently approximately 50 per cent live in the rural areas. See Abu-Lughod, *Cairo*, p. 125; Ministry of Development and New Communities, *The Population Problem and Establishment of New Towns in the Arab Republic of Egypt* (Cairo, 1979); and Central Agency for Public Mobilization and Statistics (CAPMAS), *Census of Public Housing and Establishments* (Cairo, 1986).

4   Migration is no longer a major cause of the growth of Cairo. In the period from 1966 to 1976 natural increase accounted for two thirds of the growth and migration for the remaining third. Similarly it is estimated that only 19 per cent of Cairo's population are not born in the city whereas, in a regional comparison, approximately 60 per cent of Istanbul's inhabitants were born somewhere else. See Greater Cairo Region Master Scheme, *Implementing Assessment and Updating Proposal* (Cairo, 1991), and Tekce, Belgin, Linda Oldham and Frederic Shorter, *A Place to Live* (Cairo, 1994).

5   See *Egyptian Gazette* (17 July 1993).

6   See Milad M. Hanna, 'Real Estate Rights in Urban Egypt: The Changing Sociopolitical Winds', in Ann Elizabeth Mayer, ed., *Property Social Structure and Law in the Modern Middle East* (Albany, NY, 1985), pp. 189–211, and *The Greater Cairo, Implementing Assessment*.

7   Heba Nassar, 'The Impact of Adjustment Policies on Nutrition in Egypt', in *The 29th European Association of Agricultural Economists Seminar on Food and Agricultural Policies under Structural Adjustment* (Stuttgart, 1992).

8   The city of Cairo grew at a rate of slightly less than 3 per cent in the 1980s whereas the southern area of Giza, now incorporated in the city, grew at a rate of 5 per cent. Similar areas in the north of the city, like Shubra al-Khaima grew at about 8 per cent. See United Nations, *Population Growth and Policies in Mega-Cities, Cairo*. Population Policy Paper No. 34. Dept. of International Economic and Social Affairs.

9   Sallie Westwood and John Williams, ed., *Imagining Cities: Scripts, Signs, Memory* (New York, 1997).

10 See Farha Ghannam, *Remaking the Modern: Space, Relocation and the Politics of Identity in Global Cairo* (Berkeley, CA, 2002).

11 See Timothy Mitchell, *Rule of Experts* (Berkeley, CA, 2002).

12 The authors would like to thank their research assistant Mustafa Abdallah Abdel-Rahman for his assistance with collecting field interviews in al-Darb al-Ahmar area. For a more extensive discussion regarding museumification processes in Cairo and the MENA region see Martina Rieker and Maureen O'Malley, 'Museum Effects: Politics and Practices of Heritage Inscription in the Southern Mediterranean', in Kamran Asdar Ali and Martina Rieker, ed., *TransActions: Tourism in the Southern Mediterranean* (forthcoming).

13 See Abu-Lughod, *Cairo*.

14 See Susan Stewart, *On Longing: Narratives of the Miniature, the Gigantic, the Souvenir, the Collection* (Baltimore, MD, 1984).

15 Interview with a tent-maker, *al-Khayamiyya* (8 February 2000).

19 | The contemporary labour market in Egypt: formal and informal institutions in the construction sector

Ragui Assaad

Studies of Third World labour markets have come to distinguish between formal and informal labour markets on the basis of whether or not matters concerning employment are regulated by the legal and bureaucratic institutions of society. I argue instead that even in the absence of such regulation, labour markets have a structure of informal institutions whose role has been obscured by an exclusive focus on formal institutions, at least in studies dealing with the urban areas of developing countries. The example studied in this paper is Egypt.

In Egypt the guild system was the primary instrument of economic regulation in urban areas until the end of the 19th century. The organising principles of the guilds were the customary norms, kinship and communal ties. With the introduction of alternative regulatory institutions by the British colonial authorities in the last part of the century, the existing economic regime lost the official sanction of the state and the elements of the guild system that regulated the relationship between economic agents and the state disappeared. The guilds had also organised relationships between guild members, and between guild members and other groups. However, as will be shown, these elements did not disappear with the formal abolition of guilds as the fiscal and regulatory arms of the state. Since they were no longer legally sanctioned, they became in effect informal. Although institutions based on custom, kinship and communal ties were embodied in the concrete historical form of the guilds, there are also many informal variants such as the caste system, the tribe, the clan or the village community. Like their formal counterparts, these generate distinctive labour market structures that deviate in important ways from the perfectly competitive labour market model.

Informal labour market institutions
The notion of the informal sector has received a great deal of attention in development literature.[1] Rather than review the vast literature on the subject and the ensuing debate over the definition of the term, this paper will simply concur with Castells and Portes that a strict definition may not be desirable since it would 'unnecessarily restrict a changing and complex notion that is nevertheless quite intuitive'.[2] Increasingly, the term 'informal sector' is giving way to the notion of an informal economy or simply to the general notion of informality within the economy. This shift has occurred through a realisation that informality is a quality that permeates all sectors of an economy to a greater or lesser extent. It refers to the conditions under which economic transactions are carried out rather than to specific businesses and economic agents.

An important feature of informal labour markets is the patron-client ties between employers and workers. These labour markets are also often characterised by horizontal ties of cohesion between members of the same group. By excluding outsiders from access to the segments of the labour market that they control, group members can generate monopoly rents that are redistributed to the members of the group. This kind of group solidarity was formerly the basis of guild organisation both in Europe and in the Middle East. Even with the dissolution of the guilds, however, informal ties of group cohesion remain as a result of the customary norms of conduct. These norms are internalised by group members through inter-group socialisation and institutions such as craft apprenticeships, which serve to initiate new members to the norms of the group.[3]

While craft guilds no longer exist in Egypt, craftsmen still describe themselves as belonging to *ta'ifat al-mi'mar* (the Master Mason's guild); this term came up quite often in interviews with craftsmen. Thus, while there may not be formal institutions designed to restrict access, the 'corporate spirit' prevails in the customary rules of conduct and group norms passed on from master to apprentice.

The information presented below is based on field research conducted in Egypt during 1987–1989. Data was collected in a series of in-depth interviews and a sample survey of construction workers. Interviews were conducted with workers and subcontractors in all the construction trades, with managers of construction firms, with trade union representatives and with government officials. These interviews were carried out over a period of a year, in 1987 and 1988, at coffee houses

Restoration works on the Umm al-Sultan Sha'ban complex; the AKTC project used local artisans, providing employment for the inhabitants of al-Darb al-Ahmar, an area with complex economic and social problems. The images in this chapter show the range of building skills that exists in Historic Cairo.

frequented by craftsmen, at the street labour markets where unskilled workers congregate, on a variety of construction sites, and in the offices of construction companies, trade unions and the relevant government agencies.

The sample survey was based on a national random sample of just over 800 construction workers. The sample was derived by selecting all households containing at least one manual construction worker from the 12,000 household sample of the quarterly round of the Labour Force Sample Survey.[4]

Contract and casual labour
Egyptian labour regulations allow for two types of employment contract: permanent and temporary. Permanent contracts entitle workers to lifetime employment security after an initial probationary period of three months. Temporary contracts are fixed in duration and cannot exceed one year at a time. They are renewable only once and, if upon termination of the second term, the relationship with the employer is not terminated, the temporary contract is automatically converted into a permanent contract.[5] Workers on temporary contracts can only be laid off at the end of the period specified in the contract. Like permanent contract workers, they are entitled to all the employment benefits stipulated by the law, which include social security coverage, paid vacations, disability insurance, sick leave, etc.

With such strong limitations on the employers' ability to change their work force at will in an industry characterised by severe fluctuations in demand, it is not surprising that large construction firms resort to subcontractors and labour recruiters to gain access to a flexible workforce. Subcontractors and labour recruiters hire workers solely on a casual day-to-day basis.

According to the Construction Workers Survey, 90 per cent of manual construction workers are either hired on a casual basis as wage workers or are self-employed. Among casual wage workers, 70 per cent have no attachment to a regular employer and move frequently between employers. The remaining 30 per cent work with a given

employer on a regular basis, in the sense that they have some kind of long-term relationship with that employer but with no legal contractual agreement. In most cases they are not employed continuously but get priority in hiring when their employer has work.

The social security administration realised that this system of legal employment contracts was inappropriate for the construction industry. As a result, a special ministerial decree (No. 255 of 1982) was devised to deal with the social security needs of casual workers in the building industry. For a specific set of occupations, 'temporary' workers in the private sector would be entitled to receive social security benefits if they undertook the following actions: (i) pay a monthly contribution to the social security administration based on one of three types of skills,[6] and (ii) get the signature and tax file number of all the employers they worked for during the month, or, alternatively, get the numbers of the social security files on the building permits of all the buildings they worked on during the month. A worker must have paid up and certified employment for at least ten years to qualify for the minimum pension level after he reaches the age of sixty. The social security administration collects the employers' contribution to the social security fund as a standard 2.5 per cent deduction on the gross value of all construction contracts. The employer's contribution is paid at the point of applying for a building permit.[7]

As it is currently applied, the social security system is totally unworkable for casual construction workers. If a contracting firm is involved in the construction process, it usually acquires most of its labour through small subcontractors operating informally. Sometimes there is no main contractor and the workers are hired privately by the owner of a building, either as self-employed artisans or as wage workers.[8] Given all these circumstances, being effectively freelance and self-employed, few if any casual workers take the necessary steps to get social security coverage.[9]

Even though both craftsmen and labourers are hired on a casual basis, the operation of the labour market for the two types of workers differs in many important respects. Craftsmen acquire skills in one of

the construction trades over several years of on-the-job apprenticeship. Because there is no ready way to ascertain the skill, level or reliability of a craftsman, subcontractors prefer to hire craftsmen that they know personally or who have been recommended to them by someone they trust. Consequently, craftsmen rely heavily on their personal contacts and networks to find jobs. This effectively limits their job hunting efforts to their local area, often to a particular coffee house that they frequent on a regular basis. In contrast, the market for labourers is highly impersonal and wide open. As far as employers are concerned, all labourers are alike, or at least differences between them can easily be ascertained from their appearance. Labourers can therefore spread their job search activities over a wide area. They often congregate in large numbers outside the well-known coffee houses from which subcontractors and craftsmen operate, or flock to the 'workers' markets', the major intersections in large cities where labourers congregate to offer their labour for hire. Many are not full-time construction workers, but small peasant farmers and farm workers who work occasionally in construction. Alternatively, they find employment on large construction sites through labour recruiters who hire them directly from their home villages.

Traditional apprenticeships and formal training programmes
THE TRADITIONAL APPRENTICESHIP SYSTEM
The vast majority of craftsmen (83.5 per cent according to the CWS) acquire their skills through the traditional apprenticeship system. Under this system, which dates back to the guild system that dominated economic activity in Egypt until late into the 19th century, craftsmen are trained on the job by serving as apprentices with an established member of the trade. A boy is typically sent by his family to a master craftsman in his neighbourhood for training.[10] The relationship

Interior view of the restored
top of the minaret, Historic
Cities Programme, 2004

between the master and his apprentices is quite informal and is usually based on long-standing ties between the master and the apprentice's family.[11] After an initial training period, the apprentice begins to receive wages that vary in proportion to his level of skill. At first, these wages are substantially lower than those of labourers, but gradually increase as the trainee becomes more skilled. The apprentice performs tasks that keep him in close proximity to his master, such as handing out mortar, extracting nails and cleaning tools. Gradually he is allowed to perform the easier tasks of his master's trade under the latter's supervision, eventually qualifying to become an assistant. At the point when the master feels that the trainee is ready to take on work on his own, he is promoted to the rank of journeyman. Historically, under the guild system, to be promoted to the rank of journeyman, an application had to be made by the master to the guild, the shaykh who sought the opinion of other guild members as to the skills of the candidate.[12] Whilst guild shaykhs no longer exist and many of the rules of the guilds are no longer explicit, they are still adhered to by contemporary craftsmen. Limitations on entry into the craft trades work through customary rules and norms transmitted from master to apprentice. While there are no longer any ritual ceremonies marking a novice's passage through the different ranks of his trade as in the days of established guilds, apprenticeships continue to serve as more than just a training process. The apprentice is socialised into becoming a member of the fraternity of craftsmen by learning the values and behavioural patterns that will make him an insider.

Family ties and social networks are still crucial for a boy (it is almost always a boy) to gain access to an apprenticeship. According to the cws, over 37 per cent of craftsmen had relatives in the construction trades at the time they entered the sector, whereas only 19 per cent of labourers had. There is also a strong correlation between entry into the craft trades and residence in a community that has a high concentration of construction workers. This supports the hypothesis that neighbourhood networks are crucial in providing access to apprenticeships.[13] The informal rule on the age of entry means that arrangements for an apprenticeship have to be made early in life, giving further advantages to those whose families have the requisite ties and social networks that will enable them to place a son in an apprenticeship.

THE FORMAL VOCATIONAL TRAINING SYSTEM

A wide variety of organisations offer vocational training programmes for building trades in Egypt. These include the Ministry of Housing and Reconstruction, vocational secondary schools, public sector contracting firms, local government authorities, the armed forces and private voluntary organisations. The most organised and ambitious of these programmes was that of the Training Organisation of the Ministry of Housing and Reconstruction (TOMOHAR). In response to the severe shortage of skilled workers at the start of the reconstruction of the Suez canal cities after the October 1973 war, TOMOHAR embarked on an accelerated plan to produce 'semi-skilled' craftsmen. Under this plan, workers were to be trained in one of ten building trades for a period of three months in existing training facilities, such as the training centres of public sector companies and vocational secondary schools. Trainees were to receive a small stipend, a pair of overalls and work shoes. While the programme succeeded in attracting some trainees, the quality of its graduates was so poor that they are pejoratively known among construction workers as 'October craftsmen' in reference to the October 1973 war.

In an ambitious five-year plan for 1976–1980, TOMOHAR proposed to establish sixty-two new training centres with a total capacity of 50,000 graduates per year, as well as three training centres for the formation of instructors, with a capacity of 600 graduates per year.[14]

Between 1975 and 1987, fifty of the sixty-two training centres called for in the 1976–1980 five-year plan were established at a rate of approximately four new centres per year. Three more centres began operation in 1988. From 1981, the number of graduates per year, according to TOMOHAR, increased steadily from approximately 7,000 per annum in 1981 to 18,000 in 1987; a figure that was still well below the 50,000 graduates originally planned (TOMOHAR, n.d.).

Cleaned walls showing the
original exquisite painting,
Umm al-Sultan Sha'ban
complex, Historic Cities
Programme, 2006

Restored inlay on the *mihrab*,
Umm al-Sultan Sha'ban
complex, Historic Cities
Programme, 2006

To evaluate the numerical impact of the TOMOHAR training programme on the construction labour market, I computed the proportion
of TOMOHAR graduates to the total size of the construction labour
force engaged in manual labour. Using CWS data, I also computed the
average gross rate of entry into all crafts over the five-year period from
1983 to 1987. A comparison of these two figures should give an indication
of the net impact of the training programme on the supply of new
workers entering the building trade. According to the CWS, the average
gross rate of entry into all aspects of the building trade and related trades
over the five-year period was approximately 4.4 per cent per year. Over
the same period, TOMOHAR claims to have trained 2–3.5 per cent of the
labour force for manual construction every year, depending on the year.
Thus the training programme would have been contributing 45 to 80
per cent of new entrants; a large proportion indeed.

Since the CWS inquired into the training experience of craftsmen,
I am in a position to assess the above claims. CWS results indicate that
only 5.3 per cent of current workers participated in any kind of formal
training. Among workers who joined the labour force in the five-year
period between 1983 and 1987, only 4.5 per cent had acquired formal
training. Moreover, this figure includes all types of formal training,
not just programmes sponsored by TOMOHAR. The considerable discrepancy between the two figures may be due to very high attrition
rates among graduates of formal training programmes.

Interviews with experienced craftsmen indicate that graduates of
formal training programmes find it difficult to gain acceptance from
their peers in the informal labour market. It is thought that they lack the
breadth of experience gained by apprentices in several years of on-the-job
training.[15] They also lack the contacts that are necessary for getting jobs
in the informal market once they complete their training, in contrast
to the apprentices. CWS data show that 55 per cent of the workers in the
sample who had formal training work for either a government agency or
a public sector contracting firm, as compared to 16 per cent for the sample
as a whole. Formally trained workers are thus much more likely than their
informally trained counterparts to end up in formal jobs. With the

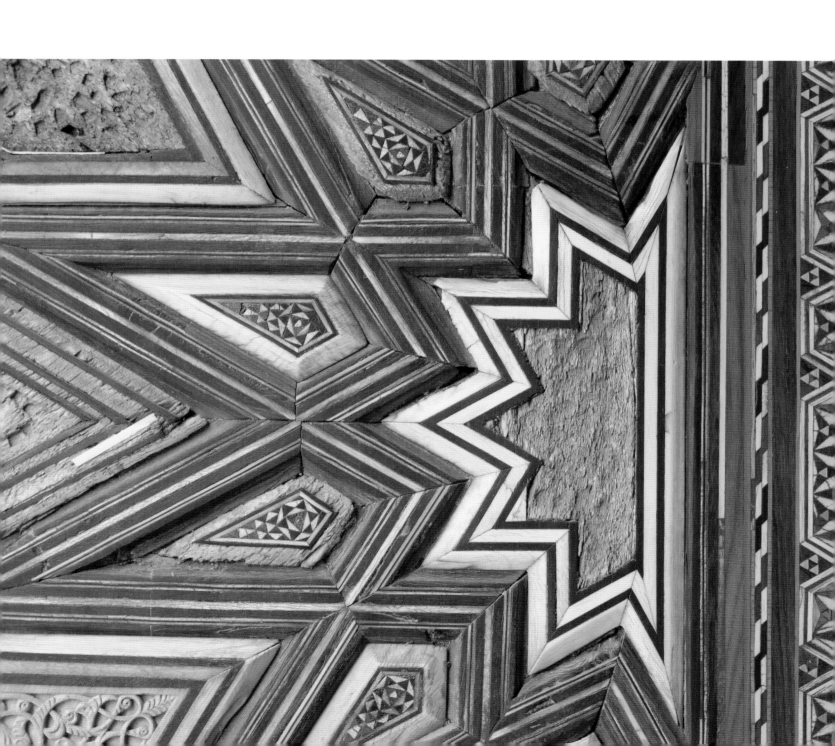

limited number of formal jobs in the construction industry, many formally trained workers may simply drop out of the construction labour market when they do not find such jobs. This may well be the explanation for their apparently high attrition rate from the industry.

None of the subcontractors and craftsmen I talked to thought that formally trained workers were as good as those trained in the traditional apprenticeship system. Since the traditional apprenticeship system is the primary means by which a worker becomes part of the 'fraternity' of craftsmen, it is not surprising if members of this 'fraternity' favour those who have also undergone apprenticeships.

Officials of large companies are somewhat less dismissive of formal training.[16] They complain that while workers trained in the traditional system are often good at what they do, it is very difficult to get them to acquire new skills or to have them work with modern forms of technology. They also blame the traditional system for the excessive specialisation in the trades and for failing to train workers to cross craft lines easily. This tends to inhibit the deployment of flexible teams of workers that can participate in several stages of the construction process. But since it is craftsmen-subcontractors trained in the traditional system (rather than the company officials) who do most of the recruiting and hiring in the Egyptian construction industry, it is their opinion that matters in the final analysis.

TRADE UNIONS AND THE CONSTRUCTION WORKERS' COFFEE HOUSES
In the literature on institutional labour economics and labour market segmentation a great deal of stress is placed on the role of formal workers' organisations and collective action in the structuring of the labour market.[17] In Egypt, union membership *per se* is practically irrelevant for most construction workers and is of little, if any, consequence in the construction labour market.

TRADE UNIONISM IN THE CONSTRUCTION INDUSTRY[18]
In 1959, unions that operated only within individual companies were consolidated to produce sixty-four general unions. Among them, were three construction-related unions: a union of building workers, a union of road construction workers, and a union of workers in the building materials and porcelain industries. In 1964, the government further amalgamated these sixty-four unions to form thirty-four unions, and the three construction-related unions were merged together into a single union, the General Union for Workers in the Building Industries. In 1973, a final consolidation took place merging the existing thirty-four unions into twenty-three. The carpenters and joiners union was merged into the General Union of Workers in the Construction Industries to yield the current configuration: the General Union of Workers in the Building and Wood Industries.

Under this current structure, the General Union includes all workers in public sector construction, road construction, construction materials, the porcelain industry and carpentry and joinery. Both blue collar and white collar workers are included up to the level of general manager. Public sector organisations are represented by union committees. 'Independent workers' (this is the way the union refers to casual workers) in construction and joinery trades are represented by geographically based occupational committees. Both self-employed and salaried workers can become union members, but registered subcontractors cannot. In January 1988, total union membership was 406,000 workers subdivided as follows: 102,000 in the public sector construction industry, 29,000 in the construction materials industry, 20,000 in the road construction industry, 4,000 in the carpentry and associated trades, 200,000 independent workers in occupational committees, and 54,000 independent workers affiliated directly with the general union. The last group consists of the independent workers from Cairo and Giza governorates – the two main constituents of the greater Cairo Metropolitan area – who are not organised into occupation committees.

Union membership is, in theory, obligatory for all workers. Union dues are subtracted directly from the pay of public sector employees. Casual workers automatically become members whenever they need to update their occupational status on their national identity cards.[19]

Detail of paintwork in the restored south-west *iwan* of the prayer hall, Umm al-Sultan Sha'ban complex, Historic Cities Programme, 2006

Virtually all the workers I interviewed have had no interaction or involvement with the union other than the occupational certification test and the payment of the required three years of dues.[20]

In fact the union's primary role is representing and serving the interests of workers mainly in public sector firms. It intervenes on their behalf, both administratively and, if necessary, legally in cases involving dismissals or termination of contracts. It participates in the tripartite adjudication of labour disputes. It sponsors some social service projects, such as medical clinics and holiday resorts. In essence, its role has been to act as a watchdog to ensure that the employment laws, which in Egypt are quite favourable to workers, are properly enforced. Since these laws are for the most part irrelevant to casual workers, who constitute 90 per cent of the construction labour force, the union itself is also irrelevant. Lengthy discussions with union officials in June 1988, led me to conclude that the only significant role the union played on behalf of casual workers, was that of representing them in negotiations with the social insurance administration. The union was attempting, at that time, to get the administration to modify the social insurance regulations in such a way that casual workers no longer need the signature and tax file number of their employers to qualify for benefits.

CONSTRUCTION WORKERS' COFFEE HOUSES

Whilst the trade unions are irrelevant to most construction workers, the coffee house is an institution that affects most workers on a daily basis. These coffee houses are the primary locus of interaction among craftsmen and between craftsmen and subcontractors.[21] Each of these coffee houses is known for having a clientele that is composed predominantly of construction workers engaged in various trades. In the past, individual coffee houses used to specialise in specific trades. Some are still known for having mostly plasterers and tile layers, others for being frequented predominantly by reinforced concrete workers, but for the most part, specialisation by trade has broken down in recent years.

As an institution, the coffee house serves many functions in the construction labour market. It is the equivalent of a union hiring hall, where potential employers or building owners come to recruit the workers they need. Coffee houses are often used by subcontractors in lieu of offices. It is there that they find and hire workers, meet the crews prior to heading to the work site, and pay their workers at the end of the working day or week. Most importantly, however, the coffee houses are the arenas where networks and contacts among craftsmen and between craftsmen and subcontractors are solidified. A craftsman has to be recognised by his peers as an insider to be able to get work. This is typically achieved through socialising at the coffee house. After long discussions with craftsmen and subcontractors, I discovered that besides having their own jargon, craftsmen also have secret signs that they would not reveal to me as an outsider. There were clear indicators that there was an insider's culture, and entry to this world was through an initiatory process.

A coffee house is usually frequented by a stable group of craftsmen who often live nearby and who rely largely on relationships they forge in the coffee house in order to get work. Most craftsmen agree that there is no point extending their job search beyond the local coffee house. Anywhere else, they are unknown quantities.

The coffee house is not only the locus for job hunting, but also where a worker spends most of his waking hours outside work. Since subcontractors and wage workers socialise together, they perceive themselves to be members of a unitary group of craftsmen, despite their different roles. Unless a subcontractor is registered, there is in fact little functional distinction between him and a craftsman working for wages since self-employment and salaried work are simply two different strategies for finding work, depending on circumstances.

Labourers usually congregate outside the coffee house in the morning waiting to be picked up by potential employers from among the coffee house clients and will take a job that starts the same day. In contrast, a skilled worker has to agree with the client or employer on the terms of employment at least one day before the start of a job. In some cases, he will go to the site to assess what is needed. If an agreement is reached, the evening the work starts he is paid an advance, called a *biyata*, which covers at least one day's wage for him and his helpers, if any are needed.[22]

Conclusion

The objective in juxtaposing formal and informal institutions performing similar functions in the labour market is twofold: first, to demonstrate that an exclusive focus on formal institutions is inadequate for understanding how the labour market functions and, second, to show that even when unregulated by formal institutions, labour markets can be highly structured.

In evaluating the functioning of the three formal institutions, the dominant factor was incompatibility with the situation on the ground. In a situation characterised by unstable levels of demand, labour contracts guaranteeing jobs for life or even temporary job security were not applicable. However, the structures of employment contracts were designed for long-term employment with large corporate employers. Formal trade union membership reflected a large constituency, but their primary purpose was to represent the interests of permanent workers in the public sector. The vocational training system, for its part, superimposed an entirely new training system upon the existing system of acquiring skills through traditional apprenticeships.

The second point is that informal labour markets cannot be assumed *a priori* to be perfectly competitive just because they escape regulation by the legal and bureaucratic institutions of society. As a result of differences in information requirements and the absence of institutions disseminating information about labour quality, the markets for craftsmen and labourers function in an entirely different fashion. The limited access to information and the need to maintain a flexible but reliable supply of workers mean that employers prefer to hire craftsmen with whom they have established personal ties. They often rely on patron-client relationships or ties of kinship and residential proximity to secure the workers they need. This effectively subdivides the market for craftsmen into a series of internal labour markets, centred on the local coffee house where workers and employers forge and maintain the necessary relationships. In contrast, the market for labourers is wide open, fiercely competitive and highly impersonal.

Besides vertical relationships between craftsmen and their employers, strong horizontal ties of solidarity exist between the craftsmen. These ties cut across the distinction between subcontractors and skilled workers who all see themselves as members of the same group. The sense of group solidarity, and the group culture and norms that go with it, are internalised by group members, first through the apprenticeships they undergo at a young age and, later, through the social life of the coffee houses.

1   G. Hart, 'Interlocking Transactions: Obstacles, Precursors or Instruments of Agrarian Capitalism?', *Journal of Development Economics*, 23 (1986), pp. 177–203; International Labour Office (ILO), *Employment, Income and Equality: A Strategy for Increasing Productive Employment in Kenya* (Geneva, 1972). See R. Bromley and C. Gerry, ed., *Casual Work and Poverty in Third World Cities* (Chichester, 1979) and R. Bromley, ed., *Planning for Small Enterprise in Third World Cities* (Oxford, 1985) for collections of articles on the topic and H.W. Richardson, 'The Role of the Urban Informal Sector: An Overview', *Regional Development Review*, 5 (1985), pp. 3–54 for a review article.

2   M. Castells and A. Portes, 'World Underneath: The Origins, Dynamics, and Effects of the Informal Economy', in A. Portes, M. Castells and L. Benton, ed., *The Informal Economy: Studies in Advanced and Less Developed Countries* (Baltimore, 1989), p. 11.

3   G. Akerlof, 'The Market for "Lemons": Quality, Uncertainty and the Market Mechanism', *Quarterly Journal of Economics*, 84 (1970), pp. 488–500, has built models to show how group behaviour and socialisation can result in the persistence of socially suboptimal institutions. See also the discussion in P. K. Bardhan, 'The New Institutional Economics and Development Theory: A Brief Critical Assessment', *World Development*, 17 (1989), p. 1391.

4   The Construction Workers Survey (CW) was carried out in conjunction with the Central Agency of Public Mobilisation and Statistics, which also carries out the Labour Force Sample Survey on a regular basis. For details of the overall study and analyses of data from the CWS see R. Assaad, 'Structured Labor Markets: The Case of the Construction Sector in Egypt', PhD Cornell University (Ithaca, NY, 1991).

5   Some employers are able to get around this provision by temporarily laying off workers at the end of their contract period and re-hiring them some time later.

6   In 1988, the monthly contribution was LE 9 for skilled workers, LE 6 for semi-skilled workers, and LE 3 for unskilled workers. LE 1 was worth $0.40 in 1988.

7   This section is based on an interview on 20 June 1988 with Mounir El Derghami and Sayed Taha, President and General Secretary of the General Union of Workers in the Construction and Wood Industries respectively. Further information was obtained from an interview with Hassan Ahmed Mostafa, the Chairman of the Occupational Committee of the union in Suez on 25 October 1988.

8   Over 75 per cent of all housing units built in Egypt are erected without building permits (GOHBPR) and The World Bank, *Construction/Contracting Industry Study*, Final Report, 3 volumes and appendices (Cairo, 1981, Annex A8), p. 15.

9   Of over 100 casual workers I interviewed in some depth, none had social security coverage and had not heard of any of their peers who did. It therefore seemed pointless to include a question on social security coverage in the CWS questionnaire.

10 The average age at entry for those who have undergone apprenticeships is 15.7 years with a standard deviation of 5.9 years.

11 This was no different under the guilds. A. Raymond, *Artisans et commerçants au Caire au XVIIIᵉ siècle* (Damascus, 1973), p. 545 ascribes the informal nature of the master-apprentice relationship in Cairo in the 18th century to the fact that there were

usually close kinship and friendship ties between the master and the apprentice's family.

12 G. Baer, *Egyptian Guilds in Modern Times* (Jerusalem, 1964), pp. 51–52.

13 In R. Assaad, 'Structured Labor Markets: The Case of the Construction Sector in Egypt', I formally demonstrate that kinship and community networks are important determinants of access to apprenticeships and the building trades.

14 The total stock of manual construction workers in Egypt in 1980 was approximately 500,000 workers. Under the plan, applicants to these centres had to be literate men aged between 16 and 30. They were to be trained for a period of six months, four of which were to be spent at one of the training centres and the remaining two at a construction site for on-the-job training (TOMOHAR, n.d., pp. 7–8).

15 Interview with Sai'd 'Ali Isma'il, Plumbing foreman, Shemto complex construction site, 31 January 1988.

16 See GOHBPR and the World Bank (1981, Annex G), p. 33.

17 See C. Kerr, 'The Balkanization of Labor Markets', in *Labor Mobility and Economic Opportunity* (Cambridge, MA, 1954), J. T. Dunlop, *Industrial Relations System* (New York, 1958) for institutional approaches to the role of trade unions. See also J. Rubery, 'Structured Labor Markets, Worker Organization and Low Pay', *Cambridge Journal of Economics*, 2 (1978), pp. 17–36; B. Elbaum and

F. Wilkinson, 'Industrial Relations and Uneven Development: A Comparative Study of the American and British Steel Industries', *Cambridge Journal of Economics*, 3 (1979), pp. 275–303; W. Lazonick, 'Industrial Relations and Technical Change: The Case of the Selfacting Mule', *Cambridge Journal of Economics*, 3 (1979), pp. 231–262 and P. Villa, *The Structuring of Labour Markets: The Steel and Construction Industries in Italy* (Oxford, 1986) for segmentation approaches to the role of trade unions.

18 This section is based on data provided by the General Union of Workers in the Construction and Wood Industries and on interviews with union officials at the union headquarters on 14 and 20 June 1988.

19 Under Egyptian law, every man over the age of 16 has to carry an identity card. Identity cards are optional for women.

20 Interview with a group of skilled workers in the Sayeda Eisha coffee house, 22 May 1988, see my PhD thesis for more details of the ideas and discussions on the unions.

21 There are usually too few construction workers in most villages to have a coffee house of their own, so these coffee houses are primarily an urban phenomenon.

22 Interview with a group of skilled workers in the Sayeda Eisha coffee house, 22 May 1988.

20 Restoration processes for historic monuments: an introduction

Robert K. Vincent Jr.

The American Research Center in Egypt (ARCE) through its Egyptian Antiquities Project (EAP) has had the good fortune to be the recipient of a major grant from the United States Agency for International Development for the conservation of Egyptian antiquities in collaboration with Egypt's Supreme Council of Antiquities (SCA). Cairo's monuments have long attracted the attention of concerned individuals. The city suffers from an embarrassment of riches; it contains more than 600 registered monuments, any one of which most cities would be proud to claim. Yet their sheer number would daunt and overwhelm the resources of any governmental authority anywhere in the world.

The 1993 award was the result of several factors. The US ambassador to Egypt Frank Wisner advocated the need for conserving these structures, and was joined in his efforts by two influential senators, Senators Ted Stevens of Alaska and Daniel Inouye of Hawaii. A major factor in ensuring the passage of the legislation through the US Congress was the Egyptian earthquake of 1992 which damaged a number of monuments in Cairo. Since this occurred while USAID funding was under consideration, it provided a real-world example of the need to act. The US legislators heeded this natural warning and approved the funding.

The project developed to encompass the broad range of Egypt's art and architecture; Pharaonic, Islamic and Coptic monuments, but also prehistoric, Graeco-Roman and Jewish contributions are included in its fifty project scope. All of the conservation work is done in collaboration with and approval of the Supreme Council of Antiquities.

Al-Darb al-Ahmar – in particular, the Bab Zuwayla area – was chosen in the earliest stages of the project as a prime candidate for area conservation by the American Research Center in Egypt. Prior efforts by the Germans in al-Darb al-Qirmiz area and the French in the environs of the mosque of al-Azhar suggested that another area should be chosen for American intervention. Consequently, ARCE decided to direct its initial efforts at an area anchored by Bab Zuwayla. The monuments needed attention; Bab Zuwayla is the southern entrance to the Fatimid city, and it dominates a busy crossroads with a substantial degree of local commercial activity.

The area includes shops brimming and bustling with traditional activity. Carpenters produce butcher's blocks from huge sycamore logs trucked in from the Nile Valley. Stonecutters shape and polish marble, granite and porphyry extracted from Egyptian quarries. Agricultural implements of all kinds are made and sold. Coopers sell their barrels; tinsmiths produce water cans and barbeque grills. A renowned natural-products pharmacy sells its remedies from a store front near Bab Zuwayla. One of the city's hubs for the sale of shishas (water-pipes) nestles at the wall of the mosque of al-Mu'ayyad Shaykh. Cairo's last covered bazaar is situated immediately to the south. From its stalls, artisans sell their famous appliqué work. In short, the area is historically important, architecturally attractive and commercially viable.

For ARCE, the concept of area conservation has meant that the improvements to buildings should reinforce each other, attract visitors, further investment and ideally lead to a general upgrading of the area. The project concentrated on a number of structures of different periods within the same urban unit. The parameter of the grant funding does not allow for spending on integrated development – only monument conservation is eligible – but ARCE has been able to work with the residents and their shops for which the monuments are a backdrop, to demonstrate that what is good for the monument is good for them.

The first monuments chosen for conservation projects were the Bab Zuwayla minarets and gate, the Sufi *zawiya-sabil* of Faraj ibn Barquq, and the mosque of al-Salih Tala'i'. Since ARCE had worked earlier at the urban palace of Bayt al-Razzaz, this was also included even through it is several hundred metres away.

Where needed, architectural documentation was conducted by the Centre for the Preservation of Islamic Heritage, directed by Dr Saleh Lamei. Patrick Godeau undertook the photograph documentation. A study of existing conditions was undertaken by Brown Morton and Alaa El-Habashi at Bayt al-Razzaz. Stone analysis and recommendations were performed by Griswold Associates, while Ian Hodkinson provided the same for fine conservation in the *zawiya*.

With these studies and relevant action plans in hand, persons and
entities were sought to conduct conservation. ARCE solicited open competitive proposals. Among the successful candidates were Agnieszka
Dobrowolska for three monuments: the *sabil-kuttab* of Nafisa al-Bayda,
the *sabil* of Muhammad 'Ali Pasha and the facade of the *wikala* of Nafisa
al-Bayda. Dr Salah Zaki, who has carried out pioneer work on historically
important though unregistered, occupied buildings in the area, received
funding to renovate four 19th-century houses. With architectural features
in sympathy with the area, these houses are important because they
constitute the tissue between the monuments. In too many instances,
such buildings were torn down to be replaced by harsh modern apartment blocks. So, in a project designed with house owner/tenant
participation, Dr Zaki set out to renovate the houses to demonstrate
their continuing value for both owners and the neighbourhood.

Throughout this volume, the reader will learn details of the four
projects of Bab Zuwyala, Bayt al-Razzaz, the *sabil* of Muhammad 'Ali
Pasha (which suffered in the 1992 earthquake and had to be closed)
and the Four Houses project. To complement those reports, this essay
will briefly discuss the four other monuments in the area conserved or
under conservation by ARCE.

1. *The mosque of al-Salih Tala'i'* (monument 116)

This important courtyard mosque was built just south of Bab Zuwayla in
1160 by Amir al-Salih Tala'i' ibn Ruzzik during the Fatimid period. In
1300 Amir Baktimur al-Jukandar presented the mosque with a spectacular wooden *minbar* (pulpit) that is still in place. Important repairs were
conducted after the 1303 earthquake which required the construction of
a new minaret, and again in 1477–1478. In the early 20th century, the
Comité de Conservation des Monuments de l'Art Arabe essentially rebuilt the
entire mosque except for the columned prayer hall in front of the *qibla* wall.

CONDITION OF THE BUILDING TODAY

The building suffers greatly from the effects of the high groundwater,
atmospheric pollution and lack of maintenance. After the dramatic

rise of the groundwater table in the 1970s, the mosque's lower portions sat in a water-filled trench for over twenty years. Rising damp
and related salt efflorescence inflicted severe damage to the structure,
including numerous cracks in the masonry walls, subsidence of the
pavement of the courtyard, and failure of the roof. The dampness also
damaged objects in the mosque, such as the 14th-century wooden
minbar. Subsequently, the Egyptian Supreme Council of Antiquities
initiated a comprehensive renovation programme, which included
complete replacement of the floor, of damaged masonry, re-plastering
of the interiors and installation of a new roof. By summer 2003 most of
this work had been completed.

THE AMERICAN RESEARCH CENTER IN EGYPT/EGYPTIAN ANTIQUITIES PROJECT'S SPECIALISED CONSERVATION INTERVENTIONS

The spectacular wooden *minbar* has been cleaned, consolidated
and restored under the direction of Agnieszka Dobrowolska. The
conservation started in June 1998 and was completed in January
1999. To do this the wooden structure was moved in one piece to a
temporary workshop within the mosque. Conservators cleaned its
nine hundred wooden panels of accumulated layers of varnish and
paint, and exposed the original carving and inlays. The internal
wooden supporting structure was thoroughly reinforced. Meanwhile,
the *minbar*'s original location was prepared to receive it back: the
minbar has been raised slightly on protective footings away from the
sources of dampness. The conservation programme also included
treatment of the exquisite medieval stucco frame of the ventilation
shaft behind the *minbar*. The building continues to function as an
active mosque.

2. *The zawiya-sabil of Faraj ibn Barquq* (monument 204)

This monument is a small Sufi establishment constructed in 1409–
1409 by one of the sultans of the Burji Mamluk era. It reproduces in
detail the architectural features of the larger mosques of the period.
The inlaid polychrome stonework and decorated wooden *muqarnas*

The restored *minbar* in the
mosque of al-Salih al-Tala'i'
(donated to the mosque
in 1300 by Amir Baktimur
al-Jukandar)

The plan of the *minbar* in the
mosque of al-Salih al-Tala'i',
showing previous restorations

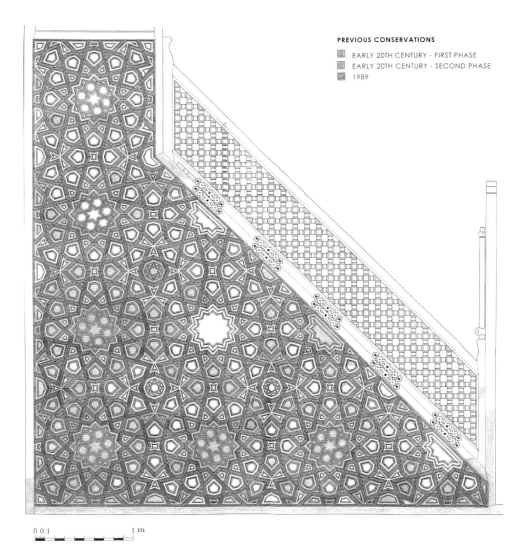

0 0.1   1 m

Exterior of the restored
sabil-kuttab of Nafisa al-Bayda,
built in 1797

ceiling of the fountain room are particularly noteworthy. The entire structure was relocated and rebuilt 10 metres south of its location in 1922–1923 by the *Comité de Conservation des Monuments de l'Art Arabe* because of road widening, with some alteration to the original plan. The building, closed to the public for years, had no present use.

CONDITION OF THE BUILDING BEFORE CONSERVATION
Rising damp and salt efflorescence seriously damaged the interior and exterior decoration. The leaking roof endangered precious medieval ceilings; water entering through roof openings had damaged the stairs and destroyed the limestone floor. Decorative stone, wood and bronze elements were covered with dirt laden with aggressive pollutants.

SPECIALISED CONSERVATION INTERVENTIONS
Hoda Abdul Hamid of ARCE's technical staff and Engineer Mahmoud El Toukhi have worked to conserve the monument, first protecting valuable decorative elements, while the stone and brick masonry walls have been repaired, repainted and grouted. Decayed parts of the stone stairs have been replaced. A waterproof course has been installed and the decaying under-floor fill was removed and replaced. Missing stained-glass windows have been replaced; doors, window frames and shutters have been treated. Repairs were carried out to the roof structure and a new waterproof roof was installed.

A community liaison specialist worked with tenants of the shops around the structure to develop a plan for their temporary removal so that new premises compatible with the architecture of the area can be built.

Further plans included cleaning, consolidating and re-attaching as necessary the exterior and interior decorative polychrome and inlaid stonework, as well as the limestone masonry; cleaning the historic ceilings of the prayer hall and the *sabil*, conserving the decorated doors, window frames and shutters, as well as the bronze window grilles. Portions of the dramatic painted and gilded wooden *muqarnas* ceiling over the *sabil* were recreated on areas where the decoration has fallen away, in order to show the glory of the original decoration.

All conservation work was completed by 2005. The building is currently being adapted for use as a visitor's orientation centre.

3. *The sabil-kuttab of Nafisa al-Bayda (monument 258)*
The public water fountain and Qur'anic school were established in 1797 by Nafisa al-Bayda, a wealthy widow of the powerful Murad Bey, when she bought and rebuilt a commercial building (*wikala*) dating back to the time of Salah al-Din. The rounded front of the *sabil-kuttab* occupies the corner of Muizz Liddin Allah Street (the Qasaba) and al-Sukkariyya Street. This is a prominent location in the historically important area, just inside the fortified gate of Bab Zuwayla. The building is a typical example of the late Ottoman style, with elaborate decoration in stone, wood and bronze. The architectural design is modelled on Ottoman Turkish patterns, but the decoration follows the local, medieval tradition of Cairo.

The project started in autumn 1995 and was completed in May 1998 under the co-direction of Jarek Dobrowolski and Agnieszka Dobrowolska. Before conservation began in November 1995, the building was abandoned, neglected and filled with garbage from the neighbourhood. The roof had failed, the ceilings deteriorated, the stairs had collapsed and the masonry was soaked with water and infused with salts.

A new, properly water-tight roof has been installed over the entire building. Walls have been grouted and stitched, and deteriorated stones replaced where necessary. Masonry was desalinated by poulticing. New wooden ceilings were installed over existing beams. Sanitary units in the neighbouring building were moved and connected to sewer lines. A medieval shaft was discovered, unblocked and cleaned and used as a ventilation shaft. A thick layer of non-absorbent gravel ventilated with a network of perforated pipes was introduced under the pavements inside and outside the building, to reduce penetration of groundwater into the walls. All decorative elements in stone, wood and bronze, were cleaned and consolidated, missing parts supplied as necessary. New electric lighting and a mechanical ventilation system were installed.

The conservation interventions were designed with reuse in mind. In 2005, a permanent educational exhibit about the building and its founder was installed in the *sabil-kuttab* by ARCE.

4. *The Facade of the wikala of Nafisa al-Bayda (monument 395)*
This conservation project started in July 2002 under the direction of Agnieszka Dobrowolska, to conserve the facade of the commercial building adjoining the *sabil* of Nafisa al-Bayda. This is a rare preserved example of the type of architecture that once defined the character of the streets of Cairo. The stone masonry of the entrance gate had deteriorated severely due to groundwater penetration, and the ground floor was disfigured by modern shop fronts. The elaborate *mashrabiyya* bay windows needed repairing; the roof cover was inadequate.

The current project completed in 2003 addresses these issues without moving the inhabitants. After conservation, the building will retain its residential and commercial use. The conservation of the facade will be a contribution to the cityscape of Cairo's main medieval street, in the location where many monuments have recently been restored, or are undergoing conservation. The project was scheduled for completion in September 2003.

In addition to its architectural conservation projects, ARCE has been conducting two projects related to Historic Cairo, with the aim of preserving cultural heritage and transmitting it into the future through documentation and recording.

HISTORIC INSCRIPTIONS PROJECT
Dr Bernard O'Kane of the American University in Cairo and his team have been conducting this project. They have recorded all the monumental inscriptions with which medieval and Ottoman period builders adorned their buildings in Historic Cairo. The team photographed, recorded and translated the undocumented inscriptions, which had become increasingly vulnerable to damage and exfoliation, largely because of the high groundwater level.

All inscriptions are now stored in a digital database that enables easy access to the data. Plans are underway to convert the database to an interactive CD or DVD so that users can call up a variety of detailed comparative information. For instance, a search formation query could result in a display of all the inscriptions containing the word 'water' from buildings from the Mamluk period. This is a powerful tool for epigraphers, art historians and architects.

THE CAIRO MAPPING PROJECT
Nick Warner has produced a large-scale map of the 5.8 square kilometres (over 1,400 acres) that contain more than 400 of the city's historic monuments. All listed historic buildings and more that a hundred unlisted ones are shown in the ground plan. Many have been surveyed for the first time, and all plans have been checked and updated. The catalogue includes descriptions of all the historic buildings shown on the map, and a list of bibliographical references for each one. The maps and catalogue were published by ARCE and The American University in Cairo Press in 2005 as *The Monuments of Historic Cairo: a Map and Descriptive Catalogue*. The result of this will be not only lasting records of this cultural heritage, but also provision of important research and planning tools for conservators, historians, architects and urban planners.

USAID has been instrumental in the area conservation project, not only in providing the funding for the work on the individual monuments but also by responding to an urgent need in the neighbourhood. The high level of the groundwater, a problem for most of the historic city of Cairo, was plainly visible at the lower level of the mosque of al-Salih Tala'i', which corresponds to the 12th-century ground level, and contains a group of shops whose rents were intended to pay for the upkeep of the mosque. As early as 1979 they were partially submerged and had become virtually unusable, a situation which prevailed in all the basements and at the foundations of all buildings, residential, commercial and monumental. Through a complex programme of 'conservation through infrastructure', USAID installed a sewer under

The restored *mihrab* in the
zawiya-sabil of Faraj ibn Barquq

the street and a drainage system around the mosque. The water table has been locally lowered and the shops are accessible again. This is a project that has benefitted inhabitants and monuments alike.

Just as in area conservation, where the conservation of nearby buildings reinforces each other, so too, contiguous projects enhance everyone's work. Since we have started, a welcome number of other major projects have commenced.

Egypt's Supreme Council of Antiquities has undertaken conservation work at the mosques of Mahmud al-Kurdi and Inal al-Yusufi. The tent-maker's bazaar has been renovated and the work on mosque of al-Salih Tala'i' is completed. At the mosque of al-Mu'ayyad Shaykh adjoining the Bab Zuwayla, the Historic Cairo Project of the Ministry of Culture is continuing its work.

Further along Bab al-Wazir Street leading towards the Citadel, the Aga Khan project worked on the mosque of Amir Khayrbak and the mosque of Sultan Sha'ban, which directly adjoins Bayt al-Razzaz. ARCE worked jointly with the Aga Khan staff to conserve a common area in front of the monuments.

Additionally, other partners have joined in. The Local Cultural Fund of the Royal Netherlands Embassy in Cairo has provided funding in two of our projects. The European Union contributed to the preparation of the exhibition for the *sabil* of Muhammad 'Ali. The Ford Foundation has also been actively involved in the work. The New York-based World Monuments Fund is assisting in the efforts of the Aga Khan Project. One of the most important developments has been the efforts of dedicated individuals and the local community (without any assistance from the donor agencies), to restore the neighbourhood mosque of Amir Qijmas al-Ishaqi.

What good are these conservation interventions? Who benefits, how and to what degree?

Ideally everyone and everything associated with a monument should benefit. At the most basic level the monument (so long as conservation is done properly) benefits. Even in this case, however, conservation provides access to the building for visitors, gives scholars a wealth of new information and preserves the monument for future generations.

Do renovation projects like this mean the monument can pay its own way? This can happen, but does it? The answer is not clear. Under current policy and institutional structures revenues from the sale of tickets to visitors at an individual monument are not returned to that monument. Nonetheless, because of the presence of visitors, both local and foreign, some degree of maintenance of the monuments is required. Proper restoration will mean that repair issues will be small and therefore, can be dealt with more easily. In turn, this will mitigate the need for major interventions, once in every generation, like those that ARCE has conducted.

Does the local community benefit from a conservation project? It can, but it might not. In a direct way it benefits since over 290 Egyptians living in the area have worked on the ARCE conservation projects. Many have been trained and now have technical skills they can transfer to other jobs.

Furthermore, if the community sees its well-being associated with the monument, it will tend to support the renovation. Our experience has been that the local inhabitants, who are 'part' of the monument, to the extent that their shops are structurally part of the monument, can benefit. They are not removed from the site, so long as their occupation does not harm the monument. They are protected from removal by the site itself, and so they in turn become protectors of the site. They are given a refurbished shop and the ability to sell their goods in a more pleasant environment. Does this help with revenue? Maybe. Those who benefit most may be those who attract increased tourist revenues, whether they sell papyrus paintings or mineral water. The revenue may not be large, but a small amount can make a great deal of

difference. An upgrade of part of the area can lead to a general upgrade, which can increase income. When the general area is upgraded, more visitors are likely to come. A case in point is the tent-maker's bazaar where many people come to purchase goods. The more presentable the whole area is – with reduced levels of garbage and well-maintained buildings – the more likely it is that more visitors will come.

Cultural heritage preservation is an important part of individual and material pride and respect. A country's cultural record in its monuments is the visible expression of a nation's identity. One needs only to look at Egypt's LE50 note, on which the mosque of Qijmas figures prominently. Protecting and preserving such treasures are reasons enough to intervene. In the larger scheme of the gross national product, preservation activities are a small price for a considerable return that has a high profile for the country itself and for visitors. Such activities also demonstrate that an entity or government cares about its history, culture and people. Foreign donors are offered an opportunity to show their non-commercial, non-political and non-military concerns.

The American Research Center in Egypt's efforts are contributing to what we believe are major beneficial changes to the monuments and the area that supports them. The discussion above has touched on the various aspects of the work. Our final act of preservation is to produce publications about each project. The series has a volume for each monument. Inscriptions are produced on a CD or DVD, and the Cairo maps published.

Thus, within the parameters of funding we have received from the United States Agency for International Development, we hope that, together with the Supreme Council of Antiquities, we are bringing added value to the monuments and the communities to which they belong.

21 Urban conservation: the inevitable task during single monument conservation in practice in Historic Cairo

Nairy Hampikian

Introduction of Urban Conservation to Historic Cairo

'Historic Cairo' is this superb urban space where the built environment and the population have survived together through a series of events that tell the uninterrupted history of Cairo from its foundation to the present. Through its one thousand years of continued existence, this same Qasaba of al-Qahira witnessed conflicts between sultans and *amir*s; the same *hara*s saw weddings, funerals, *mahmal* processions, inaugurations of conservation projects and acts of violence; the same *darb*s constantly adjusted to the changing progression of horses, cisterns, carriages, piped water and sewage systems, buses, mobile phone shops and trucks; the same coffee shops have offered the shisha, tea and coffee, now with an area for video games. The charm of Historic Cairo lies in its ability to maintain this multi-faceted coexistence: its past and its present, its material heritage and its living soul, its old buildings and new ones, and its confined area defined as 'historic' with the huge borders of modern Cairo surrounding it in all directions.

Change has always occurred in a relaxed and predictable rhythm here, where drastic intervention took place only occasionally. Today, there is an urgent need to accelerate the momentum of change in Historic Cairo. This can be reasonably justified by the abrupt deterioration of the monuments, the degeneration of houses in the area, the malfunctioning of the infrastructure and the decline in the living standards of the people dwelling and working around the monuments. But this forced acceleration in the pace of change is creating a greater imbalance between the two main constituents of Historic Cairo: the monuments and the urban fabric surrounding them. The monuments are receiving concentrated attention, whilst 'the rest' is dealt with just enough to look 'appropriate' alongside the neighbouring monuments, thus subjecting the unavoidable coexistence between the two to an insoluable formula.

Efforts to introduce urban conservation in Historic Cairo have been made mainly on a theoretical level, such as the seminar organised in 1980 by the Goethe Institute,[1] which was further extended and published in the report prepared by the United Nations Development Programme (UNDP) for the rehabilitation of Historic Cairo in 1997.[2] A comprehensive urban conservation plan was also prepared by *al-Qahira al-Tarikhiyya* (Ministry of Culture) for the rehabilitation and reuse of the area around the northern city wall.[3] Meanwhile, individual efforts were made to develop a theoretical framework designed to facilitate the legitimacy and a common sense of urban conservation, such as the idea of a new categorisation for Cairene monuments according to the degree of their incorporation into the urban fabric around them – using the idea of 'the urbanised monuments'[4] and the idea of separating Historic Cairo into 'touristic' and 'communal' nodes, to start thinking about how to deal with two different clienteles with two very different sets of requirements, and accordingly to use two different approaches concerning the application of urban conservation standards.[5] Finally, there are projects which have presented practical experiments in the field, such as the rehabilitation project of al-Darb al-Asfar,[6] which is an example for the rehabilitation of a *hara* as a whole and the ongoing housing project of the AKCSE near the eastern medieval enclosure wall of Cairo.

Different theories, concepts and practical projects are all taking their own paths towards the establishment of a new subdivision in conservation discipline in Historic Cairo: the practice of urban conservation. The main trend in the last two centuries was the practice of 'single monument conservation'. In this article, I will present an experiment conducted on the conservation of a single monument in Historic Cairo, which shows that the separation of these two practices from each other is not only undesirable and unreasonable, but also impractical and even impossible.

Urban conservation during the Bab Zuwayla Conservation Project

Bab Zuwayla, the southern gate of al-Qahira built by Badr al-Din al-Jamali in AD 1092 was representative of Islamic military architecture of the time, but it was never put to the test by a direct assault. The southern facade is composed of two massive towers connected by a bridge, unlike the northern facade, which reveals a straight masonry wall

The minarets of the mosque of al-Mu'ayyad Shaykh on Bab Zuwayla (added to the gate in 822–823/1419–1420) during restoration works

reaching a main platform placed at a height of almost nine metres above the present street level. The two facades are connected by an arched gateway covered by a shallow dome containing the two wooden leaves of the doors of Bab Zuwayla. Between 1998 and 2002 a conservation project was conducted in collaboration with the Egyptian Supreme Council of Antiquities and Egyptian Antiquities Project of the American Research Center in Egypt under the direction of Dr Nairy Hampikian with funding from the United States Agency for International Development.

The Venice Charter,[7] among other international charters dealing with historic sites, recommends the practice of urban conservation during the conservation of single monuments, but during the planning of our conservation project on Bab Zuwayla this was more than a recommendation, it was an obligatory and inevitable task.

- The original porch of the gate (covered with a semi-circular shallow dome) connecting its southern and northern facades has become the southernmost stretch of al-Mu'izz Street.
- Nearly all exposed walls of Bab Zuwayla lie directly either on Ahmad Maher Street on the south or on al-Mu'izz Street to the north
- The shops on the western side of the porch occupy the core of Bab Zuwayla.
- The shop on the northern side occupied the secondary entrance (*bab sirr*) to the adjacent mosque of al-Mu'ayyad, built in the 15th century.
- The two wooden doors of Bab Zuwayla (each weighing 4 tons) were jammed in their open position and had sunk below street level by 1.50 metres.
- It is quite obvious that when the enclosed palatial complex of al-Qahira became a part of a greater Cairo, Bab Zuwayla was left in the middle of busy streets and the main architectural elements and spaces of the gate proper became a vital part of the urban fabric around it. Therefore, if we had not brought the matter of urban conservation within the scope of the conservation project of Bab Zuwayla, we would have overlooked the conservation and the restoration of Bab Zuwayla proper.

The general plan for the treatment of the urban fabric around Bab Zuwayla
Given the limitations of this article, I will simply sketch out our urban conservation plan as a whole which included a series of action plans, and then present a relatively detailed survey explaining how we have dealt with one item – the shops. [8] The most imperative task was the general taming of the infrastructure running under the street level. This included the electricity and telephone cables and boxes, the post boxes on the gate, and the sewage and water supply pipes and systems, and was crowned by the reinstallation of the basalt pavement on the street as an alternative to modern asphalt in Historic Cairo. On both sides of the passageway, we emptied three shops permanently, and temporarily emptied, restored, remodelled and then handed back to their original tenants a further five shops. We have also removed, restored, conserved and re-installed the wooden doors of Bab Zuwayla. Another important change in the street was the restoration of the *bab sirr* (secondary entrance) of the mosque of al-Mu'ayyad, which was to be used as the main access to Bab Zuwayla after the completion of the conservation project. A final touch was the installation of a lighting system for the passageway and the two minarets. These being our broad lines of action, it is clear that what we were trying to do in the street was not an additional phase to our conservation project, but an integral part of the project proper.

Dealing with the shops around Bab Zuwayla
There were ten shops around the borders of the conservation project of Bab Zuwayla. Two were located at the eastern and western ends of the southern facade of Bab Zuwayla, six under the dome in the passageway, and two on the northern facade.

As a first step, we tried to link our system of shops around Bab Zuwayla to the entire macro system of the area. Accordingly, the shops fell into three categories:
· Shops that were directly linked to the core of the great gate, and thus directly shaped the atmosphere of the passageway proper of Bab Zuwayla
· Shops that were in direct contact with Bab Zuwayla and yet belonged to other systems, the western one being the first of more than twenty similar shops lying along the southern facade of the mosque of al-Mu'ayyad, while the eastern one was the first of a longer continuous row of shops that reach the mosque of Qijmas al-Ishaqi along al-Darb al-Ahmar
· Mobile vendors who have made Bab Zuwayla their semi-permanent station

The reason for this categorisation was to make a distinction between the shops that define the main urban spirit of Bab Zuwayla and others that belong to a neighbouring sub-system. Treatment of each category differed accordingly. This was followed by a complete physical and social survey of each and every shop separately, which included information about the business, the owner of the shop, the owner of the business, the person running the business, etc.

Moral codes to deal with the shops
The issue of dealing with the shops around monuments is a cause of great anxiety for all Cairene historic buildings under conservation for structural or aesthetic reasons. This common concern has given birth to a trend: empty the facades of all invading features, examine the walls behind them, clean and restore these, and then leave the 'un-invaded' edifice to be appreciated by monument lovers. This solution is not a new one. One of the major preoccupations of the Comité was *expropriation*. The Comité would buy all invading structures, demolish them and expose the historic walls hidden behind them. It succeeded in emptying rows of facades of historic buildings, such as the row of shops in front of the *madrasa*-mausoleum of Sultan Qalawun, the *madrasa*-mausoleum of al-Nasir Muhammad, and the *madrasa*-mausoleum of Barquq on Bayn al-Qasrayn. But it failed in other instances, such as the row of shops on the facade of al-Salihiyya *madrasa*.[9] This trend is still common in dealing with shops around monuments in Historic Cairo. It is an easy solution for conservators, but undoubtedly a heartbreaking one for the

Bab Zuwayla seen from above
during restoration works

Bab Zuwayla seen from behind
with the surrounding area
cleared for conservation work

shopkeepers and an awful end to the spirit of the historic city as a whole. Moreover, time has proved that unless occupied by a better function, empty facades are soon 're-invaded' in different forms.

Bearing these considerations in mind, and in the absence of any legal or moral code for dealing with shops situated around monuments, we have tried to establish a series of ethical restraints which will not compromise the preservation of historic buildings, yet will be both sympathetic to the built environment and responsive to the requirements of the people living or working around the historic walls. Some of these rules set by us for our own discipline, and developed during the work were the following:

· Before tackling the issue of the shops, one needs to learn almost everything about them and all those involved in each and every one of them, by collecting documentation and data.
· The collection of data must be handed over to a lawyer or a community liaison officer, whose role is to protect the rights of all the parties involved.
· Avoid the adoption of a unified solution. Personal approaches have been proved to inspire confidence between the parties involved. This is the key to finding solutions that satisfy everyone.
· Personal contact with shopkeepers is a must during the planning and the execution of the work.
· Permanent emptying of shops should take place only when absolutely necessary and only when this does not harm the atmosphere of the place as a whole.
· In the case of permanent evacuation, satisfactory compensation and/or an alternative location in proximity to the area or near the dwelling of the business owner must be legally guaranteed to the business owner.
· In the case of temporary evacuation, satisfactory compensation and/or a temporary alternative site in which to continue the business during the dislodgment, and/or an arrangement to work in the same shop after taking necessary security measures, must be legally

guaranteed to both the business owner and the customers.
· Flexibility in thinking during planning and execution to guarantee the smooth management of practical steps and the formation of a relationship built on mutual confidence between the business owners and the conservation team.
· Restoration and conservation of the shops must be fundamental and not superficial. This means that foundations, floors, ceilings and walls must be examined and treated accordingly, and remodelling must be done inside and outside the shop to these same standards. The quality of material and workmanship should be no less than those used for similar work on the monument itself.
· Finally, it is very important to make those business owners who will return to their premises in the area after their temporary evacuation participate in the process of remodelling their shops, taking into account their own needs and to the specifications dictated by their business.

These are only some of the ethical and moral obligations that were set out. The golden rule is that working in the street and with the people has its own rhythm, which calls for flexibility and patience from both the conservation team and the people.

Taking these practical steps required constant and regular negotiation with the Department of Endowments (al-awqaf), different departments of the Supreme Council of Antiquities (SCA), Department of ownership (al-amlak) or Land Registry, the shop tenant(s), the business owner(s), those who run the businesses, the conservation team, the governorate (al-baladiyya), the Department of Traffic (al-murur), the Electricity company with its three departments, the Sewage company, the Water Supply company, the Telephone company, etc. The list of departments and individuals involved is long, but all were helpful and willing to cut the time that it took to carry out procedures for the sake of the success of this experiment. It was only through the goodwill of all those involved that negotiations went on smoothly during the work.

Conclusion

Implementing a large urban conservation project requires organising the achievements of a single monument conservation to deal with the urban issues around the monument.

The purpose of this article is to emphasise the fact that conservation projects for single monuments must include urban conservation as an indispensable component of the project and not only as a matter for the final stages of the project, as a mere supplement. Urban conservation is not purely an aesthetic requirement, but is in fact a fundamental task which has to be taken seriously and placed within a larger planning framework, because when the disparate efforts of urban conservation executed on single monuments are assembled under an overall plan, then they can serve as the basis for a major urban conservation project in Historic Cairo.

Despite the poor standards of construction and the aesthetically antagonistic modern layer of building works of the last fifty years, Historic Cairo still has a unique style in which buildings and the living surroundings intermingle in harmony with the spirit of the past. Fortunately, it has always been difficult to produce any change sufficient to affect this character, and hopefully, nothing will be able to disrupt this continuity of the living spirit.

1   M. Meinecke., ed., *Islamic Cairo, Architectural Conservation and Urban Development of the Historic Center*, Proceedings of a Seminar Organised by the Goethe Institute Cairo (1–5 October, 1978) (Cairo, 1980).

2   UNDP and SCA, *Final Report: Rehabilitation of Historic Cairo* (Cairo, 1997).

3   Historic Cairo Studies and Development Centre – Ministry of Culture, *Development and Urban Conservation in Historic Cairo* (Cairo, 2002), pp. 457–500.

4   See John Rodenbeck, 'The Present Situation of the Historic Cairo: A Road not Taken', in Doris Behrens-Abouseif, ed., *The Cairo Heritage* (Cairo, 2000), pp. 328–340. Also see N. Hampikian, 'Challenges Facing Conservation Projects in Historical Cairo: Historical Buildings versus the Urban Fabric around them', *Proceedings of the 9th Conference of the Union of Egyptian Architects – Architectural Heritage and Urban Development* (Cairo, 1999). Also see N. Hampikian, 'Size of Intervention: Conservation of Isolated Buildings or Urban Conservation in Historical Cairo', in his *al-Salihiyya Complex through time* (Heidelberg, 2004), ch. 4, 4.3.

5   N. Hampikian, and M. al-Ibrashy, 'Filling in Gaps Between a "Monument" and another "Monument" in Historic Cairo - Case Study: Urban Conservation Project - Proposal for the Rehabilitation of the Area around the Southern Gate and Walls of Historic Cairo', *Proceedings of the 5th International Symposium of OWHC* (Santiago de Compostella, 1999).

6   A. Nadim, 'Documentation, Restoration, Conservation, and Development of Bayt al-Suhaymi Area', in *Historic Cairo*, Supreme Council of Antiquities (Cairo, 2002), pp. 199–212.

7   'The sites of monuments must be the object of special care to safeguard their integrity and ensure that they are cleared and presented in a seemly manner.' Article 14, The Venice Charter, International Charter for the Conservation and Restoration of Monuments and Sites (Venice, 1964).

8   For a more detailed action plan and execution report see the Progress Reports presented to the American Research Center's Egyptian Antiquities Project (15 reports, 1998–2002) and the final report and publication of the Bab Zuwayla Conservation Project.

9   N. Hampikian, *al-Salihiyya Complex through Time* (Heidelberg, 2004).

+54.62M

8.64

+45.98M

5.91

+40.07M

7.83

+32.24M

7.07

+25.17M

6.37

+18.60M
8.88
+17.92M

5.79

+12.13M

9.42

+3.71M

3.71

-00.08M 00.00M
-08.18M

Shops

7.88

0.76

1.87

3.18

0.97

1.90

0.36

3.56

0.98

1.03

2.13

0.97

1.94

1.05

1.40

0.33

1.76

0.32

3.74

1.24

15.47

South Elevation 1/50

1 0
0.5 1 3
2 4
5M

The Sam Ibn Nuh Mosque: a community support project, Cairo 2000–2001

Agnieszka Dobrowolska,
with material supplied by Barbara Drieskens

The reconstruction and renovation of two important monuments in al-Darb al-Ahmar was undertaken by Dr Agnieszka Dobrowolska, in cooperation with the American Research Center in Egypt. These were the *sabil-kuttab* of Nafisa al-Bayda, just behind the great gate of Bab Zuwayla, and that of Mahmud Tusun Pasha. A *sabil-kuttab* was a complex of a public fountain (*sabil*) and a Qur'anic school (*kuttab*) usually endowed by a wealthy patron. Nafisa al-Bayda commissioned the building of the *sabil-kuttab* named after her in 1821; the 19th-century ruler Muhammad 'Ali built the *sabil* of Tusun Pasha in honour of his son who had died in battle. Whilst Dr Dobrowolska was working on the Tusun Pasha *sabil* in 2000, the roof of the mosque next door collapsed. The story which follows is that of a community support project undertaken by Dr Dobrowolska in cooperation with the Egyptian Supreme Council of Antiquities, and financed by the Royal Netherlands Embassy in Cairo, the Ford Foundation and contributions from local merchants and craftsmen.

This is an episode in the long history of a small neighbourhood mosque set in the heart of Cairo, and in the life of the community that the mosque serves.

Cairo – the Mother of the World – is an immense city, a home and a place of work, trade and amusement for more than seventeen million people. But its medieval core, full of splendid works of architecture, of the scent of incense, of brilliant sunlight, colourful streets and picturesque sights, has never lost its links with the past – thanks to its people. Some families have been here for generations and remember a great deal of the city's history; some have come only recently to blend in with crowd. All are vivid characters and personalities; everyone knows each another and each other's family and relatives.

The mosque of Sam Ibn Nuh is an oasis of tranquillity in the medieval city's main street, and has served the local community certainly for ten centuries, if not longer. A neighbourhood mosque is not only a place for praying five times a day. There, people can gather, chat or just rest. There, they recite the verses of the Qur'an by heart every afternoon; there, their children go to school, spiritual advice can be sought from a shaykh, news and stories exchanged.

On 9 June 1999, people gathered in the Sam Ibn Nuh Mosque for the evening prayer, as they had always done. Soon after they left, a large section of the roof collapsed. Providentially, no one was killed or injured. But in an instant, the focal place of the community's life turned into a heap of rubble.

The next morning, a committee of engineers inspected the site. The authorities decided that the building was unsafe and must not be open to the public. But the congregation of the mosque could not accept the idea that their traditional place of worship might disappear. They appealed to the conservation project that I was directing in the historic building next door for help in order to keep the mosque open. After the disaster, I installed emergency shoring in the mosque to prevent further collapse which would also endanger the neighbouring monument. With this protection in place, I could give a guarantee to the authorities that the structure was safe to be used. The prayers continued, but the ultimate goal was to reconstruct the roof and bring the mosque back into normal operation, without any scaffolding and shoring inside. However, this was far beyond the financial means of the local community.

In September 2000, the Royal Netherlands Embassy agreed to sponsor a project for rebuilding the section of the roof that had collapsed. This was done in support of the community's efforts. It was a simple intervention, including the building of a new stone wall to carry the roof. All the work was done by local craftsmen and workers using traditional – sometimes almost forgotten – materials and techniques. When the construction started, it generated a lot of enthusiasm in the area and, naturally, the desire to generally renovate the entire mosque arose. This became possible when in December 2000 the Ford Foundation decided to step in and sponsor the rest of the renovation.

The remains of the old roof were removed. The walls were repaired and re-plastered; the damaged women's gallery was replaced. An experienced structural engineer inspected the building and advised against putting the load of a new roof on the weakened walls. Instead,

Prayers at the Sam Ibn Nuh
Mosque during restoration,
still from the documentary
Living with the Past

four marble columns were erected in the prayer hall, supporting stone arches on which the new roof would be carried. The cutting and carving of the columns and arches provided a unique opportunity for exchanging knowledge and sharing experiences between the local traditional stonecutters, an Egyptian marble company using the latest forms of technology and European craftsmen who brought in their traditions and techniques. This was a learning experience for everyone involved.

As the construction proceeded, the local community watched closely, discussing the work and sharing opinions. They were not just observers though. The active involvement of the community was perhaps the most valuable aspect of the project. People helped as they could. Sometimes this was volunteering their time and labour when extra effort was needed. Sometimes it involved cleaning the site after daily activities, guarding the site or helping solve logistic problems. As the project neared completion, financial contributions and volunteer work intensified: people helped to lay the new floor, built the balustrade for the women's balcony, purchased and installed new lighting and carpets. All the time, even in the midst of construction, the mosque remained open for prayers.

The building was completed, according to the wishes of the community, just before Ramadan 1422 (November 2001), and the mood in the neighbourhood was festive. Institutional and private donors contributed generously to the celebrations for the official inauguration of the newly restored mosque. It was marked by a feast that lasted long into the night, a jubilant expression of the community's joy and pride at having their mosque open for prayers for another thousand years.

Even though there are many other mosques nearby, the mosque of Sam Ibn Nuh attracts so many people that during Friday prayers they overflow onto the street. Another particular feature of this mosque is that many women come to pray here. In 2001, Barbara Drieskens, a cultural anthropologist from Belgium, interviewed members of the local community to find out why the people of the district are so strongly attracted to the mosque and consider it especially significant,

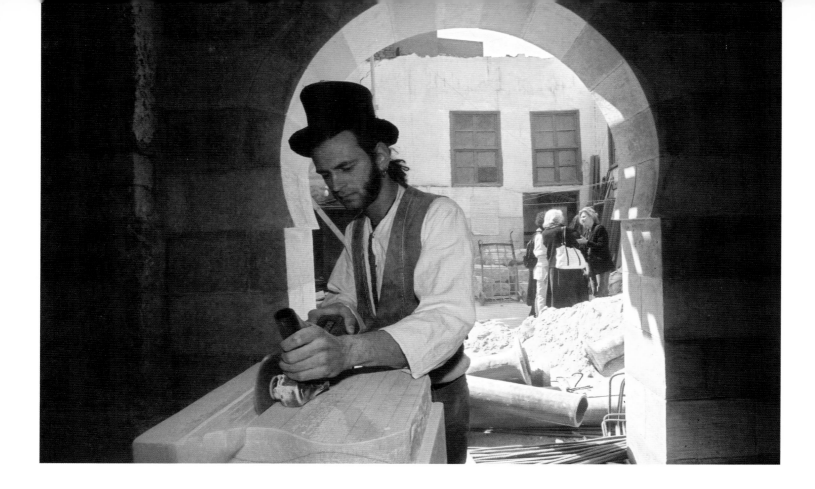

although it lacks the features typical of other similarly venerated mosques. Whilst it is true that the people who work in the area consider it practical to have a mosque so close, the study has identified many more reasons. *It was necessary* – she wrote – *to look beyond the evident, for different meanings.*

No shrine, no monument and very small
AGE AND TRADITION
'Sam is our forefather; we are all descended from him.' People referred to the antiquity of the mosque and the aura of history that it exudes. For those who come to pray here, it is very important that their fathers and mothers did so, and their parents before them. This continuity in space gives them some sense of stability in the rapidly changing life of the city.

ALMOST A HOME
The worshippers at the Sam Ibn Nuh Mosque ascribed all the qualities of a good home to it. It is comfortable and restful, and provides peace of mind, indeed even more than could be found at home. The mosque protects the people in it, and is itself protected. Another homely quality is cleanness, both its physical cleanliness and in the sense of its ritual purity.

THE BLESSINGS OF WATER
In a way, the mosque now fulfils the function of the *sabil*, which once provided clean drinking water for free. The availability of water and of toilets has a purely practical aspect, but water has a further symbolic meaning for the users of the mosque. The blessings of the water are triple: it is useful, it is pure and it is a gift: what is offered as charity carries blessings both for the giver and the receiver.

KNOWLEDGE
People value the mosque not only as a place where Islam is practised, but also where knowledge about the religion is imparted. Lessons about Islam are given every day, once a week for women. Anybody can

seek advice at any time. Many couples come to solve their disputes and often the shaykh is able to reconcile the two parties.

HARMONY

Ta'alif means harmony, familiarity and mutual affection. This was explicitly mentioned as a valuable quality of the mosque. The way it fulfills the different needs of the community makes it a place that links people together.

Why did it come down?

The underlying reason for the collapse of the roof was differential ground settlement caused by groundwater. The rising groundwater table has been an acute problem in Historic Cairo since the late 1970s, and it causes severe damage to historic monuments. Like all the surrounding buildings, the mosque sits on a man-made fill, which has accumulated over the centuries to form a layer nine metres thick. When groundwater levels change, the fill begins to settle, often unevenly. The excavation for the sewer exchange under the street, beneficial in the long term, added to the immediate instability. The whole front section of the complex of buildings which dates from 1819, including the walls of the mosque, started to lean forward and detach. This movement caused the steel beam supporting the roof to slide off its bracket on the wall. The impact of the collapse bent and twisted the tall beam into a piece of scrap metal. In the reconstructed mosque, the roof is mostly supported on new, solid foundations, and only partly on the old walls. The foundation of the front section of the entire complex was reinforced by micro-piling. Compared to the old construction, the restored mosque is far more structurally integrated, with its walls, pillars and roof solidly bound together to prevent another disaster.

The age of the mosque

In the early 15th century, the famous chronicler al-Maqrizi wrote: 'On the edge of the saddler's market is the mosque [...] called Sam Ibn Nuh, and next to it there is Bab Zuwayla.' The mosque was already ancient

by then. Its location suggests that it was already existence when Bab Zuwayla was built in 1092. Muhammad ibn al-Banna, who died in 1195, is known to have taught Qur'anic recitation here. The mosque is thus one of the oldest in Cairo, and has probably been in continuous use for a thousand years. Nothing, however, is known about the architecture of the early mosque. When Muhammad 'Ali constructed his ornate *sabil* and school complex in 1819, the entrance to the small mosque was incorporated into the new facade. Parts of its walls date to earlier times, but nothing of architectural merit was preserved. Before the collapse of 1999, the mosque was a modest, simple building that had acquired its current form in the early 20th century and had been shaped by the practical needs of the community rather than by artistic inspiration.

Historic or modern?

How does one find an appropriate form for a building that is, at one and the same time, centuries old and essentially modern? Numerous factors had to be considered: the constraints of space, the expectations of a traditional community, the surroundings of a listed monument and the crumbling walls all around. The building had to be structurally consolidated and its weakened outer walls relieved. This made internal supports necessary. The columns supporting the roof, the wall underneath the women's gallery, the arches in the entrance corridor, all have structural purposes. The architectural forms resulted to a great extent from the decision to use traditional materials and building techniques. The design uses idioms and patterns from the traditional Islamic architecture of Cairo, but in a simple, geometric form, without imitating any particular historical period or style.

Local craftsmen

The mosque was rebuilt with traditional materials and techniques, and therefore the people doing the work had to be skilled in traditional crafts. Many of the craftsmen working for the project learned their trades from their fathers. The stonecutters, stucco makers, carpenters and bricklayers, brought to the project skills and knowledge transmitted over many generations. Many of them live in the neighbourhood. The area abounds in small workshops where the same craft has often been practised for centuries. The local blacksmiths, woodworkers, masters in brass, stucco, or stone, supplied the mosque with iron and brass fittings, built the pavilion over the central columns, provided doors, floors, wooden balustrades and more.

The celebration

A *mawlid* is a celebration of a holy person's birthday when people assemble at his or her tomb. Quite apart from its religious intent, a *mawlid* in Egypt always draws crowds for a traditional feast, a festival of joyous entertainment, folk art and popular culture.

There is no tomb in the mosque of Sam Ibn Nuh. It is just a place of prayer for the local community, and not a shrine, so the celebration that marked its opening was not one in veneration of a saintly shaykh, but an expression of the neighbourhood's jubilant mood. The street called it a *mawlid* anyway – thus giving it the sense of a popular feast.

For three days, a band of musicians distributed invitations to everyone in the neighbouring streets and heralded the coming event. When it came, it began with the *iftar* or Ramadan meal for three hundred people. Later, thousands gathered in front of the mosque on the medieval city's principal street to watching musicians and entertainers until late at night.

What a night! There were crowds, lights, banners, colourful tents, whirling dervishes, tight-rope walking, juggling, fire-eating, stick-dancing, three bands, crowds of Egyptians and foreigners, distinguished guests and local peddlers, red head-dresses, a giant air-balloon, a rider on a black stallion! Men, women, children, Muslims and Christians, rich and poor, all celebrated the opening of the restored mosque.

Postscript

in the years following its restoration the mosque of Sam Ibn Nuh has re-established its role as the focal point of the district.

Even more people come every day to pray, and also to rest, to exchange news, to seek advice from the shaykh, to recite the Qur'an, or to attend the classes of religious instruction.

The mosque's attraction for the community is reflected in the care and attention it has been given. With funds raised by the community, the ablution and water-disposal facilities have been completely renovated. New electric fan systems cool the congregation in the summer, and new carpets cover the floor. Additional lighting has been installed.

The attention of the local community has not been limited to the practical uses of the building. Anonymous donors continue to embellish it: the capitals and bases of the white marble columns have been gilded with gold leaf, and the stucco of the *mihrab* now also glitters with gold. The lower sections of the walls have received a multicoloured marble facing.

As the local people successfully adapt the new building to their practical and aesthetic needs, the mosque dedicated to the son of Noah, like the Ark, continues on its journey through the flood of time.

23 Cooperative renovation of old houses in al-Darb al-Ahmar: a case study

Salah Zaky Said

Cairo has been faced with many problems when dealing with the issue of upgrading the historic city. The population of al-Darb al-Ahmar is generally poor and the city does not have an organisation devoted to the improvement of traditional vernacular architecture and historic houses. Thus it was difficult to find a system by means of which houses that are not listed as monuments could be conserved. The Supreme Council of Antiquities takes charge of only a limited number of historic houses.

In 1993 an experiment was launched by the Department of Architecture at the University of al-Azhar to provide technical assistance to owners and residents of houses of architectural and historic value in Historic Cairo. The idea, which started with a very small donation from the Goethe Institute in Cairo, was later developed into an organised upgrading procedure with the assistance from the American Research Center in Egypt under the supervision of the Ministry of Culture. As a result, a cooperative programme was launched which resulted in the conservation of four non-listed historic houses in the area of Bab al-Wazir and al-Darb al-Ahmar, from 1995 to 1997. These are Bayt Soccar, Bayt al-Sitt Awatif, Bayt Sitt Sabah and Bayt al-Nagarin.

At the outset of the programme, houses of historic and architectural value in the street of al-Mahgar and Bab al-Wazir were placed on a priority list. Architecture students helped to document the houses. The documentation included the history of the houses and their development down to their present condition, plus plans, elevations, sections and details. Conditions of deterioration were also listed and a preliminary estimate of costs for renovating the houses was established. Contributions from the residents and the owners of the houses towards the renovation were outlined. In the quarter of al-Darb al-Ahmar, forty houses were listed and photographed as subects for renovation.

The contribution and input of residents and owners

The residents of old houses in Historic Cairo prefer to live in them rather than to move into modern apartments; they generally appreciate the qualities of the old houses, especially their climatic adaptability and also the privacy they offer, particularly houses with open courtyards. This is why they are prepared to cooperate and contribute towards the renovation of these houses, and so avoid losing the house through collapse due to lack of maintenance. In such a case, they would have to move to new apartments which would probably be located far from their old neighbourhood and their work.

On the other hand, the families that live in this area are generally in the low-income bracket. They can only make a partial contribution to the expense of renovation; in the past this was usually limited to the cost of materials used to renew or install bathrooms and plumbing. (The latter, however, was the main reason for the collapse of the old houses.) Adding a shower or a sink or even an entirely new bathroom, meant that an old house was considered modernised, having new facilities.

In many cases physical labour such as digging, plastering or painting was also carried out as a participatory contribution to the project. The contributions and efforts of the residents were considered key elements in the success of the new project.

Description of typical houses of value to be saved in Historic Cairo

In Historic Cairo, a large number of houses fall into the category of historic and traditional houses that need to be saved. These houses were largely built in the 19th and early 20th century. Few of them have a central court. Mostly they consist of three or four floors. The the ground and first floor are built generally of stone; upper floors are built of red brick with an inlay of a few horizontal wooden beams on different levels as supports; these are placed usually on the level of the lintel for the window sill and also at the ceiling level. The houses usually have a common feature, which is a *mashrabiyya* (an intricate wooden screen) covering a balcony or a window.

The layout of the houses differed. If the house was built originally for one family, shops and businesses might be found on the street level, the upper level containing living quarters for men and women, laid out differently in each case according to family needs and the

The exteriors of restored
Ottoman houses near the
Khayrbak complex, Historic
Cities Programme, 2006

demands of the site itself. Houses with apartments would generally have shops on the ground level, with the apartments on the upper floors, usually laid out with a central *sala* or space for common use and the other rooms placed around it overlooking the street. The lavatory and kitchen were usually in the back, ventilated and lit from a light shaft. Most of these houses have very interesting architectural features, considered to be very rare and also very difficult for craftsmen to replicate today. These features include the *mashrabiyya*s, stonework, ironwork and painted ceilings which are found in some Turkish style houses.

Description of the procedure of renovation
The goal of the project was to renovate and adapt the old houses for reuse. The procedure depended on a few key issues, outlined below.

IMPROVEMENT OF STRUCTURAL CONDITIONS OF THE HOUSES
In Bayt Soccar, which was the first house to be renovated, but also in the next three houses, a reconstruction of the ground floor walls was undertaken to replace deteriorated segments of the walls at street level. New stone was used rather than recycled original pieces.

In some cases an entire wall had to be replaced. This task involved the considerable risk that the house might collapse totally. This risk was all the greater because most families, having no other place to go, lived in the houses during the renovation process. The entire house, and especially those parts around the wall to be reconstructed, was shored up by scaffolding, to carry the weight of the upper roofs and the adjacent walls, Generally the reason for dilapidation of walls was either the surface water at street level, or the water and sewer network of the house.

THE ROOF
Those parts of the wooden roofs that had deteriorated had to be replaced. This included wooden beams and flooring planks as well as parts of the stone or mosaic tiling in these areas. In Bayt Soccar, the wooden roof of the top floor was sagging as a result of the long term effects of rainwater, and so had to be replaced.

THE FOUNDATION
The foundations of Bayt Soccar and the other three houses were all built of solid limestone. In most cases they did not need to be replaced or restored since the groundwater level was much deeper than the foundations. Actually the ground level in this area is high because of its position at the foot of the Muqattam Hills. There was only one case, that of Bayt Sitt Awatif, where an entire wall had to be replaced, along with its foundations, due to the effects of a leaking sewer.

THE STAIRS
In the case of Bayt Soccar as well as the other houses, the stone staircases had to be replaced, using solid new Helwan limestone. The steps are cantilevered out from the wall, transmitting the load step by step to the ground.

SANITARY FACILITIES
The renovation of bathrooms was an important part of the project. Frequently sinks, showers and even entire new bathrooms were installed. Some modest apartments did not have private bathrooms but shared a common one with other families on the ground floor. In all the houses leaking drains and pipes were the reason for the disintegration of the walls. These had to be completely renewed. The project personnel provided new workshop drawings for the renovation and supervised the small contractors who carried out the works, who usually were from the neighbourhood.

PLASTER AND PAINT
The exterior walls of the four houses had a finishing of stone on the lower ground floor; this was cleaned and restored where needed. On the upper floors plaster was used as a finish for the walls; this was restored and repainted. The woodwork of windows and *mashrabiyya*s were restored to their original form and then repainted inside. Some walls had to be replaced or plastered, and then repainted. The residents took responsibility for repainting the inside of their apartments.

Social impact of the project

An economic and social investigation of the inhabitants of the four restored houses was conducted for Bayt Soccar, Bayt Sitt Sabah, Bayt al-Sitt Awatif and Bayt al-Nagarin

The results of the study indicated that
72 per cent of the inhabitants of the houses were born in the same area or the same house;
48 per cent have jobs and the rest are unemployed or living on pensions;
55 per cent go to work on foot since their work is close by;
88 per cent of the residents prefer to continue living in the same house because of the low rent, closeness to work, emotional commitment to the site and the presence of relatives in the area;
65 per cent say the area lacks public services such as a clinic, green areas and a social club;
All the residents appreciated the efforts made to renovate the buildings and believe that this intervention has prevented the collapse of their homes.

Conclusion

The project encouraged the participation of the owners and the residents in the renovation work. Whenever possible, residents either paid for or provided some of the required building materials as well as fittings for bathrooms and plumbing. The residents shared in the cost of renovation, contributing between 10 and 30 per cent of the total cost of materials. Involving the inhabitants in the renovation process proved to be quite important. Those who participated felt a sense of pride in what they had contributed through their efforts and their ideas.

Unemployment and a lack of skills and education are common among a large percentage of the residents. The improvement of people's skills in fields such as craft production would greatly assist in improving their standard of living. Opening a shop for the tourists who pass through this historic area could also be a great help to the inhabitants, who would be more appreciative of the tourists if they could increase their own income through such activity. It would be quite feasible for some houses on the main thoroughfare to open small shops as art and craft workshops or other suitable enterprises without endangering the architectural character of the area.

24 Restoring the Qijmas Mosque: a community undertaking by the residents of al-Darb al-Ahmar

Interviews with Hisham and 'Ali Mahmoud

The Qijmas Mosque was built in AD 1481 by the amir Qijmas al-Ishaqi, Sultan Qaytbay's master of horse. Usually, the patron-builder is buried in a mausoleum inside the mosque but Amir Qijmas died whilst in Syria and is buried there. The mausoleum remained empty until 1851, when the pious Shaykh Abu Hureiba was buried there. Unlike many of the mosques in the area currently under restoration, this mosque has been open and in use almost continually for the last five centuries. Hisham Mahmoud, who has a shoe repair shop, is only one of many shop owners who maintain small businesses in the shadow of the great mosque. His brother, 'Ali Mahmoud, is an electrician whose workshop is just across the street. Twenty years ago, the two brothers, with their father, Salah Mahmoud 'Ali, helped organise people from the local neighbourhood in order to restore and maintain the mosque, which had fallen into disrepair. The transcript of an interview with the brothers, describing the community activity follows:

Q: *What do you know about this mosque? Who built it? When? And so on.*
Hisham: I knew through my grandparents, my dad, and all my family that it was built in AH 881 by Prince Qijmas al-Ishaqi during the era of the Mamluks. He lived at the time of Sultan al-Ashraf Qaytbay. That great king! A lot of money was spent to construct the mosque and they used the most advanced techniques. But it had become run down.

Q: *So what happened?*
Hisham: My dad began to take care of this mosque. Before that it had been deserted. Only two or three people prayed here. Sometimes it even stayed closed. My dad made keys for all the doors. At first people said bad things about him, like he was doing it all for his personal interest. But he never took anything for himself. He began to collect money to fix the mosque. After that, everybody recognised him for his good works. He was like a father for everybody in the area.

Q: *So what has been done?*
Hisham: The mosque had one lamp only. Just one. My dad bought fans

and some *kandil*s like those lamps in Sayyida Zaynab. He collected the money from his friends and people who came to pray here. My brother 'Ali is an electrician. He put up the lights, all the new lights. All the lights you see here are new.

Q: *What connected your dad to this mosque?*
Hisham: He used to pray here all the time. He took care of opening and closing the place.

Q: *So, was he responsible for the mosque, or what?*
Hisham: No, he just loved the mosque. He liked to serve the place because he's a Muslim. All the Muslims here love the mosque. They leave their work and come. The people have bought all the furnishings themselves. All these carpets here, for example. Before there was nothing at all, only straw mats on the floor. People brought the curtains too, the lamps and everything.

Q: *Hisham, tell us what your dad has done for this mosque.*
Hisham: In 1996, the mosque had four lamps, and no carpets. The Ministry of Waqfs provided twenty-six carpets, and my dad bought more. He collected money from the people here. It was hot in summer and people used to sweat a lot while praying. My father bought fans and lamps. Many electricians were consulted before they asked my brother 'Ali to do the work. People wanted more and more lamps, and they paid a lot of money.

Q: *Why are the lamps hung down like that? Were they like that in the past?*
Hisham: Yes.

Do you remember your grandad?
Hisham: Yes.

Q: *What did he used to do?*
Hisham: He was in the other mosque, the one of 'Sidi Sad' Allah',

opposite. He loved that place because the shaykh there had some connection with Prophet Muhammad. He was his forefather. People loved that shaykh for that reason, and found blessings in that.

Q: *Is the shaykh still buried there?*
Hisham: Yes, he's still there.

Q: *Hisham, tell us about your feelings towards the mosque. You wake up in the morning and come here to do certain things. What makes you do all of that?*
Hisham: God does.

Q: *What do you gain from all this work?*
Hisham: God helps me. He blesses me with good health and money. I get the feeling that if I do things for the mosque, God will stand by me.

Q: *Did anybody ask you to do this?*
Hisham: God did. When I leave home, God guides me to do this and that. If I have no time, somebody else does my job, otherwise I come the next day and do the work.

Q: *So, the work is mostly done by the people themselves, as volunteer work. Does the government do something?*
Hisham: There are two government servants for the mosque. They're officially employed and come regularly, at prayer times. But I clean up.

Q: *Which part of the mosque do you like the best?*
Hisham: All of it. I love all of the mosque. In the summer, when I'm bored, I go up in the minaret. I take a bottle of water with me. I watch the whole of Cairo and feel comfortable. I leave when I'm feeling better. It's wonderful there in the summer.

Q: *So, the mosque is everything for you?*
Hisham: It's everything for me. I'm not married. This is all I care for.

I sit here on my own but I feel the whole world is around me. Nobody notices me, but I notice everybody.

Q: *Is the mosque visited by a certain type of people? Or do people only come to pray?*
Hisham: A lot of foreigners come here. Tourist groups love it very much.

Q: *We've noticed that most old mosques are just considered monuments, but this mosque is more than that.*
Hisham: Yes, it is a living place it's my home and everybody's home. It's the home of the whole world.

'Ali Mahmoud, Hisham's brother, took over the job of maintaining the electrics in the mosque. Since the mosque is a national and historic monument, any repairs must be approved by the government. At first, 'Ali's appointment was questioned. Was he sufficiently skilled to undertake the complicated job? But 'Ali's ability was attested to by many people, and eventually he was given the job. He was interviewed in his shop, across from the mosque.

Q: *Would you give us an idea about what you do here?*
'Ali: This is a maintenance centre. I'm experienced in repairing TV sets. Some of my colleagues work on cooling and air-conditioning equipment. Two engineers work on automatic washing machines. I've been interested in complicated technical equipment, since I was very young, Once, I had to have therapy in a jacuzzi because of a problem in my neck. It was too expensive, so I decided to make my own jacuzzi. A gentleman admired my work and bought it. Then I started to make others.

Q: *Tell us what you did for the mosque.*
'Ali: I had to replace the entire electric grid. The old wiring system in the mosque had deteriorated. Lighting was very bad. Actually, no maintenance seems to have been done to the wiring since electricity was first installed. We were afraid of fire breaking out.

Portal of the mosque of
Amir Qijmas al-Ishaqi
(built 885/1480)

Q: *So what happened?*
'Ali: We had two choices: either to close down the mosque or to cooperate and fix the electricity ourselves.

Q: *I thought the government usually did such repairs.*
'Ali: Yes. There is a government budget for the Antiquities Authority and the Ministry of Waqfs to do such repairs. But they had their own priorities and plans. They couldn't afford to do the work here. And after the earthquake, most of the wiring in the mosque was damaged even more. We couldn't wait for the authorities to do the repairs.

Q: *So?*
'Ali: Everybody here agreed we had to replace all the electrics. A lot of money was needed. One person could not pay for all that. My dad went to his friends the merchants and many people here and collected money. He would say to a man, 'Come on, give me 500 hundred pounds for the mosque, or get some wires and lamps because 'Ali is going to fix things.' We worked together as a team and collected the money needed from the people. Salah Muhammad 'Ali, my dad, bought the material and I carried out the repairs. Since it was difficult to reach the ceiling (it's eighteen metres high), we got iron scaffolds. Specialised technicians weren't available but people around here gave a hand. Everyone had great confidence in my dad.

Q: *What about the necessary government approval to undertake such an important job?*
'Ali: We got official approval from the Antiquities Authority and the Ministry of Waqfs. The Ministry of Waqfs said we could do whatever we wanted, as long as we didn't ask for money. But we also needed approval from the Antiquities Authority.

Q: *And the Antiquities Authority?*
'Ali: The Antiquities Authority approved on condition that we did the work at our own expense without touching the decoration and

under their supervision. The head of Engineering Management for the Authority came to inspect the work. Two good engineers helped us. They were ladies. They told us to save the money we paid for the scaffolding and use it for the wires. They promised to bring other scaffolding, and they kept their promise and brought us scaffolding. I worked for eight months on this project. A number of efficient colleagues in my company, including six Christians, also helped me. We all worked together. We used to come to the mosque after normal working hours, work until one in the morning and go back to work again the next day. The two engineers supervised the work. Here in Egypt, a Christian helps in the mosque and a Muslim in the church. This is the nature of Egyptians and how they behave towards each other. Everybody helped and we finished the work. We only have the main panel left now. Unfortunately, my dad died before we were finished. Only someone who appreciates this place, loves it and knows how to handle things could do this kind of work. No one else could manage it. Since the renovation the mosque has begun to attract more tourists as well as local people.

Q: *What attracts people to this mosque?*
Hisham: It's a wonderful place. The golden decoration and the beautiful calligraphy attract everybody.

Q: *Is there anything else? Are there any special feelings related to this place?*
Hisham: Oh yes. When people talk about the Qijmas Mosque, everybody thinks of Shaykh Ahmad Abu Hureiba, a holy man. And since the new lights were put up, seven years ago, we've held *mawlid* celebrations regularly to mark the shaykh's life. Meat is given to the poor. People love the place now. Only four people used to pray here. Now almost forty people attend the prayers every day. And on Fridays, we have to put extra carpets as far as where my shop is, near the staircase.

Q: *What's the story of Abu Hureiba?*
Hisham: The true story? Well, I'll tell you what I heard.

Q: *Tell us what you know. What your grandparents told you*.

Hisham: Well, you've seen the alley I live in. It's called Sid Sad' Allah alley. Down that alley is another alley, Abu Kalba. They say that long ago there used to be a bakery there. Shaykh Ahmad Abu Hureiba worked in that bakery. The dogs used to wait for him after work. Everybody knew the dogs belonged to him. He would take bread for wages. He used to save one loaf of bread for himself and give the rest to the dogs. One dog always followed him here. He used to sleep on the wide bench by the front of the mosque. That was when the final stages of construction were underway. Whenever Prince Qijmas came to inspect the work, he would notice the shaykh. When the mosque was finished, the prince decided to leave Egypt because he was building a similar mosque in Turkey, at least that's what they say. He was travelling by ship. Before he left, he told everybody that when the first kind man dies (he is supposed to have pointed to Abu Hureiba), you have to bury him here. He said, 'The first pious person.' He added that he himself would be buried in the other mosque in Turkey because he wouldn't be coming back to Egypt. But the ship sank and he died in the sea. So Prince Qijmas is neither buried here, nor in the other mosque.

Q: *What happened next?*

Hisham: They say that Abu Hureiba died the day after the prince. He was buried here upon the request of Prince Qijmas. It could be a folk-tale, I'm not sure, but that's what people say.

Q: *So tell us about the mawlid celebration here.*

Hisham: You mean, for Sidi Abu Hureiba?

Q: *Yes.*

Hisham: The *mawlid* is on the 12th day of Rabi' al-Akhar.

Q: *What happens?*

Hisham: It's like a big party. We put lights all around the mosque starting from the top on the minaret down to my shop and then along the whole street. I hang lanterns and we hold a big celebration. We serve hot drinks like canella. Shaykhs sit down here and read the Qur'an to bless the soul of the holy man Sidi Abu Hureiba and all the good Muslims who have died. Ladies sit in a corner and give out meat, *fatta*, strawberry and mango syrup. Everybody is happy, even happier than on other feast days. We have another *mawlid* the next day for Sitt Fatima al-Nabawiyya. We have also the *mawlid* of Sidi Sad' Allah, the son of Fatima.

Q: *So the area is all decorated for the celebrations.*

Hisham: Everywhere looks wonderful. In the past, this mosque was almost deserted. For seven years, no lights were hung up here. I used to decorate it with coloured paper ribbons used for wrapping up cakes. Everybody liked what I did. Now that the mosque is repaired, people come for the *mawlid* and we put up lights and people are very happy. A famous shaykh comes to read the Qur'an. A great celebration takes place.

25 The Projects of the Aga Khan Trust for Culture in al-Darb al-Ahmar area of Historic Cairo

Stefano Bianca, Francesco Siravo,
Cameron Rashti and Frank Matero

The Trust and its Historic Cities Programme

Since its beginnings, the activities of the Aga Khan Trust for Culture (AKTC) and its Historic Cities Programme (HCP) have been focused mainly around the architecture and the urban structures of Muslim societies, both in terms of historic heritage and contemporary reality. The built environment has been considered the most tangible manifestation of those essential shaping forces of a culture which are difficult to grasp (let alone quantify), but which acquire qualitative evidence through their crystallisation in meaningful architectural forms and urban spaces. Such physical support structures can, in turn, inspire and sustain matching collective values, individual attitudes and social patterns, thus giving rise to particular forms of community life and cultural identity.

The continuous mutual interchange between hidden (implicit) values and apparent (explicit) built form has always been a hallmark of traditional cultures and has enabled them to remain vibrant, creative and consistent down the centuries. Today, such connections are needed more than ever, so that local societies can find their own approach to innovation – that is to say to absorb and integrate any fresh opportunities which present themselves through the engagement of their particular internal resources, rather than being stifled by alien ideologies and procedures.

Preserving cultural values, re-interpreting and revitalising architectural traditions and strengthening the creative potential of local societies are all important challenges, therefore, in the current context of rapid change, as imposed by the worldwide impact of the uniform concepts of modern Western civilisation. Proper ways must be found to steer, control and adapt the constant process of cultural, social and architectural transformation in ways that are compatible with (and can draw from) the rich assets that Muslim communities undoubtedly possess. This will not only help preserve local cultural autonomy, but will also ensure the survival of cultural pluralism at the global level.

Through the Aga Khan Award for Architecture and the Aga Khan Programme for Islamic Architecture, the trust has engaged since the late 1970s in the theoretic debate concerning the interface between Tradition and Modernity. The many projects evaluated, selected and promoted by the award throughout its ten past cycles have become paradigms of good practice – not only in the field of architecture, but also in the domains of urban planning, conservation, adaptive reuse, improvement of social housing and landscaping. With the establishment of the Historic Cities Programme in 1992, the trust has, however, entered new ground, inasmuch as it has ventured into the active implementation of self-funded and self-managed projects covering a wide range of interventions, almost equal indeed to the scope of research covered by the award.

Over the years, the HCP has developed its own integrated approach that combines classical conservation projects with adaptive reuse, contextual urban planning, community development, strengthening of local economic conditions, institutional capacity building and skills enhancement. While overall management and supervision is centralised at the trust's headquarters in Geneva, strong local groups have been established in project countries, to facilitate proper implementation, to train local staff and to ensure eventual self-sustainability after project hand-over. In the early years of the programme, smaller individual projects tended to prevail, but soon it was realised that individual initiatives needed to be built into an integrated action-area approach, in order to generate synergies, to reach a 'critical mass', and to achieve benefits that go beyond a simple accumulation of individual actions. Accordingly, the time that the HCP and its local Cultural Service Companies can be present, in most cases, has been extended, thus enabling groups of projects to capitalise on earlier achievements with regard to local community involvement and cooperation with governmental institutions. In recent years, a number of Public-Private Partnerships with local governmental agencies have been conducted, with the aim of coordinating donor contributions with private and public investment. This approach also ensures a thorough institutional and legal back-up for HCP initiatives and increases the chances of successful modes of operation and methods being replicated later by government institutions.

The HCP portfolio now covers a large array of sites in different regions and countries. Its activities began with projects in the valleys of the Karakoram in North Pakistan, in the old Stone Town in Zanzibar, and in Cairo. These were followed by projects in the Timurid city of Samarkand, in three medieval citadels (and their surroundings) in Syria, as well as in Mostar, Kabul, Herat and Djenné. Currently, the programme is also engaged in the old cities of Delhi and Lahore. The initiatives in Historic Cairo, which are the subject of this article, constitute the Historic Cities Programme's most complex and ambitious urban rehabilitation project to date. Its scope goes beyond the restoration of individual buildings to encompass the creation of a major urban park together with the launching of a series of physical conservation and social development initiatives aimed at the revitalisation of an entire sector of the Islamic City. In this respect, the project exemplifies HCP's multidisciplinary character and its integrated planning approach. Individual initiatives covering the physical, social and economic aspects of the project are conceived of as mutually reinforcing activities. Beyond aiming at conservation and revitalisation of the built environment, they attempt to establish self-sustaining processes of adapted urban development which are designed to take into account the current dynamics of change and the need for selective adjustment and transformation.

The project's long gestation and development period illustrates another characteristic trait of HCP interventions, i.e., the gradual, incremental growth – from relatively simple beginnings to more and more ambitious undertakings in response to the requirements and new opportunities that arise during the life of the project. This pragmatic approach is based on a regular evaluation of evolving local conditions, and on corresponding feedback cycles that inform the project in its various stages. It contrasts strongly with conventional practices of planning and implementing large projects from the outset with relatively little knowledge or experience of local conditions, limited participation by the community, and no built-in mechanism to adjust the original assumptions to the constraints and opportunities encountered during implementation.

View of the Darassa Hills
before development of
the park, 1992

AKTC's involvement in Egypt began with His Highness the Aga Khan's decision to create a new urban park for the inhabitants of Cairo. The 30-hectare al-Darassa site – to be named al-Azhar Park – was selected because of its enormous potential to provide a 'lung' in the very centre of the city's historic agglomeration. By some almost miraculous coincidence, this hilly site that was formed over centuries through the progressive accumulation of debris from the neighbouring city had remained practically empty. Although the salinity of the ground caused it to remain a barren, desert-like piece of land, its topography is highly attractive, as it provides a 360° panoramic view of the major landmarks of Historic Cairo – all prime destinations for visitors to the city. To the west of the site, the original Fatimid city and its later extension including al-Darb al-Ahmar can be seen, with a wealth of *madrasa*s and mosques indicated by a long line of minarets. To the south are the Sultan Hasan Mosque and the Ayyubid Citadel. To the east lies the Mamluk 'City of the Dead' with its many mausoleums and educational and charitable complexes endowed by Mamluk sultans and dignitaries between the 13th and 15th centuries – a heritage area that has itself developed into a densely populated neighbourhood.

By 1996, the site had been cleared and three large water tanks constructed. The trust then took over the site from the Cairo Governorate, while its Historic Cities Programme began to think about a more comprehensive approach to the adjoining urban area. As a result of the Aga Khan's vision and support, the project gradually moved beyond the park boundaries to include the restoration of the Historic City Wall, the rehabilitation of the adjacent district of al-Darb al-Ahmar and the conservation of a number of important monuments that define the historic skyline seen from the site of the park. The creation of the park has thus acted as a catalyst for a whole range of associated actions in the areas surrounding it:

The *Azhar Park Project* itself has played a key role in converting the last remaining large open space in central Cairo from a marginal and derelict condition into a strategic environmental resource. The construction of the so-called *Urban Plaza* (a commercial complex combined with a Museum of Historic Cairo and an underground parking garage) on the northern edge of the park and next to the busy al-Azhar Road will generate income that can sustain the maintenance and future improvement of the park.

The scope of the new park was further enhanced by the rediscovery and partial excavation of the *Historic Ayyubid Wall* along its western slope. With a length of almost 1.5 kilometres, this is the longest and best-preserved portion of Cairo's Historic City Wall. Its excavation was facilitated by cutting back and regrading the steep western slope of the future park. These combined actions have provided a unique archeological opportunity for investigating the ancient limits of Historic Cairo and re-establishing lost urban connections through reusing the newly discovered original city gates.

As the work on al-Azhar Park evolved, the historic and social assets of the adjacent district of al-Darb al-Ahmar became more and more apparent, together with their inherent fragility and the risks associated with wholesale demolition and uncontrolled development. In order to preserve the area and orient its future development through a conscious planning effort, AKTC embarked upon a comprehensive *Urban Rehabilitation Programme for al-Darb al-Ahmar*. Its long-term strategy focused on the restoration of individual landmarks, the physical upgrading of housing and open spaces, as well as on various socio-economic development initiatives for the community that were seen as complementary, and indeed inseparable, actions aimed at the general revitalisation of the district.

By associating and integrating these different initiatives, the project stands out as an act of comprehensive urban rehabilitation that has, in many respects, changed the fate and the image of Historic Cairo. At the eleventh hour, it has saved a significant historic district from entering the terminal phase of decay. It has demonstrated how the seemingly inevitable spiral of decline can be reversed by sustainable rehabilitation procedures anchored in the local community. By connecting the revitalisation of al-Darb al-Ahmar to the prestigious Park Project (which enhances the status of the Historic City as a whole), it has turned around popular misconceptions of historic districts as hopeless slum areas.

Moreover, within the Historic Cities Programme, the project has served as a most welcome testing ground for innovative planning and conservation procedures that are now being applied in area development projects in other cities and countries.

al-Azhar Park

Development of the new al-Azhar Park got off to a slow start due to several long-standing issues of occupation and land use. Located below the escarpment of the Muqattam Hills, between the Historic City and the Mamluk 'City of the Dead', the Darassa site was for centuries a dumping ground for man-made debris and waste, eventually forming a mass some 30 metres in height and forming a major barrier to urban expansion beyond the Historic City Wall. As a result, the site was never permanently settled although, in recent times, parts of it were informally occupied.

The first plans for the Park Project were prepared in the late 1980s, but implementation was delayed until various occupants could be moved, including stables and horses belonging to the Cairo Police and a building contractor's storage compound. Further delays resulted when the General Organisation for Greater Cairo Water Supply (GOGCWS) claimed this last vacant space in central Cairo for the construction of three large drinking-water tanks for the city.

Finally, in 1990, the Cairo Governorate and AKTC signed a protocol, whereby the water tanks would be accommodated in a new design that incorporated the considerable piling and soil works needed to embed the reservoir system within the topography of the future park. The period until the reservoirs could be completed, in 1996, was used to develop a new master plan, to carry out horticultural tests and an in-depth investigation of soil conditions, and to create an on-site nursery. Earthworks and master grading began in 1997, while the detailed design of the park continued with a view to taking the best advantage of the site's opportunities, some of which became apparent only as the

work progressed. Excavation of the debris to depths of 7 to 8 metres along the eastern slope facing the Historic City Wall, and the initial discovery and exposure of a completely buried 300-metre extension of the wall, brought about renewed interest in the archeological riches in this part of Cairo. This, in turn, fostered the idea of utilising the Park Project not only to create a public green space but also as a panoramic platform, to view and reinterpret the built heritage of Islamic Cairo.

As a result, the topography and grading for the new park was designed to make the most of the higher viewpoints on top of the hills and the reservoir tanks. At the same time, the decision to keep the unearthed Ayyubid Wall fully visible called for a considerable readjustment of the original slopes, in particular reducing the incline along the western side of the site and avoid structural problems below. Yet, even with the modified incline, the western slopes remained critical in terms of the landscape treatment. Special design solutions were adopted to improve the stability of the slope, using special plantings and systems of irrigation and drainage, particularly along the relatively steep and narrow section flanking the Historic Wall. An elaborate process of partial excavation, waterproofing and compacting of soil was followed over most of the surface of the park site.

In parallel to resolving problems of soil stability and irrigation, various types of plants and landscapes were tested to determine what would best acclimatise to the particular conditions of the site. Cairo and most of Egypt falls within the extremely arid climate belt that extends westward across the North African desert. Here, the combination of high seasonal temperatures, scant rainfall and strong desert winds imposes severe constraints on planting systems. The need for a pipeline supplying water from the Nile that runs along the eastern edge of the site was fundamental. Nevertheless, the growing pressures on available water supplies in the region, the need for an efficient irrigation system and the goal of moderating total consumption were the determining factors in the choice of the plants and landscapes eventually introduced in the new park.

Initial testing of existing soil and mixtures with various additives, carried out over several months in the early investigative phases, demonstrated that a reasonable range of plant types could survive on the site with appropriate irrigation and conditioning of the soil. In order to support a greater variety of plants – beyond those which can survive in drought-like conditions and tolerate highly saline soil conditions – a programme of soil improvement including the use of nutritives and additives (sand, agricultural soils, gypsum), as well as salt flushing by initial irrigation was proposed and tested on site. Prototypes were planted on both flat and very steep terrain to test these options. Feedback from both the horticultural beds and the areas planted with prototypes was an essential part of the development of the design for the park's landscape and proved invaluable in finally determining the range of vegetation used. This varies from dry, succulent plants on the western slopes to lush, grassy meadows with shade trees, to *bustan*s, or orchards, and, finally, formal gardens. The result will be a wide variety of species, with a special focus on native Egyptian plants whose survival has been extensively tested *in situ*.

The park's conceptual design, developed by the consultant, Sites International Cairo, made maximum and skilful use of the plants found to be suitable and the very special context of the new park, including its location, dramatic topography and unique vistas overlooking Historic Cairo. The composition of these elements provides a lively contrast between flat and hilly terrain, formal and informal planting patterns, including lush vegetation at focal points on the plain and dryer stretches along the slope towards the city.

A central feature of the park's landscape is the 'spine' formed by the water channel and accompanying walkways starting at the northern hill above the central water tank and pointing towards the Citadel in the distance. This formal central axis is 250 metres long and 8 metres wide, and is flanked on both sides by a double row of royal palms and parallel side paths with lateral niches for seating. An *étoile* at the southern extreme of this sequence turns the main promenade in a south-westerly direction, towards the park's southern lower plain,

leading through a formal garden to a lakeside pavilion and cafe overlooking a large lake. The outer zones of the southern plain contain an orchard, or *bustan*, which provides shade, a stimulating variety of flowering and fruit trees, and further space through which to stroll. Water features are a traditional theme in Islamic gardens and in fact may be found along the entire length of this composition. The series of fountains, pools and carefully channelled waterways lead, ultimately, to the freer form of the large lake in the southern meadow.

The central axis of the park is anchored at each end by the two main landmarks: the hilltop restaurant at the northern end and the lakeside pavilion at the southern. The architectural language of the two buildings reflects the desire to maintain a creative relationship with the built environment of Old Cairo. The two designs were selected as a result of a limited competition between Middle Eastern and European architects.

The *Hilltop Restaurant*, by the architects Rami El-Dahan and Soheir Farid, is clearly inspired by Fatimid and Mamluk architecture. The building is almost symmetrical layout, with a central north/south axis that passes through a palm court, a portico entry and a shaded sitting area, or *takhtabush*, before arriving at a terraced garden. From there, the building opens, at the lower level, onto the park's main promenade and sweeping vistas of the Citadel. Access to the building is via the park's main entrance and an internal access drive. There is a small car park opposite the restaurant, and valet parking in the main bays off the park entrance.

The *Lakeside Cafe and Pavilion*, a composition of geometric pavilions following various rectangular patterns, designed by the architect Serge Santelli, is more abstract in its interpretation of historic Cairene architecture. On the eastern side of the complex, the pavilions enclose a square palm court with a central fountain and crossing water channels, inspired by classical Islamic gardens. Here, a shaded and informal sitting area is provided for visitors to the park, who can relax and enjoy beverages without paying cover charges. Through an intermediate space, visitors then reach the elongated poolside cafe 'floating' above the lake. This is a more formal restaurant space, which is further defined by two larger, square pavilions at each end of the pool-side terrace. The pavilions and adjacent rooms have intricate enclosing screens inspired by traditional *mashrabiyya* panels. With its ample shade and attractive courtyards, the Lakeside complex may be considered an indoor as well as outdoor space. In fact, the formal gardens, which are embedded in the surrounding orchard scheme, appear to be almost an extension of the pavilion, covering most of the southern plain.

The formal 'spine' and the two restaurant buildings are surrounded by a network of informal walkways leading in and out of all levels and corners of the park, providing visitors with a rich and varied experience. The terrain in the western half of the park is generally sloping with a gradient between 3:1 and 2:1. A continuous pathway has been carved out of the hillside at approximately mid-height (+55 metres) between the walkway along the Historic Wall (+35/+39 metres) and the summits of the hills (+74 metres), providing lateral access at strategic points to the eastern half. The western hillside is covered with flowering and succulent plants in luxuriant tones.

Finally, the sensitive and purposeful integration of the recently constructed water tanks, far from being merely functional, adds important design features to the overall landscape design. Consultation with engineers of the GOGCWS during the design phase resulted in increasing the strength of the reservoir structures to accommodate defined loads of planting and paving materials on top of each tank. With these loads and the maintenance and access requirements taken into account, the landscape design has established a sitting area and a number of trees set on top of the south tank. The top of the central tank, in line with the main promenade, carries a formal garden symmetrically subdivided into a rich geometric design. The northern tank, easily accessed from the main park as well as al-Azhar Street from the north, serves as a children's play area.

The many vantage points on top of the reservoirs and along the western slopes of al-Darassa offer unparalleled views of the Historic Wall and the city beyond. These vistas, together with the other features and landmarks contained in the park, establish a visual link and a continuity of architectural and cultural expression, and provide a new and captivating experience for residents and visitors alike. A former barren site is thus transformed into a lively destination and a catalyst for a whole range of associated projects in the surrounding areas.

The Ayyubid City Wall
During the massive re-grading of the park's western slope, where it descends towards al-Darb al-Ahmar district, a large buried portion of Cairo's Ayyubid City Wall was rediscovered, just at the edge of the Historic City. The Ayyubid fortifications were begun in 1176 by Salah al-Din, a Kurd of the Ayyubid clan who moved from Syria to Cairo, became a Fatimid vizier and then overthrew the Fatimid caliphate in 1171. The wall was built to contain the former Fatimid palace-city and its suburbs, the pre-Fatimid city of Fustat, and earlier fortifications within a single defence system linked to the new Ayyubid Citadel.

The south-east section of these fortifications forming the border between the al-Azhar Park and al-Darb al-Ahmar district is the longest surviving portion of the city wall that is integral and still visible. It measures approximately 1,500 metres from Bab al-Wazir to al-Azhar Street, and its survival is due to the fact that the city never expanded in this direction. Already during the early Ottoman period, although urban growth was vigorous on the other side of Cairo, the eastern sectors of the city gradually had become less and less important.

The area outside the walls was used as a dumping ground for debris and rubble from the adjacent city, a practice that continued unabated during the following centuries. As early as 1658, a description by the French traveller de Thevenot refers to the height of the accumulated debris, which nearly hid the high city walls. Early prints and photographic records confirm that the wall was largely buried by the end of the 19th century. Old maps made during the Napoleonic occupation at the turn of the 19th century show that buildings in al-Darb al-Ahmar were generally built right up to the wall. Many of the buildings actually abutted the Ayyubid Wall, and added rooms were constructed into and indeed on top of the former fortifications. This accretive process was common in many Middle Eastern and European cities where the old defensive systems had lost their former significance.

Following the establishment of the new park, the outer face of the Historic Wall was once again exposed to view and to the elements, while, on the city side, private development pressures and institutional demands raised complex issues of urban development. Accordingly, the question was not only how to preserve the wall, but also how best to intervene in the surrounding urban context. Comprehensive planning and design policies had to be developed for the old residential fabric of al-Darb al-Ahmar abutting the wall, as well as for the points of access and the pedestrian promenade along the western edge of the park.

The Historic Wall separates al-Darb al-Ahmar from the park, while at the same time, it provides a strong link between them – a juxtaposition which called imperatively for an integrated planning and development concept. The major stumbling block in this regard was an old decree of the Antiquities Department that established a *non aedificandi* zone and, moreover, proposed the demolition and clearing of a 20 to 30-metre wide strip of houses along the entire length of the Ayyubid Wall. The philosophy behind this decree may be attributed to the European 'modernist' aesthetic of the 1950s and 1960s, whereby historic urban centres were to be 'sanitised' and monuments 'enhanced' by isolating and stripping them of their urban context. However, for several reasons this kind of wholesale demolition was unrealistic: the cost implications in terms of compensation would be immense and the social disruption of the neighbourhoods involved dramatic. Further, the possible physical collapse of the wall (if the buttressing houses were to be removed) would have rendered such a course of action completely counterproductive. Whilst major wholesale clearance did not happen, the old Antiquities decree still impeded the establishment of an integrated conservation and rehabilitation programme covering both the wall and the adjacent urban fabric. In fact, from a strictly legal point of view, restoration of individual historic houses abutting monuments was simply not feasible according to the current approval procedures.

There was, however, one positive outcome of the Antiquities decree. It has greatly helped preserve this section of al-Darb al-Ahmar in that it imposed a *de facto* freeze on the urban strip behind the wall, preventing speculative redevelopment along the sensitive urban edge now enhanced by the Park Project. Had the demolition order implied in the decree been implemented, it would have opened the way for a new vehicular road running behind the wall, inducing all sorts of undesirable changes and further destruction in al-Darb al-Ahmar, as well as environmental problems for the park.

Given this complex situation, AKTC's policy was to negotiate, with the help of the Cairo Governorate, selective improvements and rehabilitation projects on the plots abutting the wall, with the Antiquities Department not formally approving, but 'tolerating' these case-by-case interventions. The implicit agreement was that the pilot project of joint wall conservation and urban rehabilitation should be given a chance to demonstrate its benefits, and that this might lead to a new and more integrated conservation policy for the monuments and the surrounding urban fabric in Historic Cairo.

Restoration works on the Ayyubid Wall were initiated in 1999 with pilot interventions taking place on limited sections, which were gradually extended to cover greater portions of the monument. The principles underlying the interventions may be summarised as follows:

· To research and document all evidence including physical, archival and historical information, before, during and after intervention;
· To respect the cumulative age-value of the structure by recognising the stratification that is the physical record of human activity, displaying the passage of time and embodying different materials and techniques, as well as changing cultural beliefs and values;
· To safeguard the monument's authenticity as being of cultural value reflecting the original making or re-making of the object or site, recognised as the embodiment of individual authorship or the record of a time and place;
· To avoid harm to the monument by minimising physical interference

in order to re-establish structural and aesthetic legibility and meaning, or by intervening in ways that will allow other options and further treatment in the future.

In line with these general principles, the intervention guidelines applied by the AKTC team to the conservation of the Ayyubid Wall expressed, whenever possible, preference for retention or compatible repair of original fabric over reconstruction. The recommendations for intervention on the surrounding urban fabric advocated respect for the changes accrued over time in order to preserve the integrity, scale and significance of the wall in its current configuration and context. Ultimately, the interventions promoted continuity rather than transformation. The long-term goal is to integrate and harmonise the remnants of a valuable past with present realities and future uses in ways that are compatible and sustainable.[2]

The first step in the conservation process was a comprehensive assessment of the physical condition of the entire wall and then, subsequently, a detailed study of each part of the monument subject to intervention. The general survey documented the wall's overall condition, including an analysis of the masonry and identification of areas with significant deterioration, distinguishing between loss of facing stone covering the rubble core and total loss of pieces of the wall. It also documented the presence and extent of previous repairs. The subsequent detailed condition survey provided a fuller quantitative analysis, as well as a qualitative assessment of the causes and effects of deterioration. Severity of loss, for example, was classified according to extent and depth, as well as to whether the process was still active or inactive. In addition, samples were taken for laboratory testing to ascertain the exact nature and the conditions and problems of the materials.

Together, the field survey, graphic documentation and laboratory work yielded a comprehensive record of the construction of the wall and its present state, as well as the diagnostic tools needed to formulate an intervention programme. Suggested measures included recommendations and procedures for archeological investigations,

emergency stabilisation, masonry treatment (including cleaning, removal of salt and biological growth, grouting, consolidation of deteriorating stone and selective stone replacement), as well as limited reconstruction for reasons of structural stability or visual continuity. The resulting policies and guidelines for masonry intervention were designed to achieve maximum retention of the original historic fabric, while ensuring the visual and functional continuity of the wall as an urban element.

In addition to documenting the condition of the monument itself, the general survey analysed its contextual relationship to the adjoining urban fabric. Over the centuries, the houses and monuments built against the wall on the city side had become an integral part of Cairo's urban and social history. Selective removal of encroaching elements was considered acceptable, but the wholesale demolition of the historic housing stock attached to the city wall would have contradicted prevailing international conservation philosophy and practice, and might have introduced undesirable and dangerous development pressures. Therefore, the project made a careful plot-by-plot study along the wall, defining appropriate modes of intervention for each building within the larger framework of the conservation and rehabilitation plan for al-Darb al-Ahmar.

The extent and configuration of the abutting houses was recorded by the team and assessed with regard to use, condition, date of construction, architectural integrity and significance. In addition, a series of typical sections documented the physical connection between the wall and the adjacent buildings and, in particular, whether these structures were built up against, on top of, or into the wall at the lower levels. Special attention was given to recording all cases where adjoining buildings posed a specific threat to the structural integrity of the wall, as a result of damaging industrial activity or due to water seepage from plumbing systems.

These various analyses, complemented by in-depth investigations of social and housing conditions in particular areas (such as the Aslam Mosque neighbourhood and Atfet Asaad Alley), were the basis for

interventions, including the removal of incongruous, detrimental or structurally unsound additions and accretions, rehabilitation of selected historic buildings and improvement of housing conditions to avoid the displacement of residents. The intervention policies implemented sought to selectively modify the current Antiquities law through the introduction of new building regulations, which, rather than calling for clearing any building or structure within the immediate proximity of a monument, should allow for the preservation of the historic fabric surrounding it. Altogether, the plans and interventions have advocated the conservation and harmonious integration of the Ayyubid Wall in the traditional urban fabric and contemporary life of al-Darb al-Ahmar. The joint conservation of the original structure of the wall and the preservation of the living fabric of the city around it should be seen as the best antidotes against further decay and the potentially destructive commercialisation that can be induced by excessive numbers of visitors and uncontrolled tourism.

Too often cultural resources around the world have become mere commercial commodities to be consumed by mass tourism, with the result that genuine historic sites have been compromised and emptied of meaning, and local residents have become overly dependent on an unpredictable service economy. In order to anticipate and prevent such risks in the case of al-Darb al-Ahmar and the Ayyubid Wall – particularly after the opening of the park – it was vital to implement a consistent management strategy. The Ayyubid Wall should be seen as a resource and an opportunity to deepen the appreciation and understanding of the function and the value of the old city's cultural heritage and of the traditional social fabric that has developed along it.

In pursuing this view, some questions became immediately relevant in planning for the future role of this important landmark: how could a forgotten and long-buried monument be introduced into a rapidly evolving new context without losing its meaning? How could it be reinvented as a living component of today's Historic Cairo? And, more generally, how could the tourism generated by the al-Azhar Park be reconciled with the traditional life of the community of al-Darb

al-Ahmar? Answers to these questions were not just part of an academic exercise, but were being addressed pragmatically in the search for new meanings, functions and activities around and within the wall. In particular, future actions to ensure that the Ayyubid Wall maintains its original significance and is properly re-integrated into its contemporary context were anchored to four programmatic concepts:

· Designing a system of pedestrian access and circulation along the western side of the park to enhance the perception of the Historic Wall as a dynamic edge and meeting point rather than a barrier between the community and the park.
The system of access and circulation identified the locations of the former city gates as the natural and historically appropriate connections between the park and al-Darb al-Ahmar. Three entrances were revived: Bab al-Barqiyya, close to the main traffic artery of Azhar Road, to serve as the main access from the north-western edge of the park; Bab al-Mahruq, the vanished gate and the subject of an archeological investigation, to create a mid-point entry; and Bab al-Wazir at the south-western corner of the park, providing access close to the main religious sites and historic monuments along the southern stretch of al-Darb al-Ahmar. In addition, two more connections were proposed in conjunction with the visitor's exhibits and circuits at Darb Shoughlan and Burg al-Mahruq. All of these links were conceived of as meeting points to promote visitor and community interaction, and sustain carefully planned venues in the daily life of al-Darb al-Ahmar.

· Establishing didactic programmes and experiences in order to enhance the appreciation of the wall as a monument and an important urban feature of Historic Cairo, explaining its changing role in the development of the city and introducing visitors to the life of the community that inhabits the surrounding district. Initiatives include visitor's circuits and exhibits through the Darb Shoughlan school and along the ramparts and interior galleries between towers 4 and 5, and in Burg al-Mahruq, featuring the presentation of archeological, historical, military, cultural and social elements related to past and contemporary uses of the wall. In addition, an archeological park was planned for the northernmost area, between towers 14 and 15, where there is a unique opportunity to explore the archeological remains along the city side of the wall, buried since Mamluk times. Finally, the establishment of a space for exhibitions and other cultural activities was planned in the Khayrbak complex, adjoining the southern edge of the Historic Wall. This facility offers a focal point for the community and provides visitors with a better understanding of local culture and traditions.

· Introducing activities that are relevant to promoting a deeper understanding of the cultural heritage of Historic Cairo among visitors and residents, and the development of local skills to preserve and protect Historic Cairo. The wall has supplied significant opportunities in this respect, both as an arena for demonstrating the aims and methods applied to its discovery and conservation, and as an ongoing training ground where local craftsmen, national bodies and international institutions can come together to explore and identify appropriate restoration techniques. These experiences also promote the creation of a manpower base specialised in traditional building crafts, modern restoration techniques and small enterprise development, all of which are much needed throughout Historic Cairo. Conservation can thus be linked to programmes that foster economic development and employment opportunities for the local community.

· Ensuring the future management and long-term sustainability of the wall through the establishment of permanent repair and maintenance programmes and the monitoring of future changes and transformations.
In order to be successful in the particular context of the Historic Wall, sustainability must be considered as a dynamic process of

public participation, achieved through dialogue and consensus, which ultimately leads to better stewardship of the monument. Future programmes must therefore ensure that the long-term benefits are understood and enjoyed also by the surrounding community, as the community is one of the principal stakeholders in the process of ensuring the continued life and appropriate use of the structure. In future, a garbage collection system, open space maintenance, as well as repair of the wall and rehabilitation of the surrounding buildings should not be implemented against the will of the community, but with its direct involvement and participation.

This shift in attitude, from a perception of the Historic Wall as an abstract, isolated monument to its reinvention as part of a larger urban programme, together with the gradual implementation of the plans and activities described above is turning this obsolete structure, buried for centuries and removed from the city's mainstream development, into a cultural asset and living component of the future revitalisation of Historic Cairo. The challenge ahead lies in safeguarding the remains and true significance of the Historic Wall, while shaping its new role for the years to come.

An Urban Rehabilitation Programme for al-Darb al-Ahmar District
Work on al-Azhar Park and the Historic Wall has raised the issue of how best to capture and control the dynamics unleashed onto the adjacent urban area of al-Darb al-Ahmar by the implementation of the Park Project. A densely built-up district of Historic Cairo, the area lies south of the prestigious al-Azhar Mosque and the popular Khan al-Khalili, Historic Cairo's principal tourist bazaar, and is bound by Shari'a al-Azhar, the Darassa Hills and Shari'a al-Darb al-Ahmar. Al-Darb al-Ahmar is a vital residential district which contains many artisans and small enterprises, but the area has long suffered from a lack of infrastructure and adequate community services. Although endowed with sixty-five registered monuments and several hundred historic buildings, its traditional building stock was in a very poor

condition, as a result of very low family incomes and an economic base that often lags behind that of other parts of Cairo.

Deterioration was exacerbated by the imposition of unrealistic rent controls, counter-productive planning constraints and limited access to credit. The common, though incorrect, perception of al-Darb al-Ahmar as a haven for crime and drug-related activity tended to support plans to radically clear and 'sanitise' the district, thus posing yet another threat to the survival of the historic urban fabric. With its pedestrian scale, distinctive monuments, historic buildings and active community, however, the district had the potential to become the vibrant residential and commercial area it was in the past, as well as an alternative destination for visitors and tourists. Al-Azhar Park initiative further enhanced the district's prospects and provide an incentive for parallel rehabilitation efforts in the area.

But new opportunities cannot be separated from the risks inherent in them. On the one hand, al-Azhar Park, which has become one of metropolitan Cairo's major green spaces, undoubtedly represents a powerful attraction and a catalyst for change in the old city. It is transforming and enhancing the image of the area as a whole, no longer a 'backyard' but an attractive foreground for al-Darb al-Ahmar, and this may spur increased public and private investment in al-Darb al-Ahmar. However, on the other hand, speculative pressures might determine a pattern of uncontrolled development in the area, leading to the expulsion of both the current residents and existing activities, paving the way for a total substitution of the traditional urban fabric. This undesirable trend had to be anticipated, carefully managed and properly channelled through a conscious planning effort.

To this effect, beginning in 1998, the Aga Khan Trust for Culture expanded the scope of its activities in the area and embarked on a comprehensive urban rehabilitation programme for al-Darb al-Ahmar. AKTC's long-term strategy, focusing on the physical upgrading of the building stock and the socio-economic improvement of the community, aims at the general revitalisation of the entire district. This strategy is consistent with AKTC's belief that active community development is

essential for launching a genuine process of urban rehabilitation in al-Darb al-Ahmar, capable of producing results that are sustainable and eventually independent of any external input. AKTC's funding partners, the Egyptian Swiss Fund for Development, The Ford Foundation and The World Monuments Fund, also recognise the merits of this strategy and have generously participated in the combined socio-economic and physical rehabilitation of the district.

This integrated approach is quite different from the solutions that have been proposed so far for tackling the many problems confronting Historic Cairo today. In fact, many of the planning efforts deployed over the past decade were doomed to failure because of their 'top-down' approach. They were either too abstract or consisted of grand but unrealistic proposals that never addressed the kinds of problems residents experience day in and day out. Meanwhile, more concrete recent urban renewal projects in Cairo have oscillated between opposite attitudes: the first option advocates 'beautifying' traditional houses and monuments with superficial cosmetic measures and turning the historic area into an open air museum where tourists enjoy the monuments and pay for their upkeep; the second option calls for large-scale demolition of the traditional spaces and buildings and their replacement with modern structures.

Both extremes, if carried out, would inevitably result in the dislocation of the residents, bringing about enormous social upheaval and long-term disruption of the historic area. The price in terms of compensation, alternative housing, new construction, not to mention the social cost of displacing the inhabitants, would be prohibitive. Moreover, far from resolving, they would aggravate the problems of the historic area by depriving it of the very people and economic base that sustain it. Both alternatives ignore the fundamental fact that Historic Cairo is first and foremost a living city, made up of families that have lived in the area for decades, if not generations.

However, there is a third way for al-Darb al-Ahmar, and indeed all of Historic Cairo: to accept the physical and social fabric for what it is, to acknowledge the special value of a living cultural heritage and to

provide residents with a positive prospect for their future. This solution endeavours to regenerate and revitalise the social fabric from within, mobilising its own, often hidden, potential and reshaping this potential in ways that can make it effective again. It foresees the direct involvement of national and local institutions, residents and community groups in the progressive rehabilitation of the existing fabric and the urban environment as a whole, together with a phased improvement of the underlying socio-economic conditions. It attempts to remove stifling constraints and instead to provide incentives that will release dormant resources. Moreover, this solution contributes to the progressive improvement of living conditions by creating new training and employment opportunities. It envisages a future where a stable residential district is uplifted by better housing, sustained by a capillary system of small workshops and retail activities, supported by basic infrastructure and public services, and made more attractive by the presence of well-maintained monuments and open spaces. As the general quality of the area improves, so will its prospects for attracting more visitors and their patronage, eventually leading to a general reversal of the present decline.

But how can this vision be realised? How can the manifold problems and urban issues affecting a district like al-Darb al-Ahmar be addressed concurrently and gradually brought to resolution? And are such goals realistic and at all achievable in the face of daunting socio-economic problems and physical decay? Or, more generally, is there a solution to the issue of maintaining viable and self-sustaining historic areas in Cairo, as well as in other places in North Africa and the Middle East, where the very survival of historic cities is threatened by huge population pressure coupled with crumbling buildings, infrastructure and services?

Resolving these questions is predicated on a true appreciation of what makes an historic city viable today and sustainable over the long term. Successful historic areas and cities world-wide demonstrate something that has often been overlooked by city planners and administrators: that a traditional urban context survives and thrives

not in spite, but because, of its residents, provided they are able to look after their surroundings and take pride in them. In fact, residents of these communities cherish their old houses and pedestrian environment because they feel secure and at home in these familiar and long-inhabited spaces. There can be no healthy historic city without such essential symbiosis between an established, secure social base and its traditional environment, while there are many cases where the most persistent urban problems stem from the absence of this crucial synergy.

In the historic areas of modern expanding cities, self-sustainability cannot be taken for granted, as it was in the past. It has often been discouraged or destroyed by counter-productive administrative measures, by a narrow-minded misconception of 'modernity' and through simple lack of understanding and support. Therefore self-sustainability must be reinstated through a conscious corrective effort which empowers

local communities and applies careful planning and management of a finite resource – the traditional built environment. The fragile social fabric of the depressed historic neighbourhoods must be sustained and reinforced, lest it be wiped out together with the buildings and spaces that contain it. The conservation and development of both the social and the physical fabric, therefore, cannot be separated but must be included within a single integrated planning process.

The success of this process cannot be measured in the short term – in fact it requires sustained efforts over the span of years and indeed decades. There are no quick solutions, only priority issues and activities that must be tackled and coordinated towards the gradual development of long-term, self-sustaining urban rehabilitation. Along the way, synergies and multiplier effects should be identified and exploited to increase the momentum of what is necessarily a slow process. This is what the many and diverse activities of AKTC's programme are attempting to achieve. The present overview of the project provides a summary of the major components, including institutional support and participatory planning, socio-economic development, community building, infrastructure upgrading, housing rehabilitation, restoration of monuments, adaptive reuse of historic buildings, and training.

At the institutional level, the project has endeavoured to reorganise the planning and building processes within the district, in order to include a conservation agenda as well as long-standing, unresolved issues that residents perceive as a priority. More particularly, AKTC worked with the national and local planning institutions to ensure that the district and its historic fabric are treated along specific parameters (different from those of modern Western cities), i.e., with finer-grained survey and planning work, careful attention to the special context and closer monitoring of building activities. The planning process must be geared to the requirements of an historic area at the inception of a project, beginning with plot-by-plot physical surveys and in-depth socio-economic investigations. Only such detailed work can provide the basis for the comprehensive physical planning capable of responding to the particular conditions of a given historic district.

Such an investigation was carried out prior to defining the plan of action for al-Darb al-Ahmar and its targeted interventions in the strip along the Historic Wall and the new park, which forms a corridor at higher risk of uncontrolled transformation. The proposals took advantage of special development opportunities identified during the course of the survey and focused on individual monuments and buildings, public open spaces and special residential clusters. Whether individual structures or larger sections of the district, they were viewed not only as candidates for physical rehabilitation but also as vehicles for future social and economic revitalisation.

Working with local institutions is just one aspect of the project. An equally important level of action has been to facilitate greater community involvement in planning decisions and in resolving complex administrative issues, such as the revision of building codes and building regulations, lifting of obsolete planning constraints and

coming to terms with the tenancy issue along the Ayyubid Wall. AKTC obtained from the Egyptian Supreme Council of Antiquities a partial waiver of the demolition order that had condemned the traditional houses in proximity of the monument. Alternatives to demolition were considered which would allow residents to continue to live in the area and the Ayyubid Wall to be preserved within its living urban context.

Improving the living conditions of the residents cannot be undertaken without giving the community a voice. As is the case with any depressed historic area, the priorities in al-Darb al-Ahmar are, first and foremost, social and economic. The widely-held general view that only substantial government intervention and public capital can produce results in these spheres overlooks the fact that relatively simple initiatives can have a significant if not greater impact. In fact, a 'minimalist' socio-economic approach is being implemented by the project's management and staff in al-Darb al-Ahmar with encouraging results. The project's experience has been that in order to create employment it is not always necessary to create new jobs. An efficient parallel strategy is to connect people with existing employment opportunities. With this in mind, a job placement and counselling service was established in the project's office in the district, leading to the employment of dozens of people. Acquiring on-the-job experience has also proved to be the most effective way for the unemployed young to prepare for and eventually find a job. The project made agreements with a number of existing workshops in the area to train young people, which quite often led to longer-term employment. Finally, the availability of a microcredit scheme for al-Darb al-Ahmar residents has had a very promising impact on the area, enabling people to engage in new initiatives and practise what they do best. With limited loans, the project has been able to help people, especially women, improve their businesses or start new income-generating activities.

The project also recognises the key importance of promoting community awareness and self-governance as a means of making people more aware of their cultural traditions and restoring civic pride. Self-governance of residential districts was a distinctive feature of traditional

Muslim cities. It can be at least partly restored by enabling people to share their problems and identify solutions, and by creating the confidence needed to act on their own behalf rather than passively waiting for outside intervention. Towards this end, AKTC and its partners have established al-Darb al-Ahmar Community Development Corporation (CDC). This body is operating as a self-sustaining community managed private-sector initiative, harnessing community assets within the framework of locally identified problems, needs and priorities. It combines the mobilisation of resources, technical coordination, community affairs and institution-building with physical upgrading and environmental improvement. In doing so, it strengthens the community and encourages the development of new entities capable of providing leadership, technical support and assistance in mobilising and managing resources. A case in point is the successful series of activities promoted by the group 'Women Working Together'. Building upon such promising initiatives, al-Darb al-Ahmar CDC offers the kind of support needed to help residents to become more self-reliant and take greater responsibility for maintaining and developing the district's physical environment.

Practical discussions with residents and users on how to reorganise public open spaces, infrastructure and services took place in several locations. One case in point is the Tablita Market, al-Darb al-Ahmar's principal vegetable market, where improvements to the physical organisation and long-term management of this public facility were successfully defined with the help of the vendors and potential investors. It is upon these occasions that one realises how much people's requirements are normally ignored by conventional planners.

Nowhere is the issue of participatory planning more relevant than in housing, a key sector for the future improvement of the district. The rehabilitation and provision of affordable housing is considered the best long-term antidote to the disinvestment and decline of al-Darb al-Ahmar. The realisation of better living conditions for individuals and families is the driving force for establishing cleaner and more stable neighbourhoods. In fact, housing programmes are the primer that can set in motion a positive chain reaction to preserve the traditional urban fabric and revitalise the district. The project thus focused on identifying technical solutions for housing improvements that are applicable throughout al-Darb al-Ahmar and on providing incentives for rehabilitation. A pilot housing rehabilitation credit scheme was launched in various parts of the area near the Historic Wall, which consisted of approximately 50 residential buildings. Since then, the number of requests has increased continuously. Project staff discussed priorities with the residents, identified a building programme, made funds available directly to project-approved contractors and ensured that loans were repaid to replenish the revolving fund. Moreover, the construction of new housing is presently being considered for the blighted area north of Burj al-Mahruq, in conjunction with the lowering of the road built over the Historic Wall. The development of affordable new housing opens up interesting new opportunities in a district where approximately 16 per cent of the plots are vacant or in ruins.

AKTC's efforts to rehabilitate housing are complemented by the trust's adaptive reuse of historic buildings and the restoration of several important monuments, as well as its training programme in conservation and traditional construction. These activities should be considered as related aspects of a single mission, that is, reintroducing and disseminating appropriate conservation models and methods in the district. These will find their highest level of application with al-Darb al-Ahmar's monuments. Two major structures have been restored by AKTC, the *Khayrbak* complex and the *Umm al-Sultan Sha'aban* Mosque. Works on the Tarabay Mausoleum, the Alin Aq Palace and the Shoughlan Mosque are under way. The principles and techniques applied are much the same as for any historic building, where selection of suitable building materials and identification of compatible treatments are essential. As has been proved time and again, hasty approximate interventions that ignore the nature and requirements of the historic fabric will do more damage than good, and will lead to unfortunate and irreversible results.

Training is in fact crucial to reintroducing the appropriate know-how and building up independent capacities in vanishing crafts

and skills, as well as developing local enterprises specialised in traditional construction. All of AKTC's restoration projects in the district
include a training component and make use as much as possible of the
local craftsmen and workforce, complemented, when necessary, by
external trainers.

The ability to rehabilitate the many under-used or decaying
historic structures in the district, particularly those in public ownership, should also be seen as an opportunity to revive dormant assets
and introduce needed facilities and services. In this respect, the adaptive
reuse of the former Darb Shoughlan School as a community and visitor's
centre has demonstrated to the surrounding community that old
buildings need not necessarily be associated with poverty and neglect,
and that they can still play a useful role in contemporary life.

All in all, the experience in al-Darb al-Ahmar shows that an integrated
process of urban conservation can be implemented in a poor sector
of Cairo. The results have an importance beyond their immediate setting, as they offer a living model of old city rehabilitation that may be
applied both at the higher policy level and when identifying practical
solutions throughout Historic Cairo, and indeed many other historic
cities throughout the Islamic world.

These tenets are rooted in internationally recognised and accepted
standards of conservation, namely the International Charter for the
Conservation and Restoration of Monuments and Sites of 1964 (the
Venice Charter). They build on the fundamental principles set out in
the Athens Charter (1931) with the added emphasis on the importance
of context, the discouragement of reconstruction except in cases of
anastylosis (reassembling of preserved fragments), and the integration of modern scientific technology where appropriate and useful.
More recent charters, such as the Burra Charter of 1981 established by
ICOMOS Australia, stress that the ultimate aim of conservation is to
retain or recover the cultural significance of a place and that provisions must be made for its security, maintenance and future survival.

Historic Cairo, or Islamic Cairo, basically consists of two districts. To the north lies the vibrant Jamaliyya (Gamalia), the district well known to both tourists and locals for its markets and the shrines of religious saints. Gamalia has a strong economic base and is home to the Khan al-Khalili Bazaar. To the south lies the less fortunate al-Darb al-Ahmar district, a densely populated poor residential area, once home to the elite. The wealthy residential base was replaced over the years with the poorest of the poor.

It is not surprising that both districts share a very strong religious base since there are an enormous number of mosques and *madrasa*s in the area, including the influential al-Azhar and al-Azhar University, the oldest surviving institution of higher education in the Islamic world. It is also evident in the number of annual religious celebrations (*mawlid*s) that take place here.

Al-Darb al-Ahmar district has suffered for years from the slow and steady decay of its basic services, as well as from a weak economic base. High levels of unemployment, especially among the younger generation, aggravate the situation even further. However, despite these hardships, the current residents appreciate the positive aspects of their community, aspects which keep them attached to this area and make them refuse to move. Its narrow alleys provide a safe haven from traffic for young children; mothers can safely leave their children with relatives and neighbours while running errands; and its central location allows easy access to trade and employment in other areas of Greater Cairo.

Studies carried out by international groups, including the UNDP, in the mid 1990s identified a number of community needs. In 1997, the commencement of the transformation of the old dump site of the Darassa Hills into a public park by the Aga Khan Trust for Culture (AKTC) provided an ideal opportunity to focus on the adjoining al-Darb al-Ahmar community. And so a socio-economic development programme was designed, and its implementation by AKTC's local arm, Aga Khan Cultural Services – Egypt, was set to begin in early 2000.

Assessing the local environment

How does one mobilise a community and introduce various initiatives into it without disrupting its cultural and social fabric? How will residents react to these initiatives? And how will government react?

Civil society work in Egypt in general is limited to religious and health-based endeavours, as well as services for those with special needs. Most non-government organisations (NGOs) are fragile, for the government controls them quite tightly and screens their motives and affiliations. Government control over international NGOs is even tighter and their activities are constantly scrutinised. This is probably the result of the long period of foreign occupation that Egypt experienced under the Turks, French and British. Egyptians are very suspicious of the intentions of foreign organisations conducting business in the country, and even more so in the case of international NGOs.

Furthermore, in the period after Egypt gained its independence in the early 1950s, the system of government was dominated by state planning, public ownership and administrative and social control. The government was looked upon as the provider of housing, education, health care and employment. The role civil society was marginalised, making it even more difficult for community development initiatives to succeed. A strategy dealing with both the community and the public officials had to be developed for al-Darb al-Ahmar Project to succeed.

The programmes

Based on a needs assessment, a comprehensive community development plan was formalised. The plan integrates both physical and social needs, and consists of the following programmes:

Apprenticeship and Employment: this programme aims to improve the existing skills of job seekers, and assist them in acquiring new skills. Afterwards, they are offered employment opportunities through a placement programme.

Surveying Alin Aq Palace before restoration works, with restored minarets in the background, 2004

Microcredit: this programme aims to assist two groups in the community. The first consists of small businesses that operate within the formal government system (have license, tax card, etc.) but do not have access to bank loans, which typically require certain levels of income and collateral that they do not have. The second group is the informal sector, basically those businesses that do not operate within the government system and therefore neither have licenses nor pay taxes.

Housing credit: this programme is designed to assist local residents in repairing their houses by making funds available for repairs and renovations, and allowing for repayment in monthly installments.

Restoration: this programme aims to restore significant buildings and monuments in the community that have been neglected and are currently in ruins. The buildings being restored will once again become assets that the community can use.

Health services: this programme concentrates on preventive health care and outreach programmes to serve mainly women and the elderly.

Public space and the environment: this programme deals with improving public spaces by repairing leaking pipes and sewers, replacing street paving, and instituting a garbage removal and disposal system.

Arts and culture: this programme deals with young children and youth, and aims at providing them with opportunities to learn music, art and drama.

NGO capacity building: this programme helps existing NGOs to improve their operations, and creates new NGOs to provide services not covered by existing ones.

Initiating the programmes
Two important constituencies had to be balanced for the project to succeed. The first involved the government, while the second involved the community beneficiaries. Hence, high-level officials were briefed, which resulted in an overall endorsement of the project. Subsequently, agreements were signed with the respective public agencies, such as the Cairo Governorate, the Supreme Council of Antiquities, the Ministry

View of al-Darb al-Ahmar district from the minaret of the Umm al-Sultan Sha'ban complex, Historic Cities Programme, 2006; as with all its undertakings, the trust's approach has been to work with local residents to identify priorities and then take practical steps to address these needs.

of Social Affairs, the Awqaf Institution (Ministry of Endowments), the Ministry of Education, the Ministry of Health, and their local subsidiaries. The agreements outlined proposed project objectives and expected outcomes, and included the role of the respective government agency in the project, mostly involving assistance with approvals and with reducing bureaucratic red tape

Middle- and low-level government officials were given the responsibility of periodically monitoring activities. They received a project orientation and were gradually exposed to the methods and techniques proposed for implementation. At first, when the new systems and procedures were explained they caused concern, but ultimately they gained approval and acceptance. The project was completely open in its dealings and with time this created a high level of trust.

Once this trust was developed, the project then began to suggest initiatives that moved away from traditional approaches, and were sometimes in conflict with existing outdated rules and regulations. Endorsement by middle- and lower-level officials of the new approaches paved the way for approval of the implementation of prototype initiatives, which were evaluated on their success and included in the formal system.

For example, in order to restore a landmark building on the verge of collapse which lay adjacent to the Historic Wall, approvals were required from the Cairo Governorate and its Housing Department as well as from the Egyptian Supreme Council of Antiquities. Both approvals involved exceptions to existing rules and regulations. Successful restoration of the building demonstrated to the community as well as government officials that it was in their best interests to save their architectural heritage. Had the building collapsed, current regulations would have precluded rebuilding it because of its proximity to a monument, viz., the Historic Wall. The building will be used initially for community activities and as offices for the project initiatives, but is earmarked to be transformed into the first bed-and-breakfast hotel in Historic Cairo in several years, further upgrading the adjacent neighbourhood.

This restoration offered an excellent opportunity for training many residents and new college graduates in proper restoration techniques and helped to revive high standards of quality in traditional techniques of carpentry, masonry, plastering and floor tiling. Equally important was training in plumbing, electric wiring, bricklaying and shoring. Trained workers have also been provided with the means for better employment opportunities in the future; the skills they have acquired will be used to improve techniques for repairing existing buildings in the historic district.

Introducing the project to the community
The initial step was to engage the community of al-Darb al-Ahmar in the project through an orientation and awareness campaign. To do so, a project field office was set up in the district itself, in an accessible location. All project services and programmes were offered through the local office. The ground floor of a three storey building was renovated to accommodate the offices, whilst a back yard was adapted for community meetings and functions. The office was inaugurated by the governor of Cairo, adding to the project's credibility.

Meanwhile, the project recruited ten or more young volunteers from the community, who were known as al-Darb al-Ahmar Friends. The young volunteers began by introducing the project to their friends and neighbours. Subsequently, the role of this group was enlarged to include the daily operation of the various programmes. Procedural manuals for each programme were developed, providing an opportunity to refine the programmes and receive direct feedback from the community.

Not all the programmes were launched at the same time. The project began with a series of programmes concerned with apprenticeship, employment and microcredit. These programmes and their success drew immediate attention to the project; speculation and suspicion about the project were reduced.

Early on, the project engaged the children in the community in artistic and cultural activities after school. Two main activities were

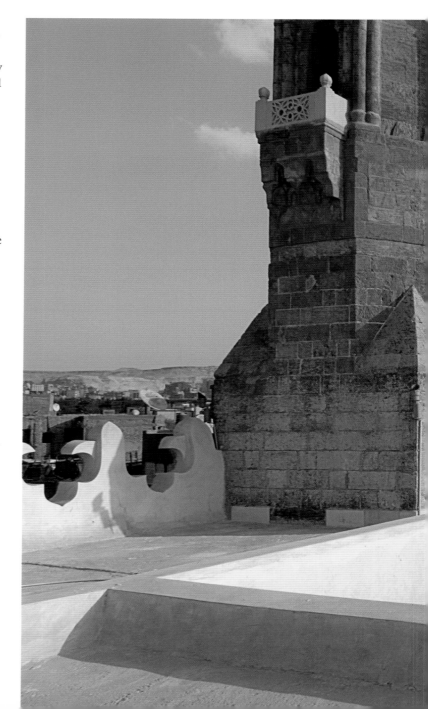

Roofscape of the restored
Umm al-Sultan Sha'ban
complex, Historic Cities
Programme, 2006

View of Cairo at night from the restored minaret of the Khayrbak complex, Historic Cities Programme, 2006; the construction of the park and the restoration of cultural monuments are meant to be catalysts for social and economic development and the overall improvement of the quality of life in the district.

sponsored by the project: singing, eventually leading to the formation of al-Darb al-Ahmar choir, and acting, leading to the formation of a theatre group which gives monthly performances. These cultural activities drew the children's parents and friends into the project, thus enabling them to learn more about project services and, more importantly, to break down barriers between the project and the community.

These initial achievements enabled the project to expand to take on more difficult and controversial programmes, such as the housing rehabilitation programme. This is one of the pioneer programmes in the city which aims to improve living conditions by negotiating between tenants, owners, obsolete laws and regulations, and government authorities. Furthermore, one of the project's main challenges is to assist current NGOs to play a more active role in their society by providing technical assistance, training and capacity building to active members. Since these programmes were launched their achievements have gained some recognition.

More important, however, is the potential long-term impact on the community and its dynamics, thus, along with the microcredit programme, providing the best circumstances in which to sustain the current initiatives in al-Darb al-Ahmar.

27 | Combatting urban poverty in al-Darb al-Ahmar: interventions and strategies for poverty reduction in Historic Cairo

Mohamed Abdel Hafiz Kotb

As one of the ten largest cities in the world, Cairo with its 17 million inhabitants, can be considered an archetype for most Third World cities and the problems they have faced in the last few decades. Recent years have seen an increase in poverty, both rural and urban. In this chapter we are concerned with urban poverty in the district of al-Darb al-Ahmar, which might be seen as the epitome of urban settlement in the city.

The concept of urban poverty as a separate category from rural poverty is problematic, given the fact that links exist between cities, small towns and rural areas, which implies that the problems of one sector cannot be treated in isolation from another. Still, it is argued that urban poverty has some particular distinguishing characteristics. First, there are two sides to urban poverty – deprivation and vulnerability. Four other interrelated attributes of urban poverty are as follows:

· Environmental health risk – hazardous daily life, no access to health care, malnutrition
· Vulnerability arising from commercial exchange
· Social diversity, fragmentation and the existence of crime
· Vulnerability arising from state intervention, such as police harassment and oppressive bureaucracy

Al-Darb al-Ahmar district displayed all these characteristics. The district contained some of the poorest of the city's population, and living conditions were among the worst in Cairo. Low family incomes, high rates of unemployment and a lack of basic community services were accompanied by deteriorating buildings, poor infrastructure and severe pollution.

How to combat this spiral of mounting and seemingly insoluble problems? In this writer's view, enablement is the answer, enablement defined as 'making opportunities/information available to others'. This involves three types of enablement: market enablement, political enablement and community enablement. It is the concept of community enablement that is applied in this essay to describe and explain the current intervention underway in al-Darb al-Ahmar, as part of the Aga Khan project for social and economic development.

The context

Investigations carried out by staff of the Aga Khan Trust for Culture and the Near East Foundation revealed that the problems of al-Darb al-Ahmar were significant.

Average family income in the area were less than 2,000 Egyptian pounds (LE) or 42 per cent lower than the already low national level of LE 3,460 (1994/1995 figures). Unemployment was rampant. A 1996 study carried out in a section of the district's al-Azhar neighbourhood, showed that 30 per cent of able-bodied male adults were unemployed. Unemployment among women was higher, a steep 45 per cent.

The area's physical and environmental conditions confirmed the dreadful picture created by these social and economic figures. Of 2,000 plots of land in al-Darb al-Ahmar, 320 plots or 16 per cent of the total were abandoned. In some neighbourhoods the amount of abandoned or vacant land was much higher, at 44 per cent. In addition, a staggering 63 per cent of built structures in the area were in deteriorating or poor condition, requiring substantial rehabilitation.

While many buildings were abandoned or only partially occupied, many others were extremely overcrowded with occupancy rates as high as four per room. Several families shared inadequate sanitary facilities. Sanitary and public health conditions were in fact a cause for much concern. Water supply networks were overextended and deteriorating. This results in a serious loss of water during distribution and a rise in groundwater levels.

Unhealthy environmental conditions were in fact widespread. Serious problems stem from the poor condition of the existing sewage system. Many of the pipes were originally laid over eighty years ago and were brittle and cracked, allowing sewage to seep into the ground. The leaking sewage mains and unsanitary conditions in local markets led to very high levels of pollution. In fact, the concentration of the various air pollutants averages between two to ten times higher than that of the recommended safety levels established by the World Health Organisation.

Pollution is also a consequence of the many crafts and small-scale manufacturing businesses found in the area. These include tanneries, carpentry shops and a multitude of workshops specialising in copper work, metal welding and marble cutting. The impact of these activities is especially harmful in an area where people, particularly children, spend much of their time in the streets.

Major socio-economic problems in al-Darb al-Ahmar relate to land ownership and historic (and planned) land-use patterns, environmental degradation, the presence of major historical monuments in vast numbers (and the resulting significant and often conflicting involvement of larger, external institutions), a declining economic base and a relative geographical isolation.

These factors resulted in continuing economic decline, the export of skilled labour to other parts of the city and a growth in unemployment and related levels of poverty. They were further reflected in the loosening of social ties, a rise in crime, drug use and increasing pressures on families and family life. Women and children carry a major part of this burden. Historic monuments, despite their potential for attracting outside investment and enhancing community life, can become the subject of neglect, abuse and often the target of community frustration and anger. The seeming lack of resources and access to opportunities seriously undermines any attempt at changing one's situation for the better.

But the district also had significant strengths and potential that are the source of the area's vibrant character. These strengths are the result of the district's closely integrated physical and social fabric, namely:

- A traditional layout and pedestrian orientation where housing, open spaces, commerce, mosques and places for social gathering are integrated
- An outstanding collection of medieval monuments and historic buildings

- A dense residential core where neighbours help and depend upon each other
- A well-established community with a population largely employed in productive activities
- An important pool of skilled workers and small enterprises

In al-Darb al-Ahmar, small production units, the dominant form of economic activity, are found in almost every street. People are involved in a wide variety of crafts, including carpentry, metal processing and metalwork, stonecutting and shoe-making. They also produce appliqué work, leather goods and furniture. Most of their activities are labour intensive and typically require skilled and semi-skilled artisans.

Reducing urban poverty: Interventions and Strategies
Reduction of poverty is generally attempted at a) the macroeconomic level, through government policies and programme interventions; or b) the micro level (working directly with community groups and non-governmental organisations). This essay is designed to generate discussion and debate on the second type of strategy.

Intervention programmes to alleviate poverty at the micro level are utilised worldwide. Generally they include generating employment and economic development, housing strategies, community services and building up the capacity of community organisation. In al-Darb al-Ahmar, all of these interventions have been employed, and in addition we have endeavoured to utilise social strategies, dealing with local customs, traditional cultural attitudes and relationships in the family and the larger community.

The application and implementation of the interventions we have introduced to al-Darb al-Ahmar in recent years are outlined below, with some of the early results of the programme:

Improving people's access to job training and job opportunities
The first step was to connect local residents in need of work to those opportunities available in the wider community.

View of the cafe in al-Azhar Park, 2009; the creation of the park is proving to be a catalyst for urban renewal

Creating and maintaining an effective localised system of expanding employment is one of the top development priorities for al-Darb al-Ahmar. A comprehensive programme of employment and job creation has been established to assist individuals – new graduates, the unemployed – to gain access to the job market through cost-effective training in practical skills, through acquisition of knowledge and skills on the job, by connecting employers with potential employees and through enhancing job search skills. Employment services allow al-Darb al-Ahmar residents to benefit from the construction and conservation works in the surrounding areas. Emphasis is given to project-related activities in al-Darb al-Ahmar such as the conservation of the Ayyubid Wall, etc. From its inception in July 2000, the programme created more than 800 apprenticeships and facilitated more than 1,770 job referrals and 1,120 job placements. Having established a framework for planning and operations, the objective of the programme was to reach 2,000 job referrals, 1,175 job placements and 900 apprenticeships by January 2004.

Providing microcredit loans to small businesses in the area
Many workshops in al-Darb al-Ahmar not only lack sufficient customers, but also access to those they might have. Although the area has a great wealth of monuments, tourists rarely visit it and local artisans sell their products through wholesalers and retailers in the central bazaar, who are the ones that harvest the profits. The effect of having only indirect access to customers also has an impact on producers of non tourist-oriented products. Carpenters complain about large retail stores that fail to offer competitive prices and frequently delay payments. This creates cash flow problems. Over the years, these various problems became real obstacles to economic growth.

In order to encourage the growth of the business sector, AKTC and Business Development Services (BDS) have established a credit programme, 'a community-based credit fund'. This helps to reinforce the local economy, ensure greater opportunities for local employment, and improve workshop operations.

Community-based credit is designed for individuals requiring relatively small amounts of funding to finance income-generating activities and the expansion of small businesses and micro-enterprise. The project has established a community-based credit fund for local residents. An advisory committee consisting of project staff and community representatives oversees the fund. Staff and community volunteers review applications, and the committee meets weekly to decide which projects will receive credit.

During the first six months, the fund received over a hundred applications and funded forty projects. In the second six months, applications grew to an average of fifty a month with twenty-five accepted. In the course of the first two and half years, the programme received over 500 applications and funded 375 projects.

In order to establish a mechanism to sustain these economic activities and to coordinate efforts to overcome problems and promote increased links and cooperation among local business people, CDS supported the community in establishing *al-Darb al-Ahmar Business Association* (DABA). DABA also aims at increasing and strengthening levels of cooperation between the community and government bodies, as well as private sector and NGO elements relative to private sector growth and consolidation. Around twenty members of the community formed the association. The project supported the association in setting a strategic plan for three years. DABA has been designed to eventually take over and run the entire activity for Economic Revitalisation and Job Creation.

Improving community services such as social education and health care programmes and supporting community-oriented recreational and cultural activities
The community service interventions target the family in general and women and children in particular. Community development approaches were used to enhance the livelihood strategy of the family. Such approaches are: Women Working Together, and Child-to-Child.

The Family Health and Development Centre is an integrated programme designed to respond to the health needs of families via a comprehensive approach to family health care. It provides sustainable

quality family health care in partnership with low-income urban communities. In the early years it was serving 185 clients a month. The centre is not meant to establish a traditional clinic; it is rather a family centre that focuses more on health and preventive social strategy. The centre has adopted two approaches that are particularly appropriate to a poor urban area. These are the Women Working Together (WWT) and (CTC) Child-to-Child programmes. The first programme targets women's needs, setting an individual woman's plan for her future, setting goals and values, and deciding on these personal goals; WWT applies learning and action group methods. The second programme targets children.

New collaborative strategies to develop community education and awareness in al-Darb al-Ahmar
These have been designed with special consideration for the historic, social and cultural values of the community. The culture and arts programme is one such strategy. This programme is aimed at enhancing the appreciation of local residents and outsiders for the culture and traditions of al-Darb al-Ahmar. Furthermore, it uses the arts as a mechanism to increase community awareness and to develop a sense of place. The project has established a wide variety of cultural activities, bringing together children and adults for recreation and training in arts, music, crafts, puppetry and theatre. There are groups of all types for people of all ages. As a result, talented young people have applied their artistic skills to the promotion of project events and to community health and awareness activities within al-Darb al-Ahmar.

Doaa was one of the girls who joined the choral group. Her father was trained and employed by the apprenticeship and employment programme. He said that his daughter joined the cultural programme before he was employed by the project. He said, 'One day Doaa came to me and asked if I would stop being a drug user. She said that it would improve her future socially and economically if I did. I acted in response to her request and stopped taking drugs.'

Kite-flying in al-Azhar Park, 2006; the Historic Cities Programme works to improve the lives of residents of al-Darb al-Ahmar district. Its Education Programme includes creative activities such as making kites.

All the direct beneficiaries of this programme, the groups who participate in the Choir, and in the Painting and Drama projects, are volunteers.

> One of the parents came to the Culture and Arts programme coordinator and asked, 'What did you do to my kid; her attitude has completely changed. She has become more organised, taking care to keep herself and the home clean.'

The attitude of the participants and their families underwent a positive change. They became more self-confident; their way of making decisions has changed and they are more likely to show initiative.

People have become conscious of the value of the open space they are using for their cultural activities. This space had been used to dispose garbage and solid waste in the past. Residents used to deny that they were from al-Darb al-Ahmar. Now they are proud of being from an area of historic value. The choir groups always start their performance with a song called *Being from al-Darb al-Ahmar*.

Like al-Darb al-Ahmar Business Association, the *Community Services Association* is a local NGO designed as a base for local management of community services and to strengthen the bonds that exist within and between families. The members of the association have set a three-year strategic plan.

The promotion of environmental, physical and housing upgrading
The strategy here is to introduce initiatives for solid waste collection, sewage upgrading and maintenance, cleaning up the area, improving environmental conditions and standards of public health in the district's main market area, and addressing the problem of deteriorating and substandard housing.

The main objective of this strategy is to facilitate community-sponsored pilot initiatives which seek to enhance environmental, health and sanitary conditions, to promote safer and cleaner manufacturing and business operations, and to encourage the maintenance of local buildings and public spaces.

Most of the poor environmental and sanitary conditions which exist in al-Darb al-Ahmar can be either corrected or significantly improved through the intervention of local residents, either acting together or in concert with district and municipal authorities. Many of the available solutions are simple in design and require little or no funds to implement them. Community concern and participation, along with a willingness to work together and share the burden, are the major ingredients required.

Such solutions are often ignored for a variety of reasons. First, many communities facing such conditions on a day-to-day basis come to accept these problems as a fact of life. Many forget that what works for one individual, a family or a small group of people, when applied at the level of al-Darb al-Ahmar with its several hundred thousand people cannot work any longer. People in a community lose sight of their own role in creating these conditions and of the need for changes in their behaviour and that of their neighbours in order to resolve the situation. It is all too often defined as a win-lose, rather than a win-win situation. The problem is further compounded in areas like al-Darb al-Ahmar when, due to a variety of circumstances, the majority of individuals feel alienated from their physical surroundings. This feeling was repeatedly expressed by the majority of al-Darb al-Ahmar residents throughout the project planning phase.

To break through this frustration and move on to new, more co-operative alliances, the project established a Local Self-Help Initiatives Fund designed to provide assistance to local NGOs and self-help groups in the identification of problems and needs to which they are seeking a solution. The programme supported four environmental campaign initiatives. Two of these initiatives were in Aslam Alley just behind Aslam Square. These initiatives received a high level of response from both community members and organisations.

The housing intervention

The main goal here is to provide residents with increased access to better housing through pilot initiatives aimed at both the rehabilitation of existing residential structures, and the redevelopment of ruined buildings and vacant land. The project initiated a pilot programme for the rehabilitation of four houses. This programme was combined with a housing credit mechanism for low-income households who wished to build, expand or buy their own homes. This approach permits them to afford better quality housing. Through this initiative, the project was able, for example, to secure tenancy for at least twenty-five families during the pilot stage. A secure tenancy generally promotes household investment in improving a house and a greater ability to negotiate with local authorities for improved services.

The upgrading of public spaces

This initiative includes interventions for improving environmental and health conditions in the local market while piloting a strategy for community involvement in large-scale environmental initiatives.

Traditionally in al-Darb al-Ahmar and in other areas of Cairo, streets and other open spaces belonged to the community. Open spaces were maintained purely by those whose activities took place in the area. Later on, the newly created municipalities often did not take into consideration these existing behavioural patterns and communal mechanisms, and as the metropolis expanded the municipal authorities found it increasingly difficult to maintain open spaces. As a result, there was a lack of cooperation between the various parties involved and no one to take responsibility. Each party began to manipulate the environment without anyone assuming the full responsibility for any, possibly detrimental, outcome to their actions.

A prime example of this scenario is Tablita Market in al-Darb al-Ahmar. Responsibility for the market is currently divided between the Governorate of Cairo which owns the land, the Central Cairo District which controls vending licenses and waste-collection services in the area, and the vendors themselves who are dependent on the market for their livelihood.

BDS together with AKTC conducted participatory design work-shops where different players in the area such as market vendors, architects and officials met together to reach agreement on upgrading the market.

The intervention in Tablita had various outcomes: a new architectural design emerged from the comprehensive and articulate design criteria outlined by the vendors, and a proposed market management scheme based on the ideas of the vendors and the propensity for cooperation on the part of the district authorities.

Strengthening local institutions through providing capacity building, training and technical assistance to local institutions
The main objective of this intervention is strengthening the capacities of local NGOs, governmental organisations and related programmes to effectively plan, implement and evaluate relevant, sustainable development projects for and with the communities they serve.

To accomplish this, a full range of training and technical assistance combined with supporting grants is being made available to local non-governmental and community-based organisations (NGOs and CBOs). This includes the district office of the Ministry of Social Affairs (MOSA). This programme seeks to help NGOs in al-Darb al-Ahmar become more effective by increasing their capacity to manage changes in the operating environment, manage organisational consolidation and growth, use resources effectively, assess and respond to the needs of clients; and to become sustainable and viable in the long term. The programme identified twenty-four community organisations, developed thirty-six proposals and provided eleven grant agreements. Moreover, the programme conducted fifteen training workshops and made more than 350 Technical Assistance visits.

If you are one of the al-Darb al-Ahmar team you can clearly see the changes that have been experienced by these NGOs and the communities. First of all, these associations witnessed a distinct evolution in their way of working together. Before, they were competing with each other. Now they believe in the advantages of networking and working together. What follows is an example of a local initiative developed by three local organisations in al-Darb al-Ahmar.

Three local NGOs (al-Hedayya Association, al-Srogyya Association, and al-Gafaryya Association) participated in an environmental study with the assistance of an outside consultancy firm. Consequently, the three associations had the opportunity to think together about how to develop and improve their community. The outcome was an initiative that requires the integration and networking of the efforts of the three associations. The associations called this initiative, 'Integrated Self-Help Initiatives Against Poverty, and for Literacy and Health'.

The idea of this project was to build on the comparative advantages of each association: al-Hedayya has the best health services in the al-Darb al-Ahmar, al-Srogyya has excellent experience in managing and organising literacy classes and al-Gafaryya is good at community outreach and building strong relationships with community leaders. The project targeted sixty families (approximately 300 members of the local community).

The strategy was based on establishing three literacy classes, one per association, with twenty individuals per class, the majority being women. All these individuals and their families (on average five persons per family) now enjoy health care provided and guaranteed by al-Hedayya Association. Al-Srogyya coordinates the literacy classes and al-Gafaryya, health and environmental awareness.

By taking into consideration the differences in the capacity of each organisation, integration allows the associations to exchange their experiences and strengthen their organisational capacities. Moreover, this project has increased the role of local associations in meeting community needs. It has also created new career opportunities through the provision of practical skills training. Importantly, the project has produced a new model for integration and networking among the three local associations.

Another obvious transformation is that these associations changed their approach from 'top down' to interaction with the community, from assuming a knowledge of the needs of the community to becoming a channel for articulating community needs. They moved away from failure to create initiatives and failure to encourage participation,

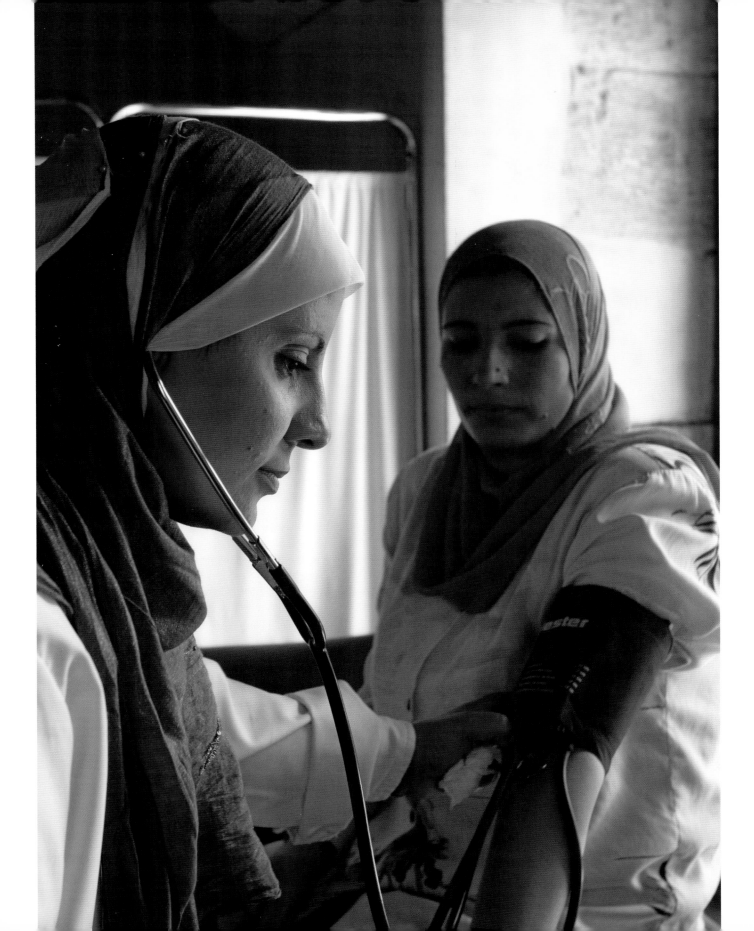

A doctor working in al-Darb
al-Ahmar: the Historic Cities
Programme has funded a
Health Programme in al-Darb
al-Ahmar

from providing physical/material resources and from offering technical solutions. They saw that their new approach increased trust and led to success in experimentation. They now believe in taking a closer look at the specific requirements of the community and are open to the community.

Ezzat, an executive director of al-Srogyya Association, is one of those who participated in all the training workshops conducted for the local NGOs in al-Darb al-Ahmar. During the Participatory Rapid Appraisal workshop he learned how to use RANKING (one of the significant tools of PRA) in setting priorities for community needs and problems. After the training he assembled all the association's staff and applied RANKING to the problems within his institution.

Training was not only offered to association members and executives. The Ministry of Social Affairs had an opportunity to participate. The director of the Association department at MOSA accompanied the Technical Assistance (TA) team on the identification visits for each association. Subsequently, having understood the approach, they promoted it in other associations.

Madam Rabaa, director of the Association department at MOSA district level, accompanied the TA team and introduced them to each association. After three visits, she said to a member of an association, 'See, these people are not going to provide you with physical or material resources, instead they are coming to develop and empower and work with people in the area.' (Association members at that time were expecting to be provided with computers and with funds to paint their premises).

What is more important, the institutional development programme experienced significant progress in creating interaction between government, the NGOs and the community. There had been a gap between MOSA, local NGOs and the community. In addition, the role of each player was unclear. MOSA's role was identified as observing in order to catch the mistakes of the supervision agencies, that is the associations. The associations were thus in a position where every visit by MOSA staff was cause for alarm. The community did not have a clear picture of the role of the associations or of what they were doing. When we asked one of the community members, 'Which agency is in this building and what they are doing?' the reply was 'This is the social affairs agency and they are taking care of children' (he meant it was a kindergarten).

The project, as an outside intervention, filled this gap by creating good channels of communications between these organisations. Accordingly, MOSA adopted a more cooperative approach to other players rather than simply controlling and observing them.

The small grants provided by the project helped to overcome the poor relations between associations and the community, and among the associations.

The ASSALA Association worked together with the MOSALAS DAHABI Association to get joint approval from the Ministry of Education for contacting and cooperating with schools in the area. Another example is the support that al-Srogyya Association gave to ASSALA in the marketing of its traditional crafts production.

One of the most obvious cases of collaborative planning for community programmes is the initiative created by the Friends of Historic Cairo Association (FHCA). This initiative was called 'increasing the children's awareness of the monuments in al-Darb al-Ahmar and the historical value of the area'. The Aga Khan Project supported this initiative with small grants and technical assistance in the areas of design and implementation. This initiative made the association work closely with community members and other different players from governmental agencies. The association built strong relations with the Ministry of Education in order to work closely with the state school in al-Darb al-Ahmar. The Ministry of Cultural Affairs represented by the National Supreme Council for Monuments provided the FHCA with official permission for thirty persons to visit twelve monuments. Members of the community, especially the parents, were very interested in sending their children to this awareness programme. Cooperating with others in implementing community activity was a new experience for the association.

Conclusion

To what extent has the integrated approach been able to alleviate urban poverty? And in what direction can it now go?

It was a challenge for all participants in the joint programme in al-Darb al-Ahmar for combatting urban poverty to introduce this approach. Working in partnership and collaboration was a significant factor in this intervention. Furthermore, ensuring the involvement of various different players, including several governmental agencies, was obviously important.

Community enablement was one of the successful outcomes of this intervention. The project, in coordination with local government and the Ministry for Social Affairs, facilitated the efforts of community and neighbourhood-based organisations to initiate, plan and implement their own projects according to the principles of self-determination, self-organisation and self-management. The impact of Self-help Initiative grants on the community living in al-Darb al-Ahmar has been very marked. Consequently, the CBOs in al-Darb al-Ahmar have been able to play substantial and multi-faceted roles in the community and these have further allowed the intervention to obtain effective access to those it was designed to benefit.

What is more, the role of local government, represented by MOSA, was positive and it supported the intervention. The MOSA officials also became aware of the programme's philosophy. This obviously had an impact on the steering committee's participation and promoted the programme among the CBOs in al-Darb al-Ahmar. However it was clear that the CBOs had the potential to take on a bigger role in the next phase, including the associations set up by the project.

However, there was a tendency in local government to focus on the physical 'hardware' side of programme implementation rather than on community participation and empowerment. Some participants, including both the local government and the CBOs had a preference for visible, tangible improvements and activities designed to foster participation, whereas awareness and community mobilisation were sometimes perceived as time consuming and the cause of delay in programme implementation. This was evident at the beginning of the intervention.

Despite this fact, *Community-based credit* has been a noteworthy strategy for offering economic opportunities to al-Darb al-Ahmar residents. The experience of this intervention demonstrates that the economy of al-Darb al-Ahmar can absorb more credit funding. However, it is essential to support credit 'as a financial service' with other, non-financial services. These include training, marketing and information facilities.

Apprenticeship, Employment and Job creation is one intervention that supports other strategies for the alleviation of urban poverty such as the housing improvement strategy. Since al-Darb al-Ahmar is a vast area and unemployment is considered the priority, requiring immediate action, further similar interventions or an expansion of the current programme has been sought by other local NGOs in the area. In its early years this programme created over 800 apprenticeships and facilitated over 1,770 job referrals and 1,120 job placements. The number of applications submitted reached almost 3,000. This programme is very successful and has helped the local community to cope with poverty.

The Cultural and Arts Programme was a new approach to the development of community education and awareness in al-Darb al-Ahmar, and one which took the social and cultural values of the community into consideration and respected the area's historic qualities. Both direct and indirect beneficiaries have greatly appreciated the programme and it has developed at a rapid rate, with a wide range of types of performance. All the direct beneficiaries of this programme are volunteers. The Cultural and Arts Programme quickly produced astounding results, far beyond the expectations with which it was initiated, and it has consistently displayed great potential for expansion.

28 Heritage protection against what? A model to explain adverse change in historic districts

Dina K. Shehayeb and Ahmed Sedky

The subject of this essay is the contemporary Arabo-Islamic city, which survives today as historic districts within the giant fabric of the modern metropolis. These districts are not just archeological sites or tourist attractions. They still contribute to and are integrated into the overall city system. The districts are clearly not playing the same role as they did a century or two earlier, when they formed completely independent cities. Instead, they have become the home for certain patterns of living and forms of activity. The historic districts in Cairo, Damascus and Aleppo, from which this paper draws many examples, have a resilient character (the heritage we would like to preserve), but which is however, in the main, responsible for the changes which have put it in jeopardy. In this paper we present a model through which we explain factors that contribute to the weakening of this local character, or heritage.

The character of these places lies in a sophisticated system of settings and corresponding meanings that can only be decoded by those who interact with them and understand the decoded messages.[1] It is therefore through those occupants, or users, that outsiders can read such environments. The character is the representation of 'cultural ideas [that] are objectively present in artifacts as much as they are subjectively present in minds'.[2] This continuing presence in the mind has been termed as the 'social logic of space'.[3] It is the only means of discerning how such areas are still able to communicate and elicit meanings, and serve functions and activities. They serve inherent functions that are perceived only by those who live in them.[4]

In short, a place is a space with varied meanings for those who use it, view it or appreciate it. Furthermore, the meaning of a place is defined not only by its built form but by the living context within and around it as well. And since one reason for maintaining architectural heritage is to use it for transmitting to future generations the meanings that comprise the local culture, the elimination of some of them would depreciate its value as heritage. This devaluation of heritage is partly caused by changes introduced by the residents or users of the historic areas, as well as by professional and officials, either through designed interventions, or a lack of intervention.

The hypothesis here is that each party is interested in a different set of perceived values. Everyday users of the place, mostly people who live and work there, are interested in maximising those values that are significant for their daily life, including social, economic, psychological and spiritual or cultural values. The users, however, tend to have a limited awareness of health issues and to lack any awareness of historic and aesthetic values. As a consequence, they often minimise these values, by using inappropriate means at hand, in their attempt to maximise the 'life-values' mentioned above.

Planners and designers, on the other hand, focus exclusively on the aesthetic and historic values of the place. The concerns of city officials may also include national security, but this is often an unrevealed aim of historic preservation schemes. In the effort to maximise these values, they minimise and abolish any other set of values as encroachments and acts of vandalism, and thus conversely they diminish the meaning of the place. Worse still, some misguided designers often enhance the aesthetic value of the place at the expense of its historic integrity.

Users as vandals[5]

APPROPRIATION OF PUBLIC PROPERTY

One form of user vandalism witnessed in historic areas involves the appropriation of public property for private use. This appropriation can simply involve extending everyday household activities or workshop activities onto public thoroughfares, and also into historic structures. For example, some residents in al-Darb al-Ahmar took over the historic Ayyubid Wall and used it as a roof top to hang out their laundry, air their bedding and sometimes just to sit to admire the sunset.[6] Others have gone further and carved rooms into the wall to expand their living space. In further appropriation, cul-de-sacs are often used by residents of surrounding buildings as areas for keeping livestock.

These are all cases where the users have perceived 'use-value'[7] in the built environment, in the thickness of the Historic Wall, the privacy of the cul-de-sac and the lack of traffic in the winding streets. However, one should not overlook the 'psychological' and 'social' gains of such territorial behaviour. Indeed, whether these acts of appropriation should be considered vandalism is questionable in the first place, since they are simply a traditional means of exercising control over the public space immediately outside one's private domain.[8] This social control serves several functions; it helps enhance a sense of safety, of belonging and it is sometimes a means of communicating one's status to others in the community.[9] Such instances of vandalism, if they are to be so considered, are ones where both users and outsiders can read the environment.

UNSUITABLE ACTIVITIES

Al-Harrika is an area within the walls of the old city of Damascus, behind the Citadel where a fire had destroyed the original fabric, which was then rebuilt as a commercial (wholesale) and manufacturing area at some point around the 1920s. As a result, commercial uses have been infiltrating the residential area inside the walled Historic City of Damascus; mansions have been converted into workshops that threaten the last remaining authentic historic fabric of the city. In Cairo, unsuitable activities jeopardising the physical condition of historic buildings and the community's health in general, are quite common in districts such as Jamaliyya, al-Darb al-Ahmar and Bab al-Wazir. These activities include welding, carpentry, marble cutting, tanning and other trades.[10] Such cases of vandalism come about when users exploit the 'economic' value at the expense of the 'historic', and 'aesthetic' values and, sometimes, the health requirements of the historic area. The problem lies in the processes and materials used in these workshops. Recently, several projects have examined ways of improving environmental and health conditions in certain workshops so they can remain in their areas. Only those workshops where adverse effects cannot be contained will have to be banned from the historic area. This is because the continuation of these workshops in those areas is vital, as well as historically valid, since they represent the economic base of the resident community.

INAPPROPRIATE IMPROVEMENTS

Contrary to the perception that residents of historic areas are unwilling to invest in improving their environment, recent research findings have shown that residents of such areas do engage in making home improvements. However, it is in the *quality* of these improvements that the problem lies.[11] These home improvements include applying new plastering on exterior facades, or replacing deteriorating window frames and lattice panels with (better performing) designs in wood or aluminum. Interiors are constantly maintained by residents, either by replastering and repainting walls, re-tiling floors, or the replacing of plumbing in parts of the building. Unfortunately these attempts at maintenance and improvement often produce an adverse effect, rather than contributing to the preservation of the built heritage. One reason is the lack of trained craftsmen with the appropriate know-how. For a long time the government and other organisations have not supported or encouraged the preservation, application and development of traditional building techniques or construction materials. As a result, these are not a widely known about and have become specialist skills available only to major restoration projects. This is largely the case in Cairo, where a gap has arisen between local craftsmen and traditional construction techniques because of the relatively long presence of colonial stylistic and technical influences. The situation in Syria is not, however, as drastic since these techniques are still alive there. Yet, an authentic construction or restoration process is still expensive,[12] and therefore it is almost impossible to restore an inhabited building of traditional value (i.e. an unregistered one) in an ideal manner, especially when the inhabitants have limited financial resources, which is usually the case.

In addition to maximising values such as 'convenience', and 'aesthetics', another motive that initiates improvements arises from the spiritual or cultural value often associated with historic areas. In Cairo, for example, a resident seeking to repent of his errors or fulfill a religious vow, will spend money to improve spiritually significant religious monuments. In one such case, the penitent had the inside

Survey of the North Advance
Tower of the Aleppo Citadel,
2002

of the *mihrab* in a mosque covered with modern ceramic tiles of the best quality available in the market.[13] This aspect of user vandalism is one where users maximise 'convenience', 'aesthetic' and 'cultural' values as they perceive them, with whatever materials, techniques, craftsmanship are available to them.

Professionals as vandals

VAGUE REGULATIONS AND SLACK IMPLEMENTATION

The regulations that apply to new construction in historic areas still fall short in the areas of rigour and articulation. This problem is compounded by lax enforcement of the regulations as they now stand. Such conditions have resulted in the introduction of modern buildings such as public housing schemes and the prototypical educational buildings in parts of Historic Cairo, such as Bab al-Wazir and al-Darb al-Ahmar, and similarly in areas of Old Damascus.

Another aspect of this problem is insecurity of tenancy. In Cairo, the struggle between the Ministry of the Awqaf and the Ministry of Culture as well as the ambiguity of the property renting laws, has left many historic buildings in a state of neglect and uncertain ownership. The most serious result is the insecurity felt by the tenants in old buildings. In Cairo, for example, owners and residents of properties in the vicinity of historical monuments are in constant fear of being moved out as were the inhabitants of houses along the excavated sections of the historic Ayyubid Wall.[14] What is more, for over a decade a plan was held by the Governorate of Cairo, which delineated a ten-metre wide street along this wall as well as the widening of an alley that runs parallel to the wall. Residents in the area were kept in a state of uncertainty, expecting any moment the implementation of this plan, while non-resident owners lost all interest in maintaining their properties, since their value had eroded. Other tenants who moved out hung on to their deserted units, believing they might be given subsidised apartments as compensation when and if the removal took place.

The fact that property values in the area were unknown due to the unimplemented plans, that conflicting regulations meant many buildings were empty, and the presence also of undeveloped lots all accelerated the physical deterioration of many historic districts. The constant insecurity that residents of historic areas experience is also a source of psychological stress.

A related issue is the lack of clear guidelines for the safeguarding of our heritage. Attempts at defining the meaning of heritage have so far addressed the matter in a very general fashion.[15] Such ambiguity has led to the absence of any concept of value estimation, which is needed in order to decide the architectural value of the building. One consequence was the long confrontation between the Cairo Governorate and the Ministry of Culture which was a topic of interest in the media because of the issue of the 1936 Al-Azhar Administrative Building. The lack of preservation guidelines also resulted in a proposal for the creation of a piazza in the heart of Historic Cairo. A possible design was discussed in the press, and was roundly rejected in some quarters on the basis that it would drastically alter the traditional physical character of the most important node in the city.[16]

MODERNISATION, 'GIVING IT A CIVILISED LOOK'

On an urban level, and carried out under the banner of modernity and giving a civilised look, one major negative change has been the dissection of the traditional urban fabric in old cities in order to introduce wider modern street systems. This can be illustrated in the walled city of Damascus, where some streets perpendicular to the ancient thoroughfare and around the Citadel were widened. Fortunately, in the 1960s, when the French planner Ecoshar wanted to emphasise the Citadel by creating vistas and space around it at the expense of Suq al-Hamidiyya, the idea was not implemented, thus saving one of the social and cultural landmarks most familiar, not only to residents of Damascus, but to Arab people generally and also to tourists.[17]

In Aleppo, the old city suffered similar dissection. Historical districts were separated to improve the street system. Thus an entire part of the old city, Bab al-Farag, was lost in a development carried out under the flag of modernity.[18]

This is also the case in the upgrading or improvement of traditional *suq*s and shopping areas in Cairo. The hustle and bustle, sounds and smells, the interweaving of cars and pedestrians in Khan al-Khalili or al-Sagha, have been criticised by certain professionals and city officials as unseemly, backward and uncivilised. There have been recurring attempts to modernise and sanitise the place. One such scheme even suggested the construction of an indoor mall. Hardly any thought is given to

simply using local taxes for improving leaking infrastructure networks and rubbish collection, and designating the area an Historic District.

BEAUTIFICATION/MUSEUMIFICATION

Planners and designers often confuse preservation of a historic building with beautification of the building and its surroundings. Their schemes usually include the elimination of other, non-architectural elements of historic areas which contribute to their current meaning; activities that may be as much a source of heritage as the buildings themselves. Such interventions can endanger the authenticity of historic areas. For example, in Cairo, the scheme for al-Ghawriyya dictated the removal of the textile shops from the area surrounding the historic religious complex in order to protect it. This threatens the livelihood and indeed the whole ambience of this area. It becomes 'museumified'. In fact, this plan removes the real spirit of the place. The area, with its location close to the main mosque of Fatimid Cairo, followed the traditional urban planning and guild division, mainly shops and *wakala*s, workshops for textiles. Textile merchants, together with perfumiers and bookshops, have surrounded al-Azhar Mosque since the 10th century. This was more than four centuries before the complex of al-Ghawri was built, as can be seen in the writings of the revered chronicler of Cairo, al-Maqrizi, in the 14th century, and 'Ali Mubarak in the 19th century.[19]

Another example of insensitive attempts at beautification can be seen in the amphitheatre added as part of the urban upgrading scheme for Qasr al-Sham', or Babylon, in Cairo. This does not fit into the socio-physical urban context. In form and function the amphitheatre has little meaning for the community. They might have benefitted more from a multi-purpose area, perhaps shaded by a few trees, somewhere children could play, or the elderly enjoy a game of backgammon. Instead, it is now a rather meaningless barren space where elements of the landscaping have become garbage collection nooks. This is an instance where the professional's intent to beautify has had an adverse effect on the character of an historic area, endangering its very integrity.

Such cases of professional vandalism occur when planners and designers maximise the 'aesthetic' value, as they perceive it, while banning all activities that often have 'life-value' for the surrounding community. In some cases, as in the latter example, actions intended to beautify may actually negatively affect the 'historic' value of the area. Furthermore, such actions are likely to be motivated by unstated hopes of economic advantage, probably through an attempt to attract tourists.

Cultural exploitation
Another domain of adverse change can be seen in the economic exploitation of historic areas for tourism. Historic areas are considered national assets, resources to be taken advantage of. Thus, development for tourism is prioritised, if not by the perceived beautification and the museumification of historic sites, then by adaptive reuse. Adaptive reuse is a concept that can either save or destroy historic treasures. For instance, in Damascus the consents issued by the 'Anbar office (the official institution responsible for the rehabilitation and revival of Old Damascus) for adaptive reuse projects are mainly ones for tourism, for it is these that in the main meet the requirements laid down. When such a strategy excludes other (non-touristic) uses and extends over areas at large, it becomes a form of cultural exploitation that threatens to change the whole character of the area. This is happening in the Bab Tuma area in Damascus where most of the old houses have been converted into restaurants and coffee shops.

The above examples reflect the tendency of planners and government generally to focus mainly on what covers the cost of preservation. Such a trend may lead to gentrification; resulting in a 'kitschy', rather than the authentic, or 'real', ambience that we still feel in the alleys of Old Cairo and Damascus despite their apparent physical deterioration. The way to manage historic areas may be to allow greater choice and a wider variety of uses, and to institute a form of monitored change in these areas so that they continue to be a 'living heritage' rather than historic artifacts no longer of any practical everyday use.

Conclusion
By realising that any intervention, use or inherent function, can either contribute to, or detract from, the heritage value of a place, and that the meaning of a place encompasses more than just its aesthetic and historic values, we ought to be able to rethink our strategies for preserving this heritage. The meaning or possible function of a place can be measured by assessing its perceived values for the different groups that make use of it, and complementing these with the values perceived by those of us who are professionals in the field and by the decision-makers at national level. The key is to balance out any disparity. Once planners and government officials comprehend the reasons behind the unintended vandalism caused by users, they can then work in a variety of ways to minimise such phenomena. On the one hand, the awareness and sensitivity of the people – both local users and visitors – should be raised using educational programmes in schools, through the media and by community events. On the other hand, the government can support the development of materials and building technologies that are more appropriate to the physical environment in historic areas and the creation of a skilled labour force to use them. On a more abstract level, it is vital that professionals rethink the very meaning of the term 'heritage'. We need to develop a more comprehensive, yet operational, definition of the term in order to guide the development of the criteria which are used to assess the value of, not only buildings, but entire traditional settings and areas, since a comprehensive participatory design may be a means of creating a two-way exchange of perceived values between insiders (users) and outsiders (planners, designers and government officials).

In conclusion, on the subject of historic areas, a balance of interests should be recognised and respected by all parties; the world has the right to see these areas, the nation as a whole has the right to benefit from them, and their inhabitants have the right to live in them. The ways and means outlined in this paper may be a first step towards reconciling value systems in order to preserve, or sustain our 'living heritage'.

1 Amos Rapoport, 'Systems of activities and systems of settings', in Susan Kent, ed., *Domestic Architecture and the use of Space* (Cambridge, MA, 1998) and idem, *The Meaning of the Built Environment* (Beverly Hills, CA, 1982).

2 Bill Hillier et al., 'Ideas Are things: An Application of the Space Syntax Method to Discovering House Genotypes', *Environment and Planning B: Planning and Design*, 14 (1987), p. 363.

3 Ibid.

4 Dina Shehayeb, 'Sustainable Housing Rehabilitation: Utilizing E-B Studies in a Historic Conservation Project', Presentation at the IAPS conference, Paris, 4–7 July 2000.

5 We use the term 'vandalism' to refer to the blurring of the local character of such places, or the weakening of their meaning and heritage, as it has been often used accusingly to describe the actions of residents and users of historic areas.

6 AKTC, 2001.

7 The term 'use-value' or rather '*valeur d'usage*' was used by the French expert on historic preservation, Professor Xavier Malverti to denote the potential of a building to accommodate different activities or uses without disruption to structural form. Lecture on Historic Preservation Methodologies as part of the HERCOMANE project inaugural Seminar. 11–13 September 2000.

8 See Amos Rapoport, *Human Aspects in Urban Form* (Oxford, 1977).

9 R. B. Taylor and S. Brower, 'Home and near-home territories', in I. Altman and C. Werner, ed., *Home Environments* (New York, 1985).

10 Moshira Mosa, 'Violations and Carpentry Workshops Threatening the Islamic and Historical Monuments in Cairo!' *Al-Ahram Newspaper* (18 September 2000).

11 See Dina Shehayeb, 'Sustainable Housing Rehabilitiation'.

12 Emmad Al-Aqqad, civil engineer who is responsible for many refurbishment projects restoring some 300-year-old mansions in al-Qimariyya, Old Damascus, an interview conducted by Ahmed Sedky, Damascus, August 2000.

13 Shehayeb, 1999.

14 Shahinaz Mekheimar and Dina Shehayeb, 'Affordable Healthy Housing', *Open House International*, 26, 2, Special Issue: Health, Housing, and Urban Environments (2001), pp. 43–54.

15 See Organisation of Islamic Capitals and Cities (OICC) Charters, Iran, 1997.

16 See Saiyyed Ali, 'In Fatimid Cairo: A New Start for a Beautiful History', *Al-Ahram Newspaper* (19 March 1998); Amal Othman and Islam Afifi, 'A Crime in the Heart of Historic Cairo: An Architectural Giant Threatening Al-Azhar Mosque and Al-Hussein Santuary', *Akhbar al-Youm Newspaper* (27 November 1999); The Burra Charter, the Australia ICOMOS Charter for the Conservation of Places of Cultural Significance, 1979.

17 This plan received governmental support because of the reputation of the French planners; fortunately it was not executed due to some amendments suggested by Dr Abdel Qader Al-Rihawi, then Department of Antiquities consultant. Interview conducted by Ahmed Sedky with Dr Abdel Qader al-Rihawi, Damascus, August 2000.

18 Based on the interview conducted by Ahmed Sedky with Mr Omar Abdel-Aziz Halaj, the Main Consultant of the Revitalisation of Old Aleppo Project. Aleppo, August 2000.

19 Shahira Mihriz, 'Al-Ghuri Complex in an Urban Context', MA Dissertation (The American University in Cairo, 1972); 'Ali Mubarak, *al-Khitat al-tawfiqiyya al-jadida li-Misr al-Qahira wa muduniha wa biladiha al-qadima wa'l-shhira* (Cairo, 1969).

Representing al-Darb al-Ahmar on film

Maysoon Pachachi

The documentary film *Living with the Past: Historic Cairo* was shot in Egypt in 2001, directed by myself, edited in London by Terry Twigg, produced by Elizabeth (B.J.) Fernea and premiered at the Middle East Studies Association annual film festival in November 2001. We have described it as a filmic portrait of the historic neighbourhood of al-Darb al-Ahmar in old Cairo, now undergoing great change and rehabilitation. And that's what it is.

A year after we finished filming, we were back in Cairo to make an Arabic version of *Living With the Past*. We had also decided to screen the film in the neighbourhood, in al-Darb al-Ahmar itself and I was full of trepidation. It is always difficult when you show people *your* version of *their* reality.

We held the screening in the late afternoon in the courtyard of the Aga Khan Centre right in the middle of al-Darb al-Ahmar, and people from all over the area came. It was the worst sound system I think I had ever heard; also it was not yet dark so it was difficult to see the screen and we had to stop halfway through while the muezzin made his call to prayer. In spite of all that, people seemed to love the film. For me, the most exciting thing was that people from one part of the neighbourhood discovered things they didn't know about another part of the neighbourhood. New contacts were made and somehow the film entered into the life of the area.

I was very pleased when the project's producer, Elizabeth (B.J.) Fernea, asked me to direct the film. I had been to Cairo many times but really only as a visitor, and I loved it. On my last trip I'd taken my stepdaughter there as a birthday present; for her it was the first time in the Middle East and everything was strange and wonderful. One early evening we found ourselves near the tent-maker's bazaar opposite Bab Zuwayla in al-Darb al-Ahmar. It was not an area I had been to before. We picked our way through the mud, avoiding a donkey cart, peering into the shops full of people working. In every tiny cubby-hole people were making or selling things. And all around them and us towered magnificent medieval mosques and *madrasa*s, stunning in their beauty, but desperately neglected and dilapidated. We were overwhelmed by

the tangible, material sense of 'history'. We stood in the street, very much in the present of car horns and Egyptian pop music, but at the same time keenly aware of the long, continuous and intimate dialogue between the buildings and the people who had lived among them for generations.

We shot the film in the spring of 2001. By then, the Egyptian Supreme Council of Antiquities, the American Research Center in Egypt, the Ford Foundation and the Aga Khan Trust for Culture were all embarked on restoration projects in al-Darb al-Ahmar. The trust was also running an innovative community development project in the area.

B.J. and I spread a map out on the dining-room table of the Cairo flat where we were staying whilst we shot the film. Tracing a triangle – al-Azhar to the north, Saladin's Wall to the east, the Sultan Hasan Mosque to the south and Bab Zuwayla in the middle – we decided that the main character in the film was the neighbourhood of al-Darb al-Ahmar itself. That meant both the people and the buildings, whose lives and stories were so inextricably linked. It was a moment of change. There was talk that people would be moved out and their workshops and houses knocked down to clear the area with its newly restored monuments, to make it easier for tourists to see them.

B.J. and her husband Bob Fernea had started researching before I arrived in Cairo. I spent the ten days before shooting began in al-Darb al-Ahmar. I would spend hours wandering around either with B.J. or Mourad el-Essawi, our production manager, sitting in people's shops and houses, drinking coffee and talking. We explained our project to the people running the Aga Khan Development Project. We drove out to the experimental farm where the plants for the big new park were being grown. We walked up and down Saladin's Wall. I knew it was essential to make people in the neighbourhood comfortable with our presence if we really wanted to hear what they thought, what their problems were, what living in the area was like.

I was aware that in Egypt, class is a big issue. Many well-intentioned middle-class Cairenes had never been to al-Darb al-Ahmar or similar working class districts. Furthermore, many thought that people from

Maysoon Pachachi
directing *Living with the Past*
during the excavation of
the Ayyubid City Wall

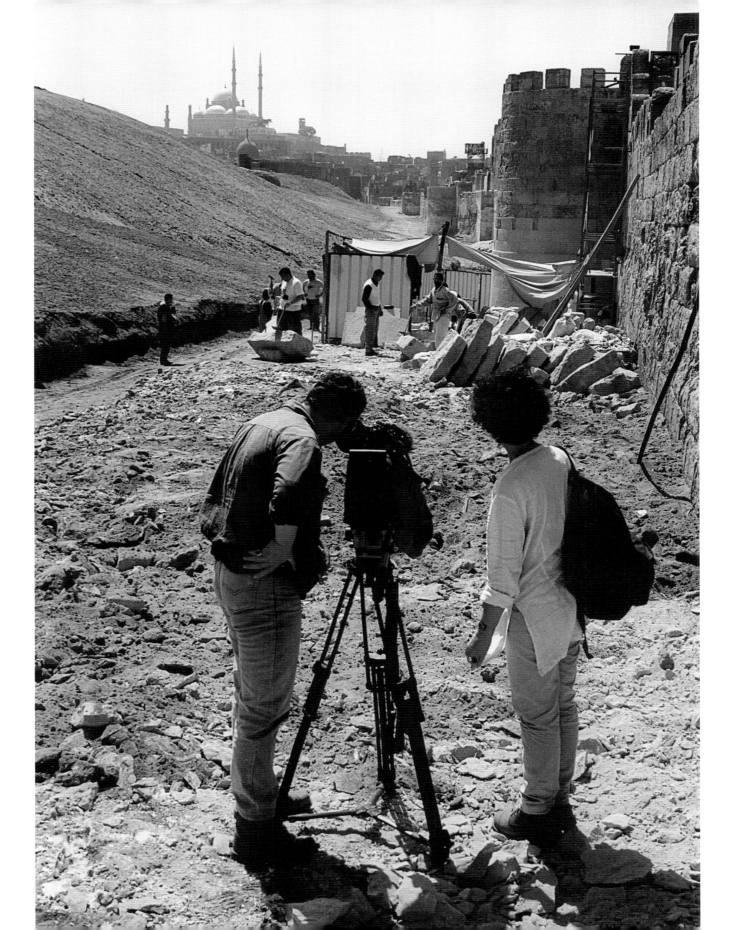

these areas had nothing interesting to say because they were uneducated and poor. I wondered if this class prejudice would be a problem for us. Our production manager Mourad dispelled any such fears the first day we went to al-Darb al-Ahmar together. Mourad had enormous charm and a democratic spirit, treating everyone with respect and warmth. He had recommended our cameraman Ibrahim el-Batout and he, too, put everyone at their ease, conducting many of the impromptu interviews on the street. Ibraham was from Port Said. For years he had covered wars all over the world. He was used to the speed and adrenalin buzz of that kind of work and I wondered how he would adjust to weeks of shooting nothing much more 'exciting' than a man repairing shoes or carving wood, people restoring buildings or sitting around in cafes and shops, a children's singing workshop, or a women's meeting.

The first day of the shoot was the day of 'Id al-Adha. We shot in the evening, wandering up and down the main street of al-Darb al-Ahmar – Ibrahim and his brother Isma'il, who was the camera assistant, myself and Diana Ruston, a very experienced and sensitive sound recordist from England. Ibrahim was getting some good material, but it seemed to me he wasn't holding shots for long enough, and was impatient to get on to the next thing. I felt that to convey the real feel of al-Darb al-Ahmar we had to reflect its pace and its texture, and this meant we had to give the viewer time to watch. Often in documentaries one senses a kind of glibness in the images – they have no resonance; such documentaries often feel like illustrated lectures. This was not what B.J. and I wanted to do. But as the shooting went on, Ibrahim slowed down. He was intrigued by al-Darb al-Ahmar and was enjoying getting to know it, and he was humouring me.

We had a clear idea about the different elements we wanted in the film and a loose sense of how they would fit together to create a picture of this particular neighbourhood at this particular time in its history. We also knew the broader issues that would be raised. We scheduled interviews and locations, but we also wanted to leave ourselves open to the unexpected, the chance meeting. As the shoot went on, and people saw us in the district practically every day, they became used to us;

after a while, we stopped causing much excitement in the streets. We became familiar, habitual visitors who happened to have a camera and sound recording equipment. We knew people and people knew us, and we seemed to know our way around. Only twice did we feel that people were edgy with the camera. One was when we followed a group of Italian tourists into the Qijmas Mosque and filmed Hisham, its informal caretaker, showing them around. I sensed the Italians were uneasy when we asked them a few questions, but they answered with good grace.

The other time was on our first day of shooting – the evening of the 'Id. We started filming down a small street strung with coloured festival lights. A man at a small tea stall started shouting at us. Why were we filming the garbage, had we come to show how filthy al-Darb al-Ahmar was? We were shocked because, we hadn't even noticed the pile of litter shoved up against the wall of a building, and it would never be seen on screen anyway, it was too dark. The man was very angry and started shoving Ibrahim around. Ibrahim tried to reason with him, but nothing helped. Then Ibrahim snapped. He handed the camera to Diana and prepared to fight. And this was our first day! Luckily, Mourad came by and defused the situation in his characteristically diplomatic way. A week later when we found ourselves in the same part of the neighbourhood, people came out of their shops to apologise to us. The tea man, they said, had been having a hard time and had been very tense.

That incident was a very clear illustration of how people hate to be shown as 'victims' and I realised that probably the people of al-Darb al-Ahmar, if they had been shown on film at all, were depicted as poor and their neighbourhood as run-down and dirty. Of course, this was the very opposite of what we were trying to do. I think one of the reasons for the delight that people in al-Darb al-Ahmar took in the film was because it showed them and their area as far more than just poor and run-down.

But the question of garbage was one of which we had to be aware. We had a representative from the International Press Centre and Ministry of Information who often came with us, particularly when we were shooting on the street. He was a nice, easy-going man, but if he thought we were filming garbage or dirt, he would get very agitated. At one point he stopped us filming a very old man, dressed in ragged oily clothes, repairing a brass lamp on the street. Another time he stopped us filming a pile of tomatoes on a market stall – because they were too small. The most important thing to him seemed to be the look of something and not the reality of it. As an Arab, it's an attitude with which I'm not unfamiliar. All over the Arab world, in one way or another, you find such concern about how you look to the outside world. I know this is partly a reaction to the way the Western media often depicts people, not only in Arab countries, but throughout the developing world.

Al-Darb al-Ahmar, was rarely silent except in the very early morning and then it was quiet, but not silent. The element of sound was very important to the film, not just as a matter of 'atmosphere', but as part of the actual experience of being in the place, an experience layered, dense with texture of all kinds. Diana had a tricky job: to record interviews so that they were clear, without losing the vital surrounding, often quite loud and complex, sound landscape. But she was an expert. We filmed several group discussions, and the most difficult took place in 'Ali's shop next to the Qijmas Mosque. Once the conversation got going, everyone was talking over everyone else. People came to vent their feelings about the area's problems; they had a lot to say and they didn't always agree with each other. Diana and Ibrahim had to get good quality images and sound down on tape without interrupting the flow. Without their skill a lot of the 'natural' and intimate quality of the film would have been lost.

What became very clear as we filmed in al-Darb al-Ahmar was people's close connection with the area, how living among these extraordinary buildings had informed their sense of who they were. Hisham's family, shoemakers for generations, had always had their shop at the bottom of the Qijmas Mosque. When we asked what he would do if he was forced to move, he said he would find a way to come back. The mosque was his home. When he is depressed, he goes up on the roof, looks over Cairo and feels better. A man who sells Coca Cola and 7Up from a stall near a beautiful restored *sabil-kuttab* up the street from Bab Zuwayla, told us

the government guardian was never there, but the people of the neighbourhood loved the building and would take care of it.

Of course, we not only filmed only the people of al-Darb al-Ahmar. Many different kinds of voices are heard in the film – high government officials, heads of foreign NGOs, architects and restorers, members of the Aga Khan Project. Unusually, several different people conducted the interviews – Bob Fernea held some of the more formal male interviews, B.J. those with the heads of foreign NGOs, restorers and architects, Mourad some of the longer Arabic interviews in al-Darb al-Ahmar, as well as the big group discussion in 'Ali's shop. Ibrahim did most of the casual vox pop interviews. I also did a few interviews in English and occasionally in my less than wonderful Egyptian Arabic. Dina Kamal did some indepth interviews with women. At first I was afraid that this might create a kind of incoherence of voice in the film, but it didn't seem to. I think this is partly because we discussed the interviews and made suggestions to each other about the questions, and partly because the film was about disparate, very different elements all coming together, but not necessarily smoothly. Each element – the people of al-Darb al-Ahmar, the restorers, the government officials – remained itself, but related to the others in telling the story of the area.

One of the stranger things we encountered in al-Darb al-Ahmar was two German stonemasons who were working on the Sam Ibn Nuh Mosque being restored by Agnieska Dobrowolska. These young men had long hair, tattoos and earrings, and were dressed in medieval German stonecutter's clothes. Their guild training required them to leave their home for three years with the equivalent of $50 in their pockets and working only for board and lodging. They had come to Cairo to learn from the Egyptian stonemasons who, in many cases, still used ancient stonecutting techniques and tools. They remained absolutely themselves, but somehow were not out of place in al-Darb al-Ahmar. They were part of the most recent layer of the history of the area, as, I suppose, we were, with our camera and our microphones.

Bibliography

Abdul Rahim, 'Abdul Rahim 'Abdul Rahman. 'The Documents of the Egyptian Religious Courts (*al-mahakim al-shari'iyya*) as a Source for the Study of Ottoman Provincial Administration in Egypt (923/1517–1213/1798)', *Journal of the Economic and Social History of the Orient*, 34 (1991), pp. 88–97.

Abrahams, Israel. 'An Eighth-Century Genizah Document', *Jewish Quarterly Review*, 17 (1905), pp. 426–430.

Abu-Lughod, Janet. *Cairo: 1001 Years of the City Victorious*. Princeton, NJ, 1974.

Abu Salih the Armenian. *The Churches and Monasteries of Egypt and Some Neighbouring Countries*, tr. B. T. A. Evetts. 2nd. ed., Oxford, 1969.

Adler, Marcus Nathan, ed. and tr. *The Itinerary of Benjamin of Tudela*. London, 1907; repr., New York, n.d.

Akerlof, G. 'The Market for "Lemons": Quality, Uncertainty and the Market Mechanism', *Quarterly Journal of Economics*, 84 (1970), pp. 488–500.

AlSayyad, Nezar, Bierman, Irene A. and Nasser Rabbat. *Making Cairo Medieval*. Oxford, 2005.

Altmann, Alexander and Samuel M. Stern. *Isaac Israeli: A Neoplatonic Philosopher of the Early Eleventh Century*. London, 1958.

Armbrust, Walter. *Mass Culture and Modernism in Egypt*. Cambridge, 1996.

Ashtor, E. 'Prolegomena to the Medieval History of Oriental Jewry', *Jewish Quarterly Review*, 50 (1959), pp. 56–57.

— *Social and Economic History of the Near East in the Middle Ages*. London, 1976.

Bacharach, Jere L., ed. *Fustat Finds: Beads, Coins, Medical Instruments, Textiles, and Other Artifacts from the Awad Collection*. Cairo and New York, 2002.

Baer, Gabriel. *Egyptian Guilds in Modern Times*. Jerusalem, 1964.

— ''Ali Mubarak's Khitat as a Source for the History of Modern Egypt', in P. M. Holt, ed. *Political and Social Change in Modern Egypt: Historical Studies from the Ottoman Conquest to the United Arab Republic*. London, 1968, pp. 13–22.

— 'Guilds in Middle Eastern History,' in M. A. Cook, ed. *Studies in the Economic History of the Middle East From the Rise of Islam to the Present Day*. London, 1970, pp. 11–30.

— *Fellah and Townsman in the Middle East: Studies in Social History*. London, 1982.

Bagnall, Roger S., ed. *Egypt in the Byzantine World, 300–700*. Cambridge, 2007.

Bardhan, P. K. 'The New Institutional Economics and Development Theory: A Brief Critical Assessment', *World Development*, 17 (1989), pp. 1389–1395.

Barrucand, Marianne, ed. *L'Égypte Fatimide, son art et son histoire*. Paris, 1999.

Behrens-Abouseif, Doris, ed. *The Cairo Heritage: Essays in Honor of Laila Ali Ibrahim*. Cairo, 2000.

— *Cairo of the Mamluks: A History of the Architecture and its Culture*. London, 2007.

Belgin, Tekce, Oldham, Linda and Frederic Shorter. *A Place to Live*. Cairo, 1994.

Belleface, J-F. 'Turat, classicisme et variétés: les avatars de l'orchestre oriental au Caire au début du xxe siècle', *Bulletin d'Études Orientales*, 39–40 (1987–1988), [pp. 39–65], pp. 54–55.

Berkey, Jonathan. 'Women and Islamic Education in the Mamluk Period', in Nikki R. Keddie and Beth Baron, ed. *Women in Middle Eastern History* (New Haven, CT, 1991), pp. 144–145.

Bianca, Stefano. *Urban Form in the Arab World: Past and Present*. London, 2000.

— and Philip Jodidio. *Cairo: Revitalising a Historic Metropolis*. Turin, 2004.

Bierman, Irene. *Writing Signs: The Fatimid Public Text*. Berkeley, CA, 1998.

Bloom, Jonathan. *Arts of the City Victorious: Islamic Art and Architecture in Fatimid North Africa and Egypt*. New Haven, CT and London, 2007.

Bloom, Jonathan M. and Sheila Blair. *Islamic Arts*. London, 1997.

Bromley, R., ed. *Planning for Small Enterprise in Third World Cities*. Oxford, 1985.

Bromley, R. and C. Gerry, ed. *Casual Work and Poverty in Third World Cities*. Chichester, 1979.

Bulliet, Richard W. *The Case for Islamo-Christian Civilization*. New York, 2004.

Burckhardt, John Lewis, tr. *Arabic Proverbs; or the Manners and Customs of the Modern Egyptians, Illustrated from their Proverbial Sayings Current at Cairo*, ed. William Ouseley. London, 1830.

Butler, Alfred. *The Ancient Coptic Churches of Egypt*. Oxford, 1884.

Caiger-Smith, Alan. *Lustre Pottery: Technique, Tradition and Innovation in Islam and the Western World*. London, 1985.

Calverley, E. E. *Worship in Islam, Being a Translation with Commentary and Introduction of al-Ghazzali*. Cairo, 1957.

Canby, Sheila R. 'Islamic Lustreware', in Ian Freestone and David Gaimster, ed. *Pottery in the Making: World Ceramic Traditions*. London, 1997, pp. 110–115.

The Cambridge History of Egypt, vol. 1 'Islamic Egypt, 640–1517', ed. Carl F. Petry; vol. 2, 'Modern Egypt, from 1517 to the end of 20th Century', ed. M. W. Daly. Cambridge, 1998.

Celik, Zeynip. *Displaying the Orient*. Berkeley, CA, 1992.

Chatterjee, Partha. *Nationalist Thought and the Colonial*

View of the Muhammad 'Ali Mosque on the Citadel with Mamluk minarets of al-Darb al-Ahmar in the foreground.

World: A Derivative Discourse. Minneapolis, IN, 1986.

Cohen, Mark R. *Jewish Self-Government in Medieval Egypt: The Origins of the Office of Head of the Jews, ca. 1065–1126*. Princeton, NJ, 1980.

— *The Voice of the Poor in the Middle Ages: An Anthology of Documents from the Cairo Geniza*. Princeton, NJ, 2005.

Cole, Juan R. I. *Napoleon's Egypt: Invading the Middle East*. Basingstoke, 2007.

Contadini, Anna. *Fatimid Art at the Victoria and Albert Museum*. London, 1998.

Cook, Michael. *Commanding Right and Forbidding Wrong in Islamic Thought*. Cambridge, 2000.

Crowe, Yolande. 'Early Islamic Pottery and China', *Transactions of the Oriental Ceramic Society*, 41 (1975–1977), pp. 263–278.

Cuno, Kenneth. *The Pasha's Peasants: Land, Society, and Economy in Lower Egypt, 1740–1858*. Cambridge, 1992.

Daftary, Farhad. 'Intellectual Life among the Ismailis: An Overview', in F. Daftary, ed. *Intellectual Traditions in Islam*. London, 2000, pp. 87–111.

— *The Isma'ilis: Their History and Doctrines*. 2nd ed. Cambridge, 2007.

Danielson, V. 'Min al-mashayikh: A View of Egyptian Musical Tradition', *Asian Music*, 22 (1990–1991), pp. 113–127.

— *The Voice of Egypt: Umm Kulthûm, Arabic Song, and Egyptian Society in the Twentieth Century*. Chicago, IL, 1997.

Dashti, Ali. *In Search of Omar Khayyam*, tr. L. P. Elwell-Sutton. London, 1971.

Davis, Stephen. *The Cult of Saint Thecla: A Tradition of Women's Piety in Late Antiquity*. Oxford, 2001.

— 'Ancient Sources for the Coptic Tradition', in Gawdat Gabra, ed. *Be Thou There: The Holy Family's Journey in Egypt*. Cairo, 2001.

Denoix, Sylvie. *Décrire le Caire Fustat-Misr d'après Ibn Duqmaq et Maqrizi: l'histoire d'une partie de la ville du Caire d'après deux historiens égyptiens des XIVe-XVe siècles*. Cairo, 1992.

Dobrowolska, Agnieszka. *The Building Crafts of Cairo: A Living Tradition*. Cairo, 2005.

Dols, Michael. *The Black Death in the Middle East*. Princeton, NJ, 1977.

Dopp, P. H. *L'Égypte au commencement du quinzième siècle*. Cairo, 1930.

van Doorn-Harder, Nelly and Kari Vogt, ed. *Between Desert and City: The Coptic Orthodox Church Today*. Oslo, 1997.

Dykstra, Darrell. 'Pyramids, Prophets, and Progress: Ancient Egypt in the Writings of Ali Mubarak', *Journal of the American Oriental Society*, 114 (1994), pp. 54–65.

El-Kodsi, Mourad. *The Karaite Jews of Egypt, 1882–1986*. Lyons, NY, 1987.

El-Nahal, Galal. *Judicial Administration of Ottoman Egypt in the Seventeenth Century*. Minneapolis, MN, 1979.

Encyclopaedia of Islam, ed. H. A. R. Gibb et al. New ed., Leiden and London, 1960–2004.

Fahmy, Khaled. *All the Pasha's Men: Mehmed Ali, his Army, and the Making of Modern Egypt*. Cambridge, 1997.

Farmer, Henry George. *A History of Arabian Music to the XIIIth Century*. London, 1929.

Feldman, Walter. *Music of the Ottoman Court: Makam Composition and the Early Ottoman Musical Repertoire*. Berlin, 1996.

Fischel, Walter J. *Jews in the Economic and Political Life of Mediaeval Islam*. Rev. ed., New York, 1969.

Frishkopf, Michael. 'Inshad Dini and Aghani Diniyya in Twentieth Century Egypt: A Review of Styles, Genres, and Available Recordings', *Middle East Studies Association Bulletin*, 33 (2000), pp. 167–183.

Fuchs, H. and F. de Jong, 'Mawlid', *EI2*, vol. 6.

Gabra, Gawdat and Gertrud J. M. Van Loon. *The Churches of Egypt: From the Journey of the Holy Family to the Present Day*. Cairo, 2007.

General Organisation for Housing Building and Planning Research (GOHBPR) and The World Bank. *Construction/Contracting Industry Study*, Final Report, 3 volumes and appendices. Cairo, Egypt: Ministry of Housing, Reconstruction, and New Communities, 1981.

Ghannam, Farha. *Remaking the Modern: Space, Relocation and the Politics of Identity in Global Cairo*. Berkeley, CA, 2002.

Ghazaleh, Pascale. 'The Guilds Between Tradition and Modernity', in Nelly Hanna, ed. *The State and its Servants: Administration in Egypt from Ottoman Times to the Present*. Cairo, 1995.

Gil, Moshe. *Documents of the Jewish Pious Foundations from the Cairo Geniza*. Leiden, 1976.

— *The Tustaris: Family and Sect*. Tel Aviv, 1981.

Goitein, S. D. *A Mediterranean Society: The Jewish Communities of the Arab World as Portrayed in the Documents of the Cairo Geniza*. Berkeley, CA, 1967–1993.

— *Letters of Medieval Jewish Traders*. Princeton, NJ, 1973.

Golb, Norman. 'The Topography of the Jews of Medieval Egypt', *Journal of Near Eastern Studies*, 24 (1965), pp. 252–270, and 3 (1974), pp. 116–149.

Golombek, Lisa et al. *Tamerlane's Tableware: A New Approach to Chinoiserie Ceramics of Fifteenth- and Sixteenth-Century Iran*. Costa Mesa, CA, 1996.

Grabar, Oleg. 'Reflections on Mamluk Art', *Muqarnas*, 2 (1984), pp. 1–12.

Graham, William A. 'Islam in the Mirror of Ritual', in Richard G. Hovannisian and Speros Vyronis Jr., ed. *Islam's Understanding of Itself*. Malibu, CA, 1983.

Gran, Peter. 'Late 18th-Century – Early 19th-Century Egypt: Merchant Capitalism or Modern Capitalism?', in *L'Égypte au XIXe siècle* (Colloque, Aix-en-Provence, 4–7 juin 1979/Groupe de Recherches et d'Études sur le Proche-Orient). Paris, 1982.

Gray, Basil. 'The Export of Chinese Porcelain to the Islamic World: Some Reflections on its Significance for Islamic Art, Before 1400', *Transactions of the Oriental Ceramic Society*, 41 (1975–1977), pp. 231–261.

Grube, Ernst J., ed. *Cobalt and Lustre: The First Centuries of Islamic Pottery. The Nasser D. Khalili Collection of Islamic Art*, vol. IX. London, 1994.

Gruber, Mark. *Sacrifice in the Desert: A Study of an Egyptian Minority through the Prism of Coptic Monasticism*. Lanham, MD, 2003.

von Grunebaum, G. E. *Muhammadan Festivals*. Ottawa, 1976.

Hallett, Jessica. 'Trade and Innovation: The Rise of a Pottery Industry in Abbasid Basra'. DPhil, University of Oxford, Faculty of Oriental Studies, 2000.

Halm, Heinz. *The Fatimids and their Traditions of Learning*. London, 1997.

Hanna, Milad M. 'Real Estate Rights in Urban Egypt: The Changing Sociopolitical Winds', in Ann Elizabeth Mayer, ed. *Property, Social Structure and Law in the Modern Middle East*. Albany, NY, 1985, pp. 189–211.

Hanna, Nelly. *Habiter au Caire: La Maison moyenne et ses habitants aux XVIIe et XVIIIe siècles*. Institut Français d'Archéologie Orientale du Caire, 1991.

— ed. *The State and its Servants: Administration in Egypt from Ottoman Times to the Present*. Cairo, 1995.

— and Raouf Abbas, ed. *Society and Economy in Egypt and the Eastern Mediterranean, 1600–1900: Essays in Honor of André Raymond*. Cairo, 2005.

Hampikian, N. *al-Salihiyya Complex through Time*. Heidelberg, 2004.

— 'Challenges Facing Conservation Projects in Historical Cairo – Historical Buildings versus the Urban Fabric around them', *Proceedings of the 9th Conference of the Union of Egyptian Architects – Architectural Heritage and Urban Development*. Cairo, 1999.

— and M. al-Ibrashy. 'Filling in Gaps Between a "Monument" and another "Monument" in Historic Cairo – Case Study: Urban Conservation Project - Proposal for the Rehabilitation of the Area around the Southern Gate and Walls of Historic Cairo', *Proceedings of the 5th International Symposium of OWHC*. Santiago de Compostella, 1999.

Haridi, Salah. *al-Hidraf wal-sina'at fi 'ahd Muhammad 'Ali*. Cairo, 1985.

Hart, G., 'Interlocking Transactions: Obstacles, Precursors or Instruments of Agrarian Capitalism?', *Journal of Development Economics*, 23 (1986), pp. 177–203.

Henein, Nessim Henry. *Poteries et proverbes d'Égypte*. Cairo, 1992.

Heyworth-Dunne, J. *An Introduction to the History of Education in Modern Egypt*. London, 1968.

Hoffman, Valerie. *Sufism, Mystics, and Saints in Modern Egypt*. Columbia, SC, 1995.

Holt, P. M. *Egypt and the Fertile Crescent 1516–1922: A Political History*. London, 1966.

Hopkins, Nicholas, ed. 'The New Arab Family', *Cairo Papers in Social Science*, 24 (2001), p. 275.

Hulsman, C. 'Tracing the Route of the Holy Family Today', in Gawdat Gabra, ed. *Be Thou There: The Holy Family's Journey in Egypt*. Cairo, 2001.

Hunsberger, Alice C. *Nasir Khusraw, The Ruby of Badakhshan: A Portrait of the Persian Poet, Traveller and Philosopher*. London, 2000.

— 'Nasir Khusraw: Fatimid Intellectual', in F. Daftary, ed. *Intellectual Traditions in Islam*. London, 2000, pp. 112–129.

— 'The Esoteric World Vision of Nasir Khusraw', *Sacred Web*, 9 (2002), pp. 89–100.

al-Hitta, Ahmad. *Ta'rikh Misr al-iqtisadi fi'l-qarn al-tasi' 'ashr*. Cairo, 1955.

Hunter, F. Robert. *Egypt under the Khedives: From Household Government to Modern Bureaucracy, 1805–1879*. Pittsburgh, PA, 1984.

— 'The Cairo Archives for the Study of Elites in Modern Egypt', *International Journal of Middle East Studies*, 4 (1973), pp. 476–488.

Ibn 'Abd al-Hakm. *Futuh Misr*, ed. Charles C. Torrey. New Haven, CT, 1922.

Ibn Bassam, 'Abd Allah b. Ahmad. *Nihayat al-rutba fi talab al-hisba*, ed. Husam al-Din Samarra'i. Baghdad, 1968.

Ibn Battuta, Muhammad b. 'Abd Allah. *al-Rihla*, ed. Mahmud Sharqawi. Beirut, 1968.

Ibn al-Dawadari, Abu Bakr b. 'Abd Allah. *Kanz al-durar wa jami' al-ghurar*, vol. 9, ed. Hans Robert Roemer. Cairo, 1960.

Ibn Duqmaq, Ibrahim b. Muhammad. *Description de l'Égypte, par Ibn Doukmak, al-juz al-rabi' wa'l-khamis min Kitab al-intsar li-wasitat 'iqd al-amsar*. Cairo, 1313–1314 [1896–1897].

Ibn Habib, al-Hasan b. 'Umar. *Tadhkirat al-nabih fi ayyam al-Mansur wa banih*, ed. Muhammad M. Amin. Cairo, 1976–1986.

Ibn al-Hajj, Muhammad b. Muhammad. *al-Madkhal*. Cairo, 1960.

Ibn Hawqal, Abu'l-Qasim Muhammad b. 'Ali. *Kitab surat al-ard*, French tr. by J. H. Kramer and Gaston Wiet as *Configuration de la Terre*. Paris and Beirut, 1964.

Ibn al-Haytham, Abu 'Ali al-Hasan ibn al-Hasan. *The Optics of Ibn al-Haytham*, tr. A. I. Sabra, vol. 1. London, 1989.

Ibn al-Haytham, Abu 'Abd Allah Ja'far ibn Ahmad. *Kitab al-munazarat*, ed. and tr. Wilferd Madelung and Paul E. Walker as *The Advent of the Fatimids: A Contemporary Shi'i Witness*. London, 2000.

Ibn Iyas, Muhammad b. Ahmad. *Bada'i' al-zuhur fi waqa'i' al-duhur*, ed. Muhammad Mustafa. Cairo, 1982–1984.

Ibn al-Ma'mum al-Bata'ihi, Jamal al-Din. *Nusus min akhbar Misr*, ed. Ayman F. Sayyid. Cairo, 1983.

Ibn Muyassar, Taj al-Din Muhammad b. 'Ali. *Akhbar Misr*, ed H. Massé. Cairo, 1919; ed. A. F. Sayyid, 1981.

Ibn al-Sayrafi, 'Ali b. Dawud al-Jawhari. *Inba' al-hasr bi-abna' al-'asr*, ed. Hasan Habashi. Cairo, 1970.

Ibn Shaddad, 'Izz al-Din. *Ta'rikh al-Malik al-Zahir*, ed. A. Hutayt. Wiesbaden, 1983.

Ibn Taghribirdi, Jamal al-Din Abu'l-Mahasin Yusuf. *al-Nujum al-zahira fi muluk Misr wa'l-Qahira*. Cairo, 1348–1391/1929–1972.

Ibn al-Ukhuwwa. *The Ma'alim al-Qurba fi Ahkam al-Hisba of Diya' al-Din Muhammad ibn Muhammad al-Qurashi al-Shafi'i known as Ibn al-Ukhuwwa (d.729/1329)*, ed. with partial trans. Reuben Levy. Cambridge, 1938.

Ibn al-Zubayr, Ahmad b. al-Rashid. *Kitab al-dhakha'ir wa'l-tuhaf li'l-Qadi al-Rashid b. al-Zubayr*, ed. Muhammad Hamid Allah. Kuwait, 1959; tr. Ghada al-Qaddumi as *Book of Gifts and Rarities (Kitab al-hadaya wa al-tuhaf): Selections Compiled in the Fifteenth Century from an Eleventh-Century Manuscript on Gifts and Treasures*. Cambridge, MA, 1996.

Ibsen al-Faruqi, Lois. *The Nature of the Musical Art of Islamic Culture*. Ann Arbor, MI, 1975.

Idris 'Imad al-Din b. al-Hasan. *'Uyun al-akhbar wa-funun al-athar*, ed. M. Ghalib, vols. 4–6. Beirut, 1973–1978.

— *'Uyun al-akhbar*, ed. A. Chleilat et al. Damascus and London, 2007–2009.

International Labour Office (ILO), *Employment, Income and Equality: A Strategy for Increasing Productive Employment in Kenya*. Geneva, 1972.

Islamoglu-Inan, Huri. 'Introduction: Oriental Despotism in World-System Perspective', in Islamoglu-Inan, ed. *The Ottoman Empire and the World Economy*. Cambridge, 1987, pp. 1–2.

Jenkins, Marilyn. 'Safid: Content and Context', in P. Soucek, ed. *Content and Context of Visual Arts in the Islamic World*. Pennsylvania and London, 1988, pp. 67–75.

— 'Muslim: An Early Fatimid Ceramist', *Bulletin of the Metropolitan Museum of Art*, 26 (New York, 1968), pp. 359–369.

al-Jiritli, 'Ali. *Ta'rikh al-sina'a fi Misr fi'l-nisf al-awwal min al-qarn al-tasi' 'ashr*. Cairo, 1952.

Joinville, Jean de. *Memoirs of John Lord de Joinville*, tr. T. Johnes. Hafod, 1807.

Juwayni, 'Ala' al-Din 'Ata-Malik. *Ta'rikh-i jahan-gusha*, ed. M. Qazvini. Leiden-London, 1912–1937. English trans. John A. Boyle as *The History of the World-Conqueror*. Cambridge, MA, 1958.

Kassem, 'Abdou Kassem. *Fi ta'rikh al-Ayyubiyyin wa'l-Mamluk*. Cairo, 2001.

— *Dirasat fi ta'rikh Misr al-ijtima'i 'asr salatin al-mamalik*. Cairo, 1994.

Kerr, C. 'The Balkanization of Labor Markets', in *Labor, Mobility and Economic Opportunity*. Cambridge, MA, 1954.

Kessler, Cristal. *The Carved Domes of Cairo*. Cairo, 1976.

Lagrange, F. *Musiques d'Égypte*. Arles, 1996.

— 'Shaykh Sayyid Darwish', *Meditérranéenes*, 8 (1996), pp. 155–177.

Landau, Jacob. *Studies in Arab Theatre and Music*. Philadelphia, PA, 1958.

Lane, E. W. *The Manners and Customs of the Modern Egyptians*. London, 1837; repr., Cairo, 1991.

Laurens, Henri, et al. *L'Expédition d'Égypte*. Paris, 1989.

Lewis, Bernard. 'The Islamic Guilds', *Economic History Review*, 8 (1936–1938), pp. 20–37.

Little, Donald P. 'Coptic Converts to Islam during the Bahri Mamluk Period', in Michael Gervers and Ramzi Jibran Bikazi, ed. *Conversion and Continuity*. Toronto, 1991, pp. 263–288.

Lutfi, Huda. 'Coptic Festivals of the Nile', in Thomas Philipp and Ulrich Haarmann, ed. *The Mamluks in Egyptian Politics and Society*. Cambridge, 1998.

— 'Manners and Customs of Fourteenth-Century Cairene Women: Female Anarchy versus Male Shar'i Order in Muslim Prescriptive Treatises', in Nikki R. Keddie and Beth Baron, ed. *Women in Middle Eastern History*. New Haven, CT, 1991, pp. 99–121.

Malter, Henry. *Saadia Gaon: His Life and Works*. Philadelphia, PA, 1921.

Mann, Jacob. *The Jews in Egypt and in Palestine under the Fatimid Caliphs*, Preface and Reader's Guide by S. D. Goitein. New York, 1970.

al-Maqrizi, Taqi al-Din Ahmad b. 'Ali. *Kitab al-suluk*, partial French trans. E. Blochet as *Histoire d'Égypte*, in *Revue de l'Orient Latin*, 6–11 (1898–1908). Partial English trans. Ronald J. C. Broadhurst, *A History of the Ayyubid Sultans of Egypt*. Boston, MA, 1980.

— *Itti'az al-hunafa' bi-akhbar al-a'imma al-Fatimiyyin al-khulafa'*. Cairo, 1967–1973.

— *Kitab al-mawa'iz wa'l-i'tibar bi-dhikr al-khitat wa'l-athar*, ed. Muhammad ibn 'Abd al-Rahman Quttah al-'Adawi. Bulaq, 1270/1853–1854.

— *Ighathat al-umma bi-kashf al-ghumma*, ed. Muhammad

Mustafa Ziyada and Jamal al-Din Muhammad al-Shayyal. 2nd rev. ed. Cairo, 1957.

Marçais, Georges. *Les Faïences à réflets métalliques de la Grande Mosquée de Kairouan*. Paris, 1928.

Marcus, Abraham. *The Middle East on the Eve of Modernity*. New York, 1989.

al-Masri, Iris. 'Harit al-Rum', in Aziz S. Atiya, ed. *The Coptic Encyclopedia*. New York, 1991, vol. 4.

Massignon, Louis. *Opera Minora*, ed. Y. Moubarac. Beirut, 1963.

— 'Sinf', *EI2*.

al-Mawardi. *al-Ahkam al-sultaniyya wa'l-wilayat al-diniyya*, tr. Wafaa Wahba as *The Ordinances of Government*. Reading, 1996.

McPherson, J. W. *The Mowlids of Egypt (Egyptian Saints-Days)*. Cairo, 1941.

Mehrez, Samya. *Egyptian Writers between History and Fiction: Essays on Naguib Mahfouz, Son'allah Ibrahim, and Gamal al-Ghitani*. Cairo, 1994.

Meinardus, Otto. *Christian Egypt: Ancient and Modern*. Cairo, 1977.

—*Coptic Saints and Pilgrimages*. Cairo, 2002.

Meinecke, M., ed. *Islamic Cairo, Architectural Conservation and Urban Development of the Historic Center*, Proceedings of a Seminar Organised by the Goethe Institute Cairo (1–5 October, 1978). Cairo, 1980.

Meinecke-Berg, Viktoria. 'Le trésor des califes', *Trésors fatimides du Caire: exposition présentée à l'Institut du monde arabe du 28 avril au 30 aout 1998*, exh. cat. Paris, 1998, pp. 96–142.

— 'Das Giraffenbild des fatimidischen Keramikmalers Muslim', *Damaszener Mitteilungen*, 11 (1999), pp. 331–344.

— 'Fatimid Painting on Tradition and Style: The Workshop of Muslim', in M. Barrucand, ed. *L'Égypte Fatimide, son art et son histoire*. Paris, 1999, pp. 349–358.

Milwright, Marcus. 'Pottery in the Written Sources of the Ayyubid-Mamluk Period (c. 567–923/1171–1517)', *Bulletin of the School of Oriental and African Studies*, 62 (1999), pp. 504–518.

— 'Gazetteer of Archaeological Sites in the Levant Reporting on Pottery of the Middle Islamic Period (*circa* 1100–1600)', *Islamic Art*, 5 (2001), pp. 3–39.

Mitchell, Timothy. *Colonising Egypt*. Berkeley, CA, 1988.

Mondal, Anshuman. 'Between Turban and Tarbush: Modernity and the Anxieties of Transition in Hadith 'Isa ibn Hisham', *Alif*, 17 (1997), pp. 201–221.

Mottahedeh, Roy and K. Stilt. 'Public and Private as Viewed Through the Work of the *Muhtasib*', *Social Research*, 70 (2003), pp. 735–748.

Mubarak, 'Ali. *al-Khitat al-tawfiqiyya al-jadida li Misr al-Qahira wa muduniha wa biladiha al-qadima wa'l-shhira*. Cairo, 1969.

al-Musabbihi, Muhammad b. 'Ubayd Allah. *Akhbar Misr*, ed. Ayman F. Sayyid et al. Cairo, 1978–1984; ed. W. G. Millward. Cairo, 1980.

Naddaf, Sandra. 'Mirrored Images: Rifa'ah al-Tahtawi and the West', *Alif* (1986), pp. 73–83.

Nadim, A. 'Documentation, Restoration, Conservation, and Development of Bayt al-Suhaymi Area', in *Historic Cairo*, Supreme Council of Antiquities. Cairo, 2002, pp. 199–212.

Nasir-i Khusraw. *Safar-nama*, ed. M. Dabir Siyaqi. 5th ed., Tehran, 1356/1977. English trans. W. M. Thackston, Jr. as *Naser-e Khossraw's Book of Travels (Safarnama)*. Albany, NY, 1986.

Nelson, Kristen. *The Art of Reciting the Qur'an*. Austin, TX, 1985.

van Nieuwkerk, Karin. *A Trade Like any Other: Female Singers and Dancers in Egypt*. Austin, TX, 1995.

O'Kane, Bernard, ed. *The Treasures of Islamic Art in the Museums of Cairo*. Cairo, 2006.

O'Leary, De Lacy Evans. *The Saints of Egypt*. London, 1937.

Pacini, Andrea, ed. *Christian Communities in the Arab Middle East*. Oxford, 1998.

Partrick, Theodore Hall. *Traditional Egyptian Christianity*. Greensboro, NC, 1996.

Philon, Helen. *Early Islamic Ceramics: Ninth to Late Twelfth Centuries*, Athens Benaki Museum Collection. London, 1980.

al-Qadi, Wadad. 'East and West in 'Ali Mubarak's 'Alamuddin', in Marwan Buheiry, ed. *Intellectual Life in the Arab East, 1890–1939*. Beirut, 1981, pp. 21–37.

al-Qalqashandi, Ahmad b. 'Ali. *Subh al-a'sha fi sina'at al-insha'*, ed. M. 'A. Ibrahim. Cairo, 1331–1338/1913–1920.

al-Qurashi, Muhammad b. Muhammad b. Ahmad. *Kitab ma'alim al-qurba fi ahkam al-hisba*. Cairo, 1976; *The Ma'alim al-qurba fa' ahkam al-hisba of Diya' al-Din Muhammad Ibn Muhammad al-Qurashi al-Shafi'i*, ed. with partial trans. by Reuben Levy. London, 1938.

Racy, A. J. *Making Music in the Arab World: The Culture and Artistry of Tarab*. New York, 2003.

— 'The Waslah: A Compound-Form Principle in Egyptian Music', *Arab Studies Quarterly*, 5 (1983), pp. 396–403.

Rapoport, Yossef. 'Marriage and Divorce in the Muslim Near East, 1250–1517'. PhD, Princeton University, 2002, pp. 67–79.

Raymond, André. *Artisans et commerçants au Caire au XVIIIe siècle*. Damascus, 1973–1974.

— 'L'Impact de la pénétration Européenne sur l'economie de l'Égypte au XVIIIè siècle', *Annales Islamologiques*, 18 (1982), pp. 217–235.

— *Cairo: City of History*, tr. Willard Wood. Cairo, 2001.

— 'The Role of the Communities (*Tawa'if*) in the Administration of Cairo in the Ottoman Period', in Nelly Hanna, ed. *The State and its Servants: Administration in Egypt from Ottoman Times to the Present*. Cairo, 1995, pp. 32–43.

Richardson, H. W. 'The Role of the Urban Informal Sector: An Overview', *Regional Development Review*, 5 (1985), pp. 3–54.

Reid, Donald. M. 'Cultural Imperialism and Nationalism: The Struggle to Define and Control the Heritage of Arab Art in Egypt', *International Journal of Middle East Studies*, 24, 1 (1992), pp. 56–72.

Reif, Stefan C. *A Jewish Archive from Old Cairo: The History of Cambridge University's Genizah Collection*. Richmond, 2000.

Reimer, Michael. *Colonizing Bridgehead, Government and Society in Alexandria 1807–1882*. Boulder, CL, 1997.

Rieker, Martina and Maureen O'Malley. 'Museum Effects: Politics and Practices of Heritage Inscription in the Southern Mediterranean', in Kamran Asdar Ali and Martina Rieker, ed. *TransActions: Tourism in the Southern Mediterranean* (forthcoming).

Rodenbeck, John. 'The Present Situation of the Historic Cairo: A Road not Taken', in Doris Behrens-Abouseif, ed. *The Cairo Heritage*. Cairo, 2000, pp. 328–340.

Rodenbeck, Max. *Cairo: The City Victorious*. New York, 1998.

Rubery, J. 'Structured Labor Markets, Worker Organization and Low Pay', *Cambridge Journal of Economics*, 2 (1978), pp. 17–36.

Runciman, Stephen. *A History of the Crusades*. Cambridge, 1951–1954.

Sabra, Adam. *Poverty and Charity in Medieval Islam: Mamluk Egypt, 1250–1517*. Cambridge, 2000.

Said, Dr Salah Zaky and Associates (United Consultants). 'Rehabilitation with People's Participation', *Final Report* for Egyptian Antiquities Project of the American Research Center. November, 2005.

al-Sakhawi, Muhammad ibn 'Abd al-Rahman. *al-Tibr al-masbuk fi dhayl al-suluk*. Cairo, 1896.

Sanders, Paula. *Ritual, Politics, and the City in Fatimid Cairo*. Albany, NY, 1994.

— *Creating Medieval Cairo*. Cairo, 2008.

Sauvaget, Jean. 'Introduction à l'étude de la céramique Musulmane', *Revue des Études Islamiques*, 33 (1965), pp. 44–50.

Sayyid, Ayman Fu'ad. *La capitale de l'Égypte jusqu'à l'époque Fatimide: essai de reconstitution topographique*. Beirut, 1998.

al-Sayyid Marsot, Afaf Lutfi. *Egypt in the Reign of Muhammad 'Ali*. Cambridge, 1984.

Scanlon, George T. *Fustat Expedition Final Report:*

Volume One, Catalogue of Filters, A.R.C.E Reports 8. Lake Winona, IN, 1986.

— and W. B. Kubiak. *Fustat Expedition Final Report: Volume Two, Fustat-C*. Lake Winona, IN, 1988.

— '1965 – Fustat Expedition Preliminary Report', *Journal of the American Research Center in Egypt*, 8 (1966), pp. 65–84.

— 'Egypt and China: Trade and Imitation', in D. S. Richards, ed. *Islam and the Trade of Asia*. Oxford, 1970, pp. 81–96.

— 'Fustat Fatimid Sgraffiato: Less Than Lustre', in Marianne Barrucand, ed. *L'Égypte Fatimide, son art et son histoire*. Paris, 1999, pp. 265–283.

Schrieke, B. et al. 'Mi'radj', *EI2*, vol. 7.

Scott, James C. *Seeing Like a State: How Certain Schemes to Improve the Human Condition have Failed*. New Haven, CT, 1998.

Serageldin, Ismail. *Very Special Places: The Architecture and Economics of Intervening in Historic Cities. Culture in Sustainable Development*. Washington, DC, 1999.

Shannon, J. 'Emotion, Performance and Temporality in Arab Music: Reflections on Tarab', *Cultural Anthropology*, 18 (2003), pp. 72–98.

al-Shayzari, 'Abd al-Rahman b. Nasr. *Nihayat al-rutba fi talab al-hisba*. Cairo, 1946; tr. R. P. Buckley as *The Book of the Islamic Market Inspector*. Oxford, 1999.

Shoshan, Boaz. 'Grain Riots and the "Moral Economy", Cairo, 1450–1517', *Journal of Interdisciplinary History*, 10 (1980), pp. 462–463.

Singermann, Diane and Paul Amal, ed. *Cairo Cosmopolitan: Politics, Culture and Urban Space in the New Globalised Middle East*. Cairo, 2006.

Stern, Samuel M. 'Cairo as the Centre of the Isma'ili Movement', in *Colloque international sur l'histoire du Caire*. Cairo, 1972, pp. 437–450.

Stillman, Norman A. *The Jews of Arab Lands: A History and Source Book*. Philadelphia, PA, 1979.

— 'Quelques renseignements biographiques sur Yosef Ibn 'Awkal, médiateur entre les communautés juives du Maghreb et les Académies d'Irak', *Revue des Études Juives*, 132 (1973), pp. 529–542.

— 'The Eleventh-Century Merchant House of Ibn 'Awkal (A Geniza Study)', *Journal of the Economic and Social History of the Orient*, 16 (1973), pp. 15–88.

— 'Charity and Social Service in Medieval Islam', *Societas*, 5 (1975), pp. 105–115.

— 'Subordinance and Dominance: Non-Muslim Minorities and the Traditional Islamic State as Perceived from Above and Below', in Farhad Kazemi and R. D. McChesney, ed. *A Way Prepared: Essays on Islamic Culture in Honor of Richard Bayly Winder*. New York and London, 1988, pp. 132–141.

— 'The Jew in the Medieval Islamic City', in Daniel Frank, ed. *The Jews of Medieval Islam: Community, Society, and Identity*. Leiden, 1995, pp. 3–13.

Stillman, Yedida Kalfon. *Arab Dress: A Short History from the Dawn of Islam to Modern Times*. Leiden, 2000.

Suleman, Fahmida. 'Ceramics', in Josef W. Meri, ed. *Medieval Islamic Civilization: An Encylopedia*. New York and London, 2006, vol. 1s, pp. 143–144.

al-Suyuti. *Husn al-muhadara fi ta'rikh Misr wa'l-Qahira*, ed. Muhammad 'Abd al-Fadil Ibrahim. Cairo, 1967–1968.

Swedenburg, T. 'Saida Sutlan/Danna International: Transgender Pop and the Polysemiotics of Sex, Nation, and Ethnicity on the Israeli-Egyptian Border', in Walter Armbrust, ed. *Mass Mediations: New Approaches to Popular Culture in the Middle East and Beyond*. Berkeley, CA, 2000, pp. 88–119.

al-Tabari, Abu Ja'far Muhammad b. Jarir. *Ta'rikh al-rusul wa'l-muluk*, ed. M. J. de Goeje et al. Series I–III. Leiden, 1879–1901. English trans. by various scholars. *The History of al-Tabari*. Albany, NY, 1985–1999.

al-Tha'alibi, Abu Mansur. *Kitab Lata'if al-ma'arif*, ed. P. de Jong. Leiden, 1867; tr. C. E. Bosworth as *The Book of Curious and Entertaining Information, the Lata'if al-ma'arif of al-Tha'alibi*. Edinburgh, 1968.

Trésors fatimides du Caire: exposition présentée à l'Institut du monde arabe du 28 avril au 30 aout 1998, exh. cat. Paris, 1998.

Turner, Bryan. *Orientalism, Postmodernism and Globalism*. London and New York, 1994.

Tyan, Emile. *Histoire de l'organisation judiciaire en pays d'Islam*. Paris, 1943.

United Nations Development Programme, Supreme Council of Antiquities, *Rehabilitation of Historic Cairo*, Final Report. December, 1997.

'Uthman, Muhammad 'Abd al-Sattar. *al-Madina al-Islamiyya*. Kuwait, 1988.

Vatikiotis, P. J. *The History of Egypt*. London, 1969; repr. 1985.

Walker, Paul E. *Exploring an Islamic Empire: Fatimid History and its Sources*. London, 2002.

Warner, Nicholas. *The Monuments of Historic Cairo*. Cairo, 2002.

Watson, John H. *Among the Copts*. Portland, OR, 2000.

Watson, Oliver. *Ceramics from Islamic Lands*. London, 2004.

— 'Fritware: Fatimid Egypt or Saljuq Iran?', in Marianne Barrucand, ed. *L'Égypte Fatimide, son art et son histoire*. Paris, 1999, pp. 299–307.

Williams, Caroline. *Islamic Monuments in Cairo: The Practical Guide*. Cairo, 2008.

— 'Transforming the Old: Cairo's New Medieval City', *The Middle East Journal*, 56 (2002), pp. 457–475.

— 'Islamic Cairo: Endangered Legacy', *The Middle East Journal*, 39 (1985), pp. 231–246.

Worman, E. J. 'Notes on the Jews in Fustât', *Jewish Quarterly Review*, 18 (1905), pp. 1–39.

Wüstenfeld, F. *Die Geographie und Verwaltun von Ägypten nach den Arabischen des Abul-'Abbas Ahmed ben Ali el-Calcashandi*. Göttingen, 1879.

Yeomans, Richard. *The Art and Architecture of Islamic Cairo*. Reading, 2006.

Photocredits

AKTC
Aga Khan Trust for Culture

ARCE
American Research Center
in Egypt, Inc.

Jacket Adrien Buchet AKTC, 2006
Title page Private collection

10 Courtesy of Special Collections, Fine Arts Library, Harvard College Library
12–13 Detail from photograph G. Lekegian, 1880, Courtesy of Special Collections, Fine Arts Library, Harvard College Library
15 Egyptian National Library, Cairo/ The Bridgeman Art Library
21 Private Collection/ The Bridgeman Art Library
26 Zangaki, 1865. Middle East Department, University of Chicago Library
29 ©Michael Maslan Historic Photographs/CORBIS
30 Zangaki, *circa* 1865. Middle East Department, University of Chicago Library
35 1880, G. Lekegian, courtesy of Special Collections, Fine Arts Library, Harvard College Library
37 By kind permission of the Procuratoria of San Marco, Venice
39 Photoglob, Middle East Department, University of Chicago Library
41 ©Metropolitan Museum of Art
43 ©The British Library Board
44 Private Collection/ The Stapleton Collection/ The Bridgeman Art Library
45 ©The Institute of Ismaili Studies
46, 49 Private collection
54–57 Asian and Middle East Division, The New York Public Library, Astor, Lenox and Tilden Foundations
58 Abdullah Frères. From Abdul-Hamid II Collection, Library of Congress
63 David Meredith/Royal Geographical Society
64 Courtesy Thomas Hartwell
67 B. O'Kane/Alamy
73 ©The British Library Board
74 Courtesy Thomas Hartwell
75 ©Ovidio Salazar
76 Henri Cartier-Bresson/Magnum
80 ©The Institute of Ismaili Studies
81 Private collection
83 Werner Forman Archive
84 Felix Bonfils/ The Institute of Ismaili Studies
85 Private collection
87 Courtesy Thomas Hartwell
87 ©V&A Images

89 ©The British Library Board
95 Robert Harding Picture Library/Alamy
99 ©2007 Museum Associates/LACMA
100 ©Courtesy of the Center for Advanced Judaic Studies Library, University of Pennsylvania
106-107 Nasser D. Khalili Collection of Islamic Art ©Nour Foundation, Courtesy of the Khalili Family Trust
110 Adrien Buchet, 2006 ©AKTC
114 Private collection
118 ©AKTC
120–121 Private Collection/ The Bridgeman Art Library
123 Gary Otte, 2001 ©AKTC
124–125 Adrien Buchet, 2006 ©AKTC
126–127 Gary Otte, 2001 ©AKTC, 2003 ©AKTC
129 2007 ©AKTC
131 Gary Otte, 2003 ©AKTC
132 ©2008 by Benaki Museum, Athens
135, 137 Nasser D. Khalili Collection of Islamic Art, ©Nour Foundation, Courtesy of the Khalili Family Trust.
139 ©1958 Elliott Erwitt/Magnum Photos
146 Asian and Middle East Division, The New York Public Library, Astor, Lenox and Tilden Foundations
147 ©RMN/Franck Raux
148 ©Alinari Archives/CORBIS
150 ©Sean Sprague/SpraguePhoto.com
157 ©1989 Chris Steele-Perkins/Magnum
158 Arabia Books 2009
161 H. Béchard, reproduced with the kind permission of Griffith Institute, University of Oxford
162 Sebah, Middle East Department, University of Chicago Library
164 Photoglob, Middle East Department, University of Chicago Library
165–168 Private collection
170–171 Adrien Buchet, ©AKTC, 2006
174 ©Monda Giruis
175 Courtesy Thomas Hartwell
177, 179 ©Ovidio Salazar
180–181 ©Alinari Archives/CORBIS
182–183 Private Collection/©Christie's Images/The Bridgeman Art Library
186–187 ©Gary Otte, AKTC, 2005
189 Robin Oldacre, ©AKTC, 2002
193 Adrien Buchet, ©AKTC, 2006
194 Gary Otte, ©AKTC, 2004
196 Robin Oldacre, ©AKTC, 2004
197–198 Adrien Buchet, ©AKTC, 2006
199 H. Béchard, reproduced with the kind permission of Griffith Institute, University of Oxford
201–202 Adrien Buchet, ©AKTC 2006
205 *Top* Photograph, Adrien Buchet, Historic Cities Programme, ©AKTC, 2006
205 *Below* Gary Otte, Historic Cities

Programme, ©AKTC, 2003
209 Reproduced by permission of ARCE Jaroslaw Dobrowolski
210 Reproduced by permission of ARCE, Patrick Godeau
211 Reproduced by permission of ARCE, Centre for the Conservation and preservation of Islamic Architectural Heritage and Erico Peintner (part 2)
212 Reproduced by permission of ARCE Francis Dzikowski
215–216 Reproduced by permission of ARCE, Matjaz Kacicnik
219 Reproduced by permission of ARCE, Agnieszka Dobrowolska
221 Courtesy Thomas Hartwell
223 Reproduced by permission of ARCE, Patrick Godeau
224 Reproduced by permission ARCE, Patrick Godeau
227 Reproduced by permission of ARCE, Centre for the Conservation and Preservation of Islamic Architectural Heritage and Erico Peintner
229–230 Courtesy Thomas Hartwell
234 Adrien Buchet, Historic Cities Programme, ©AKTC, 2006
239 Fikret Yegül, 1970, courtesy of Special Collections, Fine Art Library, Harvard College Library
240 Courtesy Thomas Hartwell
243 Stefano Bianca, ©AKTC, 1992
246–247 Christian Richters, ©AKTC, 2006
252 *Left* and *below* Gary Otte, ©AKTC, 2003, 2001
252 *Far left* Adrien Buchet, ©AKTC, 2006
256–257 Adrien Buchet, ©AKTC, 2006
260–261 ©Christian Richters, AKTC, 2006
262–263 ©Jean-Luc Ray, AKTC, 2008
265 ©Gary Otte, AKTC, 2004
266–271 Adrien Buchet, ©AKTC, 2006
274–275 ©Jean-Luc Ray, AKF, 2009
277, 280 ©Tara Todras-Whitehall, AKTC, 2006;
285 Gary Otte, ©AKTC, 2000
287 ©André Yakubian, AKTC, 2002
291, 294 Courtesy Thomas Hartwell